The
Juvenile Offender
and the Law

The Juvenile Offender and the Law

Second Edition

Paul H. Hahn A.B., M.Ed

Director, Graduate Corrections Program
Xavier University

Assisted by **John P. O'Connor, A.B., LL.B.**

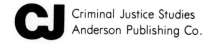

Criminal Justice Studies
Anderson Publishing Co.

THE JUVENILE OFFENDER AND THE LAW

Library of Congress Catalog Card Number: 78-58626
ISBN: 0-87084-337-0

The editor of this book was Mark Evan Chimsky, Anderson Publishing Company.

Cover Design by Dale J. Hartig

FOREWORD

The very nature of a free society invites the reassessment of values. In the process, attitudes polarize and at times generate varying degrees of conflict. Since the police officer is charged with maintaining the peace, he is often positioned in the crossfire of these opposing forces. Unfortunately, there have been occasions when his role in this context was discharged routinely and with little concern for the consequences. As a result, some segments of society emerged with an impression of the officer as an unqualified partisan. In time, this loss of respect materially influenced his effectiveness in safeguarding the very freedoms which allow for an orderly change.

Recognizing the danger implicit in the development, Paul Hahn set out to address the deficiency by providing insights for the police officer so that he might better understand one of society's alienated segments—the adolescent community.

The author is eminently qualified to explain the adolescent in the world of today. Not only are his opinions validated by the discipline of academic experience but also by a unique and dynamic service as Director of the Hamilton County Youth Center. In this capacity, he became conversant with the police officer, his rationale and the practices evolving therefrom. At the same time, he was privileged to observe the impact of these forces upon the attitude and behavior of young Americans.

Paul Hahn's work is designed to expand the police officer's body of knowledge and thus make him a more effective practitioner. This book achieves that objective in a most engaging way.

STANLEY R. SCHROTEL
Police Chief, City of Cincinnati, Retired

PREFACE

In preparing the revision of this text over six years after the preparation of the original version, your author was amazed at the applicability of the wisdom of the French philosopher who reminded us that the more things change the more they tend to remain the same. In this case, so much of that which is easiest seen and noticed has changed so drastically, and yet so many of the underlying deeper truths have indeed only been reinforced and strengthened. This seems certainly ironic if not impossible in the light of the fact that since the first edition of this text we have undergone the ordeal of withdrawing from the Vietnam war and the civil strife and division which accompanied it, the Watergate scandal, fuel shortages unimagined in a nation addicted to a lifestyle which demands ever-increasing resources, lootings in the streets, and the dramatic increase of violent crime in the suburbs, and so many other traumatic events and significant changes that one is tempted to ask what it is that really can be said to have remained the same.

And yet the basics have really indeed been the constant factor: our children and their needs, the fundamental rights of a society to have the tranquility of order and the feeling of safety, the "visions of the young and dreams of the old," basic human needs and the basic need to be human, all these and so many other fundamental foundation stones, along with our particular rights and duties in the freest and most bountiful society that man has ever developed, indeed have remained the same, although certainly the winds have blown and the storms have raged.

So, in doing this revision, your author has attempted to make careful note of those important changes in behavior, in environment, and in the law; while at the same time he has attempted to be equally as careful in preserving that which is just as true and basic now as it was in 1971.

September, 1978

PAUL H. HAHN

PREFACE TO FIRST EDITION

In our lectures to the various police academies over the past several years, we have found it quite helpful to open our remarks on many occasions by reassuring the assembled officers that: "We know full well that you see the delinquent behavior of the acting-out, aggressive youngster in the raw. When you go into a dark building on a call of man with a gun, you can be killed or injured just as easily if the gun-wielder is sixteen years old or forty-five years old. We also understand that you can suffer the expense of having your uniform ripped or your eyeglasses broken in a scuffle with a disturbed youngster, and you daily risk the hazards of automobile accident or personal injury as the result of a chase in your car or on foot, with the same cost and hazard existing whether the fleeing person be an adult criminal or a juvenile delinquent. Furthermore, we are keenly aware that by the time the various behavioral scientists see the juvenile offender in the courts and the clinics, the youngster looks better, acts better, and, in fact, on many occasions, even smells better than he did when you encountered him in a drunken state, high on narcotics or sleeping in an abandoned warehouse."

This statement is intended to bridge the gap that has long existed between many persons functioning at the level of enforcement and those who supposedly are professionally more concerned with diagnosis and treatment of the juvenile offender. We believe that juvenile delinquency can neither be prevented nor controlled without good law enforcement any more than this goal could be accomplished without good diagnosis and treatment after apprehension. The police, the courts and the correction officials should be an integral team and none can function effectively without the others.

The split that has long existed in this field between the "doers" and the "thinkers," and the suspicion on the part of the "doers" as to what the "thinkers" might be "doing," and the concern often expressed by the "thinkers" as to what the "doers" might be "thinking," has seriously hampered the teamwork that must be developed if the ever-increasing problem of juvenile delinquency in this country is to receive the official attention that it requires.

This book is dedicated to the proposition that the good enforcement officer must understand juvenile delinquency and the law applying to it, just as much, and in some cases more, than those from courts and corrections who are also concerned about it. This was well said over a half century ago in one of the classical commentaries on law enforcement and corrections: "The policeman is society's outpost in the treatment of crime. It would be well if he knew more than he does concerning the nature of delinquency and the causes of crime. His very position gives him a strategic influence upon the future of lawbreakers. He can often make or break the careers of first offenders by sympathy given or withheld, by fair or rough handling, by intelligent understanding of the forces back of a given act or by neglect of those forces."[1] It is our belief that if the police officer understands what is really happening on the "youth scene," it will make him more effective in handling the maze of problems which the delinquent behavior of youngsters presents to him each day.

For this reason, this is not a "Manual of Instructions for Police Officers," nor is it the compilation of a set of "rules of thumb" for the handling of individual situations involving an almost infinite amount of possibilities and imagined predicaments; on the contrary, it is intended to be a volume containing most of what your author believes to be necessary to understand, from a legal and a behavioral standpoint, the phenomenon that is so commonly called juvenile delinquency.

We do not intend to try to make lawyers or psychiatrists or social workers out of law enforcement officers, for to do so would be to destroy their effectiveness in their chosen profession; but we do wish to present for their thinking and study a certain amount of basic information drawn from the law and from the behavioral sciences.

There is very little original thinking in this text because so many fine observers have recorded their opinions concerning almost every aspect of juvenile behavior so well in the past. We have acknowledged the source of our opinion wherever possible. Likewise, we have tried to avoid repeating the obvious as far as

---

[1] Frederick Howard Wines, *Punishment and Reformation* (New Edition, enlarged and revised by Winthrop D. Lane, 1919), p. 314.

possible, and we have emphasized the more recent observations, especially those which we felt would be most valuable to law enforcement officers.

The complexity of juvenile delinquency as a behavioral pattern is well established. It would be impossible to present a single cause or a simple description of the misbehavior of millions of American youths exhibited through the commission of every conceivable type of offense and taking place at all hours of the day and night in places as widely separated as downtown New York City and the mountains of California. To impute the existence of the same syndrome in such circumstances would, in our opinion, be to deny the obvious and to distort reality.

Delinquency has become more complex. Prior to 1968 many behavioral scientists were stating that all juvenile delinquency was the behavior of the emotionally disturbed. Recently, however, the addition of other factors including the spread of certain offenses from ghetto to suburb and the "politically motivated" who use delinquent behavior to change the system indicate that juvenile delinquency is keeping pace with the rest of society's transformations.

At a time in history when, perhaps for the only time, we are able to see most of man's collective behavioral history laid out in front of us by viewing a man working in a field with handmade wooden instruments in an underdeveloped country and, at the same time, see a space age technology enable rocket ships to rendezvous in space with mathematical precision, unfortunately, we also witness huge numbers of alienated youth seemingly regressing from the traditional question "what shall I commit my life to?" to the more primitive query of "shall I commit my life to anything or simply squander it?"

The normal complexities of adolescent adjustment are certainly complicated by the disintegration of family life, rampant materialism, extremes of affluence and poverty existing side by side, and a disenchantment by large numbers of youngsters with a society that they seem to feel is becoming so "progressive" that it is proceeding from the notion of "throw away bottles" to "throw away people."

In these circumstances, values and attitudes change and the

behavior that results is equally different; and so the task of those who are publicly charged with the control of behavior becomes exceedingly challenging.

The lot of the policeman has never been an easy one, and at present it is becoming more difficult. This was well said in a recent joint statement by the Connecticut Bar Association and the Connecticut State Police Department: "The job of a police officer is one of the most difficult yet one of the most important callings in our society. The policeman must be aggressive and zealous in his pursuit of lawbreakers, while, at the same time, he must exercise vigilance to uphold the law to protect the rights of the innocent. Our society expects a policeman to risk his life in preserving the peace, but expects, at the same time, that he act swiftly and courageously without transgressing the limitations imposed upon his conduct by local laws and by the United States Constitution. The police officer is truly a man on a 'tightrope'."[2]

When this "walking of the tightrope" is extended to the police function in dealing with the "teen culture" and the sensitivity and "mood-swings" of youth, it challenges the professional competence and all of the personal skills and dedication of the good officer. This book is designed to help him to meet that challenge.

Among the "games" which professionals sometimes play is the "jargon game," in which a rather sophisticated, but sometimes unintelligible language is constantly used, which has meaning only to the members of one particular profession, but is of little use to laymen or even to many other professionals trained in different disciplines. This "game" probably was at least part of the reason why Herman Melville said some years ago that the true scientist "uses but few hard words, and those only when none other will suit his purpose, whereas the 'smatterer' in sciences . . . thinks that by mouthing hard words he understands hard things."[3] This observation was stated more

[2] From the pamphlet "The Police Officer and the Bill of Rights," published by the Connecticut Bar Association and the Connecticut State Police Department.

[3] Herman Melville, *I'm O.K.—You're O.K.*, Thomas A. Harris, Harper & Row N.Y. (1967, 1968, 1969), Preface, P.X.V.

graphically recently to the author by a man who said "Unless a man can explain what he is talking about in terms that could easily be understood by a nine-year-old, the man probably doesn't understand his subject."

With these admonitions in mind, and because this text is written primarily for the use of those who wish to understand the delinquent behavior of young people and the law relating to it, rather than to do an exercise in technical vocabulary, we shall attempt to use as few highly technical terms as possible while dealing with some very important behavioral principles and legal concepts.

Finally, we wish to affirm that it is because we truly love the youth of America that we wish to assist in every possible way in helping to control that portion of their behavior which causes them to harm themselves and others. Because we have confidence in the law and in due process, we wish to strengthen it by pointing out its real meaning and applicability in relation to the behavior of the young. And because we love America and the way of life which has brought such great blessings and benefits to so many, we criticize, hopefully in a constructive way, those factors that tend to destroy it or keep it from being of equal benefit to all its members.

We wish to emphasize that we believe in discipline, that which flows from inside the person and causes him to develop the necessary controls to function in society without harming others, and when necessary, that imposed from outside by parents, teachers, police and all other lawfully constituted authority who must at all times "love enough to discipline." But we also caution all those who would discipline others to remember that discipline must flow from love and justice, and that if it does not, it represents only repression; and that the right to discipline is based upon respect, but respect must be earned by being worthy of respect, just as love must be earned by being lovable.

In these troubled times, when the world so often needs "putting together" again, we might be well motivated by the apocryphal story of the dinner-meeting of many of the great minds and most powerful men of our times in a large city.

During the social hour prior to dinner, these men of means and ability worked futilely in trying to put together a puzzle, which when properly assembled made up a picture of the world. Having little success, the men went in to dinner leaving the "world" unassembled. While these leaders were at dinner, a young child came into the room and in a matter of a very few minutes had successfully assembled "the entire world." When the men returned to the room they were amazed to have found the puzzle completed so quickly by the little boy. When pressed for an answer as to how he had accomplished this, the child simply informed them that "On the back of the puzzle that made up the world, there was another puzzle that just simply made a picture of a child. It was easy. I just put the child together, and I found that the world came out all right."

It is to this goal, to help "put the child together," that this book is dedicated.

June, 1971

PAUL H. HAHN

CONTENTS

CHAPTER 1: CONTEMPORARY CULTURAL AND ECOLOGICAL ENVIRONMENT

CHAPTER 2: CLASSIFICATION OF JUVENILE OFFENDERS

CHAPTER 3: CAUSES OF DEVIANT OR DELINQUENT BEHAVIOR: DIFFERING THEORIES

CHAPTER 15: THE PREVENTION OF JUVENILE DELINQUENCY

Section

CHAPTER 16: PROFESSIONAL POLICE APPROACH TO JUVENILE OFFENDER

Section

CHAPTER 17: DUE PROCESS AND ITS SPECIAL CONCERNS RELATING TO JUVENILES

Section

CHAPTER 18: LEGAL DEFINITIONS REQUIRED FOR UNDERSTANDING THE JUVENILE'S RELATIONSHIP TO THE LAW

Section

CHAPTER 22: TREATMENT OF THE JUVENILE OFFENDER

Section

Chapter 1

CONTEMPORARY CULTURAL AND ECOLOGICAL
ENVIRONMENT

§ 1.1 Introduction

The juvenile offender cries out loudly with his behavior and the juvenile law demands with its emphatic statements that we must understand the causes of juvenile delinquency and correct them before it is too late in the life of each individual offender. Yet despite these urgings, we have traditionally approached the problem of control of juvenile delinquency with a heavy emphasis on institutionalization when the problem individually and collectively is seen by the community as being beyond control, and placed little effort into the struggle to identify the causes of delinquency, alter the conditions and circumstances which produce the problem, and obtain realistic satisfaction of the needs of the large numbers of youngsters who are identified as problem children.

For this reason, we have often been accused of being a nation that spends large sums of money to provide ambulance service at the bottom of a chasm into which our children are falling rapidly, and is at the same time unwilling to spend even a minimal amount to fence the top in order to prevent the children from falling in. More eloquently, this was recently represented as being parallel to the dilemma of the householder who spends all of his time and energy mopping up the bathroom floor, without bothering to turn off the faucet.

In many cases, the police officer is among the first to recognize a problem in the behavior of a juvenile offender, and in

1

these cases the opportunity for the officer is optimum to follow the intentions of the law in getting the necessary help for the child so that his behavioral pattern can change, and in so doing, to protect the community in the most practical way possible.

In other cases, by the time some offenders actually come to the attention of the police, they have already observed the futile efforts of parents and relatives, members of the clergy, community center and detached workers, teachers, school counselors, attendance workers, school administrators, public and private agency personnel, psychiatrists and psychologists, and in some cases even judges, probation and parole officers, to control their behavior with little success. In these circumstances, the responsibility of the police officer is greater and the need for understanding and getting practical assistance into the picture takes on the proportions of a real emergency.

Behavior can be controlled most effectively when it is understood. Law enforcement officers are charged with the control of juvenile delinquency, and consequently their need to understand the roots and the ramifications of this behavior is of great importance. It has been believed for too long that only those persons working in clinics or "treatment centers" needed to understand juvenile behavior, and the police officer simply should make arrests in a mechanical, almost unrelated sort of way. This kind of compartmentalized thinking must give way to the essential belief that each person who has any contact with a juvenile offender must understand the problems he confronts and work toward their solutions if the offender is to be helped and the law is to be fulfilled.

The police officer's contact with a young offender is often the earliest, and his impact in many cases can be the greatest. Consequently, arming the police officer with the necessary knowledge, skills and motivations is not a luxury but a necessity in controlling juvenile delinquency.

Finally, we might draw the ultimate lesson from the tragic story of the young man who was being led down the corridor to the gas chamber in a large western penitentiary some years ago and who made a very thought-provoking statement when he noticed the large number of observers who were present behind a plate glass window for the purpose of watching him die. With his last recorded statement on earth, this young man cried out, "Where were all of you? Where were all of you when I was a boy? If I would have received half this much attention then, I would not be here now."

A youngster with problems can have contact with many individuals without ever receiving the attention that is required to change his values and attitudes and influence his behavior. The needed attention can only result from someone understanding and being interested in his problem.

§ 1.2   Recent changes: Juvenile behavior and the social scene

Since the publication of the first edition of this text in 1971, there have been substantial changes in both the patterns of juvenile delinquency witnessed in this country, and in the contemporary cultural and ecological environment in which that behavior has taken place. For example, up until very recently scholars and observers of juvenile delinquency have been comfortable in saying that:

1. Most youth crime took place in the inner-city, highly urbanized areas of our society.

2. That the highest arrest rate took place within the age group of "young adults" (18 to 24 years old) and that "older juveniles" (15 to 17 years old) were distinctly in second place in relation to frequency of arrest in this country.

3. That the problem of delinquency primarily expressed itself in "crimes against property" so significantly that crimes of violence against the person were certainly not the major concern at that time.

However, very recent developments tend to challenge all three of these positions. First, within the past five years, the tremendous increase in delinquent activity in the suburbs of America, and even in rural areas, as evidenced by formal statistics and especially as indicated by "self admission surveys," present cause for very serious challenge to this previously well-accepted axiom. While the amount of delinquency still remains highest by far in the inner-city, the rate of increase in the suburbs is causing a visible narrowing of this statistical gap. Secondly, between 1970 and 1975, the arrest rate for the group of "older juveniles" (15 to 17 years old) grew so quickly (at a rate nearly three times as fast as the rate for "young adult" offenders) that the "older juvenile" group has assumed first position in the "race" for the dubious honor of being the most frequently arrested in this country. And in relation to the third statement, while crimes against property still remain by far the most frequently committed, the increase in crimes of "violence against the person" by juveniles has been dramatic within the past five years.

According to the most recent Federal Bureau of Investigation statistics, teenagers comprise about 17% of those charged with assault, 20% of those charged with rape, about 30% of those charged with robbery, and more startlingly, these same statistics reveal an increase in violent juvenile crime for non-urban areas of almost 20% during the same five-year period. Of course, at the same time, the arrest rate of urban juveniles for violent crime was still about twice that of those for non-urban juveniles although the rate of increase in the latter category is most visible. (The above statistics are based on "Uniform Crime Reports," Federal Bureau of Investigation, published August 25, 1975).

At the same time that we are currently arresting about 1.6 million teenagers each year in the United States, authorities are also advising us that we are witnessing an all-time high in teen-age suicides, vandalism, pregnancy, drug abuse, and alcoholism. While many attempt to explain the problem behavior of a large number of adolescents in our contemporary society simply in terms of the "baby bulge" (which has taken us from 24,000,000 young Americans in 1950 to 44,000,000 today), close observation seems to indicate that there are many more cultural and ecological factors which also need to be considered.

Just since the first edition of this text, for example, our children have watched this nation torn apart by the horrors of the Vietnam War and in the civil strife resulting therefrom; they have been angered and confused by a Watergate debacle and alternately confused and frustrated by a "post-Watergate morality" which has so far failed to produce a "golden age".

Before they could absorb the lack of credibility in high places, they were forced to confront the lack of energy resources in the earth itself. Their attention has been diverted in rapid-fire succession from narcotics in the suburbs to looting in the streets. The contemporary scene continues to present them with vivid examples of the most degrading poverty in the midst of the greatest affluence the world has ever known; politicalization of crime existing side by side with the criminalization of politics; and the technology to "give a man a new heart" within a system which sometimes seems not to have "sufficient heart" to give a man a job.

These "new" manifestations of the problems confronting youth in our contemporary society exist side by side with the same basic social, cultural and ecological factors which existed and influenced the behavior of our younger generation at the writing of the first edition of this text. As we have moved through several years of even greater "advancement" and change in our society, one is moved to again raise the age-old question of whether from a human standpoint change is always for the better, while at the same time dealing with the pragmatic dilemma which comes from knowing full well that we must either adapt to change or perish.

§ 1.3 Effect of technological advances on purpose of human activities

Let us look for just a minute at what man has spent his time doing in the past. One finds quickly that he spent all of his time in the remote past on survival and functions related to it. While fire-building, shelter-building and food-hunting developed into group protective-care and banding together against common enemies, all through early history we see that basically the main tasks of man have been the things connected with his survival needs as an individual or in a group.

In modern American society, these chores have been practically eliminated or reduced to a point where they consume very little time. Man today spends less time than ever before in history on anything that even comes close to the immediate filling of his survival needs. He presently spends more time in responding to pleasure stimuli and status mechanisms, and in accumulating more possessions.

There has been from the beginning of time until now, almost a complete reversal in the essential operations of the time-consuming efforts of man. Today, the entire concept of what we are attempting to do, whether we are sitting in a classroom, or on our jobs, has changed so greatly that it is difficult to grasp the old traditional human concept of what a man spent his time doing. The reason that the point merits repetition and emphasis is that this re-alignment of our time and energy economy represents graphically the extent and degree that man's world has undergone change. We are in a period of history where the very basic values that we have accepted for so long, concerning the purpose of our existence, and that of the world and life in it and what we are to spend our time doing, are changing so rapidly and have changed so rapidly that they are almost unrecognizable. Looking at just a few facts illustrative of this phenomenon, for example, we see that in the past seventy-five years, we have probably consumed more of the world's resources than we have in all previous recorded history.

In the field of transportation alone, in one person's lifetime, if a man were seventy-five years old, he would have seen us grow from the point where we used the beast of burden, which we had used in all previously recorded history, through the invention and the use of the automobile, through the airplane, through the jet age, and now into the era of outer space travel and guided missiles. Interplanetary exploration and all aspects of the aerospace age with which we are so well acquainted are only a lifetime away from the ox-cart and the mule. This period of change, unequalled, unparalleled in history, has moved so quickly that parts of the present world, and even isolated areas in the United States, have not yet begun to catch up, and so by looking around us we can see all of history laid out before us.

Looking at another field, the field of literacy or education, we observe that there is more dissemination of knowledge, whether it be good or bad information, more availability of reading matter (even if it be pornographic), more learning situations of a formal nature available than ever before in the history of mankind.

In communications, the advances are even more startling. We have passed through telephone, into television, and now into Tel-Star and transistorized marvels. The people in electronic communications tell us that the advances within the next ten to fifteen years are going to be unbelievable, so we are at the zenith of the age of communications marvels which are shrinking the world.

This tremendous change, this fantastic, almost complete turnabout from the kind of situation in which man has lived for most of previously recorded history is not only unparalleled in other centuries, but it probably outstrips the rate of advance in most of recorded history taken as a totality. Change has become the very essence of which today is composed. As multiple and all-embracing changes take place, the status quo remains secure in very few categories. Sociologically, we are well aware of what is going on. We are witnessing a breakdown in the functioning of primary social units in the face of the complexities of life.

Theologically, most of us are affected by tremendous change of discipline and questioning of doctrine. Sweeping changes are also present in education, economic patterns, production and consumption, and recreation. From another standpoint, we are faced with crises in many of the important segments of national life. We are faced with crises in the field of public welfare and law. We are faced with crises in the field of big-city government. We are faced with crises in the field of pollution and traffic hazards. We are faced with crises in practically every major area. All is seemingly in turmoil, and very little of the old, familiar and comfortable remains the same, unthreatened by impending alteration or destruction.

As we move into this tremendous period of challenge, where adaptation seems to be essential, man basically remains the same, but every single thing around him seems to be in turmoil.

This is obvious in the problems of youngsters. The generation gap is connected with unfulfilled basic security needs. One contemporary observer points out that too much change in too short a time produces a shattering stress and disorientation in individuals and in groups; and he warns that unless we are able to effect a balance between rates of change in different sectors, and especially between the pace of environment change and the limited ability of humans to adapt quickly enough, we are dooming millions to "future shock" or massive adaptational breakdown.[1]

To sum up, we have gone from a self-determined, personally geared, work-oriented society, which has existed from time immemorial, to a computer-geared, information directed, leisure-oriented society in such a few years that this change, particularly in the past fifteen years, has become so intense, noticeable, all-pervading that it has had great impact on personality development and behavior.

All of this demands adaptation. The greatest single challenge to modern mankind is: Will we be able to adapt to all this change? Will we be able to take the things that we need, and will need, and always have needed as human beings, and be able to superimpose those things over, or make those things the undergirding for the realistic use of this progress and this technological advancement? Can man learn to attain the realistic satisfaction of all the new needs that are being created? Can he translate these things into terms of being useful to him as a human being? Can he use the many new things properly, and can he understand the problems connected with their use properly? Can he adapt in general to all this change, without destroying the human values in his own life and viciously exploiting others?

§ 1.4　Nature of challenge of technological change

The challenge is to prepare a society that values people more than technology; that keeps man from being lost in mass-production and more "object relationships." Yet, the danger is that while we are getting prepared for this society which isn't going to permit people to bog down in its mechanism, to be ground in its mill, destroyed by its progress, that we ourselves are becoming less human due to the heavy pressures of im-personalization, success-orientation, and the demise of personal discipline which accompanies affluence and abundance. The real problem for us and our children is to be able to adapt our human needs and our human goals to the insecurity, the change, and the progress that is taking place in so many areas.[2]

[1] Alvin Toffler, *Future Shock,* Random House, N.Y. (1970), pp. 308-315.

[2] George A. Petit, *Prisoners of Culture,* Scribners (1970).

Are we making so much progress that in so doing we are de-humanizing ourselves? Are we getting so involved in economic and technological goals, and the building of "platforms" and levels, that we are ceasing to realize the importance of the individuality of the people, and the fulfillment of the individual as an individual? These are the pressures that set up high conflicts within society itself and within individual persons.

One of the most obvious signs of the impersonal approach to change is the problem of "uprooting," which literally means the pulling up by the roots. This is done to countless numbers of people because of the enormously fast progress that we are making. People in America are literally being torn up by the roots from most of the things of value in their lives and in their past.

And as progress becomes more rapid, we continue to uproot ourselves even from the present in our "throw-away" society. The principle of built-in obsolescence and our need for a fantastic rate of consumption, has taken us far beyond throw-away bottles and cans, and as Toffler observes so well, has launched us into the era of paper dresses in our personal lives and disposable classrooms in our schools.[3]

Attachment to things and places becomes impossible when this "throw-away" atmosphere is coupled with high mobility in society, as industry and professions require more and more family moves. Lasting relationships with people diminish rapidly as technology keeps changing our individual roles along with our location and that of our familiar possessions.

We have also been uprooted as a nation and as a society from the soil. We have been uprooted from the farm in record time. In just one ordinary life-span we have seen farm life and small town ways, where we could know people intimately, where we could have the more human type of social exchange, and the kind of emotional and personal support that we need every day, diminish from the way of the majority to that of a select few.

We don't get this kind of satisfaction in sophisticated urban living. We have been so driven through pleasure pursuits, the status drive, the desire for economic gain, that we don't "have time to take the time" for the exchanges that tend to establish

3 *Future Shock*, op. cit., pp. 47-51.

the interpersonal relationships, the sense of belonging, even the old concepts of fun.

We are uprooted now from the very cities themselves. People uprooted from the farms and placed in the cities are now being uprooted from the cities into suburbia with a speed and lack of preparedness never before dreamed possible. At the same time, we build social and economic barriers that make it impossible for large numbers to respond.

Before we have absorbed a certain type of life, our needs and desires and the pressures of the kind of environment in which we are living are pushing us to learn something new before we have fully learned about the old. We are being uprooted from all of our traditions, our religion and a cohesive family relationship. We may be suffering from a major breakdown in all of the primary units of effective social living.

It is notable that in view of social upheaval, lack of needed relationships and meaningful interpersonal communications, we have fewer problems than would be expected. A human being is not, by nature, this type of nomadic creature. He needs roots, security, a sense of belonging, first-person relationships, meaningful relationships and "gut level" communications. These are the things that are suffering because of rapid changes and we may not retain health and humanity without them.

Simultaneously, there is an assault on the individual identity of the person, the self-concept, the concept of "me as me," "me as important," "me" as being meaningful to myself, and then in relation to my God, and then in relation to other people. This is all-important to the individual.

§ 1.5　Effect of conditioning by mass media

There is an assault that we are aware of constantly by the mass media of communication—for example, with its violence and "group-reaction" conditioning. Immanuel Kant made the memorable statement that man should never be an object, he should always be a subject. Yet, in modern civilization, especially in sophisticated urban living in America today, how can one be anything but an object, when one is constantly treated like an object? We are being conditioned relentlessly. Our responses

are being conditioned day and night by the advertising, news and other communications media. We are even expected to all laugh or cry during the same programs and at the same stimuli. All of these accepted norms and fixed behavior patterns are being forced on the public. We are being literally bombarded with the demand to act "like everybody else," or at least like all the other members of the same consumer category.

This constant effort being made by various sources to place us into a consumer category is but one small aspect of the total problem. The import of this thing is seen as significant when it is evaluated in the light of our personal subjectivity and individuality. Are we remaining persons capable of our own responses, capable of our own ideas, capable of establishing a syllogism for ourselves and coming out with a proper conclusion; or are we objects that can be molded, lifted, transplanted; persons whose feelings can be mass-produced and whose responses can be conditioned? In this age of automation, it is important that we do not become automated or creatures of the very automation itself.

We are eliminating jobs at the rate of nine jobs eliminated for every one new job created. The new job created has certain very specific demands. It is either a technological job, or a "white collar job."

The "labor jobs," the jobs which bring one more into contact with reality situations, are being rapidly eliminated. As this need for the more technical skills increases, the type of training, thinking and personality that is required for the job is becoming mass-produced. And this is a tragedy, because as we train more and more people for roles, we seem to be educating less and less for human life and satisfactory living.

§ 1.6   Effect of change on family structure and children

Meanwhile, while all this is happening, what is happening to the family? It is probably being more violently assaulted than any other social unit. Under the pressure of this assault, which cannot be totally withstood by all and which is not withstood at all by some, as is easily witnessed by the divorce, illegitimacy rates, and all the rest of the rates that pertain to family life and social health, family life in America, at least as formerly known, seems to be disintegrating rapidly.

It is no longer cohesive as a unit. It is not a producing unit any longer, nor is it an educational unit. The family has become chiefly a residential and consuming unit; and it is being treated by the environment as exactly that. We pay rent or purchase a house together, and we buy the groceries for a group, but beyond that there often is little family solidarity.

The pressure is constantly on the family to remain exactly that, a mere residential group. Analyze the advertising media, the entertainment being presented, and any aspect of modern, sophisticated living, and the result will be clear.

The father, for example, formerly the principal authority, intellectually, emotionally and in every other sense, has now little or no set position. In his increasing search for more money, more status, more pleasure, for all of the "extra-familial things" which we take for granted as normal for the head of the family to seek, he is away from the home for longer periods of time and his role has changed drastically. He; in turn, reacts to his own involvement in all these other things in a variety of ways, oftentimes with a great deal of guilt. Not functioning as "head," or leader, he is often unable, when necessary, to function as disciplinarian, or as identification figure, and sometimes even as adequate male, because he has surrendered the father's role to the mother.

At the same time, the mother is subject to similar pressures. Many times, in the above kinds of situations, mother is the first to substitute for the father, and she quickly finds herself out of the feminine role and replacing the passive father. In these cases, mother goes into the aggressive, masculine role, and the results for mother, father and children are often tragic.

In situations where mother is subject to the same kind of pressures, and her own needs begin to interfere with her exercising not only her traditional role, but substituting for the father, then we often have the chaotic situation that we see existing in so many families, where both mother and father are absent from the home, if not physically, certainly psychologically. This causes the children to seek their real education, all recreation, their male or female identification, and the satisfaction of other emotional needs outside the home.

This is one of the great tragedies that is taking place, and yet oftentimes we profess to be amazed that children, even in the affluent sections of society, seem to be identifying with values and standards found on the street. This should be expected because so often they cannot identify with values in the home.

There is very little group education or even group recreational experience at home. Family meals are not as important as they used to be and family religious worship is declining. The child feels these lacks keenly; consequently, communication between the family members which used to be a natural thing breaks down.

Communication within families is breaking down every day at such a rate that it makes all of us who are concerned about child behavior in this country literally sick, because it is one of the things that we see first, and we know that total alienation follows close behind. The irony in this whole thing is that in this age of electronic communication with the planets and walking on the moon, we are not communicating with our own children in our homes across the dinner table.

Left out of all these things, the child finds that he still must function. He must grow up, mature and identify. He must establish a value system for himself. But he must do all this in a partial vacuum, where there should have been a tremendous amount of emotional satisfaction, where he should have developed a real concept of authority, and where there should have been the meaningful process of identification in which the son looks at the father and says, "I want to believe what he believes, I want to think like he thinks; in fact, I want to comb my hair like he combs his hair." Questions of personal worth, self-concept, loyalties, conscience formation, attitudes and values continue to arise as the growing up process continues, and these things, too, are often left unsatisfied. With all of the leisure time, sophisticated formal educational procedures, our technological advancement, children are left to shift for themselves "inside" in these important areas.

While this is happening, while the child is groping for a

figure to identify with, searching for the answers, seeking for the love, support, security, common-sense discipline, and the meaning of new experiences, we are bombarding him with unfortunate ideas. To take a specific one, we teach him basically and very early in life that he either has to rape or destroy a thing of beauty before he can enjoy it. What do we tell him, for example, about baseball? We tell him we don't just learn baseball because it is a good game and can be fun, we insist that he must become the best and conquer everyone else. We teach the very young that they must wring from every experience every ounce of personal achievement, from the standpoint of status, conquering others, and from a sense of winning, as far as possible.

We are teaching this all the time in the field of sex. In the field of vocations, we are teaching him constantly not just to educate himself to fulfill his innermost desires and his most personal needs, and his own sense of fulfillment, but to become the "best" of something, which we usually define as the highest paid.

This is a concept that is completely negative to happy, healthy, wholesome ability to adjust to the needs of other people, to develop the kinds of virtues that make for an ethical and satisfying way of life; but we are bombarding our children with these pressures, while at the same time, we have created the very soil in which this kind of negative pressure can thrive because the positive influences are not there.

At this point, trouble starts for society, not just in terms of the delinquent child, where it becomes so intensive and obvious that it seems a caricature, but with the normal child as well. Every person is totally immersed in his environment, and is subject to its pressures. The child, being more highly impressionable in the formative years, reacts to environmental pressures to a much greater degree than older, more stabilized persons.

§ 1.7   Environmental problems created by technological advances

The present environment, especially in the big city areas of the United States, includes so many rapid, extensive changes that they can best be described by the use of the term "explosions."

The population explosion continues at a rate that is estimated to be capable of doubling the entire world's population within thirty-nine years. The present world population of over four billion is said to be increasing by approximately 8,000 persons per hour. In our industrial country, the already overcrowded major metropolitan areas are receiving the impact of both the population growth and the migration of rural Americans to urban areas.

This overcrowding, in itself, presses people closer together in a variety of relationships for which many are poorly prepared; pressures for services that communities are not willing or able to provide for financial reasons, and causes confrontations between groups and individuals without adequate time and preparation for such group interaction.

Meanwhile, the "awareness" and "communication" explosion through TV and other mass communication media makes the availability of an amazing mass of material things vividly evident and enticingly attractive to practically the entire population. This makes the quest for things much more important to all, because it turns objects, previously only vaguely desired, into necessities, and makes things, formerly not known about, objects of desire and strong possessive urges. This is done indiscriminately, whether or not the viewing audience has the capacity to acquire legitimately the objects presented.

This creates particular pressure on the group that is economically and socially alienated in the larger society because it constantly reminds them of the "good life" which seems abundantly available, upon which the larger society places such a premium, but which they are not able to obtain legitimately.

One prominent entertainer, with a background of poverty and deprivation, said recently that when he was a youngster the hunger to which he was exposed was not nearly as severe as that experienced by severely underprivileged children today, because today a child can see more food in one-half hour on television than a youngster of some years ago would have seen in his entire lifetime.

The education and literacy explosion certainly opens new

vistas and provides a level of knowledge and sophistication to individuals and whole groups which was never before deemed possible; however, at the same time, this condition makes new demands on society as a whole to absorb as equals and integrate totally, individuals and groups who in the past, for a variety of reasons, remained uneducated and, consequently, unable to compete with the larger group.

The technological explosion continues at a rapid pace and continues to cause drastic alteration in our basic living patterns. The pollution explosion keeps pace with our expanding technology and our constant thirst for more and better things, and so we find the constant destruction of beauty and health becoming an intimate part of our everyday living and consuming patterns.

It has been estimated that because of air pollution from industrial waste and automobile exhaust fumes, the average non-smoker in our large cities inhales the toxic equivalents of from twenty-six to thirty-eight cigarettes each day. Because of pesticides and other chemicals in proximity to food products, approximately one thousand people are thought to die each year from some form of chemical poisoning, and an estimated eighty to ninety thousand people suffer disease or some form of bodily injury from the same source. It is estimated that at least one major American city suffers a forty per cent reduction in the amount of sunlight each day because of the presence of pollutants in the air; and conservation officials warn us that various important forms of wildlife, such as the bald eagle, the brown pelican, the Bermuda petrel and others, are threatened with extinction because they cannot survive amid the man made waste.

In at least one large city, school children are not allowed to run, skip or jump inside or outside the school building on "smog-alert days," and thousands of adults and children are advised by their doctors to leave the city for health reasons every year.

The explosion in space needs is intimately linked with the pollution explosion as we constantly take away more and more natural beauty in quest of space to erect buildings, to house businesses and to store our garbage. At least one source estimates that over one million acres of valuable oxygen-producing fields, forests, grass and farming lands are being gobbled up by highways, shopping centers, and urban subdivisions each year. There are an estimated one million automobile carcasses abandoned on our roads and public highways each year. About 3.5 billion tons of discards and "throw aways" are produced in the United States each year, and over one hundred million discarded automobile tires can be found dotting the landscape in or out of the confines of junkyards. Ordinary garbage is being burned in open pits, buried deeply in the earth's bosom or condensed and compressed and hidden away in caves or other natural disposal areas, and much of it is being ground or dumped into the ocean directly or after traveling through our rivers and streams. Could it be that 20th Century America will be remembered best for being a land with about 6.7% of the world's population and over 55% of the world's garbage?

The noise explosion has become critical with jet planes, sonic booms, the multiplication of radios, television sets and phonographs, and the use of electronic equipment to amplify sound in entertainment. More than one observer is warning that this problem psychologically affects millions and physically affects many, and it has been predicted that numerous teenagers will suffer hearing impairment before they reach thirty. They also warn that intense and prolonged noise can be connected with severe mental disorientation and possibly even with violence.

These problems were eloquently summarized by an Associated Press correspondent when he recently wrote:

"The standard of living rises while the satisfaction of living declines. The Gross National Product grows grosser in reverse proportions to the gross national tranquility. We have polluted the land and the air and the water, defaced the horizon with commercial clutter, and blurred our history and our symbols with dollar signs. We have suffered, in Lewis Mumford's words, 'disorder, blight, dingy mediocrity, screaming neon-lighted vulgarity. We have ceased to respect ourselves—we have ceased to cherish our own history and to enlarge our own prospects by promoting character and vanity and beauty wherever we find it, in landscapes or in people'."[4]

This, then, is the contemporary cultural, environmental, ecological scene. This is the backdrop against which, or as part of which, youth's behavior takes place. If we are to fully understand the behavior of the young, we must understand the stage on which it is acted out.

APPLICATION OF IMPORTANT POINTS EMPHASIZED FOR LAW ENFORCEMENT OFFICERS

1. In the time period since 1971 our society has witnessed substantial changes, in both the patterns of juvenile delinquency and in the contemporary cultural and ecological environment in which that behavior has taken place.

2. While the total amount of delinquency still remains significantly higher in the inner-city, the rate of increase in delinquency in the suburbs is causing a visible narrowing of the statistical gap.

3. The "most frequently arrested group" changed from "young adults" to "older juveniles" during the years 1970 to 1975.

4. While crimes against property still remain by far the most frequently committed, the increase in crimes of "violence against the person" by juveniles has been most dramatic within the past five years.

5. In addition to the problems of juvenile delinquency, youth authorities are also advising us that we are currently witnessing all time highs in other problem areas such as teenage suicide, unwed pregnancy, and juvenile alcoholism and drug abuse.

6. In our rapidly changing, technological society, the law enforcement officer must adapt to constant and abrupt change not only as a person but also as a member of a profession that changes and bears the brunt of most human problems when they affect the behavior of others.

7. Much deviant behavior represents insecurity and inability to adapt to so much change.

8. Law enforcement officers today often have to attempt to enforce the traditional law and practice an expectancy of discipline in a society and among groups and individuals that are vastly different from the society and the individuals of even a few years ago. The emotional climate of society, the methods of child-rearing, the educational system, and much of the total lifestyle of a majority in most communities has changed so drastically in a relatively short period of time that a

[4] Saul Petit, "America, the—What?"
Cincinnati Enquirer, February 15, 1970.

"communication gap" and "value gap" often exists through no personal fault of the law enforcement officer.

9. The sensitive, professional officer recognizes the changing values and new pressures, especially in dealing with the impressionable young, and he tries to adapt his methods to current problems and needs. If he remains rigid and fails to recognize change about him and the need for adaptation, his effectiveness is minimized.

10. Communication, especially with the young, and constant efforts to continue education at a practical level are the greatest assets to a good police officer in keeping up with the happenings and, consequently, with the enforcement problems and methods of each new day.

Chapter 2

CLASSIFICATION OF JUVENILE OFFENDERS

Section

§ 2.1 General statements of causality

When we discuss the important question of who are the delinquent offenders, or what is a diagnostic picture of the millions of youngsters who are in the process of detection, arrest, adjudication and correction, it is necessary that we keep in mind the fact that our complex society provides an effective nurturing ground in which an ever-increasing number of "more normal" children become involved in crime and delinquency without seemingly large amounts of internal pathology operating in their dynamics.

The influence of poverty and deprivation and the gulf between the "haves" and the "have-nots" operate as part of the picture of the social factors contributing to juvenile delinquency independently of so-called operating "psycho-pathology."

Conversely, our affluence and the resulting luxury, mobility and emphasis on material possessions create an atmosphere of frustration and confusion for many thousands of youngsters who suffer from a "value gap," "communication gap" or so-called "generation gap" as they attempt to make an orderly transition from the impulsiveness and spontaneity of childhood to the maturity and thoughtful response of adulthood.

§ 2.2　Classification according to "medical model"; popularity and limitations

However, as the theories of causality factors are discussed at length elsewhere in this volume, this discussion will deal with the multitude of offenders known to police and courts throughout the country, and determine what kind of diagnostic terminology is most often utilized as descriptive of their condition and behavior.

Unfortunately, the "medical model" has been used for so long that it still must be recognized as most popular, even though we are aware that millions of young offenders represent culturally-induced delinquency, and despite the fact that we realize many youngsters are reacting to environmental pathology much more than exhibiting "internal pathology."

§ 2.3　Complexity of task of classification

In this discussion, it also seems imperative that we deal with certain myths, or the products of wishful thinking, that have led us for so long to look for a particular and all-embracing set of behavioral dynamics operating in certain offense categories.

For example, the quest for understanding the causes of juvenile automobile larceny or for being able to list the psychological features of the "typical" sex deviant have consumed great amounts of research energy and valuable time, but have only succeeded in causing us to return to the common-sense position that most good practitioners utilize in their everyday practice, and that is that there are as many types of offenders as there are individual offenses.

On a recent day's docket in a large metropolitan area juvenile court, three automobile larcenists appeared in succession before the court. Thorough investigation at the law enforcement level and good diagnostic work in the court clinic and probation department indicated that the first youngster had stolen the automobile in order to gain status with his delinquent peer group which had great influence on his behavior; the second larcenist appearing that day had a neurotic problem with sexual confusion and grave doubts about his masculinity, and the theft of the automobile seemed very definitely to be a part of the neurotic process; and the third delinquent seemed to have stolen the car with little anxiety or concern about the violation of the law and with profit motivation as the chief reason for the behavior which was a further indication of the character disorder and anti-social development this youngster had exhibited for some years before the time of this arrest.

This brings to mind a similar situation where three youngsters were engaged in breaking windows in a suburban area about a year prior to the auto larcenies mentioned above, and in a town several miles removed from the large metropolitan court used in the example above. In this incident, the same offense, this time malicious destruction of property, again showed three totally different sets of causal factors operating.

In this case, the one young man was involved in terrific turmoil in a very unstable home situation and the window breaking seemed to be part of a continuing pattern of attempting to seek punishment and gain attention. He had recently been arrested for "exposing himself" and there were many elements of confusion, frustration and emotional disturbance in his entire behavioral picture.

The second window breaker was an apparently stable youngster who had no record of previous delinquency and no known problems in any significant area of his adjustment, but who became involved in this particular incident because of pressure put on him by the group at a time when he was graduating from a local high school with an unblemished record, never having received an official reprimand or detention in the school setting. He and his companions had consumed some beer which had lowered the inhibition level, and this, combined with the pressure to "do something bad just once" from the peer group, established the circumstances in which this youngster succumbed and became "delinquent," which was totally out of keeping with his normal behavior pattern.

The third youngster had a background of parental ambivalence and rejection and a history of being practically undisciplined in the home and consequently, a discipline problem in the school. He had had a problem with the owner of the store, whose windows were broken, and he was able to verbalize his motives for the malicious destruction of the windows as being "to get even" with the store owner. This kind of behavior had been recorded in this boy's history on several similar occasions.

Example after example of "group offenses" with totally different causal factors in the individual dynamics could be cited from arrest records as further illustration of the need to understand the offense in relation to the offender; but space does not permit the extensive use of examples, and the experience of the readers certainly calls to mind so many examples that further illustration is not necessary.

§ 2.4   Difficulty in predicting delinquency

Conversely, the presence of similar environmental factors in the life of any two or more youngsters cannot serve as positive predictors that a similar pattern of behavior will result. For example, some years ago at the Kefauver hearings in the United States Congress, a famous criminal, who was estimated to have killed scores of persons and who was allegedly one of the most feared men in the entire underworld, was shown to have been raised in an atmosphere of severe deprivation and parental alcoholism; and yet it was also mentioned that his brother, raised in the same circumstances, was a missionary clergyman who had devoted his life to helping others.

In a family well-known to courts and agencies in one midwestern city, the death of the mother in the family seems to have been the stumbling block in the life of one youngster who has a background of severe disturbances and, consequently, delinquency; and yet, a brother of similar age has made an excellent adjustment and verbalizes that the death of the mother has been one of the factors that has impelled him onward to greater achievements.

These examples, and countless others known to practically all persons working in the field of human behavior at any level, remind us of the behavioral principle that it is not so important what happens as it is important to whom the same traumatic event happens; or more accurately stated, a factor does not become a cause of behavior in anyone's life unless it is important to the person to whom it happens.

While these notions will recur wherever we are dealing with causality and psychological factors, it is important that we keep them in mind as we discuss the typologies in delinquency.

a. Effect of early labeling on behavior of juveniles

If one were to go to his family physician for assistance with a headache and be told that he has a "typical" headache and given a panacea for all headaches without the doctor expressing any interest in what kind of headache it was or how it was caused, one would be certainly tempted to seek out the services of another physician. We are all aware that one headache might be caused by nervous tension, another might be the result of having shoes that fit much too tightly, and a third could be the result of having consumed an excessive amount of alcoholic beverages on the previous evening. And yet, while we are so aware that this is true in the physical order, we are constantly dealing in generalizations and "mass labels" to describe and deal with the much more complex problems of human behavior.

This labeling of human behavior is dangerous because it causes us to view the individual not as such, with all of his complex and personal needs and problems, but as a member of a broad category with whom we can relate only impersonally and to whom we can apply certain mass standards of diagnosis and treatment.

Moreover, labeling is even more dangerous when dealing with juveniles because of the tendency to mis-diagnose or over-diagnose and because of the principle of the "self-fulfilling prophecy."

The mis-diagnosis or over-diagnosis has caused the behavior of countless of thousands of youngsters to be termed psychotic when really they were exhibiting the behavior resulting from extremes of childhood trauma, rejection, family disorganization, cultural barrenness and the resultant confusion and rebellion at the childhood or adolescent level. Numerous others have been erroneously termed sex deviants as a result of sexual experimentation at the childhood or adolescent level, or because of behavior resulting from extreme situational pressures within institutional settings, or even in individual homes. Adjustment reactions of childhood or adolescence, sometimes involving behavior approaching psychotic proportions, are often a reaction to overwhelming environmental stress in children, and unfortunately have often caused a child to be diagnosed as "psychotic" or a "character disorder," or, worse still, on occasion, as a "child psychopath."

These problems often leave the impression that those diagnosing need to place all children seen clinically somewhere within the "medical model," and there seems to be a great reluctance to admit that perhaps the child can best be handled as a social maladjustment, or as demonstrating a condition without manifest psychiatric disorder.

Secondly, there is little question in the minds of most careful observers of child and adolescent behavior that the "principle of the self-fulfilling prophecy" has operated in the lives of numerous children. A graphic illustration of this unfortunate situation can be seen in an older adolescent boy, currently a long-term ward in a large metropolitan-area mental hospital, with a long history of irresponsible and erratic behavior patterns, whose social history indicates that as early as age nine this boy had been called "nuts" by his father; and throughout his history there are recorded incidents where the father had referred to him by that term, or as "queer," or as "not like other boys." This young man now often verbalizes to doctors and other interested parties that "you know my dad always said I was crazy anyway."

Enlightened educators have long recognized, and are doing so ever more frequently in greater numbers, that the early labeling of youngsters in the primary age as "slow learners" or "retarded," and placement in a special class for such children, eventually causes the child to see himself in such a role, especially when it is reinforced by watered-down curricula and the opinions of peers and teachers. Such children eventually gravitate into the "nuts and bolts" classes or special schools or become early school dropouts, and thus a loss to the educational system and a problem to society and to themselves.

In the field of mental health, concerned observers have long emphasized that much of the maladjusted behavior of retarded or schizophrenic children must be laid at the door of the un-satisfied ego-needs of these children and not seen as the fault of the basic condition. The results of the family and peer group seeing a child as "different" or "disturbed" and thus shunting him back, visibly showing shame about his condition, or ex-pecting little or nothing in ego-functioning of him, are often far more contributory to his lack of functioning and his social maladjustment than any other factors, including the mental condition itself.

b. The need for classification and the danger of careless or inaccurate use of terms

However, despite the difficulties and dangers in using diag-nostic terminology in explaining behavioral problems of children, it is necessary for communication among professionals dealing with juveniles that some grouping and labeling be done, but we must keep in mind at all times that this grouping and cate-gorizing is for our convenience only. It is not always exact, and it is not fully expressive of the meaning of the condition to the individual or of the connection with the offense that has brought him to our attention. And, above all, it is not at all a substitute for a rich and full knowledge of the individual of-fender as a unique personality influenced in a unique way by his problems.

As emphasized earlier, it is not the purpose of this chapter or volume to attempt to make psychiatrists, psychologists, or highly technically trained behavioral specialists of the reader; but it is necessary that all professionals having any contact with delinquent children at the enforcement level or any time there-after, have a basic knowledge of some of the most popular and important terminology currently in use.

It is of even greater importance, since the use of such terms and classifications often determines the way we approach the child and many times the treatment plan for him, that all users of psychiatric terms attach the same meaning to these terms when being used. There has been a great deal of confusion and, consequently, in our opinion, a large amount of harm done because of differing meanings and connotations of terminology when used by different disciplines within the field of the behavioral sciences.

It is our belief that much of the behavior currently seen in our complex society does not fit into the traditional "medical model" because it is much more "sociogenic" than "psychogenic"; therefore, terms describing cultural deprivation, faulty socialization, reinforcement of delinquent values and standards, limited access to legitimate opportunities for upward mobility, and a whole host of other terms of a non-psychiatric type must become a definite part of the vocabulary of those who wish to accurately explain the great amount of juvenile delinquency today.

However, confining ourselves for the moment to the more traditional classifications, we feel that it is necessary to follow the guidance of the Diagnostic and Statistical Manual of Mental Disorders[1] because the traditional medical terminology is basically psychiatric, and even though many of the terms have been borrowed, and in some cases mutilated, by other disciplines, they have their roots in psychiatry.

We feel that there should be four important rules followed in using psychiatric classifications to fulfill the requirements of justice to the person being classified and to enhance the opportunity for the classification to be of service to the person:

(1) The term must be used accurately and with the same meaning for all of those using the term. Thus, for example, "schizophrenic" should mean that the person being so classified is psychotic in the strict meaning of the word; and it should not be applied before ruling out the possible use of such a lesser diagnosis as "transient situational disturbance."[2]

[1] Second edition, 1968, published by the American Psychiatric Association. Hereafter referred to as "DSM-II."

[2] The authors would like to acknowledge the fine article on this subject by Earl Parsons, M.D., "Recent Changes in Psychiatric Diagnosis in the Correctional Field," which emphasizes these very points. *Federal Probation*, (Sept., 1969), pp. 39-43.

(2) The use of the classification term must not rule out our understanding that this term has very individual meaning to the person to whom it is applied. The use of the diagnostic expression should not cause the person being diagnosed as such to be placed into a category and thus no longer be treated as an individual.

(3) Great effort should be made to understand that there are many categories and subtypes within categories, and so the blanket use of the larger classifications should never take place when there is a more descriptive definition available.

(4) Because of the severity of many disturbances caused by the complexity of life and the terrific pressures from outside the person, liberal use should be made of the diagnoses such as "transient situational disturbances" and "conditions without manifest psychiatric disorder," unless the presence of sufficient diagnostic material is definitive and sufficient to warrant inclusion in some other classification.

With these admonitions in mind, let us take a look briefly at some of the most frequently used diagnostic classifications relating to much of the juvenile delinquency that is currently being seen by law enforcement and other officials in this country.

§ 2.5   Classification closely following the medical model

a. The casual or accidental offender

This term is used for the person who commits an offense for the first, and probably the only time in his life, due to a peculiar set of circumstances. Typical examples of this type would include the conventioneer who acts irresponsibly because he is away from family and neighborhood controls and probably is influenced by too much alcohol and the "spirit of the moment"; or the high school football player who goes to a team party and drinks in violation of the law only because "we just won the state championship." These are truly situational offenders, but they can be called "casual" or "accidental" because the situation does not continue or chronically repeat.

b. Irresponsible delinquency

This term as such does not appear in the DSM-II, but it is used here to include the kinds of behavior readily seen as resulting from several classifications, including mental retardation, individuals with organic brain damage, some totally inadequate personalities, and perhaps some limited numbers of others who, for the purpose of this discussion, can be best described as simply being unable to function because of some gross inadequacy, which is congenital, organic or environmentally induced.

These classifications are placed together for discussion only. They represent a large amount of behavior and numerous psychiatric classifications and subtypes.

Within mental retardation alone can be found the following classifications: Borderline (I.Q. 68 to 83), Mild (I.Q. 52 to 67), Moderate (I.Q. 36 to 51), Severe (I.Q. 20 to 35), Profound (I.Q. under 20), and Unspecified (those whose intellectual functioning is definitely observable as below normal, but who have not been, or cannot be, evaluated accurately).[3]

It is important to emphasize that even within the subtypes of mental retardation, social, environmental, cultural and other factors cannot be overlooked. The importance of cultural deprivation, lack of a fund of positive experiences, traumatic shock, and other variables dependent on causes outside the person which severely impede intellectual functioning, must be taken into account.

From a behavioral standpoint, the outburst of temper of the person with chronic brain syndrome, the "lack of good-will" evidenced by the totally inadequate personality, or the discourtesy and lack of attention of the "borderline retarded" are constantly being seen by all professionals in enforcement and corrections; and, tragically, are often misunderstood.

c. Transient situational disturbances

These conditions by definition (including the subtypes) embrace a significant amount of juvenile delinquency. The "adjustment reactions of childhood" (or adolescence) include many disturbances of behavior that come to the attention of authori-

[3] DSM-II, pp. 14-21.

ties and individuals without any apparent underlying mental disorder, and that represent an acute reaction to overwhelming environmental stress.[4]

At the risk of oversimplification, a vivid example of this condition can be seen in the teenager, who having repeatedly committed an offense, finally explains in a burst of emotion, "You know I only do this when mom is drinking."

d. Behavior disorders

Under this grouping are contained much childhood and adolescent hostility, aggression and withdrawal. Seemingly ingrained patterns of sexual deviancy, chronic lying, theft of all types, and frequent runaways, more chronic and basic to the person's total pattern than the above described transient situational disturbances, but not as totally internalized as the personality disorders to be described next, can be placed in this classification.

e. Personality disorders

Under this heading are included several very important subtypes, many of which perhaps are more widely known and used than the general heading. Basically, all disorders contained in this category exhibit a very deeply internalized and rather inflexible pattern of behavior which interferes with normal functioning. The patterns of disturbance are more severe in this case and much more deeply ingrained than in the previously described classifications of situational reactions and behavior disorders. Some of the subtypes would include "schizoid personality," some "inadequate personalities," "explosive personalities" and others as listed in great detail in the DSM-II.[5]

1. Passive-aggressive personality

One of the most important subtypes is the "passive-aggressive personality." Much criminal and delinquent behavior can be viewed under this particular subtype classification as evidenced by the many who seem to be able to cope with life under normal conditions, but who tend to use extremely poor judgment, aggression and even psychotic-like behavior under stress.

4 DSM-II, p. 48.   5 DSM-II, pp. 41-45.

2. Passive-dependent personality

Along with the "passive-aggressives," one of the unspecified types of personality disorders is the "passive-dependent" who is attempting to cope with great hostility but who cannot express it openly in an aggressive manner.

3. Anti-social personality (psychopath)

Also, within this group, it is of fundamental importance to note the "anti-social personality."[6] Under this group is found the "crown prince" of all criminal and delinquent types, the type until recently called the "sociopath" or "psychopath."

This is the very delinquent type characterized by almost unlimited aggression under proper circumstances, little or no anxiety, anti-social to the point of seeming to possess no empathy or even ability to be concerned about the rights or feelings of others, little or no guilt about his actions, impulsiveness, and a high degree of pleasure seeking and profit motivation. He especially has the characteristic of being unable to form deep, lasting and meaningful human relationships. His loyalties seem only to himself and not to others.

Traditionally this "sociopathic type" has been viewed as a "man without a conscience" or in former times he has been called a "moral imbecile." When discussing this type of personality disorder it is necessary to understand that the condition called "anti-social personality," "psychopath" or "sociopath" does *not* involve an impairment of the intellectual functioning, but there seems to be an impairment in the "affectional" apparatus. In this condition, the offender seemingly thinks quite clearly, in many cases almost more clearly than the average person, but he is unable to make proper moral judgments and unable to "feel" as the normal person would in relation to others.

The consequences of acts are important to a person of this type only in relation to the cost to himself, and never in terms of the harm done to anyone else. Because of his need and desire to exploit others, he often has highly developed social and verbal skills. These skills are utilized in order to help him achieve whatever goals he has set for himself in a particular situation. Consequently, numerous lies can be told without the presence

6 DSM-II, p. 43.

of much anxiety, and so, ordinarily, the condition called "pathological lying" is found in these types of personality-disordered individuals. Also, because of the lack of anxiety connected with the telling of falsehoods, it is believed by some practitioners that the true psychopath cannot be validly tested on some of the currently available lie detector machinery.

It is important to note that because of the skill of these individuals in manipulating those around them, a skilled, experienced person is required in order to cope with their efforts, in interrogation and in treatment settings. The comment has been made by many that, unfortunately, in the correctional system, these types often manipulate themselves into positions of trust or into the possession of the more advantageous jobs such as librarian, chaplain's assistant or any other situation where they can achieve advantage from their position. This is not to say that any or all of those holding such positions are to be classified as having this type of personality disorder, but only to point out that many of those disordered in this way make great efforts in order to get into the so-called "soft" or profitable positions.

It is also true that individuals of this type develop high degrees of skill in responding in interviews, and there are numerous situations where such a person selects the kind of category in which he wants to be placed by the interviewer and so he manipulates the interview so that the results come out according to his expectations and design.

On one occasion, an individual of this type was heard to remark to another inmate before going into an interview situation, "this guy likes you to 'open up' about sex, so I'm going to tell him about my masturbation problem and I'll own him before the hour is up."

In the field of juvenile corrections a real problem often results in handling this type of offender because it is so easy for him to simulate the expressions and emotions of the truly dependent youngster. He is often seen as the first one to reach out for help, especially when dealing with a new worker. It is a common device for him to "open up" and suddenly "realize his mistake" at the appropriate time, or for him to make such statements to an impressionable worker as "you are the only man I can trust or talk to, etc." He is also adept at showing pseudo-emotions at the expected time, such as crying or reacting favorably to praise, criticism, etc. He is extremely competent in the area of selecting and delivering emotionally-charged messages, in writing and presenting such items as birthday cards, father's day cards and gifts when he feels these would serve his purpose.

This kind of exploitive and adaptive behavior is not only dangerous in the field of juvenile corrections because it tends to give such an offender an advantage in "case-working" with those who think that they are really dealing with him in an official capacity (and many a case worker has been effectively "worked" by such an adaptive, delinquent personality), but it presents the other problem of making a veteran worker so aware of being manipulated by this type, that he is unable to deal as effectively with the dependent who really needs close contact and an affectional relationship.

While there have been countless theories advanced as to how the sociopathic condition above described develops in a human being, there still seems to be no complete answer. However, despite any biological pre-dispositions which may determine why one individual develops such a condition as a result of great environmental stress or deprivation and another one does not, it is important to note that in a significant number of cases, the absence of meaningful early relationships with "significant others," especially with parents, is quite obvious.

An illustration of this phenomenon is a case in which a fourteen-year-old boy was apprehended in the act of setting fire to oil-soaked rags which were strategically placed in the exits of a large tenement house in which more than thirty men, women and children were fast asleep. It was established that he indeed was attempting to inflict severe bodily harm and great property damage. The apparent motive was "just for kicks."

The boy's record included several offenses of an anti-social nature including fighting, chronic stealing and abuse of animals. He was described as a "pathological liar," and he exhibited little guilt or concern about anything except his own well-being. His behavior was unsocialized and aggressive and, in most ways, seemed to merit the term "psychopathic," which was quite readily applied.

However, if the behavior presented classic ingredients, the early lack of warm and meaningful relationships with parents was equally a classic picture. One of his earliest memories was of being taken into the bathroom by his mother, where she placed him in the bathtub and was holding his head under water in an attempt to drown him. This attempt was unsuccessful only because a neighbor intervened, and the mother was subsequently placed in a mental hospital. One and one-half years later, when his mother was home from the hospital, he was taken into the same bathroom, placed in the same bathtub and, this time, burned by scalding water.

His memories of the father during the same period of time consist primarily of the child's wandering from saloon to saloon and brothel to brothel, and finding the father in one compromising or degrading situation after another. When hard-pressed to recall one positive memory of either parent, he finally was able to volunteer in reference to his father, that "he used to give 'sis' (his sister) and myself a quarter when he wanted to get rid of us because he had some woman coming to the house."

Such early total emotional deprivation and lack of meaningful relationships with parents and "significant others" is not uncommon at all as a background feature observed by those professionals working with severely delinquent youngsters. This author can recall numerous cases, including one boy who was born in a European concentration camp during World War II as a product of the rape of his mother by a Nazi guard in the camp; or another who was "given away" in a tavern at age three by his mother to a mentally retarded alcoholic; or a four-year-old who was beaten and burned with cigarettes by a step-father and then thrown into a drainage ditch on a country road and forced to stand there while the step-father threatened the trembling child with a loaded shotgun.

These cases are not mentioned, nor are the tragic background factors of deprivation and cruelty recited, in order to excuse the later anti-social behavior of the person who has been the victim of such early trauma, or to suggest a permissive attitude toward the vicious and dangerous behavior which such a person often later exhibits, but only to help us in understanding the development of such a condition in order to be able to effectively treat the individual offender, if possible, and to understand the source of his unsocialized aggression.

It is most important to note that more than just a series of offenses, or the presence of habits repugnant to "middle class standards" is required for placement in this diagnostic category. The anti-social orientation, lack of guilt, inability to establish and maintain loyalties and other identifying characteristics must be present. We may not simply place this label on offenders whose behavior frightens us or whose life-style is distasteful to us. The classifications within the various behavior disorders and situational reactions should always be utilized if at all accurately descriptive.[7]

f. Neurotic offender

In a situation where the amount of anxiety is very threatening to the person, neurotic defenses are sometimes developed in order to ward off the threat of being overwhelmed by the anxiety. When the neurotic defense embraces delinquent activities, then we have a member of the group called "neurotic offenders." These persons are disturbed in their mental functioning, but they differ from the insane or psychotic because they have some insight or understanding that there is a disturbance and that it is perhaps influencing their behavior. The neurotic remains in touch with reality, and in most cases is able to function to some degree better than the psychotic, except in extremely severe situations in which he becomes hospitalized and even practically immobilized.

Among the more common types of neuroses are the anxiety neurosis, obsessive-compulsive neurosis, hysterical neurosis (including subtypes such as conversion and dissociative), and also included in the neuroses are such conditions as phobias and neurasthenia.[8]

The symptoms in these conditions (and the psychiatric manual should be consulted for complete listing of all the neurotic conditions) include a whole variety of types, including both physical and psychological manifestations. For example, in some of the hysterical neuroses the loss of physical functions is quite

---

[7] Parsons, M.D., op. cit.   [8] DSM-II, pp. 39-40.

common, and in other subtypes the loss of some psychological abilities such as memory, personality integration, etc. is suffered. Excessive fears, acute and chronic anxiety, behavioral rigidity and a whole host of other symptoms, depending upon the particular condition, are possibly found in the neurotic delinquent.

Relating this to delinquency, at the risk of oversimplification, we can probably say that the shoplifting offense of a prominent matron, with several thousand dollars in her purse at the time of her arrest and with other neurotic tendencies in her personality makeup, could be described as neurotic delinquency. Some automobile larcenies, runaways, sex offenses and a whole variety of other acts of delinquency can be seen as attempts to avoid excessive anxiety, and thus as part of the neurotic defense.

Of course, we must emphasize that this is not to say that all those offenses, or even all of any one type of offense, are rooted in the neurotic disorder of the offender. There are, however, countless thousands of offenses originating because of neurotic conditions, just as many are caused by other disorders.

Flight, thrill seeking, revenge, guilt, status seeking, "pseudo-masculine" acting-out, and many other factors within the framework of individual needs, or attempts to cope with great stress inside the personality of the individual offenders, often must be understood within the framework of what we know about the neuroses.

g. Psychotic offender

While there has been long and intensive dispute within the legal and behavioral science professions about the exact definition of psychosis, for purposes of understanding delinquent behavior, and because an agreement is more easily reached within the general confines of this definition, in this discussion "psychotic" refers to a mental disorder which "sufficiently impairs to interfere grossly with the capacity to meet the ordinary demands of life."[9] Within this definition the word "grossly" seems to hold the key which drastically limits the number of persons to be included in this category. It is important to note that numerous conditions exist in which a person can exhibit

[9] DSM-II, pp. 32-38.

psychotic-like behavior, or have a limited "psychotic episode," but this does not mean that such a person should be classified as psychotic.

If the neurotic is seen as one desperately attempting to defend against the anxiety which might cripple or fracture the ego, or cause serious personality disorganization, the psychotic is one who has had the ego crippled or fractured, or is already the victim of serious personality disorganization. Certain audio-visual hallucinations and a highly developed delusional system can be present at times, but these are not required for the psychotic condition.

Relating psychosis to delinquency, it should be noted that two of the most frequently seen types of psychoses are schizophrenia and the paranoid states.

A schizophrenic suffers disorders in his pattern of thinking, mood, and behavior. While having delusions in his thinking, or while caught in a sudden and extensive mood swing, or while exhibiting bizarre behavior, the schizophrenic can very easily violate the law because of stealing, physical aggression, sex delinquency, or in a wide variety of other ways.

By the very nature of the paranoid states in which "delusion is the essential abnormality," an offender could very easily engage in a vicious assault upon an imagined perpetrator of evil and this, of course, would bring him to the attention of law enforcement authorities immediately.

In discussing the psychotic offender, it is of the utmost importance to keep in mind that much psychotic-like behavior is often misinterpreted as authentic psychosis. Under great environmental stress, controls often break down, and very irresponsible acts and even bizarre behavior results. This is in no way justification that the person committing the act should be classified as psychotic. A classification of psychosis should only be used when that diagnosis is absolutely necessary; and when there is doubt, normally the professional person will exhaust all other diagnostic categories before a definite classification of psychosis is made.

This discussion of psychotic offenders should certainly not be interpreted as adequate to equip the reader to diagnose based upon this reading; nor should it be considered anything more than a passing acquaintance with the condition as one of the typologies in delinquency.

h. Conditions without manifest psychiatric disorders

This "catch-all" category within the schedule of psychiatric classifications is used for many kinds of behavioral disorders and conditions which do not seem to fall readily into the other categories.[10] In the opinion of this author, this illustrates the need for many classifications dependent much more totally upon factors outside of the individual.

Many "professional criminals," narcotics "pushers," some prostitutes, some chronic alcoholics, many professional gamblers, and a whole host of other types who seem undiagnosable in other categories, can be placed together in this classification for convenience. However, it is thought by this author that many of these conditions can be much better explained by the term "cultural delinquents," and other terms reflecting deprivation, poor training, academic retardation, confusion as to goals and values, alienation from family or the entire society, etc.

APPLICATION OF IMPORTANT POINTS EMPHASIZED FOR LAW ENFORCEMENT OFFICERS

1. Not all juvenile delinquents are emotionally disturbed or have psychiatric problems. Many are reacting to bad home situations, bad example, and countless other factors in their environment.

2. Within any given offense category (i.e. auto larceny, etc.) there are countless kinds of causal factors that can be operating. Therefore, it is inaccurate to speak of a "typical auto larcenist" or a "typical delinquent type," etc.

3. Juvenile delinquency cannot be understood in general or in the abstract. It is best understood in each individual and concrete case by seeking for the cause of "this act of delinquency" and understanding the personal dynamics of "this delinquent boy."

4. Oftentimes the individual delinquents taking part in a group offense need to be handled very differently in terms of arrest, processing and disposition because the offenders are quite different even though the

[10] DSM-II, p. 51.

offense is the same.

5. The presence of the same environmental factors in the life of different individuals will not necessarily produce the same behavioral patterns. A drinking parent, a broken home, a bad neighborhood, etc. will have widely differing effects on various individuals because of "counterbalancing" and stabilizing influences within the personality or elsewhere in the environment.

6. The use of psychiatric labels never adequately substitutes for understanding the individual.

7. The use of diagnostic labels can be very dangerous if employed recklessly or indiscriminately because the individual can be "lost in the category" and a tendency to treat the individual like everyone else with the same label can easily result.

8. No psychiatric terminology should ever be used in even the most routine report unless the user is quite certain of the full meaning of the term and the accuracy of its use in the particular case.

9. Labeling of juveniles with any terminology is especially dangerous because their behavior is so complex that it is often hard to categorize accurately, and because we tend to create an atmosphere in which we expect a child to live up to our opinion of him in the schools, on the streets and oftentimes even in hospitals and clinical settings.

10. An understanding of diagnostic classifications and psychiatric terminology can be of great help to all who work with juvenile offenders if properly used and understood. The use of proper diagnostic terms can help us and those we communicate with to better understand and control the juvenile offender.

Chapter 3

CAUSES OF DEVIANT OR DELINQUENT BEHAVIOR: DIFFERING THEORIES

§ 3.1   Background of development of theories

Just as man has historically looked for ultimate answers to the important questions of life, he seems to have always been interested in explaining the "bad behavior" of those about him who have not measured up to contemporary moral and behavioral expectations. Feeble attempts over the centuries to apply the primitive science of the times to the deviant behavior of human beings can be seen in religious and secular history. Since the industrial revolution, and especially in our present science-oriented century, the attempts to take a close scientific look at criminal and delinquent behavior and to formulate theories that would explain such deviancy have become widespread.

It would require hundreds of volumes in order to fully explain all of the principal theories that have been advanced, or even to list all of the many individual extensions of such theories which have evolved into corollary theories themselves, and in some cases into whole new explanations. Since time and space do not permit, nor does the purpose of this chapter include the full treatment of all criminological theory or causal explanation, we will attempt to give a brief commentary on the multiple causes of deviant behavior as seen from the vantage point of some of the more popular theories.

Because the scholars tell us that any scientific explanation must consist of a description of conditions which are always present when a phenomenon occurs, and which are never present when the same phenomenon does not occur, we must begin this discussion by noting that, in our opinion, even the most advanced and carefully thought-out theories of causality cannot explain all delinquent and criminal behavior. Many of the theories can explain some aspects of such crime and delinquency, but none of them seems able to encompass the whole causal picture.

It is important to note at the outset that there is a great amount of overlapping in the dynamics and the content of individual theories; and so the classification of these theories into types, such as "social" or "psychological," is not at all a simple matter, because many of these terms are not mutually exclusive.

For example, the sociologist has as great a stake in carefully viewing families and their influence on delinquency as does the psychologist. The vantage point may be different, and all of the particular ingredients which come under the two respective microscopes may not be the same, but the concern about the family as a causal factor is proper to both disciplines.

With these thoughts in mind, and remembering that our purpose is not to make thoroughly trained social scientists of the readers, but to equip them with some fundamental knowledge of the dynamics of deviant behavior, let us proceed to look at some of the theories of causality.

§ 3.2 Religious theory

At the risk of oversimplification, but for the sake of the convenience of this discussion, let us say that causal factors generally have been viewed as those concerned with factors "inside" of the offender, and those concerned with factors existing "outside" of the offender.

Of the theories that focus on the causes inside the offender, probably the first, and one with widespread acceptance yet today, is the religious theory. This theory finds its basis in theology and in the acceptance of the doctrine of "free will," which posits that a human being has a conscious opportunity to choose between the good and the evil of an act which he is about to commit; and that the deliberate choice of evil is a "bad human act."

There are many refinements or particular differences within these religious theories, depending upon the various religions which approach the subject, and these thoughts range from a rather primitive consideration that man is always responsible for all of his acts, to the more advanced religious views that seem certainly reconcilable with modern science, that man is not responsible for acts concerning which he has been deprived of the use of his reason, and therefore of his "free will"; but he is responsible for those acts about which he is free to choose.

In many places where the religious theories are applied to the complexities of modern man living in highly developed societal structures, the sophistication of these theories has come to include the notion that the free choice is made extremely difficult because of social and psychological factors operating in many circumstances.

There certainly seem to be few sources that would insist that every human being is totally responsible for every act that he commits at all times; and, consequently, there would seem to be few, for example, who would insist that an obviously psychotic or severely mentally retarded individual is responsible for all, or perhaps even any, of his acts.

§ 3.3   Medico-biological theory

Medical and biological explanations have been advanced at many times and in many ways, and often in combination as "medico-biological" theories of causation. These would include an emphasis on the hereditary factors, chemical balance within the physical organism, and certainly the influence of physical illness on behavior.

The biological explanations, concerned primarily with inherited characteristics, have a famous historical example in the concern of Lombroso with measurable physiological characteristics. Such theories remain popular today in such instances as the recent studies concerning the "Y chromosome."

Contemporary medical science remains concerned with the question of chemical balance in relation to the mental disease schizophrenia, and in current research concerning such medical problems as "lymbic system disorders" and "hypoglycemia"; and it is well accepted that such conditions can influence behavior.

Modern psychiatry is a branch of medical science; and contemporary practice consists of physical examinations along with psychiatric evaluations as a matter of routine in many instances. The uncontrollable behavior resulting from recognized "organic brain syndrome," temper outbursts rooted in epileptic conditions, and countless other examples can be given of medical, biological or "medico-biological" explanations of criminal and delinquent behavior.

The psychiatric and psychological explanations of the causal factors in crime and delinquency necessarily seem to need to bridge the gap between the consideration of the causes "inside" the offender and causes from "outside" of him. Numerous psychological conditions are the subject of rather intense dispute between competent authorities as to whether they flow from some "internal pathology" or whether they are caused by "environmental factors." And, in the same arguments, equally competent authorities claim the presence of factors arising from both sources.

§ 3.4　Psychiatric or psychological theories

Keeping this in mind, let us look at some of the psychiatric or psychological theories.

Sigmund Freud seemed to see the "neurotic nucleus" developed in early childhood, and concerned himself with fixations at early levels of development, repressed infantile sexuality and internal factors of that kind. Alfred Adler gave great emphasis to man's efforts to compensate for perceived and actual biological deficiencies. Carl Jung placed great stress on the ratio of "extraversion-intraversion" within the personality makeup of the individual. Countless others have advanced versions of "psychoanalytic theory."[1] As a result, many have attempted to account for delinquent conduct because of the presence of unresolved conflicts in the area of sex or aggression, personality disorders, levels of anxiety, the quest for status, compensations for all sorts of real or imagined deficiencies, and a whole host of other internal reasons within the "psychic structure."

Most of these theories place emphasis on faulty early parent-child relationships; but even in these instances there is a great deal of difference of opinion. Some emphasize maternal separation, while others point out that separation is not nearly as bad as rejection from a present maternal figure. Others have highlighted the importance of the paternal absence or rejection.

Many have commented upon the influence of the broken home, while still others have said that it is not simply the absence of the parent, but the trauma connected with the way the absence occurred; and they advance a distinction between "delinquency proneness" in situations where natural death has disrupted the family as opposed to desertion, violent death or imprisonment of a parent.[2]

Within the framework of psychological causal consideration, great emphasis has been placed by the psychoanalytic school on the presence of anxiety, especially when this is extreme or uncontrollable;[3] while others have found a root cause of delinquency in boredom,[4] or tension,[5] or low tolerance of frustration,[6] or an almost infinite number of other internal factors.

The importance of emotional and mental illness should not be underestimated in considering the behavioral patterns of youth in our contemporary society. When we consider the recent

[1] An excellent account of early and later "psychoanalytic theories" is presented in brief form in *Personality Theory and Psychoanalysis*, Jane W. Kessler, Prentice-Hall, Englewood Cliffs, N.J. (1966), pp. 3-11.

[2] Thomas P. Monahan, "Family Status and the Delinquent Child: A Reappraisal and Some New Findings," *Social Focus XXXV*, (March, 1957), pp. 250-258.

[3] Fritz Redl, *Children Who Hate*, The Free Press, N.Y. (1951), pp. 78, 79.

[4] Arthur Miller, "The Bored and the Violent," *Harper's*, Vol. 225, #1300, N.Y. (November, 1966).

[5] Irene Josselyn, *The Adolescent and His World*, Family Association of America, N.Y. (1952).

[6] Fritz Redl, op. cit., pp. 76, 77.

statistical estimate that there are probably six million young Americans, diagnosed and undiagnosed, who are severely emotionally disturbed or mentally ill, and when we realize that about twenty-three thousand young people are being admitted to the mental hospitals in this country each month, with probably an equal number or more remaining in their homes or on the streets, the enormity of this problem cannot be overemphasized.[7]

Personality traits and deficiencies have been observed and classified in relation to their consistency in appearance in large groups of delinquents by many fine scholars and observers. Following the Freudian model, many have commented on faulty development of "super ego" or basic "ego deficiencies"; and one clinician adds the notion of strongly developed "delinquent ego-structures."[8]

Applying the learning model, observations have been made about the delinquent's classical possession of "resistance to conditioning." In 1964, Eysenck reported a study in which he had isolated a cluster or "constellation of traits" as being causally related to criminal and delinquent patterns. In this group, he listed mesomorphic physique, poor conditionability, psychomotor clumsiness, and emotional instability when combined with extraversion.[9]

Others have extended great effort in trying to develop a complex of characteristics which would enable them to predict future delinquent behavior, or in finding a "common thread" which runs through all or most criminal or delinquent patterns. (Probably most notable among these efforts has been the work of Sheldon and Eleanor Glueck who seem to use the combination of psychological and sociological factors in their predictability scale.)[10]

When Freud postulated the importance of "constitution and

---

[7] According to statistics compiled by National Association of Mental Health (February, 1970).

[8] Fritz Redl, op. cit., pp. 208-210.

[9] H. J. Eysenck, *Crime and Person-* *ality,* Houghton Mifflin, Boston (1964).

[10] Sheldon and Eleanor Glueck, *Delinquents in the Making,* Harper, N.Y. (1952), pp. 95-163.

fate" (heredity and environment) in determining human behavior, he probably very accurately reflected much of the best current thinking in psychiatric and psychological circles, which now seems to take into consideration the hereditary or constitutional features which predispose the offender in some cases for criminal behavior when those factors are present, but lay great emphasis on those features of personality or those traits which are acquired, or if previously existing, are aggravated or intensified by early upbringing and then by the opportunities presented in later environmental experience. The "strength of temptation and strength of controls" kind of eclectic causal picture seems to best stand the test of reality.

This kind of combination psychological-sociological thinking seems more and more to permeate both the psychological theories, and those called the sociological, as they take into account the dual influence areas.

§ 3.5   Theories "bridging the gap" between internal and external factors: significant others, home, peer group, environment

In looking at the factors that tend to cause criminal and delinquent behavior "outside" of the offender, it is necessary that we consider the controls exercised on behavior that are found in the home, the neighborhood and, certainly, society at large.

The influence of significant others in the schools, the church, and sub-cultural groups must be carefully considered, as well as peer pressure and the interaction of opportunities and internal control.

Emphasis has been placed by many observers on the fact that delinquency results from attitudes and techniques that are learned and transmitted by human contacts in the environment. These theories vary greatly, but they all propose that prolonged and intense contact with delinquent values is of great importance in understanding the transmission of such values. The famous theory of "differential association"[11] is an out-

11 E. H. Sutherland, (Revised by H. R. Cressey), *Principles of Criminology,* (5th Edition), J. P. Lippincott Co., Chap. IV (1955).

standing example of this school of thought.

In this explanation it must be understood that what is learned is deviant or in opposition to the accepted moral standards of the larger cultural group, and that it is learned best if it is learned at the primary level. A common sense observation would tend to verify that an extremely young child exposed to delinquent attitudes and conduct on the part of "significant others," especially parent-figures, learns with much greater effectiveness than if his contact is not so intense, or comes later in life, or is with someone with whom he is much less involved.

This deviancy then becomes fixed early in the offender's life and, of course, the earlier it is learned the more a fixed part of his personality makeup and resulting behavior it becomes. The frequency of the contacts, their duration, the degree of closeness to the "criminal role-model" and the intensity of the relationship are extremely important factors in determining the degree to which the pattern becomes fixed and operative in the life of the offender. Studies in Hawaii, Tennessee, Washington State, and elsewhere, seem to support the importance of this theory in understanding much delinquent behavior.

However, Glueck[12] and others have pointed out that this theory certainly cannot explain the origin of delinquent behavior nearly as well as it explains the transmission of values from one person to another, nor does it seem to be able to be applied universally to all offenders.

The importance of a slum environment and the many problems presented by life in the inner-city has long received and continues to receive an even greater amount of emphasis in relation to the causal picture of crime and delinquency. Early scholars pointed out emphatically that the delinquency rate is highest in the central city, and that it tends to decrease in regular gradients as it moves out from the core area. Varying emphasis has been placed by numerous observers on the importance within the urban slum of such factors as housing, a sense of alienation from the larger culture, poverty, racial prejudice, etc., as being principal or contributing causes to the

12 Sheldon Glueck, "Theory and Fact in Criminology," *British Journal* *of Criminology VII*, (October, 1956), pp. 92-98.

problems observed in these areas. However, despite some minor disagreement as to the importance of individual factors within the socio-economically deprived areas of the inner-city, most competent observers tend to agree that the "sub-human conditions" in such sections contribute very directly to the high rate of crime and delinquency which is universally reported.

In observing slum conditions as causal factors in the criminal behavior pattern, numerous theories can be applied. The socio-economic, cultural, educational and many other viewpoints, along with all possible combinations of these, have valuable insights to give toward understanding the complexity of the causal picture in this kind of deprivation-rooted delinquency. An exposition of all the applicable writings would require countless volumes; but in substance the central thesis can be summarized in the statement that there can be no human morality or even human behavior in sub-human conditions.

Various professionals from numerous branches of the social sciences have coined many names by which to refer to the underprivileged within our society. From time to time they have been called disenfranchised, socio-economically or culturally deprived, alienated, "hardcore," "hard-to-reach," "low class," and a whole litany of other unfortunate but descriptive names. All of the aforementioned terms describe the same group of persons similarly located in the social hierarchy who have rather different chances of ever being able to reach common success-goals, despite the prevailing philosophy that equal opportunity is available to all persons in this country.

Areas containing high concentrations of persons of this description are characterized by the poorest of housing, unsanitary conditions, widespread joblessness, high incidence of welfare recipiency, extremely low income rate for working members, low levels of educational achievement, family disintegration, poor standards of health, and housekeeping, erratic patterns of child rearing, and the inevitable high rates of prostitution, narcotics abuse, alcoholism and, consequently, crime.

In this atmosphere, the many pressures to engage in deviant behavior are ever-present and extreme. Despite this fact, some few youngsters because of great personal strength, or because of the intervention of some saving force from outside, or perhaps because simply of the luck or chance involved in having "longer legs" and thus being able to run fast enough to avoid arrest, do manage to avoid becoming official delinquency statistics. Some of these few are also able, despite all the odds against them, to eventually improve their status by great personal effort and education. Others manage in some way to insulate themselves, and while they do not "rise above" slum life they do survive in their own way, and they seem able to remain relatively free of criminal habits while remaining within the high delinquency-rate area.

However, these are the fortunate few. Many others, in increasing numbers every day, react and revolt; and in so doing they reinforce and perpetuate the "delinquent sub-culture." While most observers of crime and delinquency in the core areas of our big cities agree almost entirely with this observation, there are many differences of opinion as to exactly what are the "psycho dynamics" of what actually takes place.

Some have postulated that the great gulf between what deprived youth is led to want in terms of "good things" available in American society, and what is actually available to them because of academic retardation, racial prejudice, etc., is the main source of conflict within the youngsters trapped in these circumstances. Finding legitimate means unavailable to obtain the "good life" as it is constantly presented so graphically on television and in advertisements, these disenfranchised youths then develop illegitimate means to achieve the socially-approved goals, including nice clothes, spending money, automobiles, etc.[13]

Others have observed that because of the feeling of being left out of the mainstream of economic and consumer life, such delinquents actually engage in "reaction formation," reject middle class norms and values and engage in impulsive, malicious, hedonistic behavior which seeks the "thrill of the moment" and accepts little authority except that of the immediate peer group.[14]

Still others would state that the conflict has been internalized and that "lower class focal concerns" become such a part of the sub-culture that a "low-class value system" is developed

---

[13] Richard A. Cloward and Lloyd E. Ohlin, *Delinquency and Opportunity*, The Free Press, Glencoe, Ill. (1960), p. 117.

[14] Albert K. Cohen, *Delinquent Boys: The Culture of the Gang*, Glencoe, The Free Press, (1955), pp. 25, 26.

which concerns itself not at all with middle-class values and long-term goals, but sees virtue in qualities of toughness, excitement, and autonomy at all costs.[15]

In explaining the same behavioral phenomena, there are those who will emphasize the alienation of this group and point out that such "not-belonging" to the larger culture generates the feeling of powerlessness, isolation, and opportunity-denial to the point where life becomes meaningless and normless.[16] In this anomic state, illicit behavior is very acceptable, and, when reinforced by peer-approval, is much more acceptable than the kind of behavior traditionally expected by the larger society.

Most would agree that whatever the particular dynamics of each individual in these circumstances might be, the severe deprivation pressures the individual either into conflict with the larger society which then is evidenced in fighting, stealing, and antisocial acts of an aggressive nature; or an attempt is made to resolve the difference by manipulation which can readily be observed in chronic lying, flattery, and "con games"; or in many cases by retreat and escape-type behavior when the situation is seen as hopeless and overwhelming. This latter phenomenon is easily observed in the extremes of alcohol abuse, narcotics addiction, sex play, thrill seeking, etc.

§ 3.6 Two controversial contemporary theories: conflict theory and labeling theory

With the advent of so-called "radical criminology," and "liberal-cynical criminology," much emphasis has been placed on an examination of many of the traditional and principal ingredients of American society itself as playing at least a participating, and in some cases even a central role in the causation of crime and delinquency. One of the emerging theories within this frame of reference is "conflict theory." Those who adhere to this line of reasoning, with some individual variations, generally believe that the conflict begins in the community when the value system, or part of it, belonging to one group is attacked

[15] Walter B. Miller, "Lower Class Culture As a Generating Milieu of Gang Delinquency," *Journal of Social Issues,* 14, (1959), pp. 38-51.

[16] Robert K. Merton, "Social Structure and Anomie," *American Sociological Review,* III, (October, 1938), pp. 672-682.

or put in some form of jeopardy by the behavior or beliefs of another group. When the threatened group has sufficient power to have their value system protected by law, then the behavior of the other group becomes illegal; and since the other group does not have the same respect or appreciation for the particular values in question as the law-making group, it becomes very easy for them to engage in the proscribed behavior and thus become held in violation of the law. Conversely, the group whose values and beliefs are protected by law finds it much easier to be "law abiding" because long before the legal process is set in motion, usually already at "their mother's knee," that group is socialized into an acceptance of the law-protected values and behaviors, and consequently they would only rarely transgress laws in relation to those values or behaviors. In its most extreme form, conflict theorists would hold that law enforcement is in fact a self-serving system which tends to maintain power and privilege in the hands of the "haves" and keep them elusive of the grasp of the "have nots."[17]

The second theory within this frame of reference is based on the social interaction between behavior and the observance of that behavior by another group, and the consequent labeling of the behavior and the person so behaving by the observers. This "labeling theory" was perhaps best stated concisely by Howard S. Becker already in 1963 when he said, "Social groups create deviance by making the rules whose infractions constitute deviance, and by applying those rules to particular people and labeling them as outsiders. From this point of view, deviance is not a quality of the act the person commits, but rather a consequence of the application by others of rules and sanctions to an 'offender.' The deviant is one to whom that label has been applied; deviant behavior is behavior that people so label."[18]

§ 3.7   Theories of "gang delinquency"

One of the most obvious social institutions in the delinquent sub-culture is the gang. These gangs vary in size and in degree

---

[17] William J. Chambliss and Robert B. Seidman, *Law, Order and Power,* Addison-Wesley Publishing Company, Reading, Massachusetts, (1971).

[18] Howard S. Becker, *Outsiders,* Free Press of Glencoe, N.Y., (1963), p. 9.

of formal structure from city to city, and even within individual cities. In their most highly organized state, they have ruling hierarchies wielding varying degrees of real authority. Members may be linked by "blood oath" or by fear of physical reprisal. Laws are made and promulgated, and punishments are meted out effectively.

In less formalized situations there is simply the banding together of peers for protection against a hostile environment, or merely for recreation, or in many cases simply because of the innate need to "belong to something."

There have been so many extensive and intensive studies done concerning gangs that to further elucidate at this time seems to serve no useful purpose. However, it is important to note that the purpose of some "warring" or "bopping" gangs is conflict and violence, while other gangs indulge in other delinquent pursuits for economic advantage, and still others are more recreational or social in purpose and activities. All gangs within the delinquent sub-culture, no matter how antisocial their behavior and how abhorrent to the larger society, are truly functional for their members, and are a very important part of the sub-cultural life. They must be understood in the role they play in order to fully understand delinquent sub-cultures in the large metropolitan areas.

Since the delinquent sub-culture (especially as represented by delinquent gang membership) really signifies the special efforts of deprived groups to adapt to what is seen as a rather fixed and immutable position in the social and economic structure, or to overcome the desperation that results from their recognition of this position, critics have raised the question as to why all children exposed to the same situations and living at the same level of deprivation and alienation do not identify with the delinquent sub-culture. Others have rephrased the question to ask why are not all socio-economically deprived areas equally delinquent and vice-ridden.

This latter question demands answering even more when observers point to "pockets of delinquency" existing side by side with areas that seem to have equally low economic status and educational levels, but which seem to function relatively closer to the term "pockets of normalcy" in that they are literally surrounded by high delinquency-rate areas.

These questions reinforce the author's original position about the complexity of all causal factors, whether they are internal to the delinquent or external and existing in his environment. There does seem to be a maze of reasons underlying why controls handed down by tradition in the larger culture seem to reach some groups to a greater extent than others, and why control within neighborhoods and individual families seems to disintegrate in one set of circumstances and remain relatively intact in what appear to be similar circumstances in very close proximity.

There is seemingly no definite answer to the varying degrees of social and behavioral instability in areas of equally bad housing, poverty, closeness to the core area of large metropolitan communities, etc. Some scholars have thought to analyze the "toleration level" of delinquent behavior existing in the different neighborhoods by evaluating the extent of family disorganization within the neighborhood area. The sociologists have viewed the structure, the size, and the "social picture" of families. Psychologists and psychiatrists have looked at the dynamics, the mechanisms and the "psychiatric picture" inside the individual family. Broken homes, patterns of child rearing, use of physical discipline by the father, and an almost infinite number of other factors have been explored in relation to this problem.

All of these studies which are far too numerous to even list in this context, much less to explain at any length, have an immediate contribution to make at this time, which is to re-emphasize that all of the factors studied are of exceedingly great importance in understanding the behavior of the individuals concerned. Just as individuals differ as to the impact upon them which results from differences in status, education and access, so do families seem to have their own individual family strength which determines the impact of such factors upon them as a family.

It is our feeling that neighborhoods differ in the same way, and that no one theory can explain all neighborhood differentiations. While individual theories can be extremely accurate in relation to specific situations in any one particular area at the time of a particular study, generalization and wide application of findings requires great caution.

Certainly much weight must be given in considering the "tolerance of delinquency" of any individual or family or neighborhood, to the "stake in conformity" which is operating in each situation. For example, a neighborhood composed largely of persons without personal property of any significant amount could not be expected to have the same pride of ownership; nor would a community composed entirely of a minority group who sees the cultural dictates of the larger society simply as a continuation of oppression and prejudice, have the same group loyalties to the larger culture that one would expect to find in members of more privileged groups functioning as an integral part of the larger society.

These sociological, cultural and economic factors must also be kept very carefully in mind when simplistic statements are made linking the biological differences of races to high delinquency-prone areas. All too often, and for a variety of reasons, we hear the statement made that arrests in a certain section of a major metropolitan area indicate as high as a ten to one ratio in the incidence of delinquency among the members of one racial group as opposed to another. These statistics very probably are valid as cited, but the explanation that there is a causal explanation based in the biology of one racial group or another does not stand the test of reality.

§ 3.8   The need for individualizing application of causal theories

It is important to note that in connection with the escalating violence of the juvenile offender in our society, and especially in the context of considerations of alienation and racial factors, it is essential to consider the relatively recent development of the crimes of the "violent stranger." By this term we mean to include all those crimes against the person, running the entire spectrum from simple assault through homicides, which are perpetrated wantonly and without any previous knowledge of the victim on the part of the offender, often without any readily discernible explanation, in ever-increasing numbers in the very recent past throughout the entire length and breadth of this country. This unfortunate phenomenon, perhaps more than any other single factor, has contributed immeasurably to the rising fear of crime on the part of the average American, and especially on the part of those most vulnerable to criminal attack like the aged, inner-city residents, and those whose occupations force them frequently into the streets, especially in "strange neighborhoods."

Up until the recognition of this heinous problem very recently, we felt relatively comfortable with the fact that homicide and very serious personal attack usually would take place at the hands of someone we knew very well, perhaps even a family member, and certainly for reasons explainable by family conflict, business relations, or a "sex triangle." However, suddenly within the past several years, these more rational signs of attack have in many crime situations been replaced by the "crimes of the violent stranger." In this new situation, the violence is often of a very high degree and the explanation is frequently totally unavailable, if explainable at all.

After close observation of numerous cases, the analysis of information coming in through law enforcement and court sources throughout the country, and after consultation with numerous professional associates, your author feels that the best available, and perhaps the only explanation for this serious kind of offense is that in such situations the offender sees the victim, of whom by definition he has no previous knowledge or reason to assault, as simply a symbol of the frustration or rage which has long been developing within the offender. This symbol can be based on difference of race, age, ethnic or religious background, or economic circumstances. In cases of race difference, it can be more readily observed than in situations involving economics or social position, but nevertheless the difference is obviously there and the symbolism triggers the attack. Examples of such situations are available any day in the newspapers of any metropolitan area. The aged person attacked with little money on his person, the "new child" assaulted in a changing neighborhood, the person of a different race maimed or killed while experiencing automobile trouble in a strange neighborhood, all of these kinds of situations seem to fit into this pattern where there is seemingly no "utilitarian motive" for the attack and the level of violence is relatively high.

In understanding the delinquent behavior pattern of the deprived or alienated delinquent, we must be careful not to oversimplify or generalize in his case any more than we would in the case of an upper-middle-class neurotic.

While we know that in general the feeling of being "left-out" and the unavailability of legitimate means in many cases to obtain desired goals, pressures in many ways toward delinquent behavior, at the same time we observe that individuals in similar circumstances, and even entire neighborhoods, are more or less delinquent than others who share the same problems.

We also know that within neighborhoods and family groups there seems to be a varying "toleration level" or delinquency; and we recognize the importance of the "stake in conformity" as a control of delinquency within individual families and neighborhoods; and even in almost identical social groups, we find individuals who because of personal strength or even accidents of fate, seem to be more or less "delinquency-prone" than individuals in similar circumstances.

So, it is very important that we keep in mind the admonition that a factor is not a cause of delinquency in anyone's life until it is important, and only to the degree that it is important to the person in whose life it occurs.

Why two individuals react quite differently to very similar cultural pressures, for example, or to lack of opportunity, or to any other environmental conditions, remains rooted in the mystery of the individual personality. Perhaps this dilemma is best stated with the phrase that we are "ever-changing psychobiological complexities struggling to adjust to several layers of changing environment."

Should we say anything less than this, we would risk leaving out one of the significant aspects of inherited characteristics, physical construction, basic instincts and drives, learned controls, and the socializing influences of family neighborhood, ethnic groups and contemporary society; and this would prevent full understanding of the behavior of the individual which is as different in each case as the individual set of fingerprints.

APPLICATION OF IMPORTANT POINTS EMPHASIZED FOR LAW ENFORCEMENT OFFICERS
THEORIES OF CAUSALITY

1. No single theory can explain all juvenile delinquency, or even any particular kind of offense. For example, some auto larcenies are committed for thrills; some to gain status in a delinquent peer group; some for flight or escape; some for profit; some as an act of rebellion and defiance, etc., etc.

2. Some, but not all delinquents are sick emotionally or psychiatrically. Some are reacting to horrible home conditions, bad example, inconsistent discipline, alienation, boredom, etc. Therefore, individual delinquents must be understood individually in the light of their own personality and environment.

3. "An ounce of prevention" is worth many "pounds of cure" in dealing with delinquency, so every effort should be made to relieve conditions or remove pressures which cause crime and delinquency or its beginnings in the breakdown of controls or warping of personality.

4. Slums and poverty produce a tremendous amount of delinquency; but not all residents of slums or poor persons are delinquent. In fact, many such persons are quite often the victims of crime; so, enforcement services should be rendered as effectively and helpfully as possible. This helps much in overcoming the image of law enforcement officers as "oppressors" in deprived areas.

5. Many theories emphasize the importance of parental influence in either causing or preventing delinquency, despite presence or absence of other influencing factors. Therefore, every effort should be made to involve parents in control and prevention of delinquency in all areas.

6. "Significant others" can and do influence youthful behavior for good or bad. Opportunities to provide and support good example and situations providing "positive identification" should be strongly encouraged.

7. Much hostility is created and intensified in sub-human living conditions and must be understood as such in many situations where behavior seems to be difficult to understand.

8. Sometimes membership in a delinquent gang, or espousal of a delinquent life-style and set of values, is the only way a totally deprived child feels that he can survive. Often, an understanding police officer can interrupt this thought pattern or intervene practically in such a way as to help such a child rather than pushing him more deeply into the delinquent group.

9. Not all youth gangs are delinquent. They should be judged by their conduct, not by their mode of dress, meeting place, or preconceived notions of adults.

10. There are many evidences that members of particular racial groups are thought to be more "delinquency-prone" than others because of some biological or ingrained defect. This does not stand the test of reality because environment and outside influences seem to explain higher arrest percentages within some racial groups. Therefore, each person should be judged by his conduct, not by any theories or prejudices based on his race.

Chapter 4

CHILD PSYCHOLOGY

§ 4.1   In general

Because of the constantly lowering age level of the delinquent offender in most communities, and because an understanding of adolescent and even adult behavior requires some
basic knowledge of the formation of behavior patterns in the
childhood years, we will outline briefly some important aspects
of child psychology.

This chapter is in no way intended to attempt an exhaustive
treatise of any one or all of the sophisticated theories of child
development, nor is it an attempt to make psychiatrists or
psychologists of the reader. It is simply a discussion of the importance of understanding childhood phenomena and especially
early trauma, to aid in understanding later delinquent behavior.

Historically, there have been numerous attempts at the
unilateral or univocal explanation of all behavior in terms of a
single theory of child development. Many fine scholars and
practitioners have spent lives of study and practice and written
countless volumes elucidating theories which hopefully could
explain all human behavior in terms of a single set of principles.
Much attention has been given to schools of thought in this
area which originated from psychoanalysis, from learning theory,
from principles of maturation, and from numerous other sources.

There are hundreds of theories of personality and attempted
explanations of the origin of behavior patterns which cover
thousands of volumes, and which in many instances incorporate
ingredients from those basic theories mentioned above or add
numerous individual ramifications to those theories. Further

developments in some areas advance whole new postulates and theories in trying to pinpoint the cause of juvenile delinquency in early childhood.

There are some schools of thought which emphasize the importance of hereditary factors. Others put great weight on experiences during the early formative years. Some see greater significance in the absence of maternal affection; and a host of others look more carefully at total family relationships, physiological factors, lack of environmental stimulation, childhood trauma, and an almost infinite variety of other significant factors.

We tend to agree with the scholar, Dr. Jane W. Kessler, who said recently: "Most people interested in helping children usually have some ideas about why they act as they do, ideas suggested by their own childhood and by empathy. If the child has a special problem, however, one has to delve more deeply for the causes. The causes invariably are multiple, and they are thoroughly embedded in a matrix of inborn tendencies, unique past experiences, family relationships, and cultural forces which affect both the child and his family."[1]

This accurate statement of the multiple causality of problem behavior much more adequately reflects the author's opinion than perhaps any other currently available. The notion of multiple causality does not at all represent an attempt to negate the importance or to minimize the sophistication of any of the existing theories.

If one views enough children, especially those with severe problems, one can quickly find an array of cases illustrative of most of the important points contained in the writings of the best observers of human behavior. It is becoming more difficult as our society becomes more complex and the environmental factors increase in their intensity and pressure on human beings in development, to find a single theory that covers all behavior.

Remembering the purpose of this discussion, we will look at several significant aspects in the life of the child in an attempt

[1] Jane W. Kessler, *Psychopathology of Childhood*, Prentice-Hall, Englewood Cliffs, N.J. (1966), p. 1.

to understand later behavior by the use of principles drawn from much of the best available thinking in this important area. This is not an attempt to combine or integrate any or all of the existing theories, nor is it an effort to give a detailed analysis of early childhood experiences or a complete exposition of the dynamics of all child behavior. It is merely an effort to arm the reader with some knowledge of the importance of the child and his childhood in understanding the later behavior of the young offender.

§ 4.2   Immediate post-birth period: need of newborn child for physical contact and reassurance

For about nine months prior to birth, the child enjoys the most ideal living conditions and the least threatening environment which he will ever find in his lifetime. His physical needs normally are very adequately met, and the security of the womb can never really be duplicated. Suddenly, this harmonious and tranquil life-style is abruptly and, seemingly, viciously interrupted. Within the brief span of a very few hours, and with the accompaniment of some real trauma, he finds himself in totally new, unprotected, uncomfortable circumstances, subject to strange and frightening cold and noise and, seemingly alone, at least for an instant, in a strange and hostile environment.

Some scholars have stated that much or all later anxiety finds its origin at this point and have traced the beginning of future personality problems to this birth trauma.[2]

Dr. Thomas Harris lays great stress on this happening, and he calls the accompanying reaction of adults who attempt to protect and comfort the newborn baby, the time of "psychological birth."[3] Many others have commented upon this beginning, and great emphasis has come from many sources on the importance of how the infant is handled in the immediate time-span after the shock of birth. Many years ago, one of the fine nursing-nuns at a well known infant home in Ohio pointed out that many babies have been known to die simply for lack of

---

[2] Based on readings of Sigmund Freud, Otto Rank and others.

[3] Thomas Harris, *I'm O.K.—You're O.K.*, Harper & Row, N.Y. (1967, 1968, 1969), p. 41.

love and physical attention in these important months immediately after birth.[4]

Harris speaks at length of the importance of a "rescuer" coming on the scene immediately after the infant leaves the security and warmth of the womb in order to pick him up, wrap him, and begin the comforting act of stroking which he refers to as being necessary to stimulate the child's will to live.

He and numerous other authors have written about the number of children,[5] especially those who found themselves in institutions where there was no loving administration to their immediate needs, who died of the disease called "marasmus" simply because of the absence of the necessary physical contact and reassurance that enabled them to survive during this very difficult time.[6]

From a standpoint of understanding later behavior, it is important to question that if infants can literally die as a result of mishandling or the lack of warm handling in the immediate post-birth period, how much psychological damage and, consequently, how many deviant behavior patterns can develop as a result of such imporant early deprivation?

From the time of birth until about the time of walking, or at least until some real mobility is achieved, the infant is completely dependent upon adults for the important needs of physical survival and psychological existence. The child who receives only grudging attention while immobilized prior to the achievement of mobility from a parent who basically is lacking in proper love or knowledge of the needs of the infant, will then only receive less or perhaps no physical attention at all once the child is mobile and thus less dependent.

§ 4.3   Effect of treatment of child for first three years

a. Repression after mobility: withdrawal

The child who was mistreated or physically abused in the early months before mobility, will probably be abused more

---

4 Private conversation with the author, 1961.

5 Harris, op. cit., p. 41.

6 Harris, op. cit., p. 41.

often because his natural curiosity will lead him into forbidden adult territory.

The child who during the period of immobility has shown signs of intelligence, the development of ego, and other early mental, emotional and physical developmental signs, if misunderstood and mishandled when he lay helpless, will now with his new ability to crawl and walk, only experience greater misunderstanding and deprivation at the hands of ignorant or rejecting parents.

As the infant develops into the young child, the Freudians and later interpreters see the basic urges ("id") being modified by the restrictions and repression of the ever-present parent. From this the ego is said to emerge, enabling the infant to relate in some way to its environment, and ultimately advance from the uncontrolled, disorganized infant stage to the mature, controlled person because of "ego strengths." Finally, they see the development of "super-ego" which houses what is commonly referred to as conscience and our feelings of guilt.

The learning theorists see the various stimulations and reactions from the environment increasingly causing learning and consequent behavioral adjustments. Those who put great emphasis on the "process of maturation" carefully note the developing continuum and the advance through natural stages of increasing maturity.

And so, with few exceptions, most theorists and practitioners would see this important period of time as forming the basis for much personality development and the formation of future behavioral patterns. All seem to agree on the importance of the first three years, and disagreement seems merely to be as to the degree of importance attached.

It is noteworthy that Harris, in applying the theory of "transactional analysis" developed by Berne,[7] attaches great importance, and very rightly so, to this period up until about three years of age. It is pointed out that "if this state of abandonment and difficulty continues without relief through the second

[7] E. Berne, *Games People Play,*
Grove Press, N.Y. (1964).

year of life, the child concludes, 'I'm not O.K.—you're not O.K.' In this position, the 'adult' stops developing . . . . A person in this position gives up. There is no hope. He simply 'gets through' life and ultimately may end up in a mental institution in a state of extreme withdrawal and aggressive behavior which reflects a vague, archaic longing to get back to life as it was in the first year . . ." [8]

b. Development of antisocial behavior and delinquency

Harris makes the second important point that:

"A child who is brutalized long enough by the parents he initially felt were O.K. will switch positions to the . . . criminal position: I'm O.K.—you're not O.K. . . . . This is the child who has been beaten so severely that bones and skin are broken . . . . Every hour five infants in this country receive injuries of this kind at the hands of their parents.

"I believe that it is while this little individual is healing, in a sense, 'lying there licking his wounds,' that he experiences a sense of comfort alone and by himself, if for no other reason than that his improvement is in such contrast to the gross pain he has just experienced. It is as if he senses, 'I'll be alright if you leave me alone. I'm O.K. by myself . . . '

"He refuses to give up. As he grows older, he begins to strike back. He has seen toughness and knows how to be tough. He also has permission (in his parent) to be tough and to be cruel." [9]

The above quoted observations of Dr. Harris are so meaningful when trying to understand later abnormal behavior that they must be seriously considered in any discussion of this type. However, other theories are also very important and when understood properly in relation to the development of the delinquent personality, have a great deal to say.

Fritz Redl, who writes with great insight concerning the delinquent child, follows the psychoanalytic model and points out that certainly faulty super-ego development can be seen in

---

[8] Harris, op. cit., p. 46.   [9] Harris, op. cit., pp. 48, 49.

the delinquent behavior of those who exhibit faulty value systems. He also says that most practitioners encounter countless others with basic "ego-deficiencies" contributing to aberrant behavior patterns and disturbances. However, he makes the very important point that many times in viewing the most disturbed behavioral problems, what really is encountered is some or all of the aforementioned problems, intensely complicated by the development of a functional and strong "delinquent ego." This enables the delinquent child to justify and rationalize what would otherwise be intolerable behavior on the part of anyone.[10]

Dr. Robert W. Shields, psychotherapist with the London County Council, London, England, states emphatically that of the maladjusted children with whom he is so well acquainted, all had real deprivation in childhood. And he points out that faulty relationships with parents early in life cause the delinquent to build up his entire ethical life-pattern around this negative experience.[11]

Dr. Hertha Riese constantly emphasizes the almost overwhelming trauma and the consequent future behavior aberrations in the "hurt child." [12]

Numerous studies of the so-called "psychopath" or "sociopath," done by countless fine observers, indicate that the total absence of important affectional relationships with "significant others" in the child's life have been responsible for the development of this unsocialized type of disturbance in which the person is able to rationalize, but not have any real feeling.

While different writers and observers view the happenings of childhood from various approaches and with varying degrees of intensity, all seem to agree, and experience seems to verify, that early childhood environment makes deep and lasting imprints on character and personality structure which are significant in determining later behavioral patterns. Con-

---

10 Fritz Redl and David Wineman, *Controls From Within*, The Free Press, Glencoe, Ill., (1952).

11 Robert W. Shields, (tape recording), "Treating the Anti-Social Child," McGraw-Hill, (1969).

12 Hertha Riese, *Heal the Hurt Child*, University of Chicago Press, Chicago and London, (1962).

sequently, the way that parents (or parent-substitutes) who are all-important to the child in the early stages, handle such important matters as toilet training, sleeping habits, speaking, destructive tendencies, and all other problems of early childhood are of significant importance.

In later childhood, such problems as boasting, head-banging, rocking, fears of various types (even those seemingly unfounded in the eyes of adults) and all of the child's efforts to cope with the problems of sexuality and aggression, present occasions in which adults usually intervene; and depending upon the adult response, this intervention can either do very great harm or redound to the good of the developing child.

We must also never forget that such adult interventions have different meanings for, and different degrees of impact on, each individual child, depending upon his personality, needs and circumstances. This was pointed out graphically in a 1960 study of child-rearing practices in which it was stated:

". . . every experience is an individualized one for each child and its psychological influence can be understood only in terms of the environmental context in which it occurs and the primary characteristics of reactivity of the child." [13]

Harris again gives perhaps the most all-inclusive explanation when he says that the child stores up all of the responses and attitudes that the parents display and all of his childhood feelings about the parental reactions in his brain for later use just as surely as if he had stored them on a computer tape. The same scholar proceeds to point out that much behavior in adolescent and adult years is prompted by the re-play of the impressions received from the parents in early childhood and the feelings which the little child had about these happenings. [14]

It is of the greatest importance to note that whether we speak of childhood in terms of Freudian stages of development

---

[13] A. Thomas, H. G. Birch, S. Chess, & L. C. Robbins, "Individuality in Responses of Children to Similar Environmental Situations," American Journal of Psychiatry, #117, pp. 789-803

(Quoted in Developmental Psychology (A Psychobiological Approach) by John Nash), Prentice-Hall, Inc., Englewood Cliffs, N.J. (1970), p. 15.

[14] Harris, op. cit., pp. 24-36.

or as a time of intensive and extensive learning, or as that period in which the child is storing up all phenomena concerned with the parents and his own reaction to these happenings, all would agree that the periods of infancy and early childhood are times of complete dependence of the child upon the adults about him for physical and psychological survival. Because of this, the insecurity that comes from hearing the parents engaged in violent quarrels, and the damage that can be done by any direct act of brutality or rejection toward the totally dependent child is almost immeasurable in its impact on the developing personality and, consequently, on later behavior.

For this reason, most observers agree that the personality is well formed at an extremely early age, although there are differences of opinion as to exactly when and with what degree of solidity this formation takes place.

It must also be noted that while the process of personalization is taking place, the child is also learning to function as a social being. The very young child who with faltering steps learns for himself "I am me," later learns by further exploration that there are "yous," and that he must relate himself to the parents and other persons who will take on ever-varying roles as his life and horizons continue to expand.

APPLICATION OF IMPORTANT POINTS EMPHASIZED FOR LAW ENFORCEMENT OFFICERS

1. Although theories may differ on questions of how or to exactly what degree, all agree that early childhood experiences have an important influence on later behavior. Consequently, much juvenile delinquency simply cannot be understood without knowledge of the child's family and other early environment.

2. Behavior is further influenced by cultural factors and environmental pressures as the child develops. Therefore, delinquent acts are best understood in relation to the child and his environment. To leave out a consideration of either the child's personality or his environment is to only half understand his behavior.

3. Some infants literally die from lack of attention and human warmth shortly after birth. Countless others manage to survive despite neglect but their personalities and the resulting behavior show that great damage has been done. Therefore, child neglect must be under-

stood as including much more than simply physical beatings or poor nutrition.

4. The infant who is physically abused before the crawling or walking stage will probably be abused even more so when he achieves mobility because he can easily become more annoying to the abuse-prone parent and thus heighten the inadequate or rejecting parents' frustration or rage.

5. Brutality or betrayal in early childhood often causes the child to defend himself from similar hurt later in life by adopting a hard front, or by really being unable to trust any adult. If this is properly understood, it helps us to moderate our expectancy in interviewing or counseling certain delinquents, and it tends to alleviate our frustration at "not being able to reach them." Oftentimes a hostile or negative-appearing child is simply reacting to early trauma, and his attitude is not at all a personal attack upon or rejection of the person currently dealing with him.

Chapter 5

BEHAVIOR PROBLEMS IN ADOLESCENTS: THEORIES OF ADOLESCENT PSYCHOLOGY

§ 5.1   In general: reasons for conflicts of adolescence

When the philosopher said many years ago that "youth is all too often wasted on the young," he probably had in mind the uncertainty and conflict which often keeps troubled teenagers from enjoying the fresh beautiful life about them.

This uncertain period of life, the difficult period of development which we call adolescence, can best be described chronologically as the period roughly bordered on the early side by the close of childhood and roughly finished on the later side by the beginning of adulthood. In this period of change we see the setting aside of the old, traditional values of the child which have been developed through approximately twelve years of living and the substitution of whole new behavioral patterns for that which parents and other interested adults have come to consider the comfortable ways of acting of the child that they have grown to know so well.

There are no ground rules for the time of arrival or the announcement of the presence of this new stage of development; nor is there a set timetable for the speed with which the changes take place. The nature and intensity of the struggles, and even the areas in which the battle will be most severe, seem to be beyond the scope of most tables of predictability. Adolescence is a totally personal, totally individual process by which the child, over a particular span of years relative only to himself, leaves behind the life and loves of the child and walks through the threshold which, if all goes well, introduces him to the real world of the mature adult.

Because of the very nature of the experience, being a period of change or "becoming," this period is of necessity filled with uncertainty and conflict. Because the adolescent is growing but not grown, maturing but not mature, not child and yet not adult, adolescence presents great problems and contradictions to the young person undergoing the change, as well as to all of those close to him in this crucial stage.

The difficulties of adolescence seem to be heightened by an urgency in the psychological and, perhaps, even in the biological sense, which impels and thrusts the adolescent forward toward a goal which he himself does not fully understand, the goal of adulthood or maturity. When he has achieved the goal of maturity, he will have adjusted to his new surroundings and integrated all of the scattered feelings and unexplainable drives of adolescence into the adult personality; but that is *after* achievement of the goal. For the present, there is only turbulence and conflict.

The problems, stages, feelings, and crises of adolescence have been so well documented and explained by so many fine scholars and observers that it is practically impossible to present them in a new way, so let us simply state that the following brief description of the particular "ingredients" of adolescence is not only based on the experience of the author, but is drawn from the fine expositions of these phenomena in the writings of George E. Gardner, Chaim Ginott, Lydia G. Dawes, Alexander Schneiders, Edgar Friedenberg, Paul Mussen, R. G. Kuhlen, David Gottlieb, Charles Ramsey and many others.[1]

Having found in the pre-adolescent period (roughly 10 to 12 years of age) that "I am me," having learned to see each parent at that time as an individual, and having found a place for himself in the peer group through competition and the playing of games, now suddenly he awakes to find that he is rapidly changing into a new person. The world about him and all persons in it no longer look the same.

His rapid physical maturation causes great physical changes which are hard to understand; and many times they cause

[1] See Bibliography for complete listings.

anxiety and embarrassment. The physical changes in his sexual organs, along with the new fantasies and unexplainable inner feelings connected with the area of sex, cause great uncertainty and oftentimes feelings of guilt. At the same time, his new-found interests in the area of sex urge him on to exploration and to want to experience feelings and understand thoughts which are always felt to be highly personal and, in some cases, judged to be "dirty" or bad.

While this conflict continues, another new problem also comes into the picture. The teen-ager suddenly starts to understand that the behavior of others around him seems to flow from hidden internal motives, and he becomes quite unsure of how much of his own underlying motivations, his secret thoughts and desires, are known to those about him because he has revealed them through his behavior. He is quite aware of seeing "hidden things" in others, and he wonders if he is similarly exposed.

Like all human beings, the adolescent is constantly aware that instincts, drives, and motives keep determining his many needs because life is a dynamic process at all times; but now with his changing body in the changing world around him, all of these phenomena combine to cause great uncertainty and severe conflict.

If his basic survival needs in the physical and emotional order have been adequately met, then his main concern since infancy has been for satisfaction of those needs associated with the word security. He, like all human beings, needs to keep what he possesses in the physical and the emotional order. But now as his "child-love" is changing to a more mature form and as he realizes that he looks just as different to his parents and significant others as they now appear to him, his security can be severely threatened. If survival needs have not been satisfied, the turmoil of adolescence added to basic insecurity combines to cause near chaos.

Again, since the earliest stages of his infant development he has been learning to cope with his sexual and aggressive instincts. He has incorporated parental restrictions and objections into his value system and, consequently, he reflects them in his behavior. In doing this, he has had to frustrate his basic instincts. This in turn has heightened his aggressive tendencies, and now in the face of present extreme frustration, he must learn new and better ways of coping with aggression.

At the same time, the pleasures of a sexual type which have been so diffuse and general during childhood become quite localized around the genital areas during adolescence. These new physical sensations and all the psychological stimulation associated with them sorely strain his ability to meet their challenge with new control mechanisms.

While these problems which had been present since infancy present themselves in new and much more intense forms during adolescence, new problems in areas of conflict that have never existed before begin to assault the teenager. He finds very quickly that there is a considerable amount of expectancy present in his immediate environment that insists that he conduct himself as an adult; at the same time he is more aware than perhaps anyone else that there is still much of the child present in him. Other aspects of his environment constantly insist upon keeping him a child, and yet a considerable portion of his energy is used in proving that he is now "grown up."

His strong desire, and all of the biological and psychological pressures pushing him toward adulthood and emancipation from parental control and protection, force him in many ways to seek independence and freedom from parental influence even if he has to battle with great energy to achieve it. But while he is waging this ferocious struggle, something inside of himself still wishes to cling to the security and protection that has become so comfortable during dependence upon the parents physically, emotionally, and spiritually.

This conflict gives rise to the ambivalent and vacillating behavior that is seen from day to day, and sometimes from hour to hour, when an adolescent alternately asserts his manhood, and then suddenly reverts to childlike behavior and seeks parental attention, reassurance or assistance. His great need to be seen as a young adult demands that he take on responsibilities and make decisions for himself despite the fact that he has a gnawing awareness that with each new decision and independent step he is leaving childhood comfort and security behind forever.

And he is also aware that in many areas he is not yet at all ready to make certain decisions or undertake self-direction to any great degree. This is why one observer of adolescent behavior said recently that the last thing in the world even the most protesting teenager really wants is for any adult to tell him to go ahead and "let his conscience be his guide."

§ 5.2   Identification with peer groups; effect of developing sex drive

During these intense conflict situations, it is not uncommon for even the most normal of teenagers to adopt defenses of bravado and pseudo-masculinity, or even provocative demonstrations of independence, because, while he desperately wants help, he is so fearful of showing such need that he must react negatively to any offer of the help which he really seeks.

Those seeking to give advice oftentimes must be rejected and the advice must be resented when given. The adolescent will often become angry when he is given admiration, but he is hurt when no one appreciates him. His need for attention is perhaps greater than ever and yet he seems embarrassed and even embittered at any open display. His "cockiness" is most often a shallow defense for his uncertainty; and his protestations and rejections are quite often his inverted cries for help.

At some time during this adolescent process, the youngster must find his place in the peer group. At this stage his identification and preoccupation with the members of his own age group become quite intense. This is a natural need because he is seeking out his age-mates who will form the companions for his life, his work, his love and his sexual expression under most normal circumstances. For the teenager, the peer group is simply "where the action is," and to be deprived of their companionship and forced to spend his time with younger children or adults is worse than death itself.

He also, at least subconsciously, recognizes the need for his age group because of their important function in limiting his demands. His adolescent needs can make unreasonable demands upon parents, older friends, teachers and the entire adult society under certain circumstances, but he is quite aware that he cannot "get away with it" with his peers.

Another great goal of the growing up process is for his masculine (or in the case of a girl, feminine) identification. Teenagers simply must find the male (or female) role that they are going to fill during their lifetime. Past experiences have taught the boy that the male must be strong, loyal, brave, a provider, a "fixer" and, ultimately, a father. A girl has found that she must be soft, loving, gentle and, ultimately, a mother. But the recognition of the ingredients of these respective roles is not at all the winning of the battle. The adolescent has recognized that just as child-love no longer suffices in his parental relationships, so now his childhood achievements no longer fill the needs for competence in the adult role.

This problem is complicated in modern society by the fact that these basic drives and the sexual stimulation associated with this period of development cannot result in culturally accepted marriage until far in the distant future from the time they begin in the early teens. The demand for prolonged education at the adolescent level and the lack of avenues to become self-supporting and, consequently, economically capable of marriage, make the period of waiting a time of greatly prolonged struggle.

During this crucial period, there is often the frustration which comes from inability to find any effective way in most instances to prove adult adequacy and to become truly independent. Much behavior which is considered outrageous or incompresensible to adults occurs at this time because the behavioral manifestations are simply a device used by the adolescent to protest against his own feelings, or as a social outlet for feelings which he cannot really express to anyone, and cannot really understand himself.

The strong adolescent sex-drives, accompanied by day-dreams and fantasies, give the teenager a feeling of great help-lessness and aloneness. Much of this feeling-complex cannot find outlet in words; and that which could be verbalized cannot be shared because the cost in loss of independence and be-trayal of self is too great. Often this conflict is heightened by the realization, or at least the fear, that the impulses cannot be controlled alone, and this is often much more severely com-plicated by guilt resulting from any expression of pleasure re-lated to sexual stimulation.

These are very difficult times for the teenager, and these situations can become critical if there has been a false sense of shame established about sex or any bodily function. Where there has been unrealistic rigidity in parental taboos or a background of harsh punishment of any infantile sexual ex-pression, confusion or guilt in the teenager can become almost overwhelming. The feelings of guilt, rage, helplessness, and frustration can very easily cause the adolescent to make the judgment "I am bad"; and from this withdrawal into "sickness" or the development of an anti-adult, antisocial, and anti-law orientation can easily result as a defense against intolerable anxiety.

§ 5.3   Rejection of parents; identity crisis

Normally there is also a great amount of guilt associated with the realization by the adolescent that he has suddenly become a new person and is relating in totally different ways to parents and significant others.

In the process of developing to adulthood, since it is necessary to emancipate himself from the parents, the youngster reaches a stage where he must "devalue" the parents and many other familiar things and habits. During this period, open criticism of parents personally, and in relation to household practices, customs, etc., is commonplace. Identification with a family or individuals outside of the home is quite frequent, and this is often an extremely trying situation for the parents; in reality it is an essential step in the process of emancipation and growth toward maturity.

At this time, "crushes" on individuals or families outside of the home are usually developed. These serve a very useful purpose in that they provide a perspective that can readily be used in making future choices, because at home the youngster has been intimidated in choice-making by the awesome domination of the ever-present parents. By looking outside the home for a life-style and for new modes of problem-solving, the youngster has a real choice and a life-enrichment experience that he cannot obtain at home. Many serious problems between parents and adolescent youngsters could be avoided if the parents could just understand what the teenager is trying to accomplish during this process. It requires a mature and emotionally secure parent to understand this process, and not feel hurt by internalizing this as an attack or a show of ingratitude.

In his search for adults with whom to identify, the adolescent finds still further conflicts in many instances because the person who is seen as understanding, tender, and kind is often also seen as being too weak really to serve as a model for later fighting the battles of life; while at the same time the person who appears strong, is also seen as cruel, exploitative or "phony."

During all of this, the teenager feels very deeply the need for parental love, but he also has the need to belittle the parent and to emancipate himself. While doing this, he is normally quite concerned that he really has not hurt the parents too deeply; and yet the very process demands that he take the chance. Likewise, he needs ego-ideals, but he is super-sensitive to "phoniness"; and while he needs very much to reject the "phonies," he is desperately searching for ideal figures with whom to identify.

The conflict becomes so severe that often a flight from the growing-up process itself takes place in aggravated situations. The child can simply refuse to grow up any further or even regress to the infantile level by becoming extremely dependent, unclean in bodily habits, and in cases of severe disturbance, by literally returning to the physical position which he held while still in the womb.

When overwhelming conflict takes place in the area of sexual maturation, the youngsters may seek to escape by identifying all of sex with the "sinful," or by refusing to have any contact with the opposite sex or any other person at all. There are reported cases of some girls during this phase, where the disturbance becomes extreme enough that the growth of breasts or any other sign of physical maturity is rejected to the point that they might even refuse to eat in order to stop physical growth.

In less disturbed cases, such expressions on the part of boys as "I hate women" or the "tomboy stage" in girls can be seen as signs of conflict. Other youngsters have used the device of easing conflict through projection or displacement and have aggressively identified with radical political or economic movements so that the solving of outside problems could ease the unbearable inner conflict.

The quiet or aloof phase must also be understood as an important time in which much of the energy is being used on the solving of inner conflicts. During this time teenagers are seen as very moody or perhaps withdrawn. Their replies to parents might be very sharp and conversation of any length or meaning can be very rare.

Above all, throughout the adolescent period the youngster engages often in the testing process in which really he wishes to make certain that the parents do love him enough to prevent serious harm. This might take the form of the announcement of his impending participation in some very hazardous physical enterprise or the carrying out of some ridiculous scheme which would surely bring disgrace upon himself, his family or his school. It is at this time that he is crying out most loudly for help and for reassurance of parental love and the security of parental limits. It is unfortunate that in contemporary society we have often overlooked this important aspect of adolescent development and we have neglected to see that despite his loudest protestations, no teenager really wishes to be left completely to the mercy of his own impulses.

Perhaps we have forgotten to love enough to discipline; or perhaps this is just another manifestation of modern man's lack of time and energy for some of the most important human tasks, especially the task of child-rearing.

While mentioning time and energy which should be applied so generously in the life of children at all levels, it is important to note that all through childhood, and again especially at the adolescent level, we must remember that values should be "caught" not taught. And that they can only be caught when parents spend considerable amounts of time and share many experiences with their youngsters. In the same way, love has to be shown, not theorized; and those things which we perhaps can teach to a young child as the "facts of life" must be shared with a teenager as the "feelings of life." This necessarily pre-supposes a close relationship and a real bond of affection between parent and child.

In helping the adolescent to establish a workable value system, which basically means helping him to learn how to live or how to establish a philosophy of life, we are assisting him toward one of the most fundamental and necessary goals of his journey through adolescence. There is no time at which the youngster searches more for the meaning of life; and there is no time during which he is more aware of the lack of meaning in the lives of those around him. This is probably at least part of the reason why the great Dr. Albert Schweitzer said so beautifully that "example is not the best way to teach children, it is the only way."

At some point during the growth process every child becomes identified with parental figures, provided that there is a relationship positive enough to make identification desirable or even possible for the youngster. In situations where one or both of the parents are overtly rejecting, or where their per-sonal lives are such that immorality, extreme selfishness or gross lack of integrity are readily visible, the child normally looks elsewhere for more positive figures to emulate or, at least, he has an "identification crisis" of some type.

When a father personifies the qualities of a strong and adequate male, and a mother radiates the feminine qualities of woman, wife and mother, it is natural for the boy to look at the father and say, "That's what it means to be a man," or the girl to the mother, "That's what it means to be a woman"; and it follows readily that the child adds, "I want to talk like they talk, believe what they believe, and act like they act!"

In this situation of real identification, the child internalizes the parental values, and much of the behavior of the parent is the model for the behavior of the child. Ethical principles, attitudes toward other groups and individuals, religious beliefs, patriotism and even table manners are transmitted at this time with an ease and an intensity that is hard to duplicate at any other time or in any artificial setting. Such values and standards of conduct, when received by the child, normally withstand the strain of adolescence and the "contra-cultural" pressures from outside influences.

Conversely, when a youngster without such a foundation, and without the strength that is so built in, arrives at the adolescent level unsure of what is right or wrong, the "storms" and "waves" of this turbulent period very easily carry him away into all forms of trial and error experimentation and even cause such conflict that severe behavior disorders and personality disturbances can result.

When society at large, and parents and "hero models" in particular, present a standard of expediency instead of values, pliability instead of norms, and "spinelessness" instead of convictions, serious difficulties are presented to the identification-ready adolescent. This was well expressed by Friedenberg when he said that "the fundamental task of adolescence is the establishment of self-identification" and that "this process may be frustrated and emptied of meaning in a society which, like our own, is hostile to clarity and vividness. Our culture impedes the clear definition of any self-image. . . . It also makes adolescence more difficult, more dangerous, and more troublesome to the adolescent and to society itself." [2]

APPLICATION OF IMPORTANT POINTS EMPHASIZED FOR LAW ENFORCEMENT OFFICERS

1. Adolescence for all youngsters, even the most normal, is a time of extreme change and conflict. If this is understood, then much of the alarm about extreme "mood swings," and much of the frustration of adults in trying to cope with teenagers can be properly evaluated.

[2] Edgar Z. Friedenberg, *The Vanishing Adolescent*, Beacon Press, Boston (1959), p. 1.

2. Heightening interest in sex, and confusion about his own sexual feelings, often cause experimentation in sexual behavior of various kinds. This adolescent exploration must be properly understood, especially when it has caused an illegal act or an offense against a third person. The law and the rights of others must be safeguarded, but the offender must not be presumed to be a degenerate or a pervert or a fully developed "sex offender," when really he is in a transitional period and under severe situational stress in many cases. Proper help provided to a confused adolescent at such a time can perhaps prevent really serious later problems.

3. Intense feelings of guilt, dejection and even depression, extreme states of confusion, a high degree of ambivalence and vacillation, violent "mood swings" and many other signs of disturbance can cause an adolescent to be mis-diagnosed as "psychotic" or even "dangerous" at times. A certain amount of disturbance is part of the normal pattern of teenagers, and under great stress or in very bad situations, the symptoms can take on seemingly "psychotic" proportions, without such a mental condition being present at all.

4. A defense of toughness or an "I don't care" attitude is often simply a shallow mask hiding fear or feelings of inadequacy. Very frequently the "tougher the front," the more fearful and anxious the youngster really is inside. It is important to understand this so that a particular offender is not erroneously thought to be a sophisticated delinquent or a "bad actor" when really he is a frightened, dependent youngster.

5. The approval of the peer group is an absolute requirement for most adolescents in choosing behavior modes at any time. Therefore, any attempts to alienate a teenager from the peer approval or to get him to violate the group code are strongly resisted. This must especially be remembered in interrogation and investigation. An officer should not be surprised to see a youngster who was respectful and cooperative in a private interview be quite hostile and uncooperative when questioned in a group.

6. Ridicule and humiliation are never helpful in working with teenagers under any circumstances, and most often they destroy any relationship or respect that had been developed with the juvenile.

7. "Phoniness" is a particular "hang-up" of adolescents, and so honesty and frankness are the best techniques in establishing a basis for trust and respect.

8. Because of the many written and verbal attacks upon police that are circulated in the teenage group at the present, it is especially important that officers be conscious of the image they project or the example they give in contact with youth. Much good can be ac-

complished by a fine police officer presenting a positive picture of integrity, nobility, loyalty, honesty and the other virtues that are so often denied as part of the police image in hostile publications and conversations. One picture is worth a thousand words, especially to a "teen" group which is constantly challenging, "Don't tell me, man, show me!"

Chapter 6

THE MULTIPLE PROBLEM FAMILY

Section

§ 6.1   Characteristics and description of multiple problem family

It is impossible to consider the picture of causality in relation to the crime and delinquency complex in big city America, or even to fully understand the high recidivism-rate or chronicity patterns without discussing one of the major problems confronting all of the social service professions, which is the "multiple-problem family."

This group of families has often been referred to by a variety of names including "the disenfranchised," "hard-core," "hard to reach," "untreatable" and even "lower class." [1] However, no matter what descriptive terms we use to indicate their existence, we are always talking about the same family picture, which is one of disorganization, a variety of problems in several important areas, and the chronic inability to be assisted positively by existing community agencies.

These familties exhibit problems in family relationships, unity and stability, individual behavior and adjustment of members, problems in raising children, handling money, the effective carrying out of household practices and problems in the social life of the family and its individual members. Even a cursory observation of such families immediately indicates that they exhibit most or all of the problems associated with being socially disorganized and chronically poor.

[1] Helen Harris Perlman, "Casework and the Case of Chemung County," *The Multiple Problem Dilemma,* Scarecrow Press, Metuchen, N.J. (1968), p. 50.

A classic example of such a family can be seen in the following case: Two young teenage boys are currently in a local correctional school and one of them has been termed hard to handle even in that setting. An older brother is committed to the state correctional school for more serious offenses.

The father is currently on probation to the Municipal Court on a charge of child neglect as a result of a warrant being obtained by his wife. The wife is married for a second time and has four children from her first marriage and three from the present marriage, and two of the four first-marriage children are currently on probation to the Municipal Court as young adults.

During the first marriage there had been abuse of family and drinking problems which were terminated by the violent death of the first husband. The husband in the second marriage has been arrested on a hundred occasions and convicted approximately fifty times on misdemeanor charges. He has served over thirty sentences in jails and other correctional facilities and has completed probation three times. An overwhelming majority of the offenses deal with some type of family disturbance, such as abuse of wife and children, child neglect, assault and battery, or disorderly conduct.

Both the second husband and the wife have a drinking problem. The wife has been arrested several times for drunkenness and family offenses.

One of the children from the first marriage has been arrested for assaulting his step-sister who is currently in a local correctional school. Another son from the first marriage is also known for continuing the family-abuse problem and he is currently in violation of probation on a child-neglect charge.

The social service registrations concerning this family read like an alphabetical index of community resources. They include family contacts with the Juvenile Court, Welfare Department, Domestic Relations Court, two local correctional schools and one state-operated facility, the Municipal Court, the Common Pleas Court of the county, the State Parole Office, the Probate Court, the Catholic Charities, the Salvation Army, the

Bureau of Vocational Rehabilitation, the State Mental Hospital, the Municipal General Hospital, the City Work House, Children's Protective Service, Youth Aid Bureau of the Municipal Police Department, and various other agencies.

Both parents have attended hospitals and alcoholism clinics because of drinking problems. Both have used probation services at various levels with no apparent alteration in the chronicity of their behavior. Both have been evaluated psychiatrically. Both have been incarcerated.

All of the children have been termed "school problems," have been recipients of numerous agency services, and have been processed through Juvenile Courts and institutions.

To understand more fully the impact of such a multiple problem situation on the individual child, let us briefly examine the case of a fourteen-year-old boy recently processed through a juvenile court in a large mid-western city. For convenience we will call him Albert.

At the time of his arrest, Albert was alleged to have taken two boxes of frozen food from a neighborhood store. This was not his first arrest. He had seventeen previous contacts with the local police department, primarily for being out late on the streets of the city or for being away from school or his home without permission. At the time of his arrest, he was absent approximately 90 days out of a possible 102 school days, indicating that he was for all practical purposes a "non-attender" in the educational system.

A superficial review of his case would have tempted the average citizen to respond, "Here is a thoroughly bad boy. He is in trouble constantly in school, he is well known to the police department because of his truancy, late hours, and runaways; and now he is stealing from a local merchant." But before pronouncing such judgment, it is necessary that we look a little deeper into the family situation.

The boy's father is currently in the county jail awaiting trial on a burglary charge for which he was indicted. The man has a criminal record dating back to 1937 and including so many offenses that when typed single-spaced on legal-sized paper, his record covers a page and a half, including three offenses for abusing his own children. The mother in this home has been termed "functionally feeble-minded," which, from a behavioral standpoint, means that she does not understand the notes which the school sends home about the boy's lack of attendance or bad behavior in school. She cannot plan a balanced diet for her family. She cannot budget money and, consequently, the welfare voucher always runs out about the 20th of each month, leaving the family members to shift to their own resources for survival. She cannot keep a clean house. She cannot properly distribute the emotional goods of affection, consistent discipline, and a feeling of security to her youngsters; and above all, she certainly cannot cope with the very cruel and aggressive father when he is present in the home situation. She seems to be a very well-meaning woman, but she simply does not have the natural intelligence to enable her to fulfill the role of wife and mother as would be expected.

Albert's oldest brother, twenty-two years old, is currently in jail with the father awaiting indictment on the burglary charge. The second oldest brother is in an institution for the mentally retarded at the state capital. The next oldest male sibling is a run-away from a state institution. Albert is the fourth oldest child in this family, and the next two siblings in chronological order have already exhibited school problems and have been labeled "emotionally disturbed." The two youngest members of the family have not yet come officially to the attention of any community agency because they are of pre-school age and have not yet acted out any problems that would merit community concern.

A physical and psychological examination of Albert revealed very quickly not only that he had been exposed to traumatic experiences within the home consisting of vicious fighting, brutal beatings, and deprivation, but his physical care had been completely neglected. He was diagnosed in the juvenile court clinic as having a breast tumor and a heart murmur that were not previously diagnosed. He had three teeth broken off, one with the nerve exposed, and so he walked about the streets of a large city with constant dental pain as much a part of his daily life as more positive experiences are part of the lives of more normal teenagers. This last physical defect had the most devastating effect upon his behavior.

The above case examples illustrate how a definition of the "multiple problem family" is developed. Such families seem best defined as families suffering a variety of health and welfare problems, chronically dependent on community services, with some display of apathy or resistance or even a rejection of selected, or perhaps all, agency efforts to help. In the interest of simplicity, they can be more effectively and briefly described as families living under acute and chronic stress in numerous important areas of life.[2]

Because of their poverty and personal problems, these families are almost always found among the residents of the most inadequate housing, or in the public housing developments. This is not to say that all residents of such housing areas are multiple problem families, but only to say that this is a location in which most families of this type are found.

Such families have been found in houses which have been condemned for occupancy for several decades; others have been found in former commercial buildings in which plumbing and other necessities of family living are inadequate; others are found not only in tenement housing, but in shacks behind tenement buildings in many large cities.

Such housing, of course, aggravates and perpetuates their many problems. These families are, not by choice but by demands of their living situation, well acquainted with rats and vermin. In fact, more than one member of such a family has said to various workers that "the rats in our building outnumber the people five to one." In one city, an interested child-welfare worker admonishes the mothers of young children to be sure to wash carefully the mouths of the infants before putting them to bed for the evening so that the many rats would not be tempted to attack the child in order to obtain edible particles out of the mouth of the child while it is sleeping.

[2] These definitions are not original with the author. They are based on the fine thinking, discussions and writings of countless observers of the "multiple-problem family," including most notably that of Frank Arricale, Deputy Housing Commissioner, New York City, and Ronald L. Warren of Brandeis University.

Malnutrition is rampant in these situations, as any good public-health nurse can testify. The chalk-white faces of youngsters reflect the lack of protein in the diet. The gaunt expressions and the "tooth-pick thin" arms and legs of young children give evidence of the ravages of hunger.

The presence of two different groups of youngsters at lunchtime in many metropolitan areas school systems—one group going to the cafeteria and lunch-rooms because they can afford to purchase lunch or have been supplied a nutritious lunch in a lunch-box from home, while the other group goes to the auditoriums or playgrounds, or even out on the streets because they do not have the necessary money or commodities for lunch—graphically attests to the large number of children whose nutritional needs are not satisfied in such homes.

The estimated 80,000 school drop-outs in New York City alone, and the approximately 10 million youngsters who have not completed terminal education in this nation during this decade, eloquently support the thesis that large numbers of youngsters from such families are not receiving the motivation and the necessary emotional and physical goods to enable them to compete in the school system.

The fact that some 47% of all youngsters arrested and presented to the juvenile courts of America are in dire need of treatment for undetected or untreated physical abnormalities, and that over 80% of these same children need remedial dental treatment, certainly indicate that this same group of youngsters, making up such a large proportion of the juvenile court caseload, is not receiving adequate medical and dental care at home.

The third and fourth generation welfare recipients among this group testify to the failure of community services to adequately assist them to change their life-style or to drastically alter their circumstances; and yet, it is self-evident that these families are consuming a tremendous proportion of the existing services and an ever-increasing amount of community resources.

For example, in St. Paul, Minnesota, it was estimated that only 6% of all of the families utilized 77% of the public assistance dollars, 51% of health services, and 56% of corrections and mental health facilities.[3] In Cincinnati, Ohio, a study revealed that less than 800 families were providing about 57% of the juvenile delinquency and were using a comparable amount of court and agency services.[4] Additional studies in California, Minnesota, Maryland, and several other places have come to similar conclusions, and the New York City Youth Board is reported to have found that one per cent of the families were involved in 75% of the city's delinquency.[5]

For a number of such families, the municipal courts and other agencies concerned with misdemeanors become simply revolving doors. This is not hard to understand in relation to the multiple-problem family because by definition, and certainly by case analysis, we discover that these families are composed of persons under severe stress, overwhelmed, often confused and frustrated and, as a result, withdrawn. They often deny and retreat. Often they are perplexed about just how to survive. When they try to attack the many problems and fail, they react to their failure with irresponsibility and try to escape the anxiety-producing situation; and this, of course, only creates more problems.

The presence of such "multi-problems" in their lives quickly generates feelings of futility, despair and sometimes rage. The anxiety created in such circumstances becomes unbearable at times, and because of personal inadequacy or lack of education or inability to communicate, the reaction to this anxiety often results in poorly planned, crude, poorly executed solutions which quickly bring such persons to the attention of law enforcement officers and courts.

Because of past failures and rejection, a feeling of total hopelessness and inadequacy, or because positive methods of communication and problem-solving have never been learned, or a wide variety of other reasons, such persons are often seen as resisting or rejecting treatment or help when it is offered.

[3] Report of 1948 study in St. Paul, Minn. reported in *Community Planning for Human Services*, Columbia U. Press, (1952), p. 9 et seq.

[4] Richard Clendennen and Howard E. Fradkin, "Services for Delinquent Children, Hamilton County (Ohio)," (1958).

[5] Gordon E. Brown, *The Multiple Problem Dilemma*, op. cit., p. 8.

This rejection can be seen in the breaking of probation, dropping out of school, not seeking needed early medical care for serious illnesses, failure to keep job appointments, not utilizing casework services, not being home when agency visitations have been arranged, and many other "avoidance mechanisms." Of course such failure to respond or unwillingness to follow through often brings on only further rejection and negative experience at the hands of community agencies and services. Therefore the problem continues to worsen.

While much of this rejection of services is due to a past history of failure or rejection when a family was strong enough to reach out, or at least to accept services when offered, much of it can also be seen as due to the lack of means to carry out an expected function. For example, without a job there can be no "bread-winner." Without proper dishes, mops, soap, etc., there can be no good housekeeping. Without access to good medical care, health problems continue to worsen; without day care facilities a mother cannot become a working and providing mother. These lacks caused one observer to say that such families live on "budgets of despair." [6]

§ 6.2   Effect of family problems on juveniles

However, the important thing for purposes of this study is the influence of such situations upon the delinquent behavior of youngsters. This causal link was pointed out by the author in an address to the City Council of Cincinnati on the relationship between poverty and delinquency. In that report it was stated:

"In addressing ourselves to the problems of poverty, I think that it is necessary that we understand that we are using this word in a generic sense. That is to say that poverty takes on many specific forms, has many specific manifestations of itself, and acts as a manifold cause, as witnessed by previous testimony before this committee regarding housing, hunger, unemployment, medical problems, and the many other faces that poverty can and does wear. However, it is important for us to remember

[6] Id., p. 20.

that no matter how poverty exhibits itself, or no matter why it exists, the results in terms of human suffering and community costs are the same. In a family where a parent misuses the wages, or where the welfare support provides only 70% of minimal sustenance needs, or where the parent does not qualify for public assistance because of fraud or other criminal actions, or where the parents are temporarily removed from the home because of their arrest, or drinking, hospitalization, or for many other reasons—the resultant poverty is still the same. We can abhor the causes, but we must cope with the condition. A child that is made hungry because of any of the above reasons finds the hunger pangs equally as bad, whether he is responsible for the condition in which he finds himself or not.

"It is especially timely to engage in this discussion now when the importance of the group of delinquents called cultural delinquents is being ever more regularly seen as contributing a major portion of metropolitan area delinquent behavior. The day has long passed when the field of juvenile corrections was convinced that most of the problems of deviant behavior of youngsters could be resolved on an inner-psychic basis with individual therapy. The realization has dawned more and more that much delinquent behavior is rooted in socioeconomic causal factors, and that environmental situations must be remedied in order that youngsters caught in certain unfortunate circumstances can even be given the chance to survive until adolescence without succumbing to the pressure of the delinquency-prone environment already at pre-school age."[7]

§ 6.3 Understanding problems of juveniles from multiple problem families

⌐Many years ago the poet told us that "the child who lives with love learns to love, and the child who lives with hate, learns to hate." This beautiful and accurate line of literature contains a great deal of fact concerning the dynamics of child behavior.⌐ It encompasses in a simple form the basics of behavioral dynamics which have since been explored scientifically

[7] Paul H. Hahn, "Report to City Council (Cincinnati, O.) on Relation- ship of Poverty and Juvenile Delinquency," (1964).

by many scholars in great detail. It contains in its sweep the best of Freud, the environmentalists, the learning theorists, and it even embraces the essentials demanded by those of us who insist on principles of "multiple-causality," because of the wide meaning of "live with love" and "learn to love."

The child who begins life as an unwanted pregnancy; the three-year-old girl who is "given away" in a bar by her alcoholic mother; the infant who is beaten and burned with cigarettes by a sadistic step-father; the child who is placed in twenty-two different foster homes and houses of refuge by the time he is fourteen years old; the emotionally disturbed boy who is placed in a state school when he is too young to defend himself from aggression and sexual exploitation by older and more delinquent youngsters; or any one of thousands of other children that we can cite as examples of children who "live with hate," provide an eloquent and tragic example of the truth in the poet's statement.

That they learn to hate can readily be seen from the patterns of destructive, exploitative, and impulsive behavior which can be observed by any chance person who happens into their lives, and which has been carefully documented by many observers of "hurt children."

One of the best statements ever written about such children and their difficulties, reverbalizes the simple truth in the poet's statement in these words: "These children's potential and their development have been inhibited by an appalling absence of positive stimulation—sensory, motor, mental and emotional. At the same time they have been exposed to terrifying experiences and distorting influences. When later on they encounter people whose standards are impressively higher than their own, a sense of paralyzing inadequacy hampers their benefiting from belated opportunity and frustrates hope of matching these ideal figures. The flow of a beneficial source which otherwise would have been inspiring seems now to be repugnant.

"Not having learned to know in communicable terms what their feelings are, these children cannot help their mystified observers to understand why they do not react positively to good example and mental stimulation. Lacking contact with and understanding of these children, their would-be educators and benefactors become overtly and covertly annoyed and increasingly rejecting. The grapes of opportunity will move out of the children's reach with increasing momentum, and for comfort the weary child will declare them totally unpalatable." [8]

Such a child frequently often lashes out as though he needs to "get the first punch in" before a hostile environment can hurt him any further. These children seem in many cases to be driven to overt warfare from fear of assaults or from an ambush. They often show the signs of seeking a warm, accepting relationship with a positive adult figure, but when they have the opportunity to do so they immediately lapse into some obvious negative behavior in an attempt to "alienate" the person seeking to help them.

Riese discusses this point further when she says, "the children long for contact and support, but, at the same time, they fear the potential enemy in the other person. This ambivalent attitude is the carry-over of the mother-child relationship, or the relationship to all and their entire world. This ambivalence leads to a tendency to provoke what is feared, as though fear and suspense were harder to endure than the actual hurt which is anticipated. The attitude is usually generalized and the ingenuity of these children in varying the means of provoking the very trouble they fear, is impressive. It actually is their way of life—the only means by which they can feel they are living. The need to culminate the fear in concrete trouble becomes so intense that actual occurrences cannot satisfy it any more, and the aggression is imagined, nurtured by fear." [9]

Fritz Redl, one of the finest at understanding and treating the "children who hate," wrote an eloquent passage about exactly this phenomenon:

"Many of these youngsters hardly knew how to like new people any more, and they had to start learning what it means to like, and especially what it means to identify, all over again.

8 Hertha Riese, *Heal the Hurt Child*, Univ. of Chicago Press, Chicago (1967 and 1966), p. 30.   9 Id., pp. 31, 32.

This, by the way, is the reason why only a total treatment design can do the job for them. For once the machinery of identification is misdeveloped or underdeveloped, it requires a great display of total strategy to build it up anew. This is also the reason why the layman or ordinary foster parent finds such children so disappointing and intolerable to work with. A normal child with constructive childhood behind him, even though somewhat out of gear right now, usually has a good deal of identification readiness in him, just waiting for the right person around him to unfold. All you have to do in his case is to enter his life, give him affection, hold yourself in a way children understand and consider fun, and add, perhaps, an occasional bit of love-blackmail or bribery, and you won't find a child hesitating long before he accepts what you stand for and identifies with some of the values you hold." [10]

However, with the truly hurt children, reaching them is not quite so simple. Having been hurt so often and with disappointment in their basic affectional needs having been such a large part of their normal living experience, and needing to "strike out" in order to avoid further hurt, it is practically impossible for such youngsters to accept verbalizations or preliminary offerings of friendship. In such cases, the oft-repeated expression "man, don't tell me, show me!" is the rule of the day. Great patience, understanding of the dynamics of the child, and willingness to control our impulses to return hostility with hostility, are the basic requirements for reaching such an apparently unreachable child.

In treatment of various kinds in enlightened settings, it often requires literally total re-living in order to ready the child to establish any meaningful relationships; and then such would be earned only after almost constant testing by such a youngster.

For law enforcement officers who enter the life of such a child at the time of an offense against a third party in the community, or for court officials who perhaps have to process the case, and have no time for the establishment of real relation-

[10] Fritz Redl, and David Wineman,
Children Who Hate, The Free Press,
N.Y. (1951), pp. 206, 207.

ships, a great service can be performed by simply handling the offense in an atmosphere which says to the child that we cannot tolerate the offense he has committed, but we are not hostile toward him as a person. In so doing, we are able to begin to challenge his defense which tells him constantly that all outsiders are against him and that every contact he has continues to prove that he is hated by everyone.

If we can handle his offenses in an atmosphere that tells him that we do not hate him personally, that we are not insensitive to his problems, but that we really wish we had more time to get to know him better, a great deal can be accomplished. If nothing else, such an attitude on the part of the "official world" does not further reinforce his delinquent value system, and very possibly, it can reach him and establish a situation that will make treatment easier.

For purposes of handling such youngsters in investigation and interrogation, and for understanding the need for specialized treatment techniques in working with them, it is important to remember that many scholars and practitioners agree that "such children are not able to face up to fear, anxiety, or insecurity of any kind without breaking down into disorganized aggression. They cannot cope with guilt feelings produced by what they do without again becoming full of aggression. . . . As far as realizing that their own behavior contributes to a situation . . . in this they are notoriously deficient. Whatever momentary awareness they may have evaporates so quickly that, if one asks them fifteen minutes later what happened, it is always some other person or some certain destiny as they see it, that is to blame for their plight. And if one is nice to them, if one surrounds them with affection and toys and good food and adults who want to help them . . . they seem to feel that whatever shred of reasonableness they may have maintained can now be thrown to the four winds; now they can ask for anything and everything beyond what any reasonable adult can or should ever grant. If the adult does not come through . . . the inevitable explosion of hate." [11]

11 Fritz Redl, and David Wineman,
Controls from Within, The Free Press,
Glencoe, Ill., (1952), p. 17.

Keeping this observation of the dynamics of such children in mind, it is necessary to comment upon the difficulty encountered in an official offense-situation where the protection of society demands the conducting of a proper investigation and the completing of the formalities of arrest and court action, without seriously contributing to a further aggravation of the very real problems of such a totally deprived, aggressive child. This conflict can only be resolved when enforcement officers and court officials function at the highest level of professionality in which they are keenly aware of their dual responsibility to the community and to the child in their custody.

The necessary official procedures must be completed, but these must be accomplished without attitudes and actions on the part of the authority-figures which would tend to further lower the offender's self-concept or increase his hostility toward what he sees as an already hostile and threatening society.

He has learned to expect the worst from people. He has learned to play the game of "kick him while he's down." He has learned to live with a sense of failure, worthlessness and lack of interest; and his behavior and the hatred it displays are his means of showing everyone that he has learned his lessons well.

Any show of disdain, ridicule or callousness toward him and his difficulties simply reinforces his delinquent value system; and just as surely concern, fairness, professional ethics, and especially kindness in the face of his hostility, challenge his attitudes and have the chance to change his delinquent posture, even if he appears not to notice or to openly reject our efforts.

APPLICATION OF IMPORTANT POINTS EMPHASIZED FOR LAW ENFORCEMENT OFFICERS

1. The multiple-problem family is usually well known to police officers and many times is a cause of frustration and even anger because of the constant annoyances caused by the children in the neighborhood and at school. These annoyances are merely the symptoms of the many severe problems existing in the family, and the behavior will not change unless the causes are corrected.

2. Usually many social agencies and others in the community are well aware of the multiple-problem family. These families are often the

subject of much professional conversation and many agency conferences, but they seldom receive a concentrated, realistic approach to their many problems. Few areas ever focus an all-out attack, in a unified way, on the problems of health, housing, employment, nutrition, family life, education, etc. that have plagued these families for generations. Police officers usually know these families and their problems very well, and this knowledge should be constantly transmitted to responsible persons and agencies in the community until some effective effort can be made to correct these conditions.

3. Children from such families, when arrested as offenders, should be given medical attention and checked for nutritional problems so that at least some temporary relief can be given in these important areas before return to the home. It is a tragic commentary that many such children only get medical examinations or dental services or a balanced diet after arrest, and many do not receive such attention even when in official custody.

4. Degrading living circumstances and experiences of disappointment with official agencies tend to cause hostility toward official persons at all levels, and this is often very obviously shown toward police officers.

5. Suspicion and hostility have caused members of such families often to become resistant or rejecting toward offers of help. They exhibit this by refusal to keep appointments, misusing temporary financial help, dropping out of school or work programs, and not being home when interviews had been arranged. To cope with this, special understanding and skills are required, especially by police officers who are much more familiar with respect for authority and personal discipline as behavioral standards.

6. Severely emotionally deprived youngsters are not able to "reach out" to others for understanding or help in most cases. It is, therefore, necessary that the overtures of friendship or assistance come from others. The officer who understands this tries to make all his contacts with such youngsters as warm and genuine as possible, despite seeming disinterest or repugnance on the part of the youths.

7. Overtures of acceptance or friendship to such hurt youths are often rebuffed openly or evaded cleverly, or even ridiculed, by the very youngsters getting the attention. This seeming ingratitude or hostility must not be taken personally by the officer, but must be seen as part of the total defense that the child has found necessary to cope with a "tough" life situation.

8. Evaluations of any offender, or investigations of any offense, should remain professionally objective and completely independent of personal feelings as a result of not being able to reach a particular youngster on a personal basis.

9. Reaction to the hostility of a "hurt child" with hostility of our own is exactly what life has taught that child to expect; and so such conduct by officers only reinforces the delinquent attitude and encourages further hostile reactions by the child.

10. Common sense and duty to protect the community both tell us that offenses by such children should not be ignored. Permissiveness or pretended ignorance of offenses is not the answer, either for the community or the good of the child; but consistent enforcement without prejudice or personal hostility, carried out professionally, and transmitting a feeling of sincerity and interest, even under difficult circumstances whenever possible, provide a great service to the child and to the community.

Chapter 7

AFFLUENT AND SUBURBAN DELINQUENCY

Section

§ 7.1 Rise in suburban delinquency

Although for most of previous recorded history, we have taken comfort in the fact that the great majority of serious delinquency was confined to economically deprived and crowded neighborhoods, the behavior of our children in today's society makes us aware of the fact that we can no longer be comfortable in this position. Since 1970 juvenile arrests for serious crimes of all types has been increasing faster in the suburban and rural areas than in the inner-cities (with the exception of one year, 1974-75). And more alarming than the simple increase in juvenile crime in non-urban areas is the fact that the arrest rate for juvenile violence outside of the inner-city has been increasing even more rapidly.

In 1975, for example, the arrest rate of inner-city juveniles for violent crime remained almost twice as high as that of non-urban juveniles, but the rate of increase of the non-urban juvenile arrests for violence was more than doubled. (19.2% v. 7.6%).

Community leaders throughout the country have expressed great concern about the numerous indications of increasing violence and behavior patterns which lead to violence throughout the suburban and rural youth community. The open use of obscenities in the school and in community gathering places, the dependence upon alcohol and other "mind blowing substances," the venereal disease rate, episodes of horribly disruptive behavior within the schools, and especially the ever present and escalating problem of vandalism throughout affluent America, all give vivid indications that the "safety of the suburbs" is no longer nearly as certain or complete as was long taken for granted.

While the thrill seekers, the hedonists, the ordinary pranksters, the politically motivated, and the vicious delinquents who were discussed thoroughly in the first edition of this text still remain, and much of their dynamics still remain of fundamental importance to understanding delinquency in the affluent sections of our society, the evidence of today and the prior five or six years, requires us to add to that listing the notable numbers of the very seriously depressed, the completely "turned off," the nihilistic, and perhaps a more noticeable group of the anarchistic.

With the easy availability of weapons, and the violent mood swings of adolescence, offenses from homicide to suicide are very readily possible.

While assaults and robberies gained most of the national attention for the 40% increase in arrests of persons under eighteen between 1970 and 1975 (with the most rapid rate of increase being shown in non-urban areas), the rate of suicide among children and adolescents continued its dramatic increase with a notable decrease in the age-level providing perhaps one of its most shocking features. (The rate of suicides of youngsters aged 5 to 14 doubled during the ten-year period 1964-1974).

Officials in Montgomery County, Maryland, an affluent suburb of Washington, D.C., reported in a nationally publicized statement that weapons offenses among juveniles within their jurisdiction had risen 380% since 1972. And, within the same report, one of the officials commented on the case of a suburban 13-year old boy who purchased a sawed off shotgun and others spoke of the possession of "magnum force pistols and high powered rifles."[1]

This phenomenon has been reported universally throughout the country, and skilled observers of juvenile behavior have been noting it for some time. In 1967, one fine scholar noted

---

1 "America's Youth—Angry, Bored, or Just Confused?" U.S. News and World Report, July 18, 1977, p. 19.

that "recent studies have proved enlightening. The notion that delinquency is rooted somehow in the lower socioeconomic groups is much less tenable today than was the case previously. Rural and small town data (not all reported here) gathered from high school students fail to demonstrate significant differences in delinquency participation among social classes. There is good reason to believe that all children, rich or poor, engage differentially in varying kinds of delinquency, and that official statistics reveal only a fraction of the delinquency committed in any community."[2]

In the New York area alone it was recently reported that "during a three months period in the New York suburbs there were at least six similar outbreaks. Youngsters attacked a new $3,900,000 high school at West Islip, Long Island, smashing furniture, windows, throwing typewriters and tape recorders into the swimming pool, breaking up the principal's office and stealing the school station wagon. Another gang set four fires in the Uniondale, Long Island, high school, apparently in an effort to destroy truancy and grade records. A gang of seventeen youngsters attacked cars parked in the Valleystream, Long Island, high school lot. They smashed windshields, slashed tires and tops. Two police cars parked on the lot were vandalized among the rest. A gang broke into the Memorial Library at Bellmore, Long Island, and set it afire, causing $65,000 damage. A gang broke into the new $3,500,000 high school in Passaic, New Jersey, spilling acid over the science laboratories, smashing bird specimens, breaking fish tanks, ripping down shelves and hurling India ink over walls and books."

"Schools were not the only target of adolescent gang attacks. Teenagers hurled smoke grenades into the swank Parkway Casino on the Bronx River Parkway while a high school dance was in progress. Fortunately, no one was injured. Another gang near Merrick, Long Island, killed a group of swans in a reservoir by hurling lighted sticks at them. Several youngsters from good families at Greenpoint, Long Island, took a car and spent the whole evening shooting out street lights and smashing school windows with air guns. A gang of ten youngsters broke

2 Edmund W. Vaz, *Middle Class Juvenile Delinquency*, Harper & Row Publishers, Incorporated, New York, New York, (1967), p. 2.

into a beer warehouse at Sayville, Long Island, and set fire to it to 'conceal their fingerprints' after making off with several cases of beer."[3]

In other areas of the country, widely separated, a police official in the Deerfield police department, a suburb of Chicago, commented that of all of the complaints he officially sees, most of them are juvenile offenses. He comments further that there is a "lot of narcotics, even in the junior high school."[4]

The deputy chief of the police department of the town of Irvington, New Jersey, an outlying community near Newark, has noted a similar increase in juvenile offenses in his suburb.[5] Statistical reports and individual commentaries by law enforcement officials throughout the United States paint the same general picture of a tremendous increase in juvenile misbehavior throughout this nation.

While the invasion of hard drugs into the suburban area which was seen only a few short years ago no longer continues at the rapidly accelerating pace which was so horrifying to observers at that time, much of drug use has become "institutionalized" within the suburban youth culture. Marijuana, some use of hashish, and much "garden variety pill taking," especially the mixing of pills and alcohol, are still behaviors of "high fashion" in much of the teen-culture in suburban areas. And while heroin and certainly LSD have been banned altogether, or at least no longer enjoy their former popularity in many quarters, the use of cocaine and "sopors" has risen very rapidly and now enjoys a wide area of acceptance and a high degree of popularity among the affluent youth groups. (More explicit discussion of the changing narcotic pattern can be found in Chapter 10: The Drug Scene.)

While offenses by economically deprived juveniles, (those coming primarily from the inner-city portion of the urban areas), continue to dominate the headlines in most instances, middle class delinquency not only continues to account for the bulk of certain types of offenses, it also now shows some con-

[3] Id., pp. 196, 197.
[4] "Suburbia Getting a Taste of the Urban Areas' Woes," *Louisville Cour-*
ier Journal, July 19, 1970.
[5] *Ibid.*

siderable increase in many offense-types which previously had been considered "typically lower class offenses."

For example, while the deprived delinquents still tend to account for the majority of the violent robberies, grand larcenies, and severe gang assaults, a more frequent presence of these kinds of offenses in suburban areas is noted in the past several years, as the general level of violence connected with "affluent delinquency" continues to rise rapidly. Also, the delinquency patterns of the suburban group continues to reflect the hedonistic, thrill seeking, personal pleasure-oriented type of offenses, which always tended to predominate in the suburban areas, including such offenses as liquor violations, certain types of drug abuse, traffic offenses, car theft for joy-riding purposes, and so-called "senseless" offenses of vandalism and malicious destruction of property.

§ 7.2   Unreliability of statistics on delinquency

Exact statistics as to the total amount of delinquency in suburban America, or even exact estimates of the involvement of affluent adolescents in particular offense types, are indeed very difficult to obtain. This is true for a number of reasons:

First, the lack of uniform reporting which has plagued the field of juvenile offense reporting throughout the entire country, is much more aggravated in the reporting of suburban delinquency because of the varying practices of small suburban and rural police departments. This discrepancy in reporting techniques makes many of the existing statistics quite unreliable.

Secondly, it is much easier for the child from a more affluent background to have the detection of his delinquency protected. The offenses which he commits tend to be more personal and covert, and thus more easily covered; and often he receives adult help in concealing his delinquency because of family loyalties and a desire to keep any possible disgrace from becoming known to the community at large.

A third factor is seen in situations where a delinquent offense has been detected and the middle class child has an opportunity to have it "handled at the police level." This practice is widespread because of several reasons, including the ability of parents to pay for damages and thus pacify complainants, and because there is often an opportunity for the suburban police department to be personally known by families and individuals in their jurisdiction and thus cooperation in "working out" a particular problem is much more prevalent than in poorer areas.

A fourth reason is similar to the previous one, but it involves offenses serious enough to be reported to the juvenile court by the police. In these situations the same kind of disposition can often be arranged at the juvenile court on behalf of the affluent child.

A fifth factor is seen in the dual correction system that exists in our society. This system provides an opportunity for those who have sufficient funds to have even serious juvenile offenders handled through private treatment resources including out-patient psychiatric care or residential treatment centers available on a private basis. Family and friends can be mobilized in order to make private placements, and work therapy and job placement opportunities available through business and professional friends and relatives. These private treatment resources are not available to the child without funds who necessarily goes into the official public correctional apparatus.

A sixth reason involves the active or passive condoning of certain types of offenses by parents, other adults and the peer group in suburban society. Such thrill seeking episodes as "drag racing" or the "playing of chicken" with automobiles, over-indulgence in alcoholic beverages at group parties, some sexual acting out and other kinds of offenses are seen as part of the growing up process or as something which "everybody does" and therefore is not censured or reported such as would be readily done in the case of a more violent type of offense.

Finally the vast cultural difference between urban and suburban America leads many scholars to believe that the law itself and certainly the devices used to measure criminal activity are reflections of cultural taste. It was stated recently in one excellent article that "Crime is culturally defined rather than culturally determined and that it is not the fact of criminality but the form of it which varies with socioeconomic level. Thus, we have burglars and embezzlers, hold-up men and black marketeers, prostitutes and fashionable mistresses. The anti-social conduct of the 'lower classes' affronts the middle class legal norms and so leads to prison terms and criminal records. The antisocial deeds of 'respectable' folk are likely to draw much milder treatment. All this casts doubt on many research data by implying that we have not been measuring the extent of crime or of delinquency but only of the varieties we do not like. By such reasoning, no theory of delinquency or criminality can be adequate unless it explains the 'white collar' offenses as well as the more obvious forms of theft and violence. It is assumed that, if this were done, the present emphasis on the relationship of socioeconomic variables to crime might have to be discarded.

"For the field of juvenile delinquency, the existence of 'white collar' offenses is difficult to establish. We have fairly good figures on assaults, burglary, truancy and similar offenses. However, the early manifestations of patterns which could develop into bribery, bucket-shop operations, and price control evasions are not likely to draw police attention."[6]

In commenting upon the same discrepancy, another observer said, "Law in America is very likely to be middle class law, and is apt to treat middle class deviants with greater leniency than deviants within the working class. Whereas working class culture tends to emphasize verbal and behavioral spontaneity, and place nominal restraint in daily social interaction, middle class culture stresses the importance of rationality, subtlety, and control in social behavior. Therefore, middle class behavior is apt to be less violent or aggressive, and unlikely to attract the attention of law enforcement officers. By contrast, working class behavior is more likely to be noticed, disapproved, and officially recorded."[7] It is apparent from these remarks that an accurate picture of the total number of offenses committed by middle class and subur-

[6] Wattenderg & Valistrieri, "Automobile Theft: A Favored Group Delinquency," *Middle Class Juvenile Delinquency*, edited by Edmund W. Vaz, p. 149.

[7] Nancy Barton Wise, "Juvenile Delinquency Among Middle Class Girls," *Middle Class Juvenile Delinquency*, edited by Edmund W. Vaz, p. 180.

ban youngsters, or even the offenses of any one individual from that group, is not obtainable.

Many years ago, the great statesman Disraeli, told us emphatically that "there are liars, damn liars, and statistics"; and this observation was probably never more true in its application than in an analysis of the statistics available on suburban juvenile delinquency. For this reason, most of our discussion must be based upon evidence which is impressionistic, but in our opinion very reliable because of the great number of observers reporting the same impressions as to the increase and type of delinquency being observed in suburbia.

§ 7.3   Characteristics and rationale of suburban delinquency

The results of one recent study perhaps best express an overview of the entire condition. After a thorough study of suburban delinquency in one community, Tobias concluded: "(1) a noticeable breakdown in suburban middle and upper middle class adolescents' social behavior exists, (2) the situation involves a considerable number of suburban youth, (3) the condition is of serious concern to many segments of the community."[8] The same study further divides the most frequent offenses in the affluent section of the community into three categories: (1) malicious destruction of property (in which twenty-one different separate kinds of offenses are grouped), (2) larceny (in which eleven separate kinds of offenses are included in the group), (3) disorderly conduct (in which ten separate types of offenses are included in the group). Of particular significance to the reader might well be the fact that Tobias very properly points out that among the suburban affluent male delinquent there has grown up a particular type of slang terminology descriptive of some of the most popular antisocial acts. He lists a brief glossary of slang terminology which we have reprinted in the Appendix.[9]

It is quite obvious from the above listing that the thrill seeking, hedonistic, senseless (when viewed from traditional

[8] Jerry J. Tobias, "The Affluent Suburban Male Delinquent," *Crime and Delinquency*, Vol. 16, #3, (July 1970).

[9] See page 396 of the Appendix.

adult viewpoint) kinds of offenses are the most prevalent among the affluent teenagers. The seeking of the thrill of the moment is quite obvious even in particular acts which share a popularity among working class groups. For example, one might find a street gang in a socioeconomically deprived area stripping a car or a motorcycle; however, when this is done in suburbia it is usually done for totally different motives, with a heavy emphasis on the excitement or the thrill of the dangerous act. Gitchoff speaks eloquently to this point when he says:

"The speed and skill of these youths in dismantling or 'stripping' a car or motorcycle was phenomenal. Virtually no car owner was immune, regardless of his social status or political power. It appeared that the greatest challenges were those that presented the greatest difficulty, i.e., removing the transmission from a city councilman's car during his lunch hour at home; stealing hub caps from a police car and other 'senseless' property offenses. Offenses against persons were fewer, but those which took place were categorically referred to as 'senseless'."[10]

The same comment concerning the thrill seeking motive can be made about other offense types within the affluent teen group. Auto larceny, serious traffic offenses, drinking patterns, and certainly sex play and drug abuse lend themself to at least partial analysis from this standpoint, and seem to fit quite readily into the hedonistic pattern.

This obviously different and disruptive type of behavior coming in great numbers and with increasing intensity from the youth of a section of the culture known traditionally for its stability and at least verbal commitment to the Judaeo-Christian ethic, demands that we look very carefully at the immediate subcultural group in which the teenager spends his time and to the standards to which he so readily gives his allegiance. The teen culture today is indeed a group unto itself as it has never been before in history. Perhaps this is due to the affluence which has made this group an important area of the market; perhaps

[10] Dr. G. Thomas Gitchoff, *Kids, Cops, and Kilos*, p. 35.

it is due to the mass media which has permitted each member to identify himself so carefully as part of the group and which has promulgated effectively the expectations and standards of the group; perhaps because of the education and sophistication which the members have obtained they find the need for a closely knit group of their peers as they never have before in history; perhaps they simply have been provided with the leisure today in order to devote themselves to causes which they have never enjoyed in the past because of the need to work in order to survive. Perhaps it is for any or all of these and an infinite number of other reasons, but the fact is that the teen culture does exist as a large, affluent, leisure oriented, self-aware, highly sophisticated group which seemingly, in greater numbers each day, is unwilling to follow blindly the social and behavioral dictates of the total culture.

The parents and earlier ancestors of the affluent teenagers have struggled long and hard to amass a wealth and establish a standard of living in comparison with which all of the fabled civilizations of history pale into insignificance. Rapid transportation, interior and exterior comfort, easy access to education and recreation, unparalleled advances in health care and nutrition, and many other material benefits have been literally laid at the feet of the affluent teenager; however, it took a totally different type of life style or set of values and standards to carve out this wealth than it now takes the younger generation to enjoy it. As a result, we are seeing today the largest number of leisure class teenagers that society has ever known.

This group is then quite free to make choices about the use of their time, energy and resources that were totally unavailable to previous generations whose choice was made for them by economic necessity and the constant need to strive to "get ahead." Having been born into a condition of already "being ahead," and knowing that probably their very best efforts will take them no further on the economic scale than that at which they have already arrived, the affluent teenager has the several options of simply diverting all of his drives toward "having fun or kicks," of identifying with causes that before held no interest for him, or simply becoming bored with the ownership and use of his possessions and possibly choosing to reject the very system which has made them available.

A quick illustration of the above can be seen in the fact that any survey of the use of teenagers' time shows that a large part of it self-admittedly is spent "hanging around," "messing around," or "killing time." This is in shocking contrast to the previously accepted middle class values of "don't waste your time," "idleness is the devil's workshop," and "time is money." Further insight into the revolutionary change reflected in this use of time can be seen from a reminder of the fact that in times past we had always been accustomed to having street corner gangs and problems of loitering and idleness in the poorer strata of society, but today it seems that we have developed the very same phenomenon to a high degree among our affluent teenagers.

As to the use of money, a quick look at the teenage market immediately reveals that more phonograph records are purchased by this particular group than by all others combined, that an ever growing part of the deodorant, cosmetics and costume jewelry market is being taken over by adolescents each year, and that more automobiles and gasoline to operate them for nonworking purposes are purchased by youngsters than any other single group. These and countless other examples too numerous to mention bear eloquent witness to the affluence and leisure orientation of the teen culture.

Of course, this large group with vast spending power at its disposal has caused a reversal in the position of the teenager in relation to adult society. Jessie Bernard said it so accurately recently, when he commented:

"The existence of this great leisure class with so much buying power at its disposal has had profound repercussions on the relationships between teenagers and the adult world. They have had to be catered to. The values of teenage culture become a matter of concern to the advertising industry. What teenagers like and want, what they think is important. As contrasted with the traditional agencies charged with socializing youngsters, the advertisers and the mass media flatter and cajole. They seek to create desires in order to satisfy, rather than, as the parent, teacher, or minister must often do, to discipline, restrict, or deny them. The advertiser is, thus, on the side of the teenager. 'The things bought are determined by what the child wants rather than by what the parents want for him.' . . . They have the money to call the tune; they are 'patrons' of the arts and must, therefore, be catered to."[11] Thus we see very directly established the vicious circle in which literally millions spend billions each year buying "what they want and not what they need" while the mass media, the advertisers and the manufacturers constantly contribute to, reinforce and promote their "wants."

Contributing even further to this problem is the concurrent fact that within much of the adult society, actual support for this kind of "economic hedonism" is readily provided by our sensate society. As the teenagers look around them they see more and more that adults, despite some verbal protestation to the contrary, constantly teach them by example that if something does not make you feel good or if it doesn't please the senses, if it is not good to eat, smell, hear, see or feel regardless of its long term effects, it is not worth having; and conversely if it does give immediate gratification to the senses then it is legitimate to seek it, purchase it and use it immediately despite moral and intellectual inhibitions in regard to the rightness or wrongness of obtaining it. Having the economic means and the leisure and the support of widespread example within the sensate society ascribed to by numerous members of the adult community, it is little wonder that the teen culture embraces a pleasure-oriented, thrill-seeking drive toward instant gratification. This is promoted even more by the fact that traditionally the adolescent in our society has had a "role conflict" or is expected to function in a vacuum of concrete behavioral expectancy. Little responsibility has been given to him to counterbalance the many privileges which he has received. For example, he is not permitted to marry until an adult, he has no right to vote until he reaches maturity, he oftentimes is expected to buy only incidentals with his money and in countless other ways he is shown that we still permit him

11 "Teenage Culture: An Overview,"
Middle Class Juvenile Delinquency,
edited by Edmund W. Vaz, p. 27.

to be a child even though he has the physical maturity, the intellectual capacity and the earning power to function with adult responsibility. These contradictions heighten the problem even further.

In times past, this conflict situation was ameliorated because of effective controls operating through the family, the neighborhood and strong religious and ethical standards and beliefs. We have discussed the breakdown in the behavioral controls exercised by families, close relatives and neighborhood groups. At this point, we wish to emphasize that this phenomenon has resulted in less opportunity for youth to receive the traditional values and beliefs from those important sources; at the same time, due to the continuing secularization of education at all levels, we have succeeded in "debunking" most of the major religious and philosophical positions on which American society has been built. This debunking has certainly not disproved all of these beliefs, because it can be readily seen that many of them withstand our best efforts to scientifically discredit them, but it has merely undermined their usefulness as cornerstones or anchors for the development of youthful value systems. The resulting skepticism prevents religion and traditional ethics from influencing behavior during the day to day business of living. Many youths, reacting to this moral vacuum, very logically postulate that "if there is no real reason for choosing good over evil, then I might as well choose the thing which pleases me the most since nothing else really matters."

This practical hedonism is further aided and abetted by our constant preoccupation with the teaching of "how to do things" rather than "why they should or should not be done." It is quite a simple matter for youngsters in our highly sophisticated suburban settings to say "if I know how to do something and have the wherewithal financially to do it, then I can do this thing. And if I can do it I think that I shall do it." These are very easy progressions for the youthful mind to take in considering whether or not to commit any act, and if there is a high degree of promised pleasure connected with the performance of the act, it is quite difficult for the moral issue of whether he should or should not perform the act to enter into the decision-making process.

While these difficulties exist philosophically, the control of behavior that could exist through the good example of hero models has also been weakened and in some case destroyed by the "debunking process."

The mass media each day effectively pound home to youngsters a very vivid and accurate report of the obvious "clay feet" of the traditional hero models. The transgressions of high government officials, sports stars, giants of the intellectual and professional world, and of the clergy on a grand scale are constantly blared to the sensitive eyes and ears of watching youth, who have already been to a great degree removed from the control of family and neighborhood, and who have less access to their own fathers for identification purposes than ever before in history.

In our culture which has held up the accumulation of material things as "the promised land," and has established "success" as the key or map that opens up or leads to this promised land, success is readily seen, especially by the young, as the thing to seek, and those who have achieved "success" are equally viewed as those persons worthy of emulation. The success itself becomes the focal concern and the goal, and the successful person becomes the hero model without regard to how he became successful, and with equal unconcern about his own moral values and the rightness or wrongness of his personal life.

A typical illustration of exactly this kind of "antihero" was reported recently very vividly in the writing of a New York columnist concerning a very popular contemporary sports figure. James Reston reported that ". . . he is a significant symbol because he is following the contemporary notion that anything that succeeds is right. It is easy to understand why he does so. Sport is no longer sport but big business . . . to the kids, he is still a hero. He defied all the old fashioned rules. He didn't work with the 'team'." He reported late for practice. He was not like the old moral sports heroes—the Reverend Bob Richards arguing on television that sports, religion and the breakfast food for champions were all the same thing. He was not even like Babe Ruth or Walter Hagen, who tried to conceal their alcoholic adventures. He ran his bars and his football on the same track and at the same time, defying all the old assumptions and moralities, and now all he has to prove is that it will work.[12]

Whether it be identification with the antihero type which is constantly promoted by big business, advertising and mass media, or whether it is due to the ever increasing awareness of politicians who misuse funds, judges who are swayed from justice, businessmen who defraud consumers, the clergy who violate their vows and commitments or the parents who do not practice what they preach, the "debunking process" continues to go on wreaking havoc with the value systems and behavioral standards of impressionable youth.

The chasm which has developed between many youngsters and the traditional adult world has been largely characterized by the recurring use of the word "hypocrisy" by countless youngsters in their attempt to explain the value or communication gap. This problem was very directly stated by a Harvard student when he commented:

"The revolt is now taking a particular form—skepticism. When youth get skeptical, I submit, it does not indicate that anything is wrong with youth, but rather that something is wrong with adults.

". . . that 'something' is the way you usually look at and react to what is going on in the world. 'Hypocrisy' is a big word with us, and it is a mortal sin in our moral code, dooming the sinner to our version of hell—permanent eclipse of any moral influence he might have on us."[13]

This leadership vacuum and value gap created by youths' rejection of much of the traditional adult world seems to have been entered swiftly and emphatically by popular entertainers, disc jockeys and the promoters of the new teen magazines. The rock and roll groups, TV personalities and various singers have shown a fantastic ability to "turn on" this alienated group. The ability to attract vast audiences, to motivate the purchases of countless recordings, and the inciting of near riots just by

[12] James Reston, *New York Times* service by-line appearing in the *Cincinnati Enquirer*, Sunday, August 23, 1970.

[13] Steven Kelman, "You Force Kids to Rebel," *Saturday Evening Post* (1966), reproduced in *Adolescents for Adults*, Blue Cross Association, Chicago, Illinois, (1969).

their personal presence are the early signs of the leadership role occupied by these entertainers; and it is much more forcefully displayed by their continuing ability to set the styles in clothing, costume jewelry, haircuts and even language. The disc jockey, probably because of his close association with these entertainers and the reflected glory of show business has exhibited power to "stimulate teenage interest in charity drives, contests, and the like,"[14] as well as stimulate sales of recordings and countless personal items.

The teen magazines, with their emphasis upon the exclusive domain of the teen culture, exert considerable influence on adolescent taste in clothing, music, cars, personal grooming and entertainment. However, their influence, just like that of the entertainers and disc jockeys, goes far beyond these matters and seems to embrace the entire spectrum of manners, morals and behavior. One of the finest commentaries on the influence of the teen magazines was made by Ralph W. England, Jr. when he wrote:

"Young people's magazines have been published for many decades in the United States. With few exceptions, their common stamp was one of staid, moralistic conservatism which viewed adolescence as a period of preparation for an adulthood of similar qualities. Since 1944, however, when *Seventeen* began publication, a number of magazines have appeared whose kinship to the older *Youth's Companion* and *American Boy* is only faintly discernible. At least eleven of these are currently in the market, lead by *Seventeen*, whose monthly circulation is slightly over one million copies. *Co-ed, Teen, Cool, Hep Cats, Modern Teen, Ingenue* and *Dig* have combined circulations of about 1,500,000. These publications are similar in format to movie and TV magazines read by many adults, but their picture stories emphasize younger personnel from the entertainment industry, and they contain a thin scattering of teenage love stories, youth forums, puzzles and articles on automobiles and high school sports. In sharp contrast with the moralistic flavor of earlier youth magazines, the post-war group is distinguished

14 Ralph W. England, Jr., "A Theory of Middle Class Juvenile Delinquency," *Middle Class Juvenile Delinquency*, edited by Edmund W. Vaz, p. 246.

by its portrayal of hedonistic values within an essentially amoral setting: the teen years are not ones of preparation for responsible adulthood, but of play and diversion."[15]

The same author comments further that the prominence of the disc jockey, the programming of TV teen dance shows, the young people's magazines, the exploitation of the enlarged teenage market and the increased public attention directed on the youth group because of the apparent increase in juvenile problems are the five principal factors which "have speeded the development of long-nascent tendencies arising from the ambiguous status of our teenage population," and "provided means for teenagers to enter into at least secondary contact far beyond the pre-war confines of their respective communities."[16] The contacts with each other within the group, the rejection of adults and others outside of the group, the acceptance of established leadership roles, coupled with the sense of their own emergence as a power wielding group; all of these factors have made teenagers aware of themselves as a group and thus established a teenage culture with an effectiveness which probably never before in history would have been possible.

So, within the teenage culture, the youngsters recognize themselves as a power because of their affluence and the fact that they are catered to by those who wish to utilize them as a market for merchandise; they have their own leadership as mentioned above; they communicate rapidly and effectively with each other within their group by various very effective means; they are unidentified with the traditional values and standards of the adult society; and consequently they become more and more "closed," tending to keep outsiders out, and looking for the fulfillment of most of their needs for status and fulfillment within a small society strictly limited to the members of their own age group.

§ 7.4   Value system change as motivation of behavior

One of the most striking recent developments within the teen culture is the increasing influence of so-called "lower

15 Id., pp. 246, 247.
16 Id., p. 245.

class" values upon the affluent teenager. The traditional middle class values of respect for education, thrift, constant self-discipline, and especially the ability to postpone immediate gratification in order to obtain more meaningful later rewards, are rapidly being replaced by the lower class values of immediate pleasure gratification, excitement for its own sake, toughness and impulsive buying.

This phenomenon of value replacement or "value transplant," as it has been called, is one of the features of the changing adolescent picture which is perhaps more frightening to adults than any other. It also helps to explain much of the impulsivity and pure hedonism that is observed in much of current adolescent behavior.

Because of these two reasons indicating the importance of this change in the value picture in relation to adolescents in affluent society, we will explore the reasons behind this important phenomenon.

Why has our society seen the situation change so suddenly and dramatically from the traditional scene where middle class youth quite naturally embraced their responsibilities to maintain and advance the family, and to accumulate more material goods by becoming "educated and successful" to where, in such large numbers, they seem to have defected to intense pursuit of speed, unusual clothes, and instant pleasures? In our opinion, there are numerous factors involved in this change, and not the least of them is the simple fact that in our democratic society youngsters are simply less class conscious and have had far greater opportunities to mingle with members of other strata in a variety of meaningful experiences than at any other period in history and perhaps in any other place. This exposure to members of other groups has been both extensive and intensive for large numbers of suburban youth and has provided an opportunity for the cross-fertilization of ideas and standards between the two groups.

Secondly, there are factors ingrained in the lower class pattern of life itself which contribute greatly to this phenomenon, and which were stated so well in the Doyle, Dane, Bernbach, Incorporated, report, *A Study of Young People*, when they said:

"The lower class makes the best images because they have less to lose. They are the great experimenters. They invent new pictures, sounds, words, ways of dressing, dances and songs.

"Lower class life is largely a teen centered life. No behavior can be successfully prohibited the lower class teenagers. From the age of fourteen on, they are not under the control of adults. Furthermore, adulthood in the lower class is a pretty drab affair. Among the lower classes there is an identification with youth as the best time of life. Generally there is an attitude of 'let the young have fun while they can.' The excessive freedom, comparatively speaking, of the lower class teenager makes him more creative and more often the source of new styles and fads, than his middle class counterpart who has more to lose by departing from parental and class traditions. . . .

"Other factors upgrading the influence of lower class values today are: (1) The accessibility of lower class values through advances in communication. (2) The general rise of lower class standards of living, carrying with it an increased influence. (3) The idleness of lower class youth, which provides time for experimenting in new fads of dress, attitude, et cetera. (4) The vastness of numbers, which makes possible a larger incidence of social experimentation."[17]

Of course, it is of fundamental importance to add to this impressive list the fact that those who cater to the buying habits of the American public and those who advertise the wares, have long recognized the impulsivity of the lower class buying patterns and the ready willingness to spend when goods are made attractive. In our recent prosperity, even the lower class has had more money at its disposal, and this, combined with the above mentioned willingness to buy spontaneously, has caused great pressures to be exerted through advertising and the other promotion devices, which have been directed immediately and intensely at the lower class tastes. This in turn has produced a situation in which the young people who so consistently watch television, patronize the movies, and keep in tune with "what's going on" are constantly bombarded with appeals and seductions which are primarily geared at the lower

[17] "A Study of Young People," Doyle, Dane, Bernbach, Inc., (1966).

class level. Consequently a tremendous amount of lower class needs and desires have been effectively developed in the more affluent quarters of society.

William Kvaraceus and Walter B. Miller comment on this when they state that:

"As this upward-diffusion trend occurs, one can hear adult demands and pleas that the line be held on hair styles, dungarees, tight fitting sweaters and skirts, and language. Many middle class adolescents appear to have oriented to values centering around toughness, hardness, excitement, present pleasure—all reflecting the focal concerns of lower class culture. Many of these values are also strongly reinforced by the steady fare offered on the wide movie screen, on TV, and in contemporary literature. . . .[18]

"There is much selling and buying of lower class concerns and values to middle class consumers. All mass media today dig deeply into lower class culture, wrapping their plots and characters around force, trouble, excitement, chance or fate, autonomy, and present pleasure. . . ."[19]

§ 7.5   Contemporary music and the "hang loose ethic"

This phenomenon can be seen operating probably at its most effective level in the field of teenage music. And with the arrival of so-called "punk rock," which at least remained underground through 1976, but which has now begun to emerge "above ground" and become available to a greater number of teenagers, we see the dregs of despair, the promotion of anarchy, the negation of all that has previously been seen as wholesome or good, and perhaps some very definite influences of "satanism" embodied in the lyrics, the dress, and behavior of the performing groups. For example, one recent composition, "Rondi Rush," seems to be about a sado-masochist, and another called "Bad Ass Bruce" deals directly with focal concerns which certainly have not traditionally been part of the mainstream of this society's cultural values.

---

[18] William Kvaraceus and Walter B. Miller, "Norm Violating Behavior in Middle Class Culture," quoted in *Middle Class Juvenile Delinquency,* edited by Edmund W. Vaz.
[19] Ibid.

One group called, significantly, The Runaways is described in a national newspaper as a "trash talking quintet of girls who have been described as punk teenage dogmeat."[20]

Other groups named The Dead Boys, Hot Knives, Werewolves, Bitch, Crime, and The Vilestones sing such tunes as "The Auschwitz Jerk," "You're So Repulsive," and "Hit Her Wid de Axe."

As to the behavior of such groups, The Damned has at least one member who seems to frequently spit at audiences; The Sex Pistols, led by Johnny Rotten, is reported to have been dropped by a succession of "straight" record companies because of such incidences as vomiting on unsuspecting persons in an air terminal, and others have been known for alternately wearing raw meat on the outside of their clothing, uniforming themselves in Nazi symbols or items much more frequently associated with graveyards, engaging in rather overt acts of sexual symbolism if not direct sexual activity on the stage, and in short, doing just about everything which in the traditional sense had caused entertainers to lose the interest of their audiences in the past, but which, in this current frame of reference, seems to gain the appreciation of the young audiences and even to work them up into a frenzy.

A national newspaper said recently: "They sing songs about anarchy, alienation, violence, drugs, sex, teenage rebellion—in short, any and every lesion on the dark ripe underbelly of American life." And in the same article one Boston punk rocker is quoted as saying "We're not into pretty or smooth, man. We're into life. Life is ugly. Life is mean. . . ."[21]

While "punk rock" still has not become a totally accepted part of the general teen culture, it is receiving a sufficient amount of acceptance to cause grave concern among observers of the youth culture; and more importantly, ingredients from this totally counter-cultural medium are filtering into and causing negative influence upon other elements of the teen culture.

[20] *The National Observer*, June 27, 1977.

[21] Another commentator summarized recently: "Punk rock is a primal scream . . . nihilism and brute force have inspired the movement," *Time*, July 11, 1977.

And even without the influence of "punk rock," the more acceptable forms of "hard rock," "acid rock," and others contain much that tends to represent a standard of behavior for young people far short of that which can be considered ideal; and in its most extreme form, can be very seductive to sexual misbehavior, narcotics abuse and the general adaptation to a lifestyle which can be directly contributory to juvenile delinquency.

§ 7.6 Analysis of causes of change in ethics of suburban youth

With the lower class values totally permeating the teen culture, the affluence and the leisure time opportunities that had not been available to previous generations, the hedonistic philosophy and rejection of traditional goals and their own leadership and awareness of their identity as a group alienated from much of the traditional thinking of the larger society, it is easy to see how that body of values, standards and behavior which has come to be called the "hang-loose ethic" has developed both extensively and intensively within today's teen culture.

This notion of "hanging loose" instead of adhering to a program of self-discipline has provided the philosophical backdrop against which we have seen within approximately three years time the development of extensive suburban youthful drug abuse, considerable alteration in the traditional and formal patterns of dating and social events into mixed "hanging around," random selection of sexual partners and very informal "happenings," the widespread adoption of the "hip" type dress including beads and sandals, and above all the involvement in demonstrations and a new interest in politics and the causes. It is most significant to note that in this new "hang-loose scene" it seems that the alienation from traditional values and behavioral standards is so complete that the former rebellion against parental and community standards has been replaced by a feeling of "irrelevance"—a condition in which "we are doing our thing" and it does not particularly matter how that "thing" is looked upon by the larger society. This condition can probably be compared to a mythical situation in which someone might open a shop designed for the repairing of horses and buggies in the middle of a modern commercial area. It is quite doubtful that anyone would rebel against the opening of such an archaic enterprise, but it would be seen as so irrelevant to the passersby that they simply would go on about the business of satisfying their own needs and wants, and leave the anachronistic blacksmith's shop to simply "die of irrelevance." Much the same kind of thinking can be seen in the attitude of many members of the teen culture toward the traditional morals and standards.

The sociologist Lewis Yablonsky commented recently that:

"A dominant theme of the hippie scene is that its participants violate the law each day in the normal course of their behavior. For example, many are runaways, and almost all of the young people in the new community use illegal drugs.

"Despite these marked illegal behavior patterns they almost uniformly have a self-righteous, holier than thou self-concept and do not consider themselves law violators. Traditionally, delinquents have generally at minimum accepted the fact that they are 'deviant' or 'delinquent.' This factor provides a minimal starting point for correcting their behavior. Young people on the new 'hip' scene do not accept any concept of delinquent status.

". . . Most participants in the psychedelic drug scene come from a predominantly affluent middle or upper middle class background. Most of these psychedelic drug users consider themselves seekers who are turning off an ahuman-plastic society in which they find affluence—but no love or compassion. . . .

"The majority of middle and upper class young people who have adopted this life style claim to be making a conscious effort to drop out or unlearn the accepted values and goals of the society primarily through the use of psychedelic drugs. The drugs are used to unlearn the 'oppressive, machinelike' world they believe the established society and their parents are foisting upon them. Through the use of psychedelic drugs and the adaptation of the new life style they hope to become freer and more humanistic."[22]

[22] Lewis Yablonsky, "The Hippie Phenomenon: Some Legal and Correctional Issues," *Federal Probation*, (December, 1969), p. 12.

This disenchantment of youth with the adult world and the resulting alienation and skepticism are constant themes running through the entire current teen culture and seem to be at the very basis of the "hang-loose ethic." As the Harvard student wrote: ". . . The revolt is now taking a particular form—skepticism. When youth gets skeptical, I submit, it does not indicate that anything is wrong with youth, but rather that something is wrong with adults."

Another observer stated: "The major transformations of the past decades also contribute to a widespread sensitivity of today's youth to the discrepancy between principle and practice, and may help explain why the charges of insincerity, manipulation, and dishonesty are today so often leveled by the young against the old. During a time when values change with each generation, the values most deeply embedded in parents and expressed in their behavior in times of crisis are often very different from the more 'modern' principles, ideals, and values that parents profess and attempt to practice in bringing up their children. Filial perception of this discrepancy between parental practice and principle may help explain the very widespread sensitivity amongst contemporary youth to the 'hyprocrisy' of the previous generation."[23]

As one youngster, the son of a wealthy midwestern merchant, told this author shortly after his arrest on a drug and disorderly charge, "If I have to be like my old man, working all the time and only concerned about making money, not giving a damn about anyone other than himself—and if they make him a big shot in the church and in the neighborhood—if that's what the straight world is, man, then I don't want any of it." This is a pretty complete and comprehensive statement of alienation, whether or not the boy's observations about his father's behavior and motives is altogether accurate.

The numbers of runaways, truants and drug abusers found daily in practically every large metropolitan area, and especially

[23] "The Burden of Violence," from *Adolescents for Adults*, ibid.

in the large cities of California and New York, who live daily outside of the law and who many times exist at degrading levels of poverty and lack of personal care, eloquently witness, simply by their existence, the rejection of home and traditional conduct by countless numbers of young people from affluent backgrounds throughout the country.

These and thousands of others at various stages of "dropping out" of the larger society because of their alienation, frustration, personal disorientation and need to escape from the demands and pressures of normal community living, caused one youth observer to say recently that: "Another thing that is now beginning to be clear—the present population of Haight-Ashbury may well be a presage of the development of 'communities of need.' As personal experience becomes more disoriented and unsatisfying, we already find some members of our society clustering into such communities where psychic support is the basis for social organization. Synanon is for the moment the most organized model of such a community of need. Beginning as a rehabilitation program for drug addicts, it has, by means of its Synanon Games program, attracted an ever increasing number of people into what becomes for many a lifetime relationship. The nationwide popularity of communal psychiatric therapy, T-Groups, sensory awareness groups is another indication that inner anguish has become too unbearable to be endured alone."[24]

For all these reasons, the alienation from a larger group and tradition seen as hypocritical, the search for identity in a mass produced civilization, the need for personal support and orientation in a seeming nonhuman "plastic" society, or simply because they have too much money, too much leisure time and have received too little training in self-discipline, the "hang-loose ethic" has definitely arrived, is with us, is deeply ingrained in the teen culture, and is a most important part of the "youth scene."

Such expressions as "don't knock it until you try it," and

[24] Leonard Wolf, "The Legacy of Haight-Ashbury," from *Adolescents for Adults*, ibid.

"it turns me on" are essential to understanding the "hang-loose ethic" because they emphasize the importance of the present experience with total disregard for the future consequences or the danger involved in the experimentation. They are also eminently significant because of the very obvious and blatant rejection of traditional morality and prudence which are so explicit in their content. In the opinion of the author, these are the three essential ingredients of the "hang-loose ethic": (1) spontaneous experience or the preoccupation with the "now" or the "happening" along with the disregard for the morality or the consequences of the act; (2) hedonism which is closely related to the first concept but differs in that it expresses a philosophy of justifying the pleasurable whether it be past, present or future pleasure that is being considered, and that is intimately linked to the notion of the importance of sensate experiences, and a de-emphasis of the intellectual or moral consideration; and (3) irreverence, especially in relation to the traditional or formal, but rapidly coming to embrace all aspects of life. This can be expressed in so-called art form in which the most sacred or noble objects are debased and ridiculed, in language in which the most shocking and vulgar words are deliberately chosen, in personal conduct, in dress and grooming or in countless other ways. Gitchoff, following Simmons, notes five basic aspects of the "hang-loose ethic": (1) irreverence, (2) humanism, (3) experience, (4) spontaneity and (5) tolerance; and he states emphatically that "Not only are the major social institutions and values violated, but their very legitimacy is challenged. . . ."[25]

This same theme of "hanging loose" is also more frequently a recurring one within the music of the teen culture, especially in the most recent past, and again in the musical setting it is intimately linked to the notion of alienation as was observed recently:

"This poignant feeling of being a stranger moving through an alien environment comes through sometimes as a bitter indictment of the Establishment which sharply focuses upon

[25] G. Thomas Gitchoff, *Kids, Cops, and Kilos,* published by Malter-West- terfield Publishing Company, San Diego, California, (1969), p. 65.

nowhere men, universal soldiers, sounds of silence or desolation rows. At other points, the tunes are about more personal distresses; a yesterday, a solitary man, the magic missing in a supposed magic town, or the larger question, 'where do you or I go?' In still other instances, the songs express an uncertain yet determined reassurance that the new world is the rightful homeland of the modern spirit, you can walk a cat named dog, have a groovy kind of love, and catch reflections in a crystal wind.

"When combined, these themes infuse a powerful sense of seduction in the happening way of life, into the spirit if not the substance of the hang-loose ethic. The music proclaims that you, sir, are not alone in your over-all disenchantment with the state of most human relationships, that you are one of the 'seekers' searching for meaningful values without an always hollering parent or dollar sign."[26]

However, one of the differences in motivation of the youngsters which can be seen since the first edition of this book, as a result of the recession from which we are still recovering, youths do seem much more "dollar conscious" and, consequently, are much more involved in job-preparedness and money earning. When this set of motivational factors overlays the "hang loose ethic" and its hedonism, we seem to arrive at the unique situation which exists in the youth culture-at-large today, where traditional morality is no longer functioning adequately, but wherein anything that jeopardizes one's occupational future is again beginning to be seen as bad. This is a real contrast with just a few years ago where the majority of youth seemed to be concerned with "roles not goals." One sociologist who carefully observed the behavior in an affluent community very recently reported that "the adolescents live in a near vacuum of morality enclosed by the perimeter of the edict to achieve. Anything that jeopardizes their occupational future is bad; anything that furthers their career is good; the rest really doesn't matter."[27]

In summary, it is quite easy to see from all of the above

[26] J. L. Simmons and Barry Winograd, "Songs of the Hang-Loose Ethic," from *Adolescents for Adults*, ibid.

[27] Quotation taken from an article adapted from an LEAA news feature release, quoted in "Community Crime Prevention Letter," edited by Lawrence Resnick, Plainfield, N.J., Volume 4, No. 6, (February, 1977).

related phenomena, that the "table is set" psychologically and sociologically for the tremendous increase in delinquency which we are now experiencing among suburban youth.

Numerous scholars have compiled longer and more eloquent lists of the factors which they believe are directly contributory to suburban and affluent delinquency. However, the author of this text would like to suggest the following five causes based on an analysis of all of the above observations as directly operating criminogenic factors in relation to middle class and suburban youth, because we feel that there is a direct relationship between them and delinquent behavior from this population group, and because we believe that all of the other causal factors mentioned so frequently are really causes of the five points now mentioned:

(1) alienation from family and traditional values,

(2) the upward movement of "lower class focal concerns" and their adoption by more affluent youth,

(3) the "hang-loose ethic,"

(4) the disintegration of family and neighborhood as controls of behavior,

(5) the "debunking" of religion, the Judaeo-Christian ethic, and many of the principles of Western civilization.

It is of the utmost importance to note that the listing of these causes is not in any way meant to fix the responsibility for all youthful misbehavior on the youth culture or individual youngsters because it is quite obvious that any analysis of these causes individually would reveal a great need to examine the role of the adult society which caters to the teen market, the adult family members who have not met the real needs of their youngsters in their homes, the adult members of established churches who in many cases have preached religion and practiced intolerance and selfishness, and many and varied others from the adult society at large who have somehow made the image of the "straight world" so unappealing to today's youngsters.

At the same time, we must also emphatically state that such a listing is not an attempt to absolve the young in general or any youngster in particular from responsibility for his acts, because we are well convinced that the mistakes of the older generation, whether real or imagined depending upon circumstances, cannot justify antisocial behavior or violations of the law at any time. Fortunately, the task of fixing responsibility for behavior is beyond the intention and scope of this volume and must be left for others in another time or place; the above discussion has been presented at this time simply to illustrate the causal picture so that each reader might evaluate it as a part of the total youth scene in America today in relation to juvenile delinquency.

APPLICATION OF IMPORTANT POINTS EMPHASIZED FOR LAW ENFORCEMENT OFFICERS

1. There is much more delinquency in suburbia than official statistics indicate, including large numbers of offenses of types formerly considered part of the behavior pattern of lower class areas.

2. Much suburban delinquency does not become officially recorded because families cooperate in resolving problems by paying for damage, arranging private psychiatric care, etc., for an offending child.

3. Many times the cooperation of suburban families at times of detection of their child's delinquency is designed to keep disgrace away from the family, or to smooth over the trouble without due consideration of what action is best for the total community or even for the long-range good of the young offender.

4. Oftentimes provision of private counseling, or other means of adjustment outside of the official system, is a real benefit to the community and to a troubled youth because of the overcrowding and inadequacies of many juvenile courts and institutions.

5. We are currently witnessing a great amount of suburban delinquency rooted in an overt rejection of established authority and traditional values. Thus the offenders in this group no longer see themselves as deviant or delinquent, but they feel that they are rightly in opposition to a system or persons in the system who are "phony" or wrong. This attitude demands that new approaches in control and treatment be developed if successful law enforcement and corrections are to be obtained.

6. The affluence and buying power of youth have caused them to be

catered to by the business and entertainment world. The awareness of this among the youngsters themselves, combined with permissive parents and schools, have created an environment in which many of the traditional means of approaching youngsters or handling their offensive behavior, need to be reviewed and revised.

7. In counseling and admonishing offending youngsters, their sophistication level should be kept very much in mind. Old clichés, appeals to traditional hero models, and even regard for family or country often have little or no impact. Each offender should be evaluated individually and techniques should be adapted to his needs and to his level of functioning.

8. One of the greatest methods of reaching contemporary, sophisticated youth, or any youngster for that matter, is to impress on him that we are willing to honestly listen to him, to hear "his side of it," whether his "hang-ups" seem to us to be real or imagined, whether we are in a position to accept what he says and act upon it or not. This sincere listening will establish rapport and reduce hostility more than any carefully contrived techniques or planned devices.

9. The affluent teen-culture is becoming permeated with lower-class values. This is reflected in music, dress, language and many other ways. As much as this value gap may annoy or even threaten those of us with more traditional standards, simple deviance in taste should not be presumed to indicate delinquent conduct. There are enough real offenders to contend with without "seeing delinquents" where there are no real law violators.

10. It is essential that an enforcement officer's personal reaction to individual delinquents or disorderly groups whose appearance or conduct may be personally distasteful or even repugnant not be permitted to break down his professional manner. The competent enforcement officer will not return hostility for hostility, but will evaluate by objective standards and react according to instruction and necessity.

Chapter 8

CAMPUS VIOLENCE AND POLITICAL ACTIVISM

Section
8.1 Description of changes in concerns of present-day students
8.2 Reasons for involvement of students in social causes

§ 8.1 Description of changes in concerns of present-day students

When suddenly a large portion of the total youth population erupted into a political force of considerable magnitude and spent a great deal of its time and energy espousing causes, ranging from opposition to the war in Vietnam through such varied topics as support of the grape-pickers in California; promotion of higher wages for the maintenance staff of a large university; and active support of national and local political candidates, when only a few years prior to that they had seemed totally pleasure-oriented and concerned only about dates and automobiles, a major change in the vital areas of concern and the philosophy of life within the teen culture had to be carefully noted. So, in the first edition of this text, we talked at great length about the factors involved in the campus violence and political activism which was so obvious at that time. Since 1971, however, the scene has again shifted dramatically in its behavioral manifestations, and so today the campuses are quiet and the violence no longer threatens the disruption of the university scene. In fact, the recent demonstration on the campus of Kent State University in Ohio by a group of students and other supporters who wished to block the building of a gymnasium on the spot where the four students died in earlier demonstrations, is such a rare kind of occurrence that the amount of national publicity it has received is far in excess of the amount of disturbance which has been caused.

The leaders of the student movements of the sixties and very early seventies are now in their thirties, and many of the most prominent of them have been absorbed into establishment positions. (Tom Hayden, one of the founders of Students for Democratic Society, has entered politics and ran in the recent California senatorial race; Rennie Davis, one of the organizers of the "Chicago Seven" program in 1968, now sells life insurance for John Hancock in Denver, Colorado; and numerous others have abandoned the radical life style and are currently giving evidence of being "quite settled down.")

Also, the disillusionment with the Watergate scandal, and the economic necessities brought on by the recent recession have also combined to scatter the energies that have previously been so focused on political change.

However, the element of danger in the current quiet is that while the organized disruptions and the group violence seem to have abated, the rampant dissatisfaction with many of the social institutions, and perhaps even with the larger culture and its total way of life, has certainly not gone away; but the dissatisfaction seems to be evidenced in much more subdued and personally damaging ways as evidenced by the suicide rate, the drug problem, and the almost hopeless kind of feeling that is seen in the attitudes and behavior of many youngsters on today's scene.

On the brighter side, part of this new quiet can undoubtedly be contributed to the recognition by many youngsters that they must indeed prepare for a vocational future that perhaps is more competitive and not nearly as "smooth and easy" as it was before the recent recession brought them back to economic reality. Coupled with this phenomenon is the reaction of large portions of the adult community, including some educators, who are currently insisting on a higher level of discipline at all levels of training and performance, and who are emphasizing a much greater degree of return to traditional values.

Nevertheless, there is much to be learned from looking at the campus violence of the late sixties and very early seventies and analysis of the events of that period has a great contribution to make to understanding contemporary youth and their behavior. Whether the turmoil of that time in those places took place because of a feeling of alienation from the larger society by the youth group, or because it was due to their intense consciousness of their identity as a group apart from the larger culture, or because their high level of sophistication had provided them with a more intense realization of life's problems beyond their own selfish needs, or whether they became so bored with the unreal and meaningless role traditionally assigned to adolescents in the American culture, or whether it was because of their very deep concern for some of the injustices which they sensed in the Vietnam war, they were certainly vitally involved with and concerned about people other than themselves and with problems and events, many of which had no direct relation to their own life role or position in society at that time.

If this intense concern had just been confined to the poor and underprivileged, it still would have been a major force for change at the time; but in the hands of a group that was affluent, possessed of large amounts of leisure time, and secure in not needing to fight the daily battles for survival needs, and the group which had a level of literacy and sophistication that had never been achieved before by such an age group, the results in terms of demands for instant social change and for the satisfaction of real or even imagined grievances were literally earth shaking to the established order and to the traditional customs of our society.

The large universities, where many adolescents are grouped together in an atmosphere of permissiveness, skepticism about traditional values and ethics, and impersonalization and loss of identity on the part of thousands who have no sense of individual identity because of the size of the student bodies, easily became arenas in which activism and confrontation turned quickly to disruption and violence.

A lawyer who had been personally involved at that time observed accurately:

"The universities should understand the measure and the depth of the problem. It isn't just intellectual give and take on Viet Nam. Students see something which they consider an injustice. Whether it is an injustice or not doesn't make any difference; they believe it to be and their blood runs hot. The policeman on the other side hears the profanity, suffers the spitting, and his blood runs hot. Shortly, what we have is a dangerous confrontation." [1]

---

[1] Richard L. Cates, Esquire, "A Trial Lawyer's View of Student Disruption," *Student Protest and the Law*, published by the Institute of Continuing Legal Education, Ann Arbor, Michigan, (1969), p. 38.

§ 8.2 Reasons for involvement of students in social causes

This confrontation, dismissed by some as simply the work of outside agitators or a Communist conspiracy, was not just the work of one group or one particular classification of character and personality-type. While the influence of agitation from provocative sources outside the campus cannot be totally eliminated, nor can the possibility of an international Communist conspiracy be totally discounted, it was unrealistic and wrong to explain all student unrest and clashes with authority in this simplistic form.

It is always dangerous to disregard the obvious fact that the motives and underlying dynamics of any mob or large group in an active setting are usually considerably mixed. Especially when there is the opportunity for anonymous venting of hatred and anger, whether generalized or particular, the unsocialized aggressive, numerous types with character and behavior disorders, many suffering various kinds of psychotic and neurotic conditions, and the easily led, inadequate personalities and intellectually retarded individuals can quite readily be found. However, impartial observation demands that we note that in the campus violence of a few years ago and other politically-oriented, disruptive confrontations of youth groups with established authority, it was not just the social and emotional misfits that have been involved. The sons and daughters of wealthy and socially prominent families, large numbers of students with no previous record of delinquent behavior, and students with outstanding academic records indeed were present in considerable numbers in an active role.

The Illinois legislative council reported at that time that:

". . . It is the consensus that the New Left groups are the more successful in persuading idealistic students and young faculty members to make common cause with them on specific campus issues. Those who join forces with the official New Left in protest demonstrations tend to be, in the opinion of some close observers of contemporary campus movements, the brightest, most imaginative students, those most full of genuine indignation at the social and political injustices that are on display at home and abroad. They have been characterized as children of permissive parents, 'The Babies Who Were Picked Up' (by David Riesman) but also as 'Our Best Kids' (by Noam Chomsky)." [2]

It has also been said by numerous observers recently that far from being the hardened criminal-type, or being anti-social in their orientation, many of the youthful political activists are sensitized by positive factors in their background, education and personality makeup, and that this sensitivity and the outraged feelings which they suffer at the perception of injustice and deprivation of others leads them into activism and confrontation with authority. This was well said recently by one scholar who stated:

"A new middle class has emerged, composed of persons who have achieved affluence and secure status in occupations oriented to intellectual and cultural work. Families in this stratum rear children with values and character structures which are at some variance with the dominant culture. Such youth are especially sensitized to social questions, are repelled by acquisitive and nationalistic values, and strive for a vocational situation which maximizes autonomy and self expression. This sector of the youth population has been the primary constituency for the American student movement of the 1960's. . . .

"Equally important, the present movement is new in the degree to which it has expressed itself through political opposition—an opposition which has become increasingly revolutionary, in the sense that it has increasingly come to reject the legitimacy of established authority and of the political system itself." [3]

One international educator spoke directly to the same point recently when he said:

"Students are, therefore, challenging the whole fabric of present day society. . . .

[2] "Unrest on Campus," report of the Illinois Legislative Council, February 18, 1969, prepared by James T. Mooney, research coordinator, quoted from *Student Protest and the Law*, p. 57.

[3] Richard Flacks, "Social and Cultural Meanings of Student Revolt: Some Informal Comparative Observations," *Social Problems*, (Winter, 1970), Vol. 17, #3.

"They share with considerable theoretical or practical variants, a number of common ideas: distaste for the cheap glitter of a commercial society, which leads to alienation in the sociological and psychiatric senses of the word, questioning of a university education which aims at turning students into the future leaders of this alienated society, desire to give free reign to their imagination and instincts in spite of all 'repressions,' refusal to separate work and leisure and rejection of consumer culture." [4]

Historically speaking, political activism by university students has many precedents, ranging from the complete takeover of the University of Paris hundreds of years ago, at which time faculty members were executed for not obeying student commands, to more recently, the revolution against the Czar of Russia approximately one hundred years ago when it was not the oppressed poor, but the well-fed youth drawing their main strength from the student population who attempted to topple the government of Russia.

There has always been agreement concerning the fact that usually a small minority of the population is involved in creating violent confrontation, that the real causes of violence lie in social and economic ills which are often removed to some extent from the cause which precipitates the immediate confrontation, that the use of violence on the part of the group seeking to demonstrate its concern tends to breed further violence in terms of reaction by authorities and the heightening of the violent response and activities of the protesting group. And unfortunately that violence often seems to obtain for a group with a grievance the attention and sometimes relief which it might have, and in some cases should have, obtained by more legitimate means.

This is particularly deplorable in American society where our democratic principles and our state of affluence should certainly have made it possible and necessary to right many wrongs before any violent confrontation was felt to be required by any

[4] Jacques Bosquet, Deputy Director, UNESCO, Division of Education, quoted by Joseph A. Califano, Jr. in *The Student Revolution: A Global Confrontation*, published by W. W. Norton & Co., Inc., (1969).

group. However, in our opinion, this cannot excuse violence, nor can we overlook the fact that in some cases the undisciplined and the anarchistic have used the cover of "causes" to satisfy their own whims or promote other less noble purposes.

Summarizing the causes of violence in America is an extremely complex task and it has been attempted by several national commissions and task forces.[5] In a recent article, Dr. W. Walter Menninger (M.D.) attempted to synthesize many of the psychiatric and sociological factors underlying this problem. He speaks of the great visibility of violence in the mass media, the deep rooted psychiatric aspects of raw emotions, the problems of urbanization and the "packing together" of great masses in small amounts of territory, the insecurity, deprivation and sense of inadequacy felt by large groups, the loss of individual identity, the deterioration of family units, the lack of community roots, the unresponsiveness of government and numerous other causal factors.[6]

Others have listed such influences as education in which groups are taught to suspect or hate other groups, scientific advances which have outstripped mental and emotional progress, intimidation and force used to repress opposition and uphold vested interests, communication and generation gaps, and numerous other factors.[7]

One observation of great significance pointed to the philosophical "undergirding" of skepticism which seems to underlie student crises:

"Beneath all the jargon, however, I sensed a profound crisis of belief on the part of the vast majority of all students— a crisis that provides the nerve for the radical students to touch. Students simply do not know what to believe. Everywhere they

[5] Some of the more notable of these have been the National Commission on the Causes and Prevention of Violence, the National Commission on Law Enforcement and Administration of Justice, and the National Advisory Commission on Civil Disorders (commonly referred to as the "Kerner Commission").

[6] W. Walter Menninger, M.D., "Violence and the Urban Crisis," *Crime and Delinquency*, National Council on Crime Delinquency, Vol. 16, (July, 1970), #3, New York, N.Y.

[7] William L. Ryan, "Modern Violence Sparks World Concern," published in the *Cincinnati Enquirer*, August 30, 1970.

look in the society around them—the church, the university, the world of business and politics—they see hypocrisy.

"The almost total skepticism of modern western universities has had a significant impact on the students. Many professors (particularly in France) told me that they were concerned about the way they had consistently poked holes in almost every political, religious, and moral theory of western civilization. They felt this was compounded by their failure to provide students with any philosophy of life or politics beyond a sort of hedonistic and materialistic liberalism, to replace the gods whose feet of clay they had smashed.

"One professor in France noted that one of the major strengths of the radical students was that they were convinced they had the only morally right theory of life and society at this time, and that they satisfied in sensitive students the kind of guiding principle." [8]

The noted philosopher and observer of the contemporary scene, Bishop Fulton J. Sheen, sees the irresponsible activism of students and others as being part of an "identity crisis" and lack of self-awareness, with a note of personal responsibility for an immature mode of expression on the part of many. He observed recently:

"Students geared solely to activism, violence and the disruption of society, forget that time, meditation and reflection are required to interpret events. The brick thrown through a plate-glass window or the bomb exploded in a college is merely an act which is never matched with reflection. Such activism has the very serious flaw of never identifying itself with those who suffer. Instead of picking up the pedestrian who is hit by an autoist, this kind of activism strews tacks along the highway to puncture every tire of every motorist. Activism that is irresponsible and non-curative both deny that self-awareness which is the mark of a human." [9]

---

[8] *The Student Revolution: A Global Confrontation,* op. cit., n. 4.

[9] Bishop Fulton J. Sheen, "Irresponsibile Activism Denies Both Identity, Self-Awareness," quoted from the *Cincinnati Enquirer,* Sunday, May 3, 1970.

APPLICATION OF PARTICULAR POINTS EMPHASIZED FOR LAW ENFORCEMENT OFFICERS

1. Since the tremendous violence on campus in the late sixties and early seventies, the pattern has changed dramatically and so today the campuses are relatively quiet and constant violence no longer threatens the disruption of the university scene.

2. The economic necessities brought to the fore by the recent recession, combined with the maturing of the leaders of the student movements and the sense of disillusionment after the Watergate scandal, have all helped to contribute to the quieting of the "political-related violence" on the campuses that was witnessed previously.

3. There are numerous indications that while the current campus scene is quiet there is an element of real danger in that the rampant dissatisfaction, with many of the social institutions and perhaps even with the larger culture in its total way of life, has not abated. It seems to be manifest, while not in violent behavior at the present time, in much more subdued and personally damaging ways as evidenced by the suicide rate, the drug problem, and the almost hopeless kind of feeling that is seen in the attitudes and behaviors of many youngsters today.

4. During the period of great violence on campus, a great deal of the behavior which brought large numbers of youngsters into conflict with the law seemed rooted in political factors, based on a desire to overthrow or change the system of government, the promotion or denunciation of candidates or office holders, or the espousal of numerous causes at the local, state or national level.

5. Based on the experience gained during the previous period of violence on campus, and based on the few recent examples taken from scattered student demonstrations, it is probably accurate to say that because large groups want "action now" or instant change which the system is not prepared to grant, even if it were willing to do so, a clash with enforcement officials usually involves the direction of hostility and verbal or physical abuse at the police on the scene as symbols of authority or because they are attempting to control the action of the group. These situations sorely test the professional discipline of the police officers who must carry out their duty to protect lives and property, restore order or make arrests if indicated, and deal directly with physical attacks upon themselves in some instances, while remaining objective in evaluating the amount of force required, and never permitting themselves to become personally vindictive or deliberately inflammatory.

6. We should never generalize about the composition of such groups. Simplistic statements like "just a bunch of rowdy kids" or "a gang of hippies" are not only non-professional, but they are inaccurate in many cases. Experience has shown that all kinds of youngsters have

taken part in such activities at various times, including members of all social strata, economic levels, personality types, with academic achievement ranging from school drop-outs through some of the best students on campus.

Chapter 9

RACE AND THE JUVENILE OFFENDER

Section

9.1 Effect of non-acceptance of blacks by whites

9.2 Explanation of violence in behavior of black youth

§ 9.1   Effect of non-acceptance of blacks by whites

In any discussion of the influence of race in relation to understanding juvenile delinquency, it is essential to point out that while there has been significantly higher proportions of blacks involved in delinquent acts, especially those involving violence, than their numbers in the general population would ordinarily lead one to expect, two important facts must be kept in mind before one misjudges the situation and attributes some purely racial construction to this phenomenon: 1. Members of other races which have enjoyed similarly disadvantaged status in America also showed much higher rates of delinquency until they reached a stage of upward mobility which removed them significantly from the underprivileged group and absorbed them more fully into the larger society's opportunity structure. 2. Most black Americans have so much of European and other "mixed blood" in them that many who are called racially black are simply being identified because of a minority part of their composition and are not being recognized as "more European than black" in relation to their full racial heritage.

Also, it is important to point out that several significant studies recently have adequately demonstrated that the strength of association between race and violent offenses varies extremely with geographical location, and tends to come close to statistically disappearing altogether when the two groups are found in more privileged suburban communities living side by side. (A recent study conducted by the Vera Institute and others done under the auspices of the Ford Foundation tend to dramatically support these conclusions.)

When we consider the identity crisis, the group feeling of alienation, and all of the many factors mentioned in considering the teen culture and the current causes of violence and delinquency among young people today, it is impossible to ignore the race question because it brings with it two significant added factors that are not present in any of the other considerations—an "acceptance gap," and the constant, easy and continuing identifiability of the members of the group because of their color.

The acceptance gap has been so wide in this country that all defensive attempts to minimize its existence or extent notwithstanding, we need merely to be reminded that it was only in the very recent past that we were willing to have members of the black community eat in the same restaurants and ride in the same section of the bus with members of the larger community; and in some places at this very time, members of the white community still do not wish to attend school or participate on an equal basis in social activities with black persons.

These facts speak so eloquently for themselves in regard to the non-acceptance of the black person in the mainstream of American society, that no detailed discussion of cases or methods of overt or subtle discrimination and avoidance needs to be undertaken at this time.

Also, in view of the fine reports of federal commissions and committees, foundations, self-study groups and others, it is doubtful whether anything could be added to the documentation of this problem. It suffices to say that a consciousness of a lack of acceptance in the larger culture is an added burden that the black youngster has long carried, and continues to carry in most places, in addition to all of the other emotional and environmental conflicts and problems that he shares with other adolescents. To deny this, in our opinion, is to deny the real situation.

At the same time, it is equally self-evident in our opinion, that members of the black community have never been able to become fully immersed in the larger culture because their identity as members of the minority group is so readily visible because of skin color. This has not been true of many other immigrant and national groups who at one time or the other in American history have been looked down upon by the members of the larger community, but who have managed to disperse themselves throughout and immerse themselves thoroughly within the major culture, where eventually their membership in the low-status group has become very difficult, if not impossible, to detect. On the contrary, the easy identification of the black person as part of the minority group has most certainly contributed to the continuation of his status as such.

The late Mr. Whitney Young of the Urban League made an emphatic statement, and asked several soul-searching questions on this subject recently when he said:

"The sickness of racial hatred is a problem white people have had to live with for years, without the benefit of anyone studying it.

"What kind of person panics because a Negro family moves into his neighborhood? What sort of sickness is it that makes a man fear Negro children going to his child's school? What form of madness is it that makes an employer or a union leader try to keep Negroes from a decent job?" [1]

Because hatred breeds hatred, and violence breeds violence, unfortunately we are now at the point where many young blacks see the situation as totally hopeless and unable to be changed by traditional or non-violent means; and they use this rationalization for unleashing the most violent verbal and physical attacks indiscriminately upon random members of the white community. Some others see their newly found group identity and strength as providing the opportunity to attack, revile, and "pay back" for past abuses. Unfortunately, after the 1977 showing of the television novel "Roots," besides the great good that was accomplished in helping many whites to understand the black dilemma and in heightening the awareness on the part of both groups for the need to work together to overcome problems caused by past abuses, there were some blacks who obviously had their hostility-level heightened, and in some communities there were vicious physical attacks, and in many cases a higher frequency of verbal abuse of white students by blacks citing elements from the television program in justification for

[1] *The Michigan Chronicle*, (1968), A:15.

their hostility. While at the same time, equally unfortunately, some members of the white group, resenting the attention given to the past problems of blacks and the newfound feeling of racial solidarity on their part, engaged in increased acts of hostility and overt prejudice to members of the black community.

§ 9.2   Explanation of violence in behavior of black youth

In a particularly unfortunate incident of this kind, recently, in a large midwestern city, a police officer was shot while seated in his police cruiser in a large black ghetto, and while many responsible members of the black community spoke out against irresponsibility, hatred and violence on both sides, other influential blacks took the position that previous white violence justified this act; or they simply refused to recognize the act as lawlessness in any sense of the word. This indeed is tragic, especially because it so severely hampers the efforts of all people who have in the past, and continue in the present, to work for true equality and racial understanding.

On the one hand, many whites simply refuse to acknowledge the fact that if the black community had been granted legitimate rights out of a sense of justice and love long before the present crisis, there would have been no need for "black violence" at all in this country. On the other hand, many members of the black community because of frustration, disenchantment with continual meaningless promises, and a sense of outrage at many of the injustices, in some cases simply refuse to recognize the authority of the law or the fact that "violence breeds more violence" and that all irresponsible acts at this time tend to promote the polarization of feeling that is threatening to divide the nation.

An unfortunate result of the polarization taking place is the fact that many who in the past had seen the issue not as racial but as "right against wrong," are now being pushed into a position of seeing the entire problem as one of "black against white."

The young black who has the normal conflicts of adolescence, with the tremendous environmental pressures weighing upon all teenagers in today's culture, has the added stress of trying to resolve the conflict which he sees all about him in the area of race relations, and of searching desperately for his identity as a black man. As a result, many black youths rebel against what they visualize to be the "selling out" of their parents and elders to a white-dominated culture; still others remain within the larger culture and attempt to change it from inside; many place great emphasis on ingredients from their black heritage and emphasize this in modes of personal dress, grooming, music, language and in other ways which often are misunderstood by older members of the black community as well as by members outside of their racial group. The black youth finds himself, at a time of normal adolescent strife, immersed in a world, and often in the more immediate environment of the neighborhood and the family, that is in a constant state of turmoil in relation to his position, role and identity.

One psychologist spoke on this point recently when he said:

"In the transition from the deep feelings of inferiority to the goal of an effective positive identity, they seem at times to be driven to extremisms, to the illogic of rejecting not only 'whitey' but rejecting all other Negroes who do not share their present form of extremism. In the enthusiasm and impatience of youth they are not above name calling. Even as they insist upon Negro history as a firm foundation for positive Negro identity, they reject the recent history and the sacrifices of those Negroes who made it possible for them to reach this stage of realistic quest for personal and racial affirmation.

"But these are the unavoidable symptoms of any positive transition. They're signs of health and the persistence of the struggle for life and justice. To understand the positives of these young people, one must understand that no group of human beings can move from being the victims of extremes of injustice and inhumanity to the goals of self-acceptance and positive personal and racial identity without a transition period being marked by turmoil." [2]

[2] Kenneth B. Clark, "The Search for Identity," *Ebony Magazine*, (August 1967).

On the other hand, the long tradition of law in this country has insisted that all men conduct their quest for freedom, justice and happiness within the framework of the law, and that the grievances of any man, however serious, may only be redressed as far as the law allows and in the way that the law allows. Thus, it is easy to see the special conflicts that need to be understood and resolved in relation to the black juvenile offender and the law. This is especially true at the present juncture of history when enormous pressures are being exerted in some quarters on black youngsters to view all law as simply "white man's law," and when on the other side, unfortunately, many injustices and continued abuses still exist and tend to give a degree of credibility to this dangerous pattern of thinking on the part of many young blacks.

APPLICATION OF IMPORTANT POINTS EMPHASIZED FOR LAW ENFORCEMENT OFFICERS

1. The black teenager has all of the emotional and situational problems of other adolescents plus the serious conflict arising from his minority group status and the reactions of many of the majority group.

2. The highly sensitive adolescent is quite conscious of racial hatred, even if it is displayed in subtle ways or hidden behind a mask of formal, verbalized acceptance.

3. Since "hatred breeds hatred," unfortunately many young blacks are striking out at white society by unprovoked attacks on the streets and in the schools, property damage, and many other offenses which are rooted in racial hatred, or in their feeling that the system which has produced such prejudice must be overthrown. (Such lawlessness and violence can never be permitted, but in fairness, we must try to understand some of the causes.)

4. Many young blacks are struggling to find or to assert their identity as "black men." This causes them to emphasize their black heritage by mode of dress, language, music, and in many other ways. Unfortunately, this practice often offends the sensibilities of some members of the larger society. Law enforcement officers must be professional enough to separate any personal feelings they might have about life-styles from an objective evaluation of the conduct of any group.

5. The law enforcement officer, because he so obviously represents the official authority of society, is in an extremely advantageous position to demonstrate the equality of justice and the equality of concern for the rights and safety of all citizens that the U. S. Constitution guarantees; and by so doing, often in very difficult and even

dangerous circumstances, he can do more than any other professional person to lessen the problems of alienation and hostility which exist for so many black youngsters in our society.

Chapter 10

THE DRUG SCENE

Section

§ 10.1   Use of drugs by juveniles; general survey of narcotics

With the exception of marijuana use, which continues to grow rapidly among the young population, drug abuse in general seems to have stabilized during the last two-year period. According to the National Institute on Drug Abuse, while the use of marijuana has risen to the point of where 53% of all high school seniors have tried the drug at least one time and about 30,000,000 Americans of all age levels have done likewise, the use of amphetamines, LSD, barbiturates, and some of the more "exotic" drugs has actually decreased among the youth population, and juvenile use of heroin has at least stabilized if not decreased.[1]

Additionally, an interesting phenomenon took place about 1973 when the abuse of "sopors" (a brand name which has become popular on the street for methaqualone, a sedative hypnotic drug) made a meteoric entrance into the drug abuse scene to the point where, at that time, many authorities were calling it the "most frequently abused drug by high school students" in several sections of the country; and after just several years of popularity, when the potentially lethal effects of this drug, especially in combination with alcohol, became a matter of accepted knowledge among the youth group, the abuse of this drug now is in a period of great decline. However, it still maintains its popularity with individual users and in some specific groups.

While there is no longer the "shocking numerical increase"

[1] For complete details of the 1976 report, contact National Institute on Drug Abuse, 5600 Fishers Lane, Rockville, Maryland 20852.

in across-the-board drug abuse within the youth culture that we mentioned in the first edition of this text (1971), the intensity of the search by many youngsters for "mind blowing experiences" and for the chemical solution to all of life's problems and the horrible individual cost to the young drug abuser in terms of the physical and psychological debilitation which eventually accompanies the established drug habit, and the economic cost of the crime required in some cases by addicts to support their drug habit, continue to compel us to give special attention to this most important problem in relation to juvenile behavior in this country.

As the late 1960's and early 1970's brought us to an awareness of the emergence of severe narcotics abuse from the deprived areas of the inner-cities into the more affluent areas of suburban America and into the "very best schools and homes" in our society, the present period certainly shows us the continuation of this condition, and especially the "institutionalization" of marijuana abuse at all levels of the contemporary youth and adult culture. A vivid example of this can be seen from the recent statement in a metropolitan daily newspaper: "The drug scene, especially the marijuana scene, has indeed changed. Eight years ago, the scene was part of rock and roll, a symbol of the counter-culture. Smoking was a political act, a deliberate breaking of a law to protest the mores of a whole society. The majority of people who smoked then were college students. Today, they are doctors and lawyers, investment counselors and corporation junior executives.

"Robert Carr, senior program officer for the Drug Abuse Council in Washington, DC, says 'If you look at marijuana as a consumer product, the demographics are enough to light up the heart of any marketing expert.' According to the Council's studies, users tend to be young, live in cities, work in a handful of prestige professions and have a lot of money to spend on nonessentials."[2]

The "low-class" stigma and the picture of the violator as part of the "out-group" continues to break down as the edu-

[2] "Pot Smoking No Longer Limited To Defiant Counter-culture," article by Glenda Daniel, the *Cincinnati Enquirer*, September 5, 1976.

cational and social levels of the user are rising and drug abuse is looked upon more and more by young people as an accepted practice. One veteran enforcement official, commenting upon this trend, said very accurately that "the police officer today is experiencing an unusual situation. During the arrest or shortly thereafter, he sees his young prisoner change from a confident, defiant, rebellious young boy or girl to a shaken, uncertain individual who still knows how to cry. It is not easy for the officer or the violator. This state of affairs remains even more true today."[3]

The summary given by one researchist in 1970 also remains true today:

"We are seeing more and more bright young people from the so-called middle class. They are wholesome, clean-cut—the boy or girl next door type. They are now part of an expanding drug culture."[4]

As the scene changes and the picture becomes more confused, official thinking and planning in all disciplines from enforcement through treatment is in a state of flux. At all levels, from the local police agencies to the United States Congress, reaction has been taking mixed forms. However, most of the difference of opinion and variety of proposed solutions is due to the fact that use of drugs does not present a unified or simple picture. It represents so many things to so many people in so many different ways that it is a most complex collection of happenings rather than one particular pattern of behavior or one syndrome. This idea was expressed very adequately in a government publication some years ago which said that:

"Drug abuse is so many things. It is the heroin user injecting his bag of 'H,' a methedrine user high on 'speed,' the teenager smoking 'pot,' the 12 year old sniffing model airplane glue. But it is also the adult starting his day with an amphetamine for needed pick-me-up and ending it with several drinks to unwind and a barbiturate to put him to sleep. The problem

3 Albert D. Cook, Chief, Division of Dangerous Drugs and Narcotics, Office of the Ohio Attorney General, quoted in "Keep off the Grass," (pamphlet published by Attorney General of Ohio, 1970).

4 Ibid, Dr. Harold T. Conrad, Chief, Clinical Research Center, NIMH, Lexington, Ky., Clinical Research Center.

of drug abuse reaches deeply into our values, aspirations and fears. It is an emotionally-charged area for almost all of us, making effective communication difficult.[5]

"Drug abuse, because it takes many forms and involves many different kinds of substances, is not an easy term to define. In one instance, drug abuse refers to the consumption, without medical authorization, of medically useful drugs which have the capacity for altering mood and behavior. A truck driver who takes a stimulant to maintain wakefulness is abusing drugs. A student who has decided on his own to take a tranquilizer before an exam is also abusing drugs.

"The problem of drug abuse also refers to the ingestion of a medically useful mood-altering drug for a purpose other than that for which it was prescribed. A patient who has been prescribed a barbiturate for insomnia, but who uses it to get intoxicated at a party, is abusing drugs.

"Drug abuse also describes the use, except for medical research, of mind-changing drugs and substances having no legitimate medical application. Anyone who smokes marijuana or takes LSD is abusing drugs. Anyone who uses heroin is a drug abuser. Anyone who chews 'morning-glory seeds' is abusing drugs. (Note that the consumption of alcoholic beverages, which in some cases technically could fall into this category, is not considered drug abuse in our society.)

"The term drug abuse is also applied to the inhalation of fumes from gasoline, various types of adhesives and household cements, and other solvents. Since the inhalation of these fumes can result in mood and behavior changes, this practice should be considered along with the other types of drug abuse.

"Obviously, all forms of drug abuse are not equally dangerous to society; nor can every type of drug abuse be equally controlled; but as far as possible, laws have been passed to

---

[5] "Teaching About Drug Abuse" from the pamphlet "Students and Drug Abuse" (reprinted from *Today's Education*, NEA Journal, March, 1969) by National Institute of Mental Health, U. S. Dept. of HEW, (U. S. Gov't. Printing Office, 1969), p. 2.

curtail what society feels are the most dangerous forms of this practice."[6]

It is also important to note that the terminology has often contributed further to the confusion. "Addiction" has traditionally been used to describe involvement with those drugs which produce physical dependence, for which a physical tolerance is developed, and to which there are physical and psychological problems associated with discontinuing use, commonly called "acute withdrawal syndrome."

"Psychological dependence" or "habituation" are terms which apply to those drugs which basically do not produce a physical dependence. "Narcotics" has differing meanings when applied in the chemical or legal framework (e.g., legally cocaine is considered a narcotic while chemically it is considered a stimulant).

This matter of terminology has been further complicated in the very recent past by the high incidence of abuse of the non-narcotic drugs such as stimulants, depressants, tranquilizers and a number of other household products. As a result, the Expert Committee of the World Health Organization recommends scrapping much of the traditional terminology and embracing the use of the more general term "drug dependence." They define drug dependence as "a state arising from repeated administration of a drug on a periodic or continuous basis."[7] And they further qualify these terms for diagnostic purposes as "drug dependence of the morphine type," "drug dependence of the cocaine type," "drug dependence of the marijuana type," and "drug dependence of the amphetamine type," etc.

While the adoption of this terminology requires that we discard many traditional expressions, it seems to have a definite advantage in that it gives us accuracy and precision in discussing the different types of drug abuse which are currently prevalent among the juvenile offenders.

While the number of drug abusers in America is hard to

6 *Drug Abuse (A Manual for Law Enforcement Officers)*, (Revised 5th Edition), Smith, Kline and French Laboratories, Philadelphia, Pa., (1965, 1966, 1968), p. 1.

7 Id., p. 3.

accurately estimate, the National Institute of Drug Abuse estimates that there are about 13,000,000 "regular users" of marijuana and the publisher of "High Times" (a magazine dealing exclusively with matters of the drug market and related information) estimates that the number of such "regular users" of marijuana is as high as 15 to 20 million. With the addition of estimated "occasional users" this would bring the figure to within 25 and 35 million who have experimented with marijuana alone in the United States at the present time.[8]

In the business community there is an increased alarm at the number of workers at all levels who are absent from work or who are performing ineffectively on their jobs because of narcotics-related problems. Recently the Wall Street Journal reported that the Metropolitan Life Insurance Company had openly acknowledged an alarming increase in the number of employees who had to be dismissed because they were using drugs.[9] The same source further reported that the New York Telephone Company has begun using private plain-clothes police officers to detect employees' dope pushing efforts.[10] Similar reports are also coming to public attention from locations all over the country.[11]

Most of the opiates, including heroin, come to this country from two major sources, the Middle East and Southeast Asia. Opium poppies grown in Turkey in great quantities are converted into morphine and much of it is then processed into heroin after having been transported to France. The heroin then is smuggled directly into the United States, or it is diverted through Italy, Canada or Mexico to arrive eventually in the United States.

In the Far East, large quantities of opium are grown in the Yunan Province of China, and the Shan and Kachin states in Burma. While much of this supply is consumed in Asia by opium smokers, large amounts find their way to the United States directly or indirectly through Hong Kong and Macao.

[8] Reported in *Behavior Today,* Vol. 8, No. 2, January 24, 1977.

[9] "Drugs on the Job" *Wall Street Journal,* May 4, 1970.

[10] Ibid.

[11] "Firms Beginning to Take Note of Employees' Use of Drugs," *Cincinnati Post and Times Star,* July 10, 1970.

There is some opium produced illegally in Mexico where it is converted into heroin in hidden laboratories and smuggled across the border.

Most of the marijuana supplying the United States market is grown in Mexico, although there are sources in the near and middle-Eastern countries, and also some illegal marijuana fields in the United States itself.

The cocaine supply originates in the Andes Mountain region of Bolivia, Chile, Peru, Colombia and Ecuador, where the leaves of the coca plant are processed into cocaine and enter into the United States normally through Miami or New York, although some comes across the Mexican border into California.

Most of the amphetamines and barbiturates used illegally in this country are diverted from legal channels, although some of these drugs are smuggled into the United States from Mexico. The diversion of these drugs sometimes is the result of theft from legal sources or is the product of illegal laboratories, and some is made available by unscrupulous dealers and suppliers.

Many of the hallucinogenic drugs (other than marijuana and hashish) are smuggled into this country from Europe, Mexico, Canada and Australia, since they cannot be produced legally in the United States.

Many drugs which are legal for medicinal uses find their way into the illicit market because of dishonest employees who steal or overproduce, as a result of theft from warehouse supplies and dealers' shelves, as a result of forged prescriptions, and because of illegal sale by unscrupulous persons who have some legitimate access to the drugs.[12]

In this entire discussion of drugs we are intentionally omitting alcohol, although it is probably the most readily available, one of the cheapest, and one of the oldest and most effective

[12] "Illegal Traffic in Narcotics and Dangerous Drugs," (Fact Sheet #3) from the publication "Fact Sheets," Bureau of Narcotics and Dangerous Drugs, U. S. Dept. of Justice, Washington, D.C., (1969), pp. 3-1, 3-2.

of all the drugs, because it is treated separately in relation to youthful offenders in another place in this volume.

The history of drug abuse is indeed a long one. One of the first recorded legitimate uses of drugs dates back to the fourth century BC when Hippocrates, the "father of medicine," spoke of the use of "white poppy juices for many illnesses." Later the Spanish Conquistadores cited examples of American Indians using the leaf of the coca plant. Later, the explorers of the southwestern United States and South America spoke of American Indians inhaling "toxic humors" coming out of a "hole in the ground" and seeming to be stimulated or narcotized by these inhalations, especially prior to certain religious rites or before going into battle. There are also early references to the Catholic Church banning the use of certain substances by the Indians for narcotizing purposes.

In 1729, the Chinese Emperor, Yung Cheng, prohibited the smoking of opium. By the year 1902, China was producing an estimated 44,000,000 pounds of opium each year, primarily promoted by Western business interests.

Before the Revolutionary War, the use of opium in this country was reported, but the supply was minimal. After the Civil War, morphine addiction was rampant in this country and by the late 19th century it was estimated that millions of Americans were addicted to the narcotic effect of certain kinds of patent medicines.

By 1874, diacetylmorphine (also called diamorphine-hydrochloride), now known as heroin, was being produced in England; and at the end of World War I, heroin addiction in the United States was a well-known fact.

In 1938, a Swiss scientist accidentally developed lysergic acid diethylamide. About five years later it was discovered that this had a mind-altering effect, and by the 1960's it was in widespread use among young people, especially on college and university campuses throughout the United States.

More recently, the diversion of all sorts of legitimate medical drugs and household items, ranging from the amphetamines and barbiturates to nutmeg and airplane glue, for purposes of becoming intoxicated or "expanding the mind" have come into a high degree of popularity.

Just as all societies have engaged in law-making, education, or some other method to control the abuse of alcoholic beverages, especially by the young, there have been many legal efforts to control the use of drugs. In the United States, while there are many local ordinances pertaining to certain aspects of drug abuse (e.g., the 1965 *glue* sniffing ordinance enacted by the city of Cincinnati and surrounding communities) most of the more effective legislation has developed at the federal and state levels.

There have been two major sets of federal laws, passed at different times, to control the abuse of drugs in the United States. The earlier group of laws was intended to control the traffic in and use of narcotics, drugs and marijuana; the later group was intended to control the manufacture, sale, and use of the "dangerous drugs." These laws are outlined and summarized by the Bureau of Narcotics and Dangerous Drugs of the U. S. Department of Justice as follows:

§ 10.2   Federal narcotic and marijuana laws

In 1971, all of the previously existing federal laws controlling the use and sale of narcotics and other controlled substances were superseded by a new sweeping piece of legislation entitled The Controlled Substances Act of 1970 (which went into effect September 1, 1971).

This Act replaced the Narcotics Drug Import and Export Act, the Harrison Narcotics Act, the Narcotics Manufacturing Act of 1960, and the Marijuana Tax Act—laws previously designed to cover the entire spectrum of chemical substance control.

In the new Controlled Substances Act of 1970, there are two major elements of great concern to readers of this text. These are: 1. A schedule of drugs and controlled substances (listed according to their "redeeming value in terms of socially acceptable use"). 2. Penalties associated with the abuse or illegal use of any of these substances.

To summarize the vast amount of material contained in this

new code of drug-related laws, your author will, at the risk of over-simplifying, list the schedule of the drugs and controlled substances and simply comment that as to penalties, they vary depending upon the purpose, amount, and nature of the substance involved: The classification of drugs is as follows: 1. Those substances which apparently have no medicinal use (for example, heroin). 2. Those substances having some medicinal value with a high degree of abuse potential (for example, morphine). 3. Those substances having medicinal use, with a lesser degree of abuse potential (for example, aspirin with codeine). 4. Those substances having medicinal use, but with a still lesser abuse potential (for example, pentobarbital). 5. Those substances having medical use with a still lesser or very low abuse potential (for example, cough syrup with codeine).

It is of great significance to note, (although a fuller discussion of marijuana will take place later in this chapter), that in this newer Federal Code, while marijuana and related substances are in the most serious schedule, that is Schedule No. 1, and while the penalties for possession with intent to sell still remain relatively high, simple possession of small amounts for personal use has been reduced out of the felony range and is now considered a misdemeanor only by the federal government.

§ 10.3   Types and effects of various narcotics

Drugs as related to juvenile offenders are only one contributing factor in juvenile delinquency, and space limitations require that only brief mention be made of individual drug pharmacology, specific methods of detection and evidence which should be gathered for prosecution of drug offenders. Many outstanding authorities have written accurately and eloquently on these subjects and an extensive bibliography is listed at the end of this volume for those who wish to pursue the subject further. We will confine our discussion to the relation of drug abuse to the type of juvenile offenders in this area and the effects the various types of drug abuse have on the juvenile offender.

The use of chemical substances which can be grouped together under the term "narcotics" (we include cocaine in this group, although chemically it is a stimulant, but legally is termed a narcotic) has recently mushroomed among youngsters. That it has come out of the ghetto and is now found in the high schools, and even in the junior high schools, is a fact well known to law enforcement and correction officials throughout this country.

This drastic alteration in the traditional pattern of drug abuse existing only in the inner-city and among the deprived groups became evident already in the late 1960's and "blossomed" in the early 1970's. Prior to that time, the use of heroin, morphine, the other opium derivatives, and cocaine had been considered the problem of a few readily identifiable "hard core" drug abusers who were estimated to be about 100,000 or less in the entire country. After the drastic change of the late sixties and early seventies, we now see some forms of drug abuse fully accepted in the youth culture within suburban America in many places and it is unfortunately often surrounded with a high degree of peer approval. However, that is not universally true, and fortunately those drugs which are seen as having severely debilitating physical effects (for example, heroin and especially LSD) are now meeting with a high degree of disapproval in many youth quarters, and the users of these substances are once again feeling the withdrawal of peer support and are identified as members of an "out" group.

The use of these hard drugs by youngsters is not only dangerous because of the almost 100% probability of their physical addiction to the drug, but also because of the physical and psychological deterioration which results from their habituation. Besides the tearing-down of physical and mental health which accompanies long-term addiction, there is the immediate danger of serious physical illness and death because of the use of narcotics mixed with toxic adulterants. Variance in the amount of pure narcotics in the mixture can cause the youthful user to suffer severe physical results if he suddenly acquires the narcotic in "too pure" form after being accustomed to a "cutdown" mixture of the narcotic, at which times the more pure mixture slows down vital bodily functions too quickly and may stop these functions altogether. A young addict can very easily suffer death within a matter of hours, for example, because of an acute depressive effect on the respiratory system.

Indirectly, many youngsters are becoming seriously ill or dying because of infections resulting from the use of unclean tools of administration of the narcotic, such as needles and razor blades which have not been sterilized. And, needless to say, death is often the result of the deteriorated life style which goes along with drug addiction and which makes the addict a ready victim for pneumonia, malnutrition, and a variety of other diseases.

Hard narcotics are used by the youngsters in a variety of ways including "sniffing," "skin popping," and up to and including "mainlining," a practice in which a chemical substance is injected, usually by hypodermic needle, directly into the blood stream. In this latter practice of mainlining, after repeated injections, overworked veins eventually collapse and the youthful addict is forced to look beyond his arms to his legs, feet, hands, and even between the fingers and toes in order to find veins suitable for insertions of the narcotic.

The cost of a hard narcotic habit is estimated to be anywhere from $15 to $20 per day for the light habit, up to $100 or more per day required to support a severe habit. Few of the addicted youngsters have this kind of money available to them, and they are forced to resort to crime in order to purchase drugs. Ordinarily, the boys resort to theft and the girls to prostitution to finance the cost of their narcotic addiction, although both sexes have resorted to practically every known crime to obtain money needed to purchase a "fix."

Another major classification of the drug abuse problem among young people has been called the "inhalation of solvents" or the problem of "toxic inhalation," which includes the practice of inhaling fumes or vapors from glue, gasoline, paint thinner, and household solvents of many types. Because of the widespread practice of inhaling airplane glue this practice has been termed "glue sniffing."

The solvent normally is squeezed or poured into a cloth or into an open bag and the container of the solvent is then placed over either the nose or mouth and the sniffing operation begins. This practice is extremely prevalent among the young, with cases reported down to the age of approximately eight years. It is especially popular among the youngsters who do not have the money to purchase other forms of narcotics or dangerous drugs. It is also significant to note that in at least one survey of this practice it was found that a substantial amount of airplane glue was obtained by shoplifting.[13]

The practice is dangerous both physically and psychologically, and serious effects can be noted in bodily and behavioral changes. As the result of one study involving over 700 children, the following report was made:

"Our findings reveal among other things, that anemia has a particular manifestation among glue sniffers. There are changes in form, shape, and color of the red cells, increase in the number of white cells, and decrease in white blood count. They reveal basophilic stipplings and target cells which indicate a toxic condition. The urinalysis reveals pus, albumen, casts, bacteria, and blood, and examination of several glue sniffing children revealed evidence of liver and kidney damage.

"Preliminary observations on the effect of chronic, recurrent sniffing of organic solvents were also made in Sweden on 32 boys between the ages of 12 and 15, of whom at least one-half had practiced glue sniffing frequently. A number of bone marrow aspirations indicate such abnormalities as inhibition of maturation of blood cells. Electroencephalographic changes resulting from acute inhalations of these solvents appear to be related to somnolence, a common side effect with inhalation.

"The juveniles will experience some of the following after sniffing glue: (1) buzzing sensation, (2) dizziness, (3) headaches, (4) euphoria, (5) somnolence at times, (6) loss of weight, (7) diplopia, (8) nystagmus, (9) dullness with poor concentration, (10) forgetfulness, (11) tremors at times simulating a condition of alcoholic intoxication, (12) spasmodic condition of muscles, especially neck muscles and the muscles of the lower extremities, (13) dilated pupils, (14) decreased reflexes, (15)

---

[13] "Glue Sniffing Study," (Cincinnati, Ohio, 1965, under the direction of the author, who at that time was Director of the Hamilton County Juvenile Court).

numbness of the extremities, (16) sneezing, (17) coughing, (18) chest pain.

"Loss of weight is not uncommon—in one case, 30 pounds were lost during indulgence of the glue sniffing habit.

"While under the influence of glue and especially in the euphoric stage, these children are dangerous to society and themselves."[14]

Behavior is altered emphatically as glue sniffers tend to deteriorate in their ability to effectively control their impulses. When under the influence of these toxic vapors, the youthful inhalers become extremely aggressive, easily sexually aroused, and have little respect for authority or the personal and property rights of others. Fighting, sex offenses, and rebelling against parents and other authorities often become a part of the behavior pattern of youngsters who are habitually practicing this activity. Their interest in wholesome activities, their ability to concentrate, and their total personality and adjustment level, tends to deteriorate rapidly.[15]

We can summarize the glue sniffing problem among children and adolescents by stating that it has become a serious problem throughout the nation, especially in larger urban areas. The result of inhaling such toxic vapors can be acute brain syndrome resembling alcoholic intoxication, with addition of serious side effects which include hallucinations and delusions. Judgment deteriorates and sometimes serious accidents and death result. The possibility of chronic physical and mental morbidity is widely accepted. The question of addiction is disputable, but development of dependence is frequent.

Because of the widespread dangers of this problem, the young age at which it can begin, and the danger to health and behavior, results of a study describing the symptoms connected with inhalation of toxic solvents were made available in one large city in order to alert parents, teachers, and other interested adults to the possible presence of this problem.

---

[14] "Glue Sniffing," Jacob Sokol, M.D., Chief Physician, L.A. County Probation Dept. (first published in *American Journal of Correction* and reprinted in *Youth Leaders' Digest*, April, May, 1966).

[15] "Glue Sniffing Study," (Cincinnati), op. cit.

"The symptoms that are clearly observable are: (1) extreme changes in the conduct and interest of the child, (2) lack of ability to concentrate or remain attentive for any length of time, (3) restlessness or irritability, (4) rapid loss of weight, (5) sleepiness, (6) tendency to withdraw from the observation of parents or teachers, (7) inexplainable misuse of lunch money or other funds available to youngster, or desperate need for additional pocket change, (8) association with delinquency-prone groups, where this association was not previously the practice, (9) unexplainable outbursts of temper or violent reaction to authority with no previous history of this type of behavior, (10) inability to get along with all the child's former friends, (11) repeated episodes of fighting."[16]

A third large group of drugs which are commonly abused by youthful offenders can be identified best by the slang term, "uppers and downers." This refers to those drugs which are normally legally available for proper medicinal use, but which are in considerable demand for the illegal purposes of "getting high" or to gratify the urge to escape or withdraw.

Generally speaking, the "uppers" are stimulants which are intended to directly stimulate the central nervous system and which are capable of producing the feeling of excitement, a rise in the respiratory rate and blood pressure, and a state of physical and mental alertness. The amphetamines are probably the best known of this group which includes phenmetrazine, denzthetamine, methamphetamine, digethylproprion and many others (including cocaine which legally is a narcotic, and was mentioned previously in this chapter under that heading).

The amphetamines and stimulants closely related to them are widely used in medical practice for treatment of many kinds of mental and emotional disorders, overweight and certain illnesses resulting in muscular rigidity. These stimulants are widely abused at the juvenile age level by "speed freaks" and "meth users," which are popular slang names for abusers of stimulants.

When abused, the stimulants can be highly dangerous both physically and psychologically. While there is no physical addic-

16 Ibid.

tion resulting from the abuse of these drugs, psychological and emotional dependence and all sorts of physical symptoms, ranging from inability to sleep, restlessness, and excitability, to a truly psychotic-like state characterized by delusions and hallucinations can develop very readily. Minor symptoms include talkativeness, restlessness, excitability and inability to sleep.[17] Behavioral changes including severe aggression and poor impulse control frequently follows heavy and chronic abuse.

The severe effects physically, psychologically and in behavior have often caused "speed freaks" to be excluded from other drug using groups; and it has led, at least on one occasion, one chronic drug-abusing group to post signs warning their members not to abuse the stimulants because "speed kills" and "meth is death."

The "downers" frequently abused are the barbiturates. These are depressants and sedatives which act upon the central nervous system in such a way as to slow down the vital processes. They are widely used in the legitimate practice of medicine because of their beneficial effect in cases of sleep disturbances, and in treating high blood pressure. When these "downers" are abused they can be more dangerous than hard narcotics. In a manual prepared by a prominent drug manufacturer this important set of observations about barbiturate abuse was outlined:

"High doses of barbiturates may be more dangerous than narcotics. Both tolerance and physical dependence develop with excessive use. Tolerance to high doses of barbiturates is never complete. The symptoms of toxicity which characterize the barbiturate abuser include slurring of speech, staggering, falling, quick temper and a quarrelsome disposition. Overdoses produce coma during which pneumonia is an ever-present danger.

"It should be kept in mind that an unsteady gait and speech problems may be signs of illness—neurological disorders, diabetes, or other diseases. However, an unsteady gait without an alcoholic drug may be indicative of barbiturate intoxication.

[17] *Drug Abuse*, op. cit., p. 30.

"Although physical dependence does not develop with dosages normally used in medical practice, it does occur with the excessive dosages encountered in drug abuse. When barbiturates, taken in large quantities are suddenly discontinued, withdrawal symptoms develop which may be far more dangerous than those resulting from narcotic withdrawal. Barbiturate withdrawal can, in fact, end in death. That is why a physician must be contacted whenever barbiturate dependency is detected. Withdrawal should always be carried out under a doctor's care. Barbiturate users often take the drug in combination with alcohol to hasten intoxication. When an officer suspects an alcohol-intoxicated person is also under the influence of barbiturates, he should immediately summon medical aid. The intoxicated person faces two distinct dangers: (1) death due to the combined effects of alcohol and barbiturates. This can occur in people who are not dependent on barbiturates as well as those who are, (2) death due to barbiturate withdrawal—a distinct possibility in persons dependent upon barbiturates.

"In withdrawal, the barbiturate-dependent abuser appears to improve during the first 8 to 12 hours after his last dose. After this there are signs of increasing nervousness, headache, anxiety, muscle twitching, tremor, weakness, insomnia, and nausea. Changes in blood pressure when the person stands up suddenly often cause him to faint. These symptoms are quite severe at about 24 hours. There are changes in the brain wave (electroencephalographic) readings and, within 36 to 72 hours, convulsions resembling epileptic seizures may develop. Such conditions occasionally occur as early as the 16th hour of withdrawal or as late as the 8th day.

"Convulsions, an ever-present possibility with barbiturate withdrawal, distinguish barbiturate from narcotic withdrawal. (Unlike barbiturate addiction, narcotic addiction is not characterized by a failure of muscular coordination—staggering during drug use or convulsion upon drug withdrawal.) Convulsions are a sign of a dangerous, perhaps fatal, condition. After convulsions, there may be a period of mental confusion. During succeeding days, delirium and hallucinations, similar to the delirium tremens (DT's) of alcoholism may develop. Delirium may be accompanied by an extreme agitation that contributes to exhaustion. The delirium may persist for several days after which a long period of sleep follows. (Delirium may also develop early in the course of withdrawal.)"[18]

A new "downer" with a "numbing effect" suddenly swept into prominence about late 1972 and blossomed into a very serious problem in 1973. This drug, called by its street name "sopors" (methaqualone), was highly marketed and frequently prescribed as a sleeping pill. It was most often advertised as non-addicting and its effects were generally expressed to be benign. However, under the onslaught of juvenile abuse of the drug, it was quickly noted that it was in fact addictive and that, far from being benign, it could have very dangerous effects, especially when combined with alcohol.

Its easy availability and cheap price (about 75¢ to $1.25 per day) made it extremely attractive to younger students who formerly would "get high" on marijuana or some other more expensive drug before going to school in the morning, and then suddenly would find that the "high" would wear off before the school day was out. With sopors, the high was found to last much longer, and in effect for 75¢ per day one could remain high.

Additionally, within the youth group, the word was spread that the advantages of sopors abuse included the fact that there was no odor, vomiting, and unconsciousness did not result from over use; also, there was no "hangover" effect after its abuse.

As a result of all these factors, very quickly the drug became extremely popular and presented such a real problem that several communities estimated that it was the most frequently abused drug "almost overnight" among the youth population in their areas. School officials estimated that from 20% to as high as 80% of their "problem students" were involved in this habit in various locations.

Then, just as suddenly as the appearance and popularity of the drug, the facts became known about its potential danger and fortunately the use has begun to decline. In the initial promotion among youthful abusers, sopors were billed as an aphro-

18 Id., pp. 8, 9.

disiac. Part of the beginning disillusionment with the drug came in about 1973 when the word was spread that this effect did not take place. It actually offered no performance which would justify its street reputation as "heroin for lovers."

Immediately following this revelation, various prominent medical authorities began pronouncing its potential physical danger up to the point of death. When it finally became known that withdrawal from a sedative hypnotic drug like sopors is more severe than withdrawal even from heroin, and that in heroin withdrawal, while one felt like one might die, in withdrawal from sopors it was entirely possible that one might actually become physically unable to survive, the popularity of the drug began to wane.

Today, the use is still found in scattered quarters, and the hold on individual users still exists, but the popularity of the drug as a major source of abuse seems to be diminishing very rapidly within most youth groups.

Another area of drugs commonly being abused by youngsters in the United States is the group called the "hallucinogens." The most commonly abused drug in this category is marijuana. It is known by many familiar subcultural names such as "pot," "grass," "reefers," etc. It is by no means the only hallucinogenic drug, although by far it is the most popular in use in the general drug culture, and especially among the youth groups.

For purposes of discussion we will follow Szara[19] who has classified the hallucinogens into three groups: (1) phenylethylamine group, including mescaline, TMA and MDA; (2) tryptamine group, including DMT, DET, DPT, psilocin, psilocybin, harmine and LSD twenty-five; (3) chemically heterogeneous group including ditran, N-allylmorphine, phenylcyclidine and tetrahydrocannabinol (which is the active ingredient of marijuana, hashish, and cannabinol).

There are also a number of other more exotic hallucinogens which probably can best be treated in this same section. These

[19] S. Szara, "The Hallucinogenic Drugs—Curse or Blessing?" *American Journal of Psychiatry*, (June, 1967), pp. 1513-1518, as quoted in "Drugs for Kicks," James L. Chapel, M.D. and Daniel W. Taylor, *Crime and Delinquency*, Vol. 16, #1, (January, 1970), p. 20.

include Jimson weed, peyote, morning-glory seed, nutmeg, and numerous other substances which reportedly are either ingested or injected in order to produce a mind altering effect.[20]

This "mind blowing" effect is so called because when under the influence of hallucinogenic drugs the user can experience hallucinations, illusions, and certainly a distortion of the various senses and mental processes which makes the perception of objective reality unreal or altered to some degree.

Most of the hallucinogens are imported illegally or are manufactured in clandestine laboratories. The hallucinogens can be dangerous when abused because of their unpredictability and because they heighten sensitivity to a great degree. Normal anxiety can quickly be heightened into panic and a passing depression could quickly be changed into despair. The conflicts and frequent mood-swings of adolescents create a fertile ground in which these highly dangerous conditions can quickly take place under the influence of the hallucinogens.

There has been no evidence accumulated to indicate that physical dependence is developed by users of hallucinogenic drugs, but there seems to be a great likelihood that psychological dependence does develop, often quickly and to a high degree.

LSD-twenty-five (lysergic acid diethylamide), commonly called "acid," is a tasteless, odorless, colorless, extremely powerful hallucinogen which can have a highly pleasant or terrifyingly painful effect upon the user after the ingestion of a microscopic size dosage. It has been estimated that almost 250,000 doses can be contained in one ounce of this substance; and it is so powerful that at one time it was studied by the United States Army for a possible use in chemical warfare, since a package of pure LSD twenty-five the size of a normal pack of cigarettes, if properly dispensed through the water supply or in the air, could possibly have serious effects on the inhabitants of a city of one-half million persons.

Physical reactions can include nausea, increased heartbeat,

[20] "Drugs for Kicks," Id., pp. 27-31.

perspiration, dilated pupils and possible damage to the blood cells and alterations of chromosomal patterns. Psychological effects can range from dreams and distorted perception through panic, psychotic-like states and even suicidal attempts. Residual effects can include either anxiety or depression, and the recurrence of psychotic-like states, panic reactions, and other behavioral aberrations which are unpredictable and have been reported to occur for months and perhaps even several years after the last dose of LSD twenty-five has been taken.

This highly dangerous substance can be taken in a variety of ways, but normally it is deposited in sugar cubes or in a liquid form although it is known to have been placed on crackers or even mixed with the glue contained on the flap of an envelope.

Reports of the frequency and extent of its usage vary widely, but it can probably safely be estimated that at the height of its popularity LSD twenty-five was especially prominent on college campuses, with perhaps between one and two percent of all college students having had some experience with it. It is now estimated to be less frequently used, probably because of the widespread dissemination of information as to the great danger resulting from its use.

Another hallucinogen known popularly as STP appeared on the scene about 1967 amidst wild claims that it was the "coolest thing yet," and would produce all sorts of results for the user. The Bureau of Narcotics and Dangerous Drugs confirms that "doses of more than three milligrams can cause pronounced hallucinogenic effects lasting 8 to 10 hours."[21] They also report that at least one investigator claims that STP is 200 times as powerful as mescaline, but about 1/10 as potent as LSD,[22] while Chapel and Taylor seem to consider its effects more intense than the effects of LSD.[23]

§ 10.4 Marijuana problems

From a standpoint of the extent of the abuse of marijuana,

---

[21] "Hallucinogens," (Fact Sheet #9), U. S. Bureau of Narcotics and Dangerous Drugs, op. cit., p. 9-3.

[22] Id., p. 9-3.

[23] "Drugs for Kicks," op. cit., p. 20.

as well as from the intensity of feelings surrounding the use of marijuana, this is probably one of the most important topics to be discussed and understood when considering the whole picture of juvenile behavior in our contemporary society. Estimates of the extent of "pot smoking" have recently ranged from about an estimated thirteen million to approximately thirty million Americans. Of this number, the experience of most enforcement officials indicate a great number, if perhaps not a majority, are juveniles and young adults.

The National Institute on Drug Abuse currently estimates that about one-third of all high school seniors (graduating in spring of 1977) regarded themselves as regular users of marijuana, and more than half of that same group are estimated to have sampled the drug at some time.

The recent survey by the Institute (covering 17,000 students in 130 schools) indicated that the current 53% of high school seniors admitting to having tried marijuana indicates an increase of 5% since 1975.[24]

The active ingredient in marijuana is tetrahydrocannabinol, which comes from the flowering tops of the hemp plant (cannabis sativa). Marijuana is the most popular form of this drug in the United States, although hashish is imported from the Middle East and is found in use in some places in this country. Hashish contains a much more potent dosage of the active ingredient than marijuana does, and the same is true of the artificially manufactured "cannabinol" form, which is only recently finding its way into use in this country.

While in many places movements to decriminalize possession of marijuana for personal use have been successful to the point where the Federal Controlled Substances Act regards such possession as only a misdemeanor and many localities have such minimal penalties that they can be paid as simply as a "traffic ticket," arguments continue to take place as to whether or not marijuana is harmful, and especially as to how much legal control government should place upon its possession and use.

[24] Report of National Institute on Drug Abuse, op. cit.

Perhaps one of the finest summaries of thoughtful opinion by a knowledgeable person has been prepared by the Honorable G. Joseph Tauro, Chief Justice, Superior Court of the Commonwealth of Massachusetts.

Justice Tauro presided over the celebrated *Leis* case,[25] and after having decided the case, he presented his opinion on the full matter of marijuana and the law in an article prepared first for the American Criminal Law Quarterly[26] and from which we now present excerpts for the consideration of the reader:

COMMONWEALTH V LEIS[27]

© 1969 by the American Bar Association. Reprinted from the Spring, 1969 *American Criminal Law Quarterly*, Volume 7, No. 3, with permission of the ABA and the Section of Criminal Law.

"First let me discuss briefly the *Leis* case, the so-called Marijuana Case over which I presided—something I can now do with propriety because it is no longer pending in our courts. This case, as you may remember, was a protracted hearing in September of 1967 on pretrial motions which sought to challenge the constitutionality of our Narcotic Drug Act as applied to marijuana. The challenges were predicated on a variety of complex and interrelated constitutional theories. Without delving into all of their ramifications, it would be well to outline for you my conclusions which were affirmed, without dissent, by the Supreme Judicial Court of Massachusetts this past January.

"At the conclusion of the evidentiary hearing, I found marijuana to be in fact a harmful and dangerous drug and ruled that its possession and use do not rise to the level of a fundamental right of a United States citizen. I also ruled that the inclusion of marijuana in our statutory scheme regulating narcotic drugs was permissible; that its total prohibition was within the limits of the state's police power; and that the treatment accorded by law to other drugs, such as heroin or

[25] Commonwealth v. Joseph D. Leis, Mass, Superior Court, 69 Mass. advance sheet 97, aff'd by the Supreme Judical Court (Spiegel, J. presiding) 243 NE(2d) 898.

[26] Tauro, G. Joseph, "Marijuana and Other Relevant Problems, 1969," *American Criminal Law Quarterly*, Vol. 7, #3, (Spring, 1969), pp. 174-194.

[27] Commonwealth v. Joseph D. Leis, op. cit.

alcohol vis-a-vis marijuana, did not constitute a denial of the equal protection of the laws.

"However, more pertinent to our purposes here today than the legal rulings in the *Leis* case or the underlying constitutional foundations is the manner in which I arrived at my factual conclusions. The legal issues to be resolved were framed by the scope of the defendants' motions and the restraints wisely imposed upon judicial inquiry into the validity of legislative acts and whether there was a rational basis for the legislation being challenged. But central to the whole dispute was a factual determination of the nature and effects of marijuana which, on the basis of the evidence produced at the hearing, I found to be a dangerous and harmful drug.

"For two weeks the defense and prosecution presented a series of eighteen expert witnesses from this country, Great Britain, Greece and India. These learned and articulate men represented the fields of medicine, botany, pharmacology, psychiatry, sociology, psychology, philosophy, religion and law enforcement.

"Ordinarily the opinions of such experts would be presented under favorable ground rules of their own choosing without fear of confrontation or contradiction. However, in the *Leis* case the opinions of the experts were subjected to the scrutiny of a judicial process. Nothing was accepted at face value. Every statement and opinion proferred for creditability and acceptance was contested by opposing counsel. Their testimony was alternately elicited under the careful guidance and systematic interrogation of a skilled advocate and then subjected to the relentless searching and probing of an equally capable cross-examiner. The rules of evidence, predicated on centuries of Anglo-American jurisprudence, were strictly invoked to exclude and cull out irrelevant matters. The examination and cross-examination of some witnesses was completed in a matter of hours. Others testified for a day or more. The net effect of this painstaking, time-consuming inquiry was a full and complete exposition of the opposing contentions of experts, enabling the court to evaluate the issue at hand with a broad perspective.

"Thereafter the attorneys argued the merits of their respective positions with art and determination and submitted comprehensive supporting briefs to me. I also had available a complete transcript of all the evidence. Then, and only then, solely upon the evidence received by me and the reasonable inferences to be drawn from it, I was required to render my judgment on the issues raised by the defendants' motions to dismiss. To the best of my knowledge, this was the first time that so extensive a judicial hearing had been conducted anywhere on this subject. To me, after long deliberation on the evidence and the applicable law, the conclusion was inescapable. Marijuana, *on the basis of what is now known and understood*, is a harmful and dangerous drug. As a consequence, I ruled that the Narcotic Drug Act as applied to the facts of the case before me was a valid exercise of the state's police power.

"Recently, Dr. John C. Ball, an eminent professor in the Department of Psychiatry at Temple University, wrote to me, 'Since appearing in your Court as the last expert witness in the case of *Commonwealth v. Leis and Weiss*, I have often thought about the issues involved and wondered about your personal opinion on the subject. It is a pleasure to learn that it will soon be forthcoming.'

"This is more than lingering curiosity. Dr. Ball's incisive and analytical comment recognizes the fact that my conclusions in the *Leis* case were necessarily restricted to the admissible evidence and by the legal issues then before me. He now indicates an interest in my *personal* views divorced from legal technicalities. This is, I feel, a proper forum to express my views.

"Here, I am not subject to the restraints imposed upon me by the formal proceedings of the *Leis* case. I am free to call upon my total experience as a judge and information derived from other sources in expressing my personal views on the dangers of marijuana and on the wisdom of our present approaches to it. I might add parenthetically, however, that nothing in these other experiences causes me to have any doubts about the validity and propriety of my decision.

"As I indicated earlier, my contact with marijuana is not limited to this single case. It is my practice, whenever compatible with the discharge of my administrative duties, to preside over the First Criminal Session in Suffolk County. Unlike the *Leis* case the great bulk of the business there goes unnoticed. This is the Superior Court session where indictments are returned by the Grand Jury, arraignments held, pretrial motions heard and pleas received. In the case of a guilty plea, sentence is imposed there; and in the event of a not guilty plea, the case is thereupon assigned to another session for trial before another judge. In addition, the judge presiding in the First Session frequently presides over appeals of findings of juvenile delinquency in the lower courts and the commitment of persons to mental institutions for observation or treatment as narcotic addicts or sexually dangerous persons.

"In each case, after receiving a plea of guilty and before imposing sentence, I am required to examine the record compiled by our probation department on every defendant and the circumstances surrounding the commission of each offense. This process includes a survey of the defendant's prior criminal record, if any, reports prepared by the arresting officer, probation officers and possibly correctional officials, parole officers and psychiatrists concerning his family background, educational achievements, employment history, military experience, religious training and an evaluation of his current mental and physical condition, personality and attitudes. In most instances, it also involves the reception of testimony from witnesses and police officers and an in-court interrogation of the defendant himself. Only then can I determine the disposition most beneficial to the defendant and to society.

"This daily observation of the pathetically tragic experience of others over half a decade has, I believe, given me a background of first-hand knowledge and an insight sufficient to form valid opinions on the narcotic problem *as it is* and as it relates to criminal activity.

"AREAS OF AGREEMENT

"There are certain important areas on which there is no substantial controversy among reputable and informed authorities.

"First, marijuana is universally recognized as a mind-altering drug which in varying degrees and with unpredictable effect produces a state of intoxication sometimes referred to as 'euphoria.'

"Second, in the United States marijuana is customarily used for the explicit purpose of inducing this state of intoxication.

"Third, in varying degrees this state of intoxication can cause a lessening of psychomotor coordination and a distortion of the ability to perceive time, distance and space. However, there is usually no interrelated diminution of muscular strength.

"Fourth, the habitual use of marijuana is particularly prevalent among individuals with marginal personalities exhibiting feelings of inadequacy, anxiety, disaffiliation, alienation and frustration or suffering from neuroses, psychoses or other mental disorders. Such persons constitute a significant percent of our population, and it is precisely among this type of individual that marijuana may cause psychological dependence.

"Fifth, marijuana may have a disinhibiting effect upon the user which tends to aggravate or exaggerate his pre-existing mental state or disposition. Thus, its effects can vary with individuals and can vary during different occasions of use by the same individual.

"Sixth, marijuana has no accepted medical use in modern medicine and serves no useful purpose in any other way.

"Seventh, the use of marijuana is not part of the dogma of any recognized Western religion.

"Eighth, marijuana has had a growing attraction for the young and the adolescent.

"Last, but probably most significant, no one can guarantee with any degree of certainty that continued use of marijuana will not eventually cause permanent physical injury. Incidentally, none of the witnesses, including those for the defense, in the *Leis* case advocated its use.

"Again, it must be emphasized that *on the basis of these*

areas of agreement alone it should be obvious that marijuana is a dangerous drug possessing a potential of harm both to the user and society *irrespective* of any other disputed qualities or unproven attributes.

"DISPUTED AREAS

"Why, then, if there is general agreement on these properties of marijuana, do we find ourselves in the midst of a social debate? I contend that, within any realistic meaning of the word, there is no substantial or rational debate about the *harmfulness* of marijuana.

"There is a great deal of ignorance and misunderstanding about the effects of marijuana. There are irrelevant comparisons of it to alcohol, nicotine and heroin. There are numerous persons who seek to justify or rationalize their involvement with marijuana or other drugs. There are also others who exploit the drug cult for purposes of notoriety, publicity, protest or profit. The net impact of such theories and positions serves to foster a distorted image of marijuana among the curious or the gullible.

"One oft repeated contention is, absent positive scientific proof that marijuana *invariably* leads to criminal activity, permanent physical injury and use of hard core drugs, it is no worse than alcohol or tobacco and, therefore, should be regulated rather than prohibited.

"The marijuana debate often bogs down because of semantic arguments and rigid preconceptions, especially in the areas where *scientific* proof is unavailable. If the word "harmful" is defined to mean permanent organic injury, addiction to heroin or the occurrence of criminal activity, then the debaters have, by their own terms, made *any* debate futile. Manifestly, the word 'harmful' is legitimately subject to a much broader interpretation, and apart from any such artificially limited concept, marijuana has been shown to be harmful. Furthermore, since the debaters are often trained in different disciplines, they frequently tend to resort to the jargon of their own technology. By so doing, they not only talk past one another, but unfortunately provide mighty-sounding phrases which, when taken out of context, serve to compound the problem by further misleading the uninitiated and unsophisticated.

"I have already outlined significant points upon which there is no substantial disagreement. There are other areas where we do encounter some measure of disagreement and where scientific proof is lacking. Basically, they constitute three issues:

1. Does marijuana cause physical injury as opposed to functional harm?
2. Does its use lead to addiction to hard core drugs?
3. Does its use cause crime?

"None of these questions can be answered with the scientific proof presently available.

"By taking each of these points in the abstract and strictly applying the *scientific* concept of efficient causality, the use of marijuana has not yet been shown to lead *inevitably* and *invariably* to *physical* harm, the commission of crime or addiction. The first is subject to such proof eventually; the second and third, in my opinion, are not. Human activity cannot be so neatly and clinically dissected. A human act or condition cannot be easily attributed to one specific, discernible cause except on the mechanical level of reflex action. That marijuana does not *necessarily* cause these social evils *all of the time* in all cases does not entirely eliminate its causative or contributing influence in those instances where the sequence does occur. In many instances, I believe the use of marijuana does ultimately lead to physical harm, crime and hard core addiction and is a contributing factor, at least, in the wrecking of many promising careers and lives. The lack of precise, scientific proof does not sway my considered judgment based on what I have seen and heard in court.

"There is a regrettable tendency to minimize or even deny the dangers of marijuana because its use has not been proven *scientifically* to cause permanent, organic injury. But neither does heroin for that matter. The pivotal word here is 'proven.' Although in the *Leis* case some expert witnesses for the defense insisted that the answer to all three questions enumerated is in the negative, none of them would state unqualifiedly that marijuana is not harmful.

"The public is continually exposed to the results of 'scientific studies' concerning marijuana. Undoubtedly, some have added to our total knowledge and, therefore, serve a useful purpose. Others confuse and compound the problem, especially where the attendant publicity presents a distorted or incomplete picture. In my view, the reporting of the recent study, 'Clinical and Psychological Effects of Marijuana in Man' falls in this category. Some of the news media and other publications reported one aspect of the study by headlining, 'Marijuana is found to be a mild intoxicant.' The impact of emphasizing the word 'mild' on young marijuana users or potential users, particularly where the investigation was conducted at a large university, must have been great indeed.

"It is tragic that such publicity places a potent weapon in the hands of those who seek to legalize the sale of marijuana. It serves also to encourage its use—especially by the adolescent and the submarginal person with underlying personality disorders.

"The study itself, published in 162 *Science*, 1234 (Dec. 13, 1968), is flawed in several other respects. It purports to be directed at 'acute marihuana intoxication in human subjects' and is described by its authors as:

'. . . the first attempt to collect basic clinical and psychological information on the drug by observing its effect on marihuana-naive human subjects in a *neutral laboratory setting.*'

"The basic inconsistency in the entire approach of the study is most clearly seen by considering the goals of the study in light of the reality of the situation. The implicit goals, i.e. to carefully and in detail analyze the 'American experience' with marijuana, are certainly not fulfilled in the sterile atmosphere of a laboratory. By the scientists' own admission,

'. . . All indications are that the form of marihuana intoxication is particularly dependent on the interaction of *drug, set, and setting.*'

Despite this realization, the experiments were performed in such manner that,

'Greatest effort was made to create a neutral setting. That is, subjects were made comfortable and secure in a pleasant suite of laboratories and offices, but the experimental staff carefully avoided encouraging any person to have an enjoyable experience.'

"The scientists criticize other studies for their use of 'psychedelic' environments and suggestive questions. However, these factors which influence a positive response to marijuana seem more consonant with the American experience than 'strict adherence . . . to a prearranged set of conventions.'

"The validity of a 'neutral' environment is further debased by Result #2. Here, the authors state that the eight chronic users became "high" but nine naive subjects did not, except for one who expressed a desire to get 'high.'

"Various other weaknesses in the study are admitted, although the significance of these weaknesses cannot be determined until future studies are completed. A sample of tobacco-smoking males who admitted their desire to smoke marijuana seems patently 'non-neutral.' The age of the participants is not truly representative, but even more significant is the relatively minute size of the sample. Employing chronic users as rating machines does not appear to be the most scientific measuring device.

"Perhaps the statement most likely to be misunderstood and to cause controversy is found in the discussion section:

' . . . we would like to comment on the fact that marijuana appears to be a relatively mild intoxicant in our studies.'

"This highly qualified statement, read out of context, without recognizing the limitations of the whole experiment, is greatly misleading. The word 'relatively' is used loosely, no indication being given as to the nature of the relationship. It is certainly true that the naive subjects were mildly intoxicated; however, the 'chronic users'

' . . . became "high" by their own accounts and in the judgment of experimenters who had observed many persons under the influence of marihuana.'

This statement minimizing the effects of marijuana should at least be expressly limited to naive subjects tested under clinical circumstances.

"It is questionable whether a neutral setting can truly measure marijuana-induced responses in a realistic and helpful manner. The study may, however, be of value, even considering its inherent weaknesses, so far as it establishes certain physical facts concerning pupil dilation, heartbeat, and blood sugar content. Even these findings, however, must be used cautiously until they are confirmed by 'field' study. The scientists were certainly correct in calling their experiments 'pilot.'

"Further serious and unresolved questions are apparent from the following excerpt from the study.

'Our finding that subjects who were naive to marihuana did not become subjectively "high" after a high dose of marihuana in a neutral setting is interesting when contrasted with the response of regular users who consistently reported and exhibited highs. It agrees with the reports of chronic users that many, if not most, people do not become high on their first exposure to marihuana even if they smoke it correctly. This puzzling phenomenon can be discussed from either a physiological or psychosocial point of view. Neither interpretation is entirely satisfactory. The physiological hypothesis suggests that getting high on marihuana occurs only after some sort of pharmacological sensitization takes place. The psychosocial interpretation is that repeated exposure to marihuana reduces psychological inhibition, as part of, or as the result of a learning process.'

"Of much significance is their finding that:

'The researcher who sets out with prior conviction that hemp is psychotomimetic or a "mild hallucinogen" is likely to confirm his conviction experimentally, but he would probably confirm the opposite hypothesis if his bias were in the opposite direction.'

"Physical Addiction vs Psychological Dependence

"The issue of addiction raises two completely distinct questions:

1. Does the repeated use of marijuana lead to addiction to more potent drugs?

2. Can a person become addicted to marijuana itself?

"I have previously indicated that in my view these questions, like that of physical harm, are not yet susceptible to *scientific* proof. As a matter of fact, the existence of persons who have used marijuana and have *not* gone on to experimentation with or addiction to more potent drugs is living proof that these results do not *necessarily* follow the use of marijuana. By the same token, alcoholism does not *inevitably* result from drinking, nor lung cancer from smoking, but we recognize the dangers inherent in those habits. Our Supreme Judicial Court has recognized that, '[t]he progression from marijuana to heroin or LSD is a frequent sequence.' Not automatic, but frequent. Words such as *'necessarily'* and *'inevitably'* point to the fallacy in this method of analysis. In effect, it again demands mathematical precision and I do not believe this is possible. Who can assure a youngster that he can use any of these drugs with safety?

"A study of 970 white, male drug addicts admitted to the Addiction Research Center at Lexington, Kentucky from sixteen states, including Massachusetts, disclosed that 764 of them, or nearly 80 percent, had prior histories of marijuana use. On the average, they were two years younger than other addicts at the time of their first arrest and were determined to be twice as likely to become heroin addicts as were nonusers of marijuana.

"A California study of 1,034 young adults arrested solely for marijuana use revealed that within five years nearly 13 percent had become involved with heroin, 11 to 13 percent with other dangerous drugs and another 50 percent were re-arrested for other nondrug offenses. Only 25 percent were not re-arrested during that period.

"Matthew M. O'Connor, supervising agent for the California Bureau of Narcotic Enforcement, conducted a 'back run' survey of a random sampling (5 percent) of heroin arrests in that state during 1967. Over 22 percent had been previously arrested on marijuana charges.

"Dr. Victor Vogel, chairman of the California Narcotics Addict Authority, determined that 95 percent of inmates released on parole after commitment for opiate addiction had first tried marijuana. Dr. Vogel is the first to point out that this figure does not mean 95 percent of marijuana users will eventually use heroin but unfortunately too many will.

"Despite the fact that these figures do not prove conclusively an automatic progression from marijuana to heroin, I can derive no sense of comfort and security from them. On the contrary, using the yardstick of probabilities, it would seem that a significant percentage of marijuana users do progress to hard core drugs. It is no more possible to determine in advance who will succumb to hard core drugs than it is to predict which of those who drink will become alcoholics or which cigarette smoker will develop lung cancer. Nonetheless, the danger is real and substantial.

"The following report was recently received by me with regard to a young defendant whom I ordered committed to a state hospital for observation. Of course, he must remain anonymous; but he typifies many cases which pass through the courts.

'This twenty year old white, single male was admitted . . . for examination to determine if he is a drug addict. Information volunteered by the patient elicits he has been a user of harmful drugs since the age of sixteen when he was introduced to marijuana by friends. He gradually progressed to the use of cough syrup with codeine, barbiturates and the intravenous use of amphetamines. In the past year subject was introduced to heroin and used it intermittently. He had also used LSD, mescaline, demerol, morphine, opium, dilaudid, pantapon and cocaine and indicates a preference for methedrine. . . . Diagnosis: Drug addiction.'

"I cannot in conscience and in the discharge of my office disregard the conclusions of reports such as this.

"The question of possible addiction to marijuana itself is
another matter entirely. If we restrict ourselves to the concept
of physical addiction characterized by the alteration of bodily
functions and the suffering of withdrawal symptoms upon cessa-
tion of drug use, then marijuana cannot be considered an
addictive drug. Yet, among knowledgeable scientists this definition of addiction is no longer considered determinative. The
extent of recidivism among narcotics addicts who have broken
the hold of physical addiction emphasizes that the basic problem
lies much deeper than physical addiction. Accordingly, most
scientists now subscribe to the World Health Organization's
definition of 'drug dependence,' which eliminates some of the
previous hairsplitting between 'habituation' and 'addiction.'
'Drug dependence' is defined as 'a state of psychic or physical
dependence, or both, arising in a person following administration of that drug on a periodic or continuous basis.[28]

> '[P]sychic dependence can and does develop . . . without
> any evidence of physical dependence. . . . Physical depen-
> dence, too, can be induced without notable psychic de-
> pendence. . . . Psychic dependence . . . is more parti-
> cularly a manifestation of the individual's reaction to the
> effects of a specific drug and varies with the individual
> as well as with the drug.'

"Dr. Benjamin Kissin, director of the Downstate Alcoholism
Division in New York, writes, 'Marijuana can cause a state of
"psychic dependence" which may be stronger than physical addiction. It may result in the most intensive craving and perpetuation of chronic abuse. Simply because it doesn't cause
physical dependence, does not mean that it is not "addictive."
Continuation of use tends to become chronic.'

"Since the World Health Organization lists marijuana as
one of the drugs capable of inducing 'psychic dependence,' it is

[28] Drug Dependence; Its Significance and Characteristics, Bull. Wld.
Hlth. Org., 1965, 32, 721-733.

critical to ascertain among what personality types such dependence—which is as real as addiction—may occur.

"The American Medical Association in 'The Crutch That Cripples,' has remarked that '[t]he roots of such dependence lie within the individual, but the drug feeds these roots and makes them grow. . . . Most chronic drug abusers are dependent personalities, who feel insecure and inferior, and may start out on marijuana, but find that it does not blot out their emotional pain, so they turn to heroin.'

"Dr. Henry Brill, vice chairman of the New York State Narcotic Addiction Board, has observed that taking marijuana is a sign of psychiatric instability or problems and then, having taken it, there is a tendency for those problems to be aggravated. There is, according to him, a tendency to relapse with the individual throughout his life in psychological dependence.

"A study at the Bellevue Psychiatric Hospital in New York disclosed that the '[u]se of marijuana is disproportionately higher among unstable persons or those with established psychiatric records than among those without these characteristics.'

"As we witness the seepage of marijuana smoking down through our society and educational system to a point where it now enters the junior high schools, we would have to be totally insensitive not to be alarmed.

"In the light of these observations, whether the use of marijuana can become addictive in the physical sense is, for all practical purposes, an irrelevant abstraction totally divorced from the established fact of its harmfulness and dangerousness. Furthermore, given the character of those who habitually use marijuana and develop a psychological dependence on it, its involvement with other criminal and anti-social activity is more readily appreciated."

Those who feel that the official position toward marijuana use by individuals should be tolerant, (almost the same as the official position toward cigarette smoking or at least the use of alcohol), frequently base their argument on the sincere conviction that unless we do maintain a non-repressive official

attitude in this whole area of behavior, a greater degree of
alienation will take place among large groups within the young
population and, as a result, great damage could accrue to the
legal system itself; also, individuals may argue that they are
convinced that there has been no effective rebuttal to the
argument that marijuana use is in fact "harmless."

§ 10.5　Scope of drug abuse

The concerns expressed are particularly relevant at a time
when we are concerned with the typologies of drug abusing
juvenile offenders.

For all too long in this country we have taken comfort in
believing that drug addiction was strictly just another symptom
of the old disease of social, economic and emotional deprivation. It is true that there are still many drug abusers and drug
addicts who are members of the severely deprived sections of
our communities, especially the ghettoes; but there are many
others outside of the ghetto areas also.

Historically drug abuse presented a convenient way for
certain antisocial personalities, especially the sociopathic type,
to resist the accepted norms of society, and today we continue to
see drug abuse flourish among this group.

Also, some emotionally unstable and severely disturbed
youngsters who have always had a great deal of difficulty in
channeling their various drives into acceptable pursuits have
traditionally found recourse to drugs an avenue of escape,
and this pattern continues to endure.

Many inadequate personalities, attempting to escape their
problems and daily frustrations, continue to abuse drugs in one
form or another, just as they have at other times during the
history of narcotics abuse, and so they present no new phenomenon either.

The late sixties and early seventies showed us the shift of
drug abuse, including the use of hard narcotics. Now, at this
particular point in history, this trend has continued and solidi-
fied itself so extensively that drug abuse in general, and marijuana in particular, is "institutionalized" and receives great

peer support at practically every level of society.

It would seem that juvenile drug abuse has "leveled off" during about the last two years and now after having seen a period of about ten years during which it increased dramatically, the number of juvenile users appears to be stabilized. But lest we confuse the word "stabilized" with the phrase "under control," we must note emphatically that the current level implies that over half of all high school seniors have in fact used some illicit drug at least once and about one-third are using at least one drug regularly. At the same time, the cost of drug abuse to our society in terms of the crime required to support the habit and even to support occasional use by those who cannot afford such experimentation, the medical treatment, the lost man-hours of work, and the cost of criminal prosecution and the jails and institutions, currently amounts to over ten billion dollars per year (with heroin addiction accounting for well over half of that total).

Heightened adolescent anxiety complicated by the increasing pressures of complex urban living, alienation from or disillusion with family and traditional groups, rampant insecurity heightened by a sense of imminent nationwide or worldwide disaster, the gnawing feeling of being unwanted, useless or out of place; diminution of parental authority, and overt challenges to traditional morality; frustrations and disenchantment resulting from war, national problems and international policies; or a desire to escape the responsibility and boredom of the day-to-day business of living; any or all of these factors seem to be involved in pushing narcotics into the lives of our youngsters much more quickly and emphatically than all of the more traditionally identified and loathed "pushers" ever dreamed possible.

Consequently, all persons who are concerned with young people feel a great urgency to reach an understanding of their problems and give them the needed support. For the enforcement official this means that efforts to curtail supply and eliminate sources are still important, but that community education at all levels and effective dialogue with youth must be established and emphasized.

The greatest single deterrent to drug abuse at this time, in our opinion, is anything that will help to give meaning and orientation to the present, and hope and motivation for the future to our youngsters. As was said before in this volume, values and attitudes determine behavior; and unless we reach these underlying causal areas, control of the surface problems is difficult, if not impossible.

More and more the drug picture tells us graphically that the young are rejecting our values and standards; and it is tragic that many of us are not yet willing to recognize that we must change our own approach to their problems if we are to be accepted by them. Enforcement and control of sources are certainly important, as is education and community awareness, but it seems that self-evaluation and real involvement with the issues as a greater number of youngsters present them to us, present the greatest challenge to our professionality and our dedication.

APPLICATION OF IMPORTANT POINTS EMPHASIZED FOR LAW ENFORCEMENT OFFICERS

1. Drug abuse in all its various forms is an intimate part of the current life of young people and it takes on changing appearances from place to place and time to time. What is most popular today changes to something else tomorrow; the most frequent abuse in one town or on one campus is different somewhere else; but the overall problem remains always present.

2. With the exception of marijuana use, which continues to grow rapidly among the young population, drug abuse in general has seemed to stabilize to some extent during the last two-year period.

3. Narcotics abuse is seen as an acceptable practice among large segments of the youth group, and there is no stigma attached to the habit. In fact, in many groups there is a high status rating connected with drug abuse.

4. Typical stereotypes of the user and the pusher certainly no longer apply to many young abusers. Many appear normal and well adjusted, and many sell to each other, just as youngsters formerly exchanged clothes or sold legitimate items within the intimacy of the group.

5. Drug abuse has taken on so many forms, and it is practiced by so many for widely different reasons, that there is no typical drug-abuser. Depending on who he is, what he is using, and why he is so

doing, some individual diagnosis can be made, but generalizations seem futile.

6. Some abused drugs do cause physical addiction, and some do not. Among those which do not, there are still severe physical problems associated with chronic abuse in many cases. The officer should be aware of the need for medical assistance when encountering toxic reactions, acute withdrawal syndrome, and other medical problems resulting from drug abuse.

7. "Mood swings," deterioration in judgment and behavior aberrations are usually encountered in dealing with youthful drug abuses and the skilled officer is aware of how to handle the problems related to these.

8. Symptoms of barbiturate intoxication so closely resemble an alcoholic state that the officer must be aware of the problems this presents. Severe illness and even death can easily result if this situation is not handled properly by competent medical personnel.

9. The effects on behavior, and the danger to mind and body of each drug differ, and the competent officer needs to acquaint himself thoroughly with these matters, because of the frequency of encounter with drug abusers in the current society, and because of the dangers which can easily result in many cases from mishandling of the real problem.

10. The behavior and life-style of many drug-abusing youngsters violates the sensibilities and is repugnant to the value system of the enforcement officer. It requires a high degree of professionality to deal objectively with persons in such circumstances, and yet this must be done if the effectiveness of the officer is not to be minimized completely.

Chapter 11

THE ROLE OF ALCOHOL IN DELINQUENCY

§ 11.1   Legal control of use of alcoholic beverages

In discussing the influence of alcohol on juvenile delinquency, it is important to keep in mind some general notions about the efforts of society to control the use of alcohol at all levels, and especially as it relates to juveniles.

First of all, history and a survey of current practice, indicate that all societies have found it necessary to attempt to control the use of alcoholic beverages in some way. The most obvious explanation for this is that alcohol is one of the oldest, most easily available, most widespread in its use, and the cheapest of all the forms of narcotics.

Secondly, alcoholic beverages exist and have been used, at least by some, illegally or legally, throughout the entire world and during most of history. This can be verified by most international travelers and in the writings of most historians.

The efforts to contain or control the use of alcoholic beverages seem to be based on an almost universal desire to maintain an orderly use, increase the chances of a pleasurable experience and reduce the chances of disorder or painful experiences.

In the United States, several of the states make it illegal for a juvenile to consume alcoholic beverages; in other states the law is not so specific as to prohibit consumption by juveniles. However, in practically all jurisdictions, it has been declared illegal for a juvenile to purchase (and in some jurisdictions to receive in any other way) alcoholic beverages.

These laws differ widely from state to state and in the various municipal codes. Because of the widely differing cul-

185

tural and ethnic backgrounds within jurisdictions, the problem of the legal control of consumption and purchase of alcoholic beverages seems best handled at the local level.

§ 11.2   Education on effects of misuse of alcoholic beverages

As is true in the case of all social problems, prevention is preferable to punishment for violation. Therefore, programs using parents and other adults to teach the benefits of moderation in the use are most effective to control the problem of misuse of alcohol in America.

Five studies from five separate geographic areas involving almost 8,000 adolescents completed about ten years ago told us dramatically that at that time:

1. Average age for first drink is 13-14 years (although tasting may have occurred before).
2. Place of first drink is usually at home.
3. Practically all have experimented with drinking before graduating from high school.
4. One in four reported having been "high" in the month before interview.
5. One in ten reported having been drunk in the month before interview.
6. Beer was by far the most common beverage used.
7. Laws had little relation to the actual drinking practices.[1]

Today, the National Institute on Alcohol Abuse and Alcoholism estimated that 1.3 million boys and girls between the ages of 12 and 17 have serious drinking problems, not to mention the fact that 60% of those killed in automobile accidents involving drunken driving are adolescents.

The same source also states that about 10% of American teenagers can be categorized as "heavy drinkers," and even more unfortunately, about 25% of American teenagers do at

[1] George L. Maddox, "Teenage Drinking in the United States" in Pittman & Snyder, *Society, Culture and Drinking Patterns* quoted in "Alcohol and Alcoholism," Public Health Service, Publication #1640, U.S. Dept. of HEW, Washington, D.C., (1968), p. 15.

some time experience personal problems as a consequence of their drinking. The horrendous increase in youthful drinking, coupled with the lowering of the age level and the tremendous increase in the number of girls drinking at an early age presents great cause for alarm to all those who are genuinely concerned about American youth. A recent California study showed that boys using alcohol more than fifty times per year had doubled since 1970 while at the same time the same rate for girls had tripled.[2]

Similarly, Dr. Ernest Noble, Director of the National Institute of Alcohol Abuse and Alcoholism, informed the same Senate Sub-committee that the incidence of drinking among high school aged girls in California had risen from 25% in the late 1960's to 69% in 1974, which was the same level reported for boys at that time.[3]

And recently Dr. Patricia O'Gorman, Director of the National Council on Alcoholism, Department of Prevention and Education, stated alarmingly: "Girls' drinking patterns are becoming more like boys'. We used to think that a girl didn't drink unless she was on a date and a boy twisted her arm. Now girls get together in groups without boys to drink. Everybody is starting to drink at a younger age. Twelve or thirteen now has become the age where large groups of adolescents begin to drink on their own."[4]

Programs of widespread community education as to the harmful effects of over-indulgence and the dangers of performing certain functions, such as driving, while under the influence of alcohol, should have priority in any successful campaign.

Many communities have found efforts to educate vendors as to the role they can play in properly controlling the sale of such beverages to irresponsible individuals have met with some success.

[2] Reported in an address by William Hathaway, Chairman of the Senate Subcommittee on Alcoholism and Narcotics, reported in "Youth Alternatives" Vol. 3, No. 11, Washington, D.C., November, 1976.

[3] Ibid.

[4] Quoted in *Alcoholism and Alcohol Education,* Vol. 6, No. 10, July 27, 1977.

Education of youngsters in the school system and through other agencies, along with safety programs and health education, also seems to hold promise of some effectiveness in achieving control.

Uniform and proper enforcement of the various codes, both within the legal framework and the alcoholic beverage industry, can be an effective aid.

§ 11.3   Extent of problem drinking and physical effects

All of the above mentioned efforts can accomplish much, and all are underway to some extent in many areas, but this country continues to witness an increasing consumption of alcoholic beverages, and a staggering rise in the number of problem drinkers. While in past years many have estimated that we have about five million alcohol-abusing persons in this country, more recent statistics seem to indicate that that number might be approaching ten to twenty million.

In the very recent past, at least one source of information concerning problem drinking in this country estimated that we are currently approaching the point where we have about twenty million problem drinkers.[5] It is also currently estimated that there are about as many as 100 million Americans who are making some use of alcoholic beverages.[6] Most unfortunately, of this number at least 1.3 million are adolescents who are recognized as being problem drinkers, and most sources agree that the "great majority" of American teenagers have at least experimented with alcohol use.

The problem of alcohol abuse as a public health problem seems to have been neglected because of a tremendous amount of misunderstanding about the meaning of "problem drinking," and a great deal of emotionalism surrounding the problem drinker. Many have taken comfort in the belief that only the "skid-row" type individual has been properly presented as the alcoholic type; but this is manifestly untrue, and most recent studies seem to indicate that alcohol abuse is becoming a more

---

[5] "Alcohol and Alcoholism," ibid, p. 10.   [6] Ibid, p. 9.

prevalent problem among the highly educated, the ranks of the junior executive, and others higher on the socio-economic scale. The presence of heavy drinking in suburbia has been noted by many observers.

From an enforcement standpoint it was estimated in 1965 that alcohol-related offenses comprise about 45% of all arrests in America.[7] In one large metropolitan area in 1970, it was estimated that the population of the local jail and workhouse is composed of about 40% directly alcohol-connected offenders, and that when one includes those offenses involving family abuse, disorderly conduct and other indirectly alcohol-related offenses, the percentage of inmates in those correctional facilities rises to as high as 55%.[8] There are probably some jurisdictions where as high as 70% of all police time is consumed in alcohol-related matters.

In attempting to explain the dynamics of problem drinking, every conceivable explanation has been offered historically by a wide variety of academic disciplines. The moralists have seen it as caused by sin; the biochemist has spoken of potential defects of a biochemical nature in physical organisms, such as the liver or the brain; sociologists have from time to time explored alcoholism as antisocial behavior; and by legislation (and perhaps by default in many cases) it has been inherited as a problem for enforcement officials because it has been declared a crime.

Many attempts have been made to isolate and identify the "alcoholic personality." This type has been described as passive, dependent, egocentric, and sexually immature. However, such description seems to fit more accurately the personality of the alcoholic after chronic involvement with alcohol abuse has taken its toll. It seems that these descriptive phrases are applied much more accurately as the results, rather than conditions found within the personality of the person before he is involved in long-term alcohol abuse.

The experience of those working in detoxification units,

---

[7] "Uniform Crime Reports for the U. S., 1965," FBI, Department of Justice, Washington, D. C., (1966).

[8] Conversation with the chief caseworker, Cincinnati Workhouse, November 12, 1970.

alcoholism clinics, and other agencies working directly with a large number of persons with alcohol problems, seems to indicate that there are as many types of personalities who become involved in alcohol abuse as there are in any other kind of deviant behavior. More and more, current professional opinion agrees that there is no "alcoholic type;" but there are certain characteristics that the personality tends to take on after long periods of alcoholic abuse.

Just from a standpoint of the number of persons involved in problem drinking in this country alone, it would seem inaccurate to defend the position that there is one particular personality disorder common to from 5 to 20 million Americans that has led them to develop problem drinking as the primary symptom of their condition. With the amount of acceptance within our general culture surrounding the use of alcohol, especially in times of stress, the use of alcohol in excess very easily becomes the symptom of a breakdown in controls for a wide variety of personality problems and character disorders.

Unfortunately, the general population and many professionals in the past, have tended to place all alcoholics in the same category just as we have placed the homosexual offenders into one large group, which we then consider to be a particular personality and character type; we then use the alcoholism or the homosexuality to explain all other ingredients of personality and all manifestations of behavior disorders, no matter how varied or dissimilar they may be. This has been costly to us because it prevents proper understanding and appropriate treatment of such offenders.

§ 11.4   Recognition and treatment of juvenile offenders

As we attempt to understand the problem of the juvenile alcohol abuser, it is important that we keep in mind that youngsters turn to alcohol for all of the many reasons for which adults make the same choice; they also frequently have their motivation complicated by attitudes of adolescent rebellion, thrill seeking, value confusion and a desire to drop out of the mainstream of the dominant culture.

For many years, it was not recognized that the "skid-row"

type really does not drink as much as many members of the middle and upper middle class; nor did we properly understand that many of this "skid-row" type were not addicted to alcohol, but simply were using alcohol and the resulting arrest for alcohol abuse as the "tools" to remain in, and show their addiction to a sub-cultural style of life.

Today, as we recognize that the age level of the "skid-row" type is becoming increasingly younger, and as we see countless youngsters throughout the big cities of America adopting the life styles of the society dropout, it is imperative that we understand the social, cultural and ecological causal factors operating in the dynamics of the teenage alcoholic, as much as we need to recognize these same causal factors in the teenage narcotic addict.

Alcohol abuse as a sign of "dropping out" of the cultural mainstream is increasing at an alarming rate. At the same time, the more affluent sections of our society seem to be condoning, and making readily available, much greater use of alcoholic beverages to the young. As a result, hospital admissions for acute and even chronic alcoholism keep reflecting a greater lowering of the age level; at the same time, arrest records show shocking increases in alcohol-related offenses of large numbers of youngsters outside of the socio-economically deprived group.

For the police officers, and for a variety of court intake and detention personnel who see youngsters shortly after the time of their arrest, it is becoming increasingly important to recognize the symptomology of "acute alcohol withdrawal," and to be able to distinguish this condition from some of the states induced by the use of barbiturates, hallucinogens and other mind altering narcotics.

In the classic case of delirium tremens one normally finds psychomotor agitation (shakes, high blood pressure, etc.), hallucinations (audio-visual, tactile, and of a very frightening or threatening type), disorientation as to time, place, etc., perhaps delirium and/or amnesia, and seizure activity (whether grand mal, petit mal, bizarre, etc.).

It is also important to remember that in today's youth culture, excessive use of alcohol is often accompanied by "garden variety" pill-taking or the use of some form of narcotic. This phenomenon makes diagnosis and treatment complicated at many times, and even detection of juvenile alcohol abuse is difficult because while most adults drink leisurely, openly, and in familiar comfortable surroundings, most teenagers' drinking tends to take place quickly, in hidden places, often in automobiles, and generally in circumstances which makes detection extremely difficult.

It is of the utmost importance to understand that acute alcoholism is often accompanied with other complicating physical conditions brought on by the life style of the person during the weeks or months of heavy drinking. Malnutrition, the effects of exposure to the elements and to very unsanitary living conditions, and numerous types of infections are often part of the physical picture of the alcoholic at the time he is first seen by enforcement officials or court personnel.

Consequently, effective treatment in such cases calls for providing good medical management, including sedation if the symptoms are acute; restoration of the fluid and other chemical bodily balances; the use of antibiotics to control undiagnosed infection, and anticonvulsants to prevent or control seizures if indicated, and to assist in restoring chemical balance. These are medical functions and, consequently, require proper medical staff for their administration. The neglect of such important needs at a crucial time could result in severe illness and even death. This should be remembered in those settings where the only treatment of the acute alcoholic problem is to place him in the "tank" until he "dries out."

After proper medical care for the physical problems, good psycho-social services are necessary, including individual and group therapy and counseling for the purposes of assistance with problem-solving, encouragement in attempting to overcome the addiction, in order to re-educate the person to be able to more properly adjust to pressures. The use of professional staff, the clergy, interested lay groups (such as Alcoholics Anonymous), and the focusing of many community resources are required if such a program is to really assist the severely addicted alcoholic in achieving success in his battle to overcome this habit.

In summary, it is necessary to re-emphasize that alcoholism and alcohol-abuse among the young is not caused by any one factor, but like so many behavior problems, it has its root in both the environment and the personality of the offender. In its acute form, it must be treated with good medical management because there are very serious physical problems involved. However, it is not only an illness of the body. There are numerous mental, emotional and environmental factors involved in the causal picture, and so a wide range of psycho-social services are necessary in support of the treatment program.

APPLICATION OF IMPORTANT POINTS EMPHASIZED FOR LAW ENFORCEMENT OFFICERS

1. Alcohol is a narcotic and its easy availability and widespread acceptance make it particularly a problem for youngsters.

2. Laws governing alcohol consumption and sale differ widely in various jurisdictions, and drinking patterns also differ widely based upon ethnicity, religion, etc., but all areas seem to recognize need to control the use of alcohol by juveniles.

3. Education of vendors, the adult community and the youth group, when combined with uniform enforcement practices, seem to help in controlling juvenile alcohol abuse.

4. Alcohol abuse is not confined to socio-economically deprived areas, but is a large problem among the more affluent and better educated portions of the population.

5. The causes of alcohol abuse, like most problem behavior, are multiple, and there is a great variety of personality types represented in the alcohol-abusing population.

6. Alcohol abuse is frequently associated with problems of life-style and alienation.

7. Acute alcohol withdrawal symptoms are a medical problem, and should be recognized and treated as such.

8. Officers should be alerted to the medical problems presented by the practice of youngsters ingesting pills of various kinds while consuming alcohol.

9. Alcohol-related problems consume so much valuable police time that enforcement officials should be leaders in attempting to secure

adequate treatment of offenders through provision of proper professional care and establishment of detoxification centers.

10. Simple arrest and jailing, repeated court appearances, and threats, scorn and ridicule can never be therapeutic in a condition where there are severe medical and/or psycho-social problems existing at the causal level.

Chapter 12

JUVENILE SEX OFFENDERS

Section
12.1 Sexual development of child and factors in adolescent sex behavior
12.2 Distinguishing between normal and abnormal sex behavior in juveniles

§ 12.1 Sexual development of child and factors in adolescent sex behavior

The sex drive, one of the most potent and intense of all instinctual motivating forces of behavior, is especially important in understanding adolescent behavior. Deeply rooted in human biology, the physiological nature of the sex drive is quite obvious; but it is equally true that the psychological needs which the sex drive embraces are of equal importance.

Opinions within the behavioral sciences differ concerning the exact steps with which the "sexual being" develops, or an exact time-table for psycho-sexual development. The simple fact that with the onset of puberty the physical sexual apparatus matures, and its full functions are available for use by the individual, is not enough information to enable us to understand the full scope of sexual behavior or the depth of the problems of adjustment which sexual maturation, or lack of it, presents to countless teenagers.

Sexual development, and the proper control of the functions and urges that go with it, must be understood along with the total picture of the physical, psychological, social and moral development of the youngster. Whether the observer accepts the full Freudian explanation of the stages of psycho-sexual development and the resulting problems created by the "Oedipus complex," "castration anxiety" and fixation at the various levels, or whether one more fully accepts the "learning theories" with their stress on environmental factors and transmitted attitudes, there seems to be abundant evidence, borne out by the experience of numerous investigators, that psycho-sexual development begins long before the onset of puberty.

195

The many questions of a sexual nature asked by children of the pre-school age or primary grades, the many studies which have continually indicated the presence of the practice of masturbation by youngsters in the earliest ages of childhood, the sexual nature of some childhood games, and many other indications point to sexual awakening long before puberty begins.

Combining the childhood interest in sex and the arrival of the physical capacity to engage in sexual activity in its fullest sense at the time of puberty, the dilemma created by contemporary society's demands that the gratification of such urges and the use of such physical abilities be prolonged until marriage, which in many sectors only takes place after the completion of many years of higher education, can easily be seen as creating many hazards and conflicts in the whole problem of sexual control by adolescents.

While this treatise is not intended to be an exhaustive consideration of the entire notion of psycho-sexual development, it is necessary to understand some of the problems connected with the change of a child from a relatively non-sexual to a sexual pattern of living, if we are to understand sexual behavior and its relationship to delinquency. It must also be remembered that psycho-sexuality does not commence with adolescence, but has been existing in a vague and generalized form throughout most of childhood; and it has existed to a greater or lesser degree dependent upon environmental factors surrounding the child in terms of the attitudes of "significant others" and the opportunities for sexual expression and possible seduction which have been present in his early life.

The awakening of sexual feelings, curiosity, fantasies and the desire to indulge the urges accompanying these, is part of the general developmental pattern which is not sudden or rigidly definable in the life of any individual, but which takes place gradually along with other developmental signs and patterns. The glands and other physical elements seem to come to the fullness of their development only after the psychological and emotional sexual awakening has already taken place in most children.

Even a casual observation of a large group of youngsters immediately makes evident the wide range chronologically at which varying degrees of physical sexual maturation takes place. The evolution of the psycho-sexual person requires an even wider range of age span than the physical because it seems to depend on so many factors not only inside the person, but on such outside elements as attitudes within the family, and the inhibitions and taboos of the larger culture. Consequently, our comments about sex and behavior are the same as our statements about behavior in general, and that is that it seems determined by a mixture of the biological, the physical, the psychological from within the person, and the environmental factors outside of the person, including familial and neighborhood influences, sub-cultural standards and the attitudes and general expectancy of the larger culture.

Just as all of these factors determine the makeup of the intellectual, social and emotional maturity of the individual, so they influence his sexual adjustment.

This is especially significant in understanding the sexual misconduct of many adolescents because, just as we see immature responses in many other areas of a youngster's life resulting in deviant behavior, so in his sexual misbehavior, we are often looking simply at sexual immaturity.

In analyzing any particular sex offense committed by an adolescent, we might well find that there has been a physical root for his problem associated, perhaps, with some childhood disease which has inhibited his physical development; or we might well find that unwholesome parental attitudes, or even seduction into sexual practice at an early age within the family itself, has taken place; or equally possible, and becoming ever more important, we might find that a physically normal child with a relatively normal childhood environment at the time of adolescence has simply been influenced by a prevalent philosophy in the general culture of "doing your own thing" or "expressing yourself" as this permissive philosophy tends to replace some of the older community demands for self-control.

We should not underestimate the importance of the ever-present seduction and temptation in the lives of youngsters through advertising, the movies, the readily available pornography, the mass media of communication, and the so-called "new morality."

The turbulence of the conflict which this presents was stated well in a recent article: "Still, putting down Hugh Hefner is not of much help in coping with our present stresses and no amount of enlightened perspective can argue away the anxiety that even a mental health professional may feel today when confronted with the depth, turbulence, and individual impact of the sexual upheaval that is part and parcel of a revolutionary period in human relationships. . . . What we appear to be wrestling with, in other words, at the individual end of the collective level, is the extent to which traditional monogomous and rigidly heterosexual behavior has been superseded by a more tolerant morality, whose tolerance genuinely reflects a lessened need for rigid taboos in the handling of interpersonal relationships, and the wrestle is not made any easier by the easily demonstrated facts that around the better motivated proponents of a new maturity and autonomy in the handling of one's sexual needs there orbits a fearsome array of pornographers and outright criminals, whose well-paid lawyers can zero in on a loophole in less time than it takes a hawk to spot a chicken."[1]

The increased stimulation provided by the widespread wearing of provocative clothing, and the ever-increasing knowledge of available contraceptives, occurring at the same time that the family has less control over whereabouts and behavior of children, and the fact that traditional morality is philosophically and practically challenged on every front, also contribute to increased control problems for youngsters in the sexual area.

The easy availability of the automobile as a means of transportation for young people, and the anonymity which results from being able to go to far away places or drive to secluded areas, is certainly of great importance in considering the patterns of adolescent sex behavior in contemporary society.

[1] "The New Sexual Morality," *Behavior Today*, Vol. 8, No. 32, August 22, 1977.

Also, greater availability of spending money in large amounts, and the ability consequently to purchase alcoholic beverages and narcotics, also needs to be considered in any examination of the total causal picture.

In looking at the kinds of juvenile offenses and the offenders so involved, it is necessary first of all to state that many young offenders whose only crime was having had sexual relations of a normal type with a girl of his own age or perhaps younger, who was physically mature and a very willing partner, primarily is delinquent and an "offender" only because of the fact of having been unlucky enough to be detected and apprehended by public authorities.

Such a couple are probably psychologically normal, and in the area of social adjustments, educational achievement and even their willingness to abide by the law in other areas, probably are functioning at a level equal to or perhaps even higher than many hundreds or thousands in a metropolitan area who conduct themselves the same way, but under circumstances which are not brought to the attention of law enforcement.

Typical of these cases are the youngsters who feel that they are "in love" and who choose a public park or a drive-in theatre or some other place for sexual activity where they are observed by a citizen who feels it is his duty to report their activity to the proper authorities. Many such situations are also called to the attention of law enforcement and the courts because of irate parents, family quarrels, or as a result of a disagreement between the young people.

The laws determining what constitutes a sex offense differ so greatly from society to society, and even from state to state and community to community within this country, that perhaps the only workable definition of sex offense is "any conduct of a sexual nature which is forbidden by law in a particular jurisdiction."

In a case tried not so long ago in a northern city, a probation officer recounted for this author the sad facts in a situation where a young woman was arrested under a municipal ordinance which forbade "sexual relations" under certain circumstances. The woman was brought to the attention of the authorities by a landlady who, under interrogation, admitted that she observed the girl's sexual activities by climbing a tree in the back yard of her home and looking into the window where the accused was in bed with her boy friend.

From a legal standpoint, the difference between a sex offender who is reported to the authorities and his peers who may have committed the same act can be the accident of discovery of the sexual behavior.

However, from a standpoint of interest in the general well-being of our young people, all those concerned about youth are greatly alarmed by the tremendous increase in the incidence of venereal disease among adolescents, which has been estimated to be approaching epidemic proportions in many large metropolitan areas in the past several years, and by the emotional and moral problems presented by sexual promiscuity.

The rising increase in teen-age marriage, of which it is estimated over one-half terminate in divorce within one year of the time of the consummation of the marriage, and the fact that the number of illegitimate births attributed to young mothers has risen to the point in this country where now forty percent of all illegitimate mothers are under nineteen years of age, are also matters of grave concern.

However, when we consider the fact that the tremendous amount of sexual promiscuity among the deprived persons in our ghetto areas has long been taken for granted as just another manifestation of cultural differences, "lower class focal concerns," and the pleasure-seeking behavior of persons who are desperate in their total life and environment, while at the same time we recognize the permissiveness and breakdown in traditional morality in the affluent segments of our society, this increase in sexual activity is not surprising.

§ 12.2   Distinguishing between normal and abnormal sex behavior in juveniles

Considering sex offenses related to heterosexual behavior, excepting the kinds of offenses mentioned above, there is only a very small percentage of adolescent offenders who become involved in violent sexual assaults or in the exploratory kind of behavior that leads an older teenage boy to perhaps tamper sexually with a much younger girl.

Law enforcement officials are often involved in complaints of statutory rape, or rape with consent, in which a person over the age of a juvenile in a particular jurisdiction has sexual relations with a youngster under juvenile age. No matter how willing or even seductive the victim may have been in many of these cases, parents and neighborhood groups are quite upset, and arrest and court action are indicated.

In looking at abnormal sex offenses, it is well to keep in mind that sexual behavior can be perverse or abnormal, for purposes of discussion, traditionally divided into two classes: (1) deviation in the manner in which relations are carried out; and (2) deviation in the selection of a sexual partner.

In the first case, the object is a member of the opposite sex, but normal intercourse is not the mode of sexual expression. Such offenses can include sodomy or acts of a sado-masochistic nature, etc. When these offenses involve children, often there is an adult committing an offense against a child, although childhood or adolescent deviance of such a type does occur.

In the "object perversions," the object of sexual gratification is not a member of the opposite sex. Such offenses can include all sorts of acts such as homosexuality, bestiality, fetishisms, etc. In homosexual acts there is often an adult involved with a juvenile, but often such acts involve only juveniles.

Exhibitionism, in which one obtains sexual pleasure from displaying genitals to others, usually a member of the opposite sex, quite often involve adolescent boys when a complaint of such type is received. Occasionally, these offenses are the result of a nonsexual set of circumstances such as "college hazing" where nudity is a part of the hazing, or where someone is not careful about urinating in a rather public place, but these are not to be considered truly exhibitionistic offenses. Exhibitionism in its true form sometimes involves teen-age boys with problems of real or imagined sexual inadequacy, high anxiety and confusion.

Voyeurism, commonly called the offense of "peeping,"

often is the result of an adolescent responding to intense sexual pressures, exploration or deeper psychological disturbance.

Since this is not intended to be a complete treatise of adolescent sexuality, in conclusion it should be stated emphatically that sex is an area of great concern to the adolescent and one which consumes much of his time and energy. The complexities of the process of sexual maturation are such that no two adolescents mature at exactly the same time or in exactly the same set of stages; nor do any two handle the problem in exactly the same way.

In cases of maladjustment, it must be remembered that the laws vary greatly from jurisdiction to jurisdiction, and that some things which are a crime in one area are not so considered in another. Also, the amount of control that is expected of an adolescent in dealing with his sexual impulses is determined heavily by family attitudes, cultural standards, and the amount of permissiveness and outright seduction present in the total environment.

In considering heterosexual offenses, there are many normal youngsters who are caught doing things that are pretty well accepted in the general behavior pattern of an increasingly large number of persons in our permissive society. Many times such behavior is merely a reflection of accepted adult values and standards.

In discussing offenses of an abnormal sexual type, it is well to remember that whenever a juvenile is involved, it is quite probable that exploration, adolescent confusion and simple "sexual immaturity" are operating; and so it is well not to consider such juveniles as confirmed sexual offenders, but rather to look at such behavior as situational reactions or stages in development from which the youngster can go on with the proper help to a healthy normal life. This is not to say that society does not have a legitimate concern about such cases; and it is important to note that the earlier that realistic assistance can be obtained for the youngster engaged in deviant sexual activities, the better are the chances for him to gain sexual maturity and thus to refrain from any further abnormal sexual behavior.

APPLICATION OF IMPORTANT POINTS EMPHASIZED FOR LAW ENFORCEMENT OFFICERS

1. Sexual development is not merely a physical growth process, but it includes a lot of internal changes and adjustments that must be considered as emotional and psychological.

2. This process is a continuing one. which begins long before physical signs of puberty appear.

3. Family attitudes, religious training and early experiences affect the development of attitudes and habits.

4. The conflict between control and sexual freedom after puberty is heightened and complicated by constant stimulating through seductive advertising, dress codes and the mass media; while the voices of family, religion and the law urge restraint.

5. Individuals mature sexually at different rates of maturity dependent upon their particular personality, physical development and circumstances. Therefore, they react differently to pressures and exhibit varying degrees of control. For this reason, one youngster might get into trouble as the result of a source of stimulation which another youngster is able to handle without extreme difficulty.

6. We cannot generalize about sexual misbehavior of youngsters, or the individuals involved, any more than we can about other forms of human behavior. In fact, sexuality and its expression is so much a part of the individuality of each offender, that a special effort must be made to understand the strength of the temptation and the strength of the controls if we are to understand youthful sexual misconduct.

7. The permissiveness and sexually charged atmosphere currently prevalent in the total culture contributes to the problem of sexual acting-out of a type that brings youngsters into conflict with the law. Consequently, there are many "sex delinquents" who are simply doing what countless others are doing, but they have the misfortune of being apprehended and brought to public attention.

8. Great care should be taken before considering a juvenile a sex offender or labeling him as such. Many such offenders are not exhibiting sexual abnormalities at all, and even much abnormal behavior by youngsters is exploration or the result of temporary confusion or immaturity. Great harm can be done by giving a juvenile a "sex offender" record in many cases.

9. The early detection, apprehension and provision of treatment for those youngsters who do have serious sex problems which cause them to commit sex offenses is the best protection for society, and the best opportunity for the offender to have a chance to grow into normal adulthood.

10. The professional police officer must constantly be aware of his own attitudes and values in relation to sexual behavior, and he must never permit these personal factors to interfere with his objective and competent dealing with the juvenile sex offender.

Chapter 13

ROLE OF THE SCHOOLS IN JUVENILE DELINQUENCY

Section

§ 13.1   In general

According to the U.S. Office of Education, in 1976, half the elementary and high schools surveyed in a nationwide study reported at least one school-related crime each during the five-month period of the survey.[1]

This finding was reinforced by a report of the National Education Association during the same year which indicated that there were one hundred homicides in the schools in the United States, 9,000 rapes, 12,000 armed robberies, and over $600,000,000 in damaged property.[2]

In a compilation of the most frequent kinds of offenses in the schools, the U.S. Office of Education reported the order of frequency of offenses as follows: burglary, personal theft, drug abuse, disorderly conduct, assault, bomb threats or actual use of explosive devices, alcohol abuse, weapons offenses, arson, robbery, and rape.[3]

As early as 1939, the relationship between the schools and juvenile delinquency was pointed out in a report by the New Jersey Delinquency Commission.[4] This study found that of 2,021 inmates of prisons and correctional institutions in the state of New Jersey, two out of every five had first been com-

[1] Reported in *Juvenile Justice Digest*, Volume 4, No. 24, December 17, 1976.

[2] Reported in "Vandalism, Teacher Militancy, Fiscal Troubles Foreseen," a nationally syndicated article by G. G. LaBelle, Associated Press writer (The Cincinnati Enquirer, September 5, 1976).

[3] Report of U. S. Office of Education, op. cit.

[4] *Justice and the Child in New Jersey,* report of the New Jersey Juvenile Delinquency Commission, (1939), page 110.

mitted because of truancy as a child.

We have seen this relationship develop so steadily that we now have come to accept the existence of extortion, gang assaults, constant malicious destruction of property, and the need for the presence of police personnel in corridors, and even classrooms, as a part of the modern school scene.

It would be unfair and inaccurate to say that the school system itself is responsible for all of the delinquency that takes place in its buildings and in conjunction with its activities. It is well established that some of the contributing factors are: (1) the failure of home and family to act as behavioral controls, (2) the pressures toward delinquent conduct in criminogenic sub-cultural groups, and (3) the permissiveness and skepticism rampant in the larger society.

Certainly much "preparation for delinquency" takes place before the child enters school.

The preschool education of youngsters was graphically pointed out in the preparatory discussions for the 1970 White House Conference on Children in the "forum on learning," when the assembled observers stated:

"Schools and teachers have been with us for so long that we now equate them with education and, worse, with learning. The infant learns to walk and to talk, to trust and to distrust; he learns fear and love and hate—all without benefit of school. The irony is that we know all this and still equate learning with school. By age five, the child has sat before a television set for at least the number of hours he will spend in the first three grades of school. And still we equate learning with school."[5]

§ 13.2   Reasons for failure of school system in preventing delinquency

Fortunately in some cases the relationship of the school to delinquency has been one of prevention and the school setting has been one in which an obviously "hurt" child has found

5 "Learning Into the 21st Century," Report of Forum 5 (Working Copy- Subject to Modification) White House Conference on Children, Washington, D. C., (1970), p. 5-2.

some positive experiences. In the cases where this has taken place, the school has obviously been successful in utilizing the individual relationships between school personnel and the child, and in providing a curriculum which met some very basic needs in the lives of the individual students.

However, in analyzing the caseloads of the police agencies and the juvenile courts, or from an observation of the many serious problems currently confronting the large school systems in this country, it is quite apparent that in all too many cases, not only have the schools been unable to prevent delinquent conduct, but they have shared in contributing to its development.

Many volumes have been written on the inadequacy of the slum schools to meet the real needs of the severely deprived youngsters who have either dropped out or been "pushed out." The insistence upon testing and classifying based upon verbal skills and cultural enrichment, the teaching of irrelevant matter to youngsters who are struggling each day with the need to survive and other procedures used as adhesives to the middle class model have caused the schools to be seen as irrelevant at best to many children from deprived backgrounds.

With the presence of the "hang-loose ethic" in suburbia among ever-increasing numbers of sophisticated youth, and especially with their intense unwillingness to follow blindly the social and behavioral dictates of the establishment, it is easy to see that the serious school problems are not at all limited to any one type of school.

The increasing presence of narcotics on the campuses of high schools and junior high schools, the open defiance by groups and individuals of rules and authority, and the "sit-ins" and "walk-outs," give eloquent testimony to the fact that many students find schools unrelated and undesirable outside of the ghettoes also.

This was emphasized recently by one group of scholars who stated emphatically: "The schools have been poked and probed, judged and weighed—and found wanting. . . . The overall failure is glaringly apparent in dropout rates, in barely minimal learning on the part of many who do remain in school, and in growing alienation among the young of all colors and classes."[6] Countless reasons have been advanced for the existence of these problems, and they probably are all accurate in part, but none of them seem to apply totally to the entire situation throughout the country.

Some children seem to be affected by a sense of failure resulting from learning disabilities in the lower grades, classification due to IQ testing, and a whole host of other reasons related to lack of success. Others seem to be reacting to the inflexibility of programs or people within the system, to the permissiveness of adults which many times is simply a cover for disinterest or fear, or to punitiveness or repression disguised as fair discipline, and the pseudo-professionality that has been substituted for personal contact at times.

One of the chief causes of alienation in the schools is the obvious gap between what is taught in the classroom and what the child sees and senses in every other experience of his daily living. This problem was also emphatically stated recently by the group preparing for the White House Conference on Children when they said:

"The subject matter of today's schools is both narrow and antiseptic; we ignore and denigrate the rich variations in our culture and we paint pretty, half-real pictures of life for our children. We have adhered to the outworn notion that certain subjects are to be learned by all children at successive stages of growth at stipulated times and in sterile places.[7] . . . We paint and show only putty pictures of life, out of deference, supposedly, to the tenderness of children. In so doing, we magnify our hypocrisy for all to see. Even the youngest of our offspring soon become aware that we wage war while talking peace, that children go hungry in the richest land on the face of the earth, that even leaders cheat and lie. They come to understand that what we say and what we do are very different things."[8]

There are countless other reasons for maladjustment in the schools. The causes of delinquent conduct in connection with or resulting from the educational experience have all been

---

[6] Ibid.
[7] Ibid.

[8] Ibid, p. 5-3.

thoroughly treated in the works of many fine commentators on the contemporary educational scene. The huge mass of misbehavior in America today is simply the "top of the iceberg." Beneath it lies an almost infinitely greater conglomeration of causal factors resulting from personality problems, behavior disorders, environmental conditioning with roots in the homes, families, neighborhoods and gangs, the breakdown of controls and traditional value-systems in the larger culture, and sometimes in the inadequacies of school programs and the personal failings of school administrators, counselors, and teachers.

Despite the complexity of the causal picture, delinquent behavior must be controlled, and so today's schools are in close contact with the police agencies and the courts. In the past, there was a tendency among many school administrators to keep any knowledge of serious delinquent activities within the school, and to "not air our dirty laundry in public" because of a desire to uphold the reputation of the school and maintain public confidence in the school program. Today, however, because of the magnitude of the problems, the pendulum seems to have swung in the other direction and there is an almost constant police presence in some schools.

§ 13.3   School liaison law enforcement officer: pro and con

The recently established practice of having a "school liaison officer" or "school-resource officer" assigned to a particular school, or to several schools in the area, is a much debated practice. The pros and cons in relation to the school liaison officer were eloquently presented in an article by two United States Children's Bureau law enforcement consultants when they said: "The school liaison policeman's purpose is five-fold: (1) to establish collaboration between the police and school in preventing crime and delinquency; (2) to encourage understanding between police and young people; (3) to improve police team work with teachers in handling problem youth; (4) to improve the attitudes of students toward police; (5) to build better police community relations by improving the police image."[9]

[9] George Shepherd and Jesse James, "Police—Do They Belong in the Schools?," *American Education*, (September, 1967).

Despite these stated purposes, the same observers commented that much criticism of this program has arisen from parent-teacher organizations, civil rights groups, the American Civil Liberties Union, and to some extent from personnel of the Children's Bureau of the United States Department of Health, Education and Welfare.

They further point out that in order to accomplish the kind of attitude change that is part of the goal of this program, the assigned police officer would have to be persuasive to the point of faultlessness, while at the same time he would have to be able to compete with all the outside stimuli, including home, parents, companions, and any other negative influences in relation to the student's opinion of police; and they point out that very few police officers are equipped either by experience or training to accomplish this task.

They observe also that the drain on essential police manpower to implement such a program effectively would be considerable since if, for example, only 15 percent of the junior high schools in this country utilized one such officer, this would demand over one thousand highly trained police officers drawn from existing sources which are already inadequate. On the same subject of manpower they also mention that such officers, being on duty during the day in the schools, would not be available to departments during the evening hours when juvenile crime reaches its peak proportions.

They discuss possible legal complications related to the interrogations and inspections of students in the school building, where by law the school acts "in loco parentis"; and they are concerned about the necessity of properly informing parents and guardians regarding interrogation of juveniles. They cite additional arguments against the school liaison officer program including the possibility of a stigma being attached to the school that requires police presence; the fact that he can be diverted from his primary mission into becoming practically the school disciplinarian and handling trivial non-police matters; and finally that in so doing he can be conceptualized by the students as a repressive force which in turn would defeat the primary purpose of his mission, which was initially explained as being to enhance the police image among the youngsters in the school setting.[10]

It is the opinion of your author that close school-police relationships must be maintained in order to provide maximum benefits for the students and the community at all times. However, it seems that the school liaison-officer program is certainly not the only way to achieve this, and for the reasons expressed by the law enforcement consultants cited above, it can present some very real problems. Nevertheless, when properly utilized, it can be a very effective program.

One of the outstanding examples of a successful effort of this type is the "Police-School Liaison Program" which is operated as part of the "Mott Program" of the Flint (Michigan) Board of Education.[11] Its purpose, goals, functions and methods are best explained in the words of those responsible for the program:

"Juvenile delinquency is a social ill, and like other diseases it can be minimized by early treatment. This is the theory of the Police-School Liaison Program established in Flint's eight junior high and four senior high schools.

"It has been found that juvenile crime can be greatly reduced by early detection, a fact that makes it imperative that the pre-delinquent child be reached before he develops an attitude vulnerable to delinquency.

"Because all children attend school, this is the most logical place to reach them with preventive measures. The school and the police are the two largest agencies to combat delinquency, and in Flint their efforts are united by means of a Regional Counseling Team. On this team is a police liaison detective.

"THE POLICE-SCHOOL LIAISON OFFICER

"The Mott Program of the Flint Board of Education subsidizes one-half of each detective's salary and car, and provides him with office space in the school building. The City Police Department provides the other one-half of salary and car.

10 Ibid.

11 "The Police-School Liaison Pro-

gram," (brochure prepared by the Flint Board of Education, Flint, Michigan).

"The Police-School Liaison program is administered and supervised by a detective lieutenant.

"Vital to the success of the program is the detective's relationship with faculty, students and parents. He must earn acceptance from them. This is accomplished in great part by his attending numerous school functions, by knowing countless people in the school neighborhood including merchants and members of civic and church organizations, and by ultimately becoming an integral part of the school community.

"POLICE LIAISON DUTIES

"The detective has his office in the secondary school, not only for convenience, but also because he finds the bulk of his teen programs and student contacts at this level.

"Before classes begin in the morning, he makes a regular patrol of elementary schools in his area. He does this again during the noon hour and after school in order to observe and correct infractions of safety rules or loitering by suspicious adults and older students.

"He checks on the complaints that come in from the downtown juvenile bureau, relating to his area, and follows them up during the day. This may involve conferences with the student or contacts with the parents.

"BENEFIT OF POLICE-SCHOOL LIAISON

"Three major benefits accrue from having a plain-clothes detective in the school: (1) Good communications are developed between the schools and the police department, and a cooperative program for the guidance of young people is available. (2) When the detective becomes a friend of the youth of a community, a greater respect for law enforcement is created. (3) Preventive work gives a partial solution to the problem of juvenile anti-social behavior.

"REGIONAL COUNSELING TEAM

"The liaison detective does not work alone. He is part of a

Regional Counseling Team. Before 1958, when the first liaison detective was added to Bryant, there had existed a team composed of principal, nurse, dean, and community school director. The results of their efforts were good; it is admitted that the addition of a liaison detective increased the strength in dealing with delinquency and pre-delinquency.

"So successful was Bryant school's program that in 1960 another school added a liaison detective to its counseling team, and by 1965 all secondary schools had similar Regional Counseling Teams with a liaison detective.

"The team is composed of the principal, assistant principal for students, assistant principal for counseling, nurse counselor, school social worker, school nurse, community school director, principals of elementary schools that feed the junior high, and a liaison detective.

"Whether a child has academic, health, or social problems, there is a member of the team who can coordinate special knowledge toward the team effort of helping the child who needs guidance.

"The liaison detective has no academic responsibility toward the school, but he does work closely in counseling and delinquency prevention within the junior high school community. His major duty is to ascertain causes and prevent crime before it materializes."

The field of police-school relations has not been fully explored, although there have been some very interesting projects in the recent past, and there is much room for continual experimentation and exploration in a sincere effort to find more effective ways for the schools and police to work together in controlling the complex delinquency problem in the schools.

It must be remembered that the primary role of the school is education, and that this concerns itself with the creation of the atmosphere in which learning can take place, instruction, motivation of students and the many tasks that are properly the domain of the educator; however, in relation to juvenile delinquency the school probably functions best in the role of prevention, and this is carried out through meaningful personal relationships at the individual level between staff and students and by ingredients in the curriculum which encourage positive experiences in the lives of the youngsters.

§ 13.4   Community-centered schools

More formal preventative work can be done by the schools in conjunction with the many public and private agencies in the community, if these agencies are actually functioning and are not simply giving lip-service to their interest in delinquency prevention. Early referral of students with problems can be a real tool of prevention.

It also seems apparent that much can be accomplished by involving the community with the school in a cooperative effort toward neighborhood improvement, mutual assistance programs and opportunities for positive interaction.

When community schools are properly programmed, staffed and funded, they can produce excellent results in terms of delinquency prevention. In one area where an outstanding program of this type has been in operation since September, 1969, and where there had been riots and extensive vandalism in 1968, the principal of an elementary school stated recently that there has only been one cracked window at his school from September to December of this year, and that this one incident was an accident; and the director of the community schools program in the area added that: "In my two years as community school director in a predominantly black inner-city school our vandalism was literally ended. In the previous year the school had three break-ins and window replacement was a weekly occurrence."[12]

In this fine program, 18 community schools are operated for 11 months from 3:00 p.m. till 11:00 p.m., five days per week and on Saturday mornings. Six junior high, two senior high, and ten elementary schools are involved in the effort, and programs are specifically designed for the respective needs

[12] Steve Stark, Director, Springfield (Ohio) Community Schools in a letter to Paul Hahn, December 9, 1970.

of teenagers, senior citizens, elementary age children and adults. The total program is based on the belief that the community must be involved in the school and vice versa; and to achieve this, the day school and the night school become a unit whose function is to program for a wide variety of needs in meaningful and innovative ways.

Not only are volunteers, senior citizens and indigenous workers of various types utilized according to their various skills, but police officers volunteer their time to supervise a Teen Program, and on "Police Day," during this past year, 600 inner-city youngsters were provided with refreshments and given the opportunity to inspect equipment and meet with staff of the police department.[13]

The accomplishments of such a program are easily observed through interviews with youngsters, neighborhood leaders or others in the immediate area who benefit from this realistic approach.

The schools, as such, should be properly staffed and programmed to be able to handle problems that are essentially school problems, including much truancy, without continually burdening the already overloaded police and courts with purely school matters. When there is serious delinquency, and police and courts are properly utilized, the schools can be of great help by creating an atmosphere in which these legal agencies can properly perform their respective tasks.

While the schools as such are not in the business of treatment, they can be of great service to youngsters with problems long before such youngsters become officially delinquent, and they can be of great assistance in cooperating with courts and other agencies when a youngster has returned to the school system after his arrest by a police agency and his hearing and disposition in the juvenile court.

An example of a cooperative "after-care" program which seems to hold great promise in assisting to rehabilitate adjudicated delinquent offenders is found in the "Community Guid-

---

[13] Ibid.

ance Project" of the Ohio Youth Commission. Federally funded for a modest cost of $35,800,[14] this project provides for close cooperation between the state agency responsible for community-care of youngsters released from the state facilities for juvenile delinquents and the schools in the Columbus, Ohio, school district. It is designed to improve the adjustment of the child returning to school by providing special consulting services to the schools, special counseling services to the child, and a high degree of cooperation between the schools, the state institutions and the bureau legally responsible for after-care.[15]

This program deals directly with the problems presented by youth returning to the community from institutionalization meeting experiences which might reinforce their feelings that school is threatening or intolerant. As a result of such a program, attendance, achievement and conduct at school should improve, and the drop-out rate should be significantly lowered.[16]

Another practical program for effective treatment of juvenile delinquents within the school setting is the rapidly developing use of "school probation officers" (SPO) or "teacher probation officers." This program was established in a formalized way in Shelby County, Ohio, in 1964 by John M. Pettibone, Chief Probation Officer, and it was extended and further developed in a major metropolitan area by the same man in 1965 in Columbus, Ohio.

This program attempts to literally turn the daily school experience into an individualized treatment program by providing a competent, interested "on the scene" probation officer, readily available for crisis intervention and constantly involved in efforts toward emotional support and effective limit-setting.

The program is explained very simply in an article entitled: "Salvaging the In-School Delinquent"[17] (and again in the book

14 Title III, p. 1. 90-247. Project #45-70-008-1, "Community Guidance Project," Ohio Youth Commission.

15 Ohio Youth Commission, "A Project Proposal for a Pilot Operational Grant (April 30, 1970) (Title III E.S.E.A.) for a Community Guidance Project" (Submitted by K. R. Baskerville for O.Y.C.)

16 Ibid.

17 John Pettibone, "Salvaging the In-School Delinquent," Ohio Schools, (May, 1966).

Managing the In-School Delinquent—the Volunteer SPO Program).[18]

In describing the program and explaining its basic advantages, Pettibone says:

"The TPO is able to give extremely intensive probation supervision with an absolute minimum of effort. This intensive supervision includes being on the scene to take instant action in cases of probation violation committed during school hours. The personal control, contact and observation under the TPO program is considerably greater than under even the most intensive of conventional supervision programs. In fact, these factors are probably stronger in the TPO program than they are in any but the most intimate, structured, and treatment-oriented institutional setting."[19]

The results of such programs should be carefully evaluated; and similar experimental efforts must be encouraged if the schools are to be effectively utilized as an effective preventative and rehabilitative instrument in many lives. Needless to say, such constructive efforts make the work of law enforcement easier and more effective.

APPLICATION OF IMPORTANT POINTS EMPHASIZED FOR LAW ENFORCEMENT OFFICERS

1. Many youngsters exhibit problem behavior for the first time to a serious degree in the school setting.

2. Delinquent conduct often readily manifests itself in the behavior of a child at school because of the need to observe rules, to relate to authority-figures, and to get along with others in a variety of circumstances.

3. A child with a behavior disorder or personality disturbance developed before entry into school often acts out his problem very quickly under the pressures of the school setting, even though the origin of his problem is totally unrelated to the school.

4. Feelings of failure, rejection by teachers, learning problems, and many other school-related factors often contribute to delinquent conduct within the schools.

[18] Published by Davis Publishing Company, Santa Cruz, California (1975).

[19] "Salvaging the In-School Delinquent," op. cit., pp. 15, 16.

5. In some instances, schools as a whole, and especially individual teachers, do their utmost to assist deprived children through providing warm personal relationships and satisfying physical needs for food, medical care, jobs and even clothing. Such efforts are often extremely valuable in delinquency prevention. Alert and interested police officers often cooperate in such efforts by identifying children needing special help, and even by playing active roles in obtaining and distributing resources.

6. There is an absolute need for close communication between area police and the neighborhood school officials; however, the often-proposed "school liaison officer" is not necessarily the only answer at any time, but when properly utilized it has proven effective in some places.

7. When asked to provide service on a school campus, the police officer must remember that the law and a long tradition place a certain expectancy as to what can be done with a child at school, and as to who is responsible for his care and control in that setting.

8. No matter how close the cooperation with the schools, police officers should never become school disciplinarians, nor should they take on the responsibility for primary enforcement of compulsory school attendance laws or other functions that are properly those of school personnel.

9. Police officers can provide many services to youngsters, and contribute greatly to better community relations, when invited into schools for lectures, safety demonstrations, movies, discussions and other events in which the officers can share their talents and display their interest in constructive ways.

10. The police officer can be extremely effective by participating actively in programs arranged by "community schools," in areas where such programs are available.

Chapter 14

RELIABILITY OF JUVENILE DELINQUENCY STATISTICS

§ 14.1   Statistics on juvenile delinquency

a. Reasons for inaccuracy

When discussing how many juvenile offenders are currently known to the police departments of America, or in analyzing what offenses they commit, one must keep in mind that all official statistics concerning crime rate are confined only to describing the gross amount of crime reported. This is especially true concerning juvenile delinquency and youth crime, where the differences in laws and the reporting practices are often even wider from jurisdiction to jurisdiction than those involving adult offenses.

Some of the most obvious reasons for the discrepancy between crime reported and the real crime rate are the following:

(1) The unwillingness of victims or witnesses to report to or cooperate with the police. This can be the result of a belief that the police are powerless (this was cited as the most frequent reason given in the survey published in "The Challenge of Crime in the Free Society"),[1] or it can be the result of fear, hostility toward police officials, etc.

(2) The accessibility of victims and witnesses to police officers and the approachability of the officers.

(3) The varying degrees of efficiency and methods of detection.

---

[1] "The Challenge of Crime in the Free Society," a report by the President's Commission on Law Enforcement and Administration of Justice, U. S. Government Printing Office, Washington, D. C., (February, 1967), p. 22.

(4) The large amount of victimless crime (such as narcotics, prostitution, drunkenness, etc.). The crime rate regarding these kinds of offenses can soar at times when there is a "crackdown" or special drive to enforce certain laws, and the rate lowers very drastically at other more normal times.

(5) The philosophies within varying police departments (on the part of administrators and field officers) concerning what should be reported and what should not.

(6) Community pressures for enforcement in various areas.

(7) The kind and amount of training and supervision received by the enforcement officers.

(8) The confidence which the arresting officers have in the local courts and corrections system. (Often if the feeling is that the courts are too lax or in some cases too strict, the pattern of arrest will deviate sharply.)

(9) The amount and availability of accurate record-keeping services within the police department.

(10) The centralization of control and policy-making (for example, district stations located far from the center of administrative control, especially if they have a juvenile officer accustomed to operating in an independent manner, might handle many offenses with no record of contact in a very informal way).

(11) The size of the city. (Reporting practices vary greatly between larger metropolitan areas and small rural areas.)

(12) All of the differences between suburban and inner-city statistics discussed in Chapter 7 "Affluent and Suburban Delinquency."

Many other factors influence the number of official records that are established and kept, depending on local politics, various changing conditions and, in some instances, even on the average age of the officers in any given department. With the amount of variables differing so greatly as to how much and what is reported, it seems quite fair to say that we have no real picture of the juvenile delinquency-complex in America today. In fact, one study recently indicated that about three percent of all juvenile delinquents are actually apprehended.[2]

The most accurate compilation of reported crimes, including juvenile delinquency, is contained in the Uniform Crime Report issued by the Federal Bureau of Investigation, but even this fine work reflects the inadequacies and the inconsistencies in the reporting practices and the many other variables discussed above.

For this reason, and because of the ready availability of the Uniform Crime Reports to all of those who wish to study in depth the current reported delinquency statistics, your author will make only a few general comments on the total delinquency picture at this time, and urge each reader to carefully analyze the real picture of what is actually happening in his particular area.

It is significant to note that during the decade 1960-70, the arrest of juveniles increased 90% while the population of this age group increased only 27% (during the same time span adult arrests went up 57% in this country).[3] In the same time period, total arrests were up approximately 71%, while arrests for narcotics law violations rose 492%, primarily due to the involvement of the youth group.[4] At the same time, in just one year, this country saw a 13% increase in reported crime in the suburban areas.[5]

Since that time, however, juvenile delinquency seems to have reached some sort of "plateau," at least in regard to the overall rate of increase. With the postwar baby boom beginning to level off at the "prime arrest age" level, and with a noticeable slowdown in the growth of juvenile property arrests, the present stabilization in the rate of increase seems to be encouraging. However, there is an accompanying rise in the rate of violent crimes by juveniles which seems to give rise to continuing concern.

---

[2] Gold, Martin, Belmont, "Delinquent Behavior in an American City," Brooks-Cole Pub. Co., Calif. (1970).

[3] *Uniform Crime Report*, FBI,

(1969).

[4] Ibid.

[5] Ibid.

For example, between 1970 and 1975, the arrest rate for the "older juveniles" (15-17 years old) grew nearly three times as fast as the rate for young adults (18-24 years old). As a result, the older juveniles became the most frequently arrested group and the reason for this increase seemed primarily to be based on a horrendous increase in the number of robberies and aggravated assaults by this group.

It should also be noted that arrests for all serious crimes has been increasing faster in non-urban areas than in the inner-cities since shortly before 1970, and the increase in the arrest rate for violence in the non-urban areas has been noticeably at the greatest rate.

All of these statistical trends and conclusions must be considered in relation to the fact that there are often serious discrepancies between the "officially reported crime" in any category and the "actual amount of crime." Some of these differences are most easily seen when official statistics are compared with "self-report surveys." When such discrepancies are located, it is often necessary to deal with such factors as "police willingness to arrest juveniles" in a particular area, changes in reporting practices, the amount of community concern and consequent demands that "something be done" about certain offense categories, etc.

b. Differences in juvenile crime by sex and residential area

With these admonitions in mind, the need for each enforcement official to look carefully at his own particular area of jurisdiction to determine what the current patterns are, and how much delinquency he actually has to face, seems an absolute necessity if any effective methods of prevention and control are to be instituted. This is especially true when we consider that most acts of delinquency are committed close to home. (One recent study reported three-fourths of offenses studied occurred within one mile of the offender's place of residence.)[6]

Although some of the formerly accepted statistics about juvenile delinquency do still apply, although even some of the most

6 Stanley Turner, "Delinquency and Distance," *Delinquency: Selected* *Studies,* Sellin & Wolfgang, John Wiley & Sons, N.Y. (1969).

"hallowed" of these might also be swept away at some date in the near future because of the constantly changing picture of youth misbehavior, there are many changes in trends currently important to note. We can still safely say that among the officially recorded group, the delinquent offenders are predominantly male, with boys being arrested much more frequently in all offense categories. However, there is a definite trend, in the past several years, toward more frequent arrest of girls in all categories. This is especially true in the commission of violent offenses by girls under eighteen. From 1970 to 1975, for example, the arrest rate of girls in that age group for serious offenses climbed 40% while at the same time the arrest rate for boys in similar offense categories increased only 24%. This trend culminated in 1975 when a full 11% of all juveniles arrested for violent crimes were female. This is an unprecedented rate of female juvenile violence in this country.

Also, while there is still a great difference in the frequency of kinds of offenses committed, and in the case of girls it still can be normally accepted that more than half of their offenses are "status offenses" (offenses which would not have been offenses if committed by adults), but at the same time, the trend toward "across the board" increases in all other offense categories by girls is very noticeable.

Boys continue to be referred to juvenile courts primarily for larceny, burglary, and motor vehicle theft, in that order of frequency; while girls tend to be referred for running away, ungovernable behavior, larceny, and sex offenses. However, as mentioned above, with the tremendous rate of increase in arrests of juvenile females for very serious and especially violent offenses, it is not unrealistic to see some of these frequency categories undergoing great change in the near future.

Despite the tremendous increase in delinquent behavior in the suburbs, the inner-city areas still tend to have a disproportionately high concentration of serious delinquency; and this is especially true in the large cities, although sharp increases in suburban delinquency, especially drug offenses, are currently reported. (Further discussion of this topic can be found at length in Chapter 7 Affluent and Suburban Delinquency.)

The rural areas tend to have much lower delinquency rates than the inner-cities and the nearer suburban areas.[7] The change in the nature of the statistical picture and the offense patterns will be discussed much more fully in the sections treating particular problem areas such as the drug scene, and suburban and affluent delinquency, elsewhere in this volume.

For further statistical review of the reported delinquency picture, the reader is referred to the Uniform Crime Reports and to the Juvenile Courts Statistics, which give a very complete picture and thorough statistical breakdown of all offenses which reach the juvenile courts in this country.[8]

APPLICATION OF IMPORTANT POINTS EMPHASIZED FOR LAW ENFORCEMENT OFFICERS

1. Reported or official delinquency statistics often reflect many factors other than actual amount of delinquency in any jurisdiction.

2. Self-criticism or planning by any department should not be based on comparison with statistics from any other jurisdiction unless those statistics are fully understood and interpreted properly.

3. Public attitudes toward the police and the courts influence the amount of reported delinquency in many ways; thus emphasizing another reason for good community relations.

4. Enforcement actually can be very good in an area with a bad statistical report, and vice versa; thus it is always desirable to professionalize statistical procedures as much as possible.

5. The rapidly changing juvenile offense pattern requires that we take a closer look at the number of actual offenses within each jurisdiction in order to adequately plan prevention and control.

---

[7] "The Challenge of Crime in a Free Society," a report by the President's Commission on Law Enforcement and Administration of Justice, U. S. Government Printing Office, Washington, D. C., (February, 1967), p. 56.

[8] *Juvenile Court Statistics*, Children's Bureau Statistical Series, published by the U. S. Dept. of HEW, op. cit., Washington, D. C.

Chapter 15

THE PREVENTION OF JUVENILE DELINQUENCY

Section

§ 15.1 Summary of various prevention methods

The concept of juvenile delinquency prevention is complex because, like the notion of juvenile delinquency itself, it depends upon factors inside of persons and factors outside of them in the various strata of their environment. Consequently, any effective program of juvenile delinquency prevention must address itself to the personal needs of the potential offender as well as to the control of conditions in which an act of delinquency might develop.

There are four possible approaches to prevention:

(1) the universal or global approach—concerned with strengthening any area of life that is beneficial for children, including families, religion, discipline, recreation and education;

(2) primary prevention or control of proximate causes of delinquency—concerned with the alleviation of conditions which directly contribute to delinquency, including narcotics education programs, organized group activities in high delinquency rate areas, "detached workers" programs, surveillance of undesirable places and control of outlets for illegal merchandise;

(3) early identification and treatment of youngsters with problems—concerned with the danger signs seen in children at early ages which indicate that a present minor infraction might be the beginning of a serious delinquent pattern. This approach concentrates on getting realistic services for the child with severe personality disturbance, for the alleviation of hun-

ger or vicious situations of child neglect and for the provision of needed professional and academic assistance to the child with an obvious learning disability;

(4) realistic treatment and adequate programs of rehabilitation for the identified, adjudicated juvenile delinquent—this approach concerns itself with an intense effort to prevent recidivism in the lives of known juvenile delinquents. It emphasizes the importance of providing the services that are necessary to change the values and attitudes, and if necessary the life style of those youngsters who without such help would continue a severe and chronic pattern of juvenile delinquency. This approach must necessarily include the whole range of services at the noninstitutional or community-based level for offenders on probation and parole and through the provision of meaningful programs within the institutional setting for those who are incarcerated.

Within the confines of the universal or global approach to prevention, while there is an infinite variety of elements in a child's life and total environment that could be emphasized, there are three areas which will be discussed briefly because of their importance as agents of delinquency prevention.

§ 15.2 The family

It is known from the common experience of all mankind that the family is the first and most influential nurturing place of all values and attitudes, and consequently of all behavior. It is within the confines of the family that the first experiences with "good people and a happy world" normally take place or where these are sorely missed if they are lacking in a child's life. It is within the family that the great bulk of early learning, be it for better or worse, normally takes place, and it is in this setting where a life-style is adopted and where values and attitudes are firmly fixed. If there is love, security, understanding, protection from a hostile environment and the satisfaction of all the other physical and emotional needs, then the family insulates the youngster against many of the pressures and negative influences outside of the home and the child shows a remarkable ability to mature free of delinquency despite many outside pressures. If the child is frustrated and disappointed in his basic family relationships, and the family atmosphere is found wanting in the essentials of good child development, then the child must necessarily look for the satisfaction of these needs in many "strange places" and his behavior can quickly mark him as a "stranger in the house."

§ 15.3 Religion

If the term "religion" is understood in its strictest sense as a bond or relationship between a creature and a Creator who brought him into being out of love and remains vitally concerned about his happiness, then religion can provide a basis of security, a source of hope and a motivating force for real achievement in life that can be stronger than any other influence in the life of a human being. On the other hand, if religion is understood in the narrow sense as a formal membership in a particular church with little relativity to our day to day life and to our most intimate goals and aspirations, then it is meaningless as a control of behavior, and in fact it can produce further frustration and disillusionment in the lives of many.

History is replete with the evidence of religious persons who have behaved in a heroic manner under the most difficult of circumstances motivated by a strong belief in a personal God and the relevance of their religion. Likewise, there are numerous examples of men living the lives of utmost degradaation at practically an animal level, somehow coming to realize, when other sources of motivation such as family or hope of material success had failed, that there is "something more important" to live for, and consequently changing the entire pattern of their lives in such unlikely places as "skid row" or the death house of a large penitentiary.

Just as the most learned efforts of some men have failed to disprove the existence of the God upon whom all religions are based, so too have all the most sophisticated efforts failed in their attempt to show that He is not the great motivator in the lives of untold thousands who, without Him, would be tempted to live lives of delinquency.

§ 15.4   Discipline

There is probably no other single area of child rearing that has been so misunderstood at such a great cost to so many than the area of discipline. Despite the common experience of mankind for all preceding centuries of human history, despite the writings of the learned philosophers of the ages including Aristotle, Cato, the fathers of Zen Buddhism, despite the exhortations of the Old Testament, the Koran and practically all of the writings of the major religions, in the twentieth century, especially since the 1930's, parents and all others charged with the responsibility of rearing and educating children have exerted less and less discipline and extended more and more permissiveness to the youngsters of this country. This trend has taken place under the guise of a myth that it had been scientifically established that discipline, especially any form of corporal punishment, caused emotional disturbances in children. This myth has been perpetuated and intensified by a series of gratuitous assumptions on the part of certain writers, despite the fact that the overwhelming experience of most practitioners indicates that we are seeing many young people with disturbances of all sorts in whom at least part of the problem can be traced to a lack of discipline, and to the resulting lack of a sense of security and conscience development. Peter Cranford, speaks eloquently of the subject when he says "Discipline is the wand by which the kind goddess of learning guides the child through the bewildering and sometimes terrifying maze of life. Skillful discipline is indistinguishable from love—and this is both its glory and its meaning." [1]

Of course, those who have sought to discredit discipline over the years have always sought to separate it from the notion of love, which is impossible, and so they have often cited cases of harsh physical abuse as examples where strict discipline was not effective, or was harmful, in the lives of youngsters. Such persons never bother to point out the obvious fact that such harsh physical abuse is not discipline but simply brutality.

[1] Peter G. Cranford, Ph.D., *Disciplining Your Child: The Practical Way,* Prentice-Hall, Inc., Englewood Cliffs, New Jersey, (1963), p. 18.

Discipline without love and common sense always becomes something other than discipline; and at the same time love without discipline ceases to be love and becomes mere sentimentality or permissiveness. The truth is that one of the first things a child senses in a loving parent is that he "loves me enough to keep me from hurting myself or someone else."

Despite the fact that the promoters of the permissive doctrine claim John Dewey and Sigmund Freud as the authors of many of their theories, it is quite evident from the later writings of both Dewey and Freud that they had a great desire to correct the misinterpretations of their positions which had resulted from their earlier writings and both said emphatically that discipline was essential. John Dewey stated: "The effect of overindulging a child is a continuing one. It sets up . . . an automatic demand that persons and objects cater to his desires and caprices in the future. . . . It renders him . . . incompetent in situations which require effort and perseverance in overcoming obstacles. . . ."[2]

And Sigmund Freud slapped strongly at permissiveness when he said: "Let us get a clear idea of what the primary business of education is. The child has to learn to control its instincts. To grant it complete freedom so that it obeys all impulses without restriction is impossible. . . . It would make life impossible for the parents and would do serious damage to the children themselves."[3]

Self-opinion polls from youngsters, the experience of those administering programs for the delinquent or emotionally disturbed children, material gathered in interviews with youngsters with severe behavior problems and countless other sources have emphasized the child's awareness of his own need for discipline and the sense of security and love which it fosters when properly administered and understood. Perhaps the most eloquent testimony was received by your author when he was

[2] John Dewey, "Experience and Education," (1938), quoted by Peter G. Cranford, op. cit., p. 28.

[3] Sigmund Freud, "New Introductory Lectures on Psychoanalysis," Vol. 54, *Great Books of the Western World,* *Encyclopedia Britannica,* Chicago, (1952), p. 870, quoted in the book by Peter G. Cranford, op. cit., p. 29.

chief probation officer in a large metropolitan area juvenile court some years ago, when he made it a practice of interviewing a large number of the youngsters who were being permanently committed to the state institution because their behavior could no longer be controlled at the local community level. Practically without exception these children who had the longest records and the most serious offenses would make such statements as: "If only Mom or Dad would have made me come in at night!" Or "If only they would not have let me run around with Johnny Smith or with Mary Jones!" These examples, coupled with the youngsters' insistence that we cease telling them things with words and start showing them with concrete actions as they constantly remind us "Man, don't tell me, show me," certainly must reinforce us in the notion that if we really love our children we show them by doing the best we can to control their behavior.

§ 15.5　Predictability of juvenile delinquency

When the early identification of youngsters with problems is considered, the subject of "predictability scales" and whether or not we can predict who will become a delinquent offender comes into focus. There have traditionally been two approaches to the notion of predictability, statistical (actuarial) and clinical. The statistical or actuarial method is totally based on group experience and it is entirely empirical and coldly numerical without regard for the individual involved or without applying any particular theory of delinquency causality to any of the individuals in the group. This method represents the accumulation and classification of statistics concerning the delinquent population. From statistics which provide a profile of the delinquent population, an attempt is made to establish a chart of probability as to the entrance into the delinquent group of anyone bearing a certain number or percentage of the traits identified in the large statistical group. Probably the first such attempt took place in 1923 [4] and the methods for accumulating and classifying the data are constantly continuing

---

[4] Warner, Sam, Bass, "Factors Determining Parole from the Massachusetts Reformatory," *Journal of Criminal Law and Criminology*, No. 14, (1923), pp. 172-207.

and being improved. One of the most important of such studies was done for the first time in 1930 by Sheldon and Eleanor Glueck and in 1959 they reflected twenty-nine years of progress in their published report.[5]

The clinical method is far older than the statistical and it has probably been in use in at least a crude form since the first time that any human being was interested in understanding the behavior of anyone else. It relies intensively on the knowledge of the individual as it comes to apply theories of causality to his life.

While there is much good to be gained from the kind of scientific knowledge that can be obtained from the accumulation and classification of data as required in the statistical method of predictability, for purposes of preventing delinquency it seems that the more valid of the two methods is the clinical because of the many intangibles and variables that are involved when one attempts to relate a cluster of traits to the life and behavior of an individual. There are too many examples of differences in basic constitutional features and differences in responses to environmental stimulation, and we know too well that a factor is not a cause unless it is significant to the person in whose life it is present.

§ 15.6　Diversion

In the 1970's a whole new concept of diversion began developing within the total criminal justice system, and especially in relation to juvenile delinquency. As with most new concepts, there has been a considerable amount of confusion, and even open conflict as to the meaning of the term itself and certainly in relation to its implementation in the juvenile justice system.

The traditional meaning of the word diversion, in general use, is "to change directions or alter courses" (Webster's Unabridged Dictionary). When this is applied to the juvenile justice system, it is generally accepted to mean the changing of the direction or the altering of the course of an offender, or

[5] Sheldon and Eleanor Glueck, *Predicting Delinquency and Crime*, Cambridge, Harvard University Press, (1959).

alleged offender, from the normal procession into and through the juvenile system. The reason your author words this so carefully, is that some diversion takes place after adjudication and some takes place at the "pre-trial" level before the adjudicatory process.

Probably the best available definition of the diversionary process was formulated by Dr. Joe Hudson, Director of Research Planning for the Minnesota Department of Corrections, and his associates as follows: "Structured informal intervention into the criminal justice process as a result of which the individual is referred for treatment or supervision to a community agency which is at least partially outside of traditional criminal justice establishments."[6]

In the same article in which that definition was expounded, the authors proceed to identify two ways in which the term diversion is used: "The first is true diversion in which any direct action on the part of the criminal justice official is avoided except that of referring the individual for some kind of action to agencies outside of the criminal justice system. . . .

"The second, and the more common, use of the word diversion refers to minimizing the offender's penetration of the juvenile or criminal justice system. By this definition, any action short of serving the full sentence in a correctional institution can be regarded as diversionary. To a great extent the distinction between true and partial diversion programs corresponds to diversion prior to conviction as compared to post-conviction diversion programs."[7]

Your author tends to favor the second interpretation, especially when considering diversion in relation to or distinct from concepts of "prevention." For this reason your author has utilized the following definition in teaching graduate courses on this subject recently: "Conscious effort to prevent further penetration into criminal justice or juvenile justice system." This obviously implies that at least the beginnings of systemic re-

---

[6] "Diversion programming in criminal justice: The case of Minnesota," Joe Hudson, Burt Galaway, William Hen- schel, Jay Lindgren, and Jon Penton, *Federal Probation*, March, 1975.

[7] Ibid.

sponse have taken place in terms of a child being brought to the attention of authorities. By using this understanding of the term, clear distinction from "global prevention" efforts is possible.

The purpose of diversionary programs, no matter how they are defined or understood in most cases, is generally accepted to be an effort to minimize or prevent altogether the stigmatization or any other harmful effects of the process of the juvenile justice system. Needless to say, these diversionary efforts are most effective with, and can probably only be justified in relation to, those offenses and offenders who do not require the full impact of the system.

There are several very weighty implications, both systemically and legally connected to the concept of diversion. Some of these are: 1. An implied admission of at least partial failure of the system itself. When we adopt a policy of "keeping people out of the system" as a positive step this certainly seems to constitute less than a "vote of confidence" in the system in its entirety.

In those places where long delay, clogging of the docket, inequality of treatment, ruthless plea bargaining, and hasty careless justice are a few of the more obvious problems, this implication can be founded in reality; conversely, where those negatives in the system are minimized or absent altogether, there is certainly less real ground for this assumption.

2. In the diversionary process, some of the basic concepts of our legal system can be challenged. For example, in pre-trial diversion we do considerable violence to the concept of "the presumption of innocence," in diversion at other levels we certainly effect "adversary procedure," due process in some cases, etc.

3. The diversionary concept tends to return emphasis to the "actor" instead of simply expressing systemic concern with the act. In this regard, diversion seems to fit beautifully into the original concept of the juvenile court, which itself was instituted as a "diversionary process" to "head off" juveniles from entering the criminal justice system.

4. An emphasis on diversion in any community certainly demands a change in community attitudes toward offenders in many instances, this especially is true in relation to the public desire for revenge or for a continuation of the "away syndrome" in which segments of the public want all offenders "sent away" (which implies that they would proceed very deeply into the justice system).

APPLICATION OF IMPORTANT POINTS EMPHASIZED FOR LAW ENFORCEMENT OFFICERS

1. Anything that an officer can encourage or support that is good for proper growth and development of children (be it physical, educational, recreational or whatever) is a real step toward prevention of juvenile delinquency.

2. Surveillance and control of persons and places which tend to cause delinquency can contribute much to a sound prevention program by removing temptations from the path of youth.

3. The police officer first recognizes the danger signs of serious disturbance in youngsters, and proper referral to sources of realistic assistance can be a very significant contribution toward preventing future delinquency.

4. Adjudicated delinquents, youngsters on probation, recent returnees from correctional institutions and all other known juvenile offenders in the community require special programs and services to assist them to avoid recidivism. Merely token supervision, "punch-card probation," or other meaningless programs are of no real help. Open hostility and harassment by authorities can do great harm and are never a substitute for realistic, positive programs.

5. Discipline is a necessary part of child-rearing; but physical abuse is not discipline, nor is it effective as a positive behavioral control.

6. Over-permissiveness, protectiveness and sentimentality are not effective as behavioral controls, in fact they only serve to confuse and create greater problems than the ones they seek to evade. Love without discipline is as unrealistic and ineffective as discipline without love. Neither meet the real needs of youngsters for the emotional security provided by the setting of limits for behavior by a person who understands and cares about him.

7. In attempting to predict future delinquents, we must always keep in mind that we are dealing with individuals who might resist many of the same pressures which have caused others to become delinquent. Also, we must remember that there is an almost infinite number of variables within the individual and his environment which

make it extremely difficult to categorize him or predict his future behavior.

8. There is always a great danger in labeling any child because of our tendency to react toward him in ways best designed to encourage the fulfillment of the label. For example, if a child is unfortunately stated to be the possessor of all the characteristics which we feel make him delinquency-prone, we might so react to him that he is pushed into actual delinquency.

9. There is value to understanding the kinds of factors that cause delinquency, so that efforts can be made to understand delinquent behavior and to alter the undesirable conditions.

10. Much good work in prevention can be done by the police officer communicating with groups and individuals so that they can better understand his work and relate to him as a person. Above all, his good example of concern for people, respect for law, fairness to all, and professional competence on the job have tremendous impact on sensitive youngsters.

Chapter 16

PROFESSIONAL POLICE APPROACH TO
JUVENILE OFFENDER

Section

16.1 Rules of police department in handling juvenile offender

16.2 Methods of disposition of juvenile matters by police officer

§ 16.1 Rules of police department in handling juvenile offender

The degree of professionality with which the problems of juvenile delinquency and individual juvenile offenders are approached can be judged to a great extent by the very structure and administrative policies of the department, but can be determined almost infallibly by the habitual attitudes and personal conduct of the individual police officers in dealing with juvenile delinquents. Professionality first and foremost is concerned with a level of conduct or performance which obviously flows from the values and attitudes of the officer performing. This was eloquently stated in the definition of a professional police department expounded by James Q. Wilson: "The professional police department is one governed by values derived from general, impersonal rules which bind all members of the organization and whose relevance is independent of circumstances of time, place and personality." [1]

It follows logically from this definition that such a department sets the standards of conduct in relation to the juvenile offender, as well as in all other areas, and it expects the police officer to carry out his duties in accordance with the stated policy, independently of his personal feelings, political pressures or any other considerations.

Various outstanding police departments throughout the nation have stated these general, impersonal rules for handling the juvenile offender in many different ways. However, they

[1] James Q. Wilson, "The Police and Their Problems: A Theory," *Public Policy*, No. 12, (1962), pp. 189-216.

all translate the spirit of the law of the various states concerning the treatment of juvenile delinquents into operating philosophies and procedural language. The general orders of one large metropolitan area police division state:

"(1) When a juvenile comes to the attention of police because of some act of delinquency, the officer may use any of the following methods, provided it complies with the condition set forth in this order. In making his decision the officer shall bear in mind that the purpose of the juvenile program is to give youth the help they need to make the social adjustment necessary for acceptable behavior, and not to administer punitive actions.

"This action should be one that will be of the greatest benefit to the juvenile and to the community both now and in the future. Every police contact and every police disposition has an influence on a juvenile's future. It is important that each police officer exercise understanding judgment in his treatment of youth so our juveniles do not develop ingrained feelings of hostility against those in authority." [2]

When general orders of this type are carried out properly within a department, a high standard of professionality results, and innumerable abuses are eliminated before such unfortunate situations even arise.

Within various police departments, normally dependent upon size, administrative attitudes and the presence of a professional approach in relation to handling the juvenile offender can be seen in many instances in the presence or absence of a "juvenile bureau" (also called youth aid bureaus, juvenile aid divisions, etc.) and by the availability (or lack of availability) of special training for any or all officers in relation to the handling of the problems presented in processing juvenile matters.

A vast store of knowledge and a high degree of skill is required to cope with the many juvenile problems that might arise. The department's contact might be with a delinquent

---

[2] *General Orders of the Cincinnati Police Division*, Cincinnati, Ohio,   16.005, § B, "General Information," (revised July 1, 1968).

offender, with a dependent or neglected child, it could involve handling truancy or incorrigibility, or many times, it involves apprehension of run-aways or absconders from other jurisdictions. In all of these separate instances, the professional standards must be applied in specific ways, depending upon the particular demands of each situation, or great harm can result to the juvenile and to the community at large.

§ 16.2   Methods of disposition of juvenile matters by police officer

A high degree of professionality is required in order for the officer to keep constantly in mind that he is trying to help the child, not just if he is dependent or neglected, but even if he has violated a law. This is exceedingly difficult in most cases where a violation of the law is involved, and it especially taxes the professionality of the police officer in those situations where he is dealing with a very hostile, "foul-mouthed," perhaps even physically dangerous offender. However, when the officer is capable of conducting himself professionally in such circumstances he not only is functioning at a high level as a police officer, but he is carrying out the mandates of the laws of the several states as they relate to the handling of the delinquent offender. Furthermore, in so doing he challenges the delinquent values and contempt for authority which is part of the make-up of the offender and also enhances the reputation of the police division in the eyes of onlookers or of any who later become aware of the situation through the reports in newspapers, reading of transcripts, etc.

In dealing with the child who has broken a law the police officer is often the first official contact, and many times he takes on the additional responsibilities of being the "on-the-spot" prosecutor, judge and correctional system combined.

Each year, there are thousands of cases in which youngsters engage in a minor violation and are apprehended by a police officer who proceeds to counsel and release the child, with no further official contact being continued and oftentimes with no record being made of the contact. This unofficial counseling touches large numbers of children, has considerable influence for better or worse in the lives of many of those contacted, and thus makes up a very important part of the juvenile correctional system.

Secondly, oftentimes before even such an informal procedure as mentioned above, a disposition is administered at the time of the violation in terms of a cursory warning or admonition. These are very brief, often impersonal contacts, always without benefit of counseling, and many times consists simply of "get off the corner," "break it up," or simply "go home." As brief as such contacts might be, and assuming that the very informality of the contact prevents any record keeping, still these are very real police-juvenile contacts and they can be classified as a disposition administered as a result of juvenile misbehavior.

Other dispositions without prolonged contact involve such procedures as taking names for future reference, the filling out of field interrogation reports, and the filing of "closed referrals," which usually involves the filling out of a form similar to a court referral form but without any further procedure being required and the intention being that the closed referral serves practically the same purposes as the traditional warning ticket.

If properly used, one of the most frequent and effective dispositions available to the police is the "referral home" or the simple procedure of taking an errant child home to the parents or guardians with an explanation of the offense, in the hope that the child will receive closer supervision from the home and perhaps some disciplinary action in that setting as a result of the offense.

Referrals to public and private agencies for help with problems obviously rooted in the need for medical assistance, vocational training or job placement, welfare problems, and a whole host of other problems of youngsters which require immediate assistance but outside of the police and court frame of reference is a standard procedure, and it requires a high degree of communication and cooperation with existing agencies in the community. Unfortunately, because of many problems, including lack of funds and proper staff, policies of "selective intake" which screen out truly delinquent young-sters, disputes resulting from "role jealousies" and "vested in-terests," many times agencies which normally would be expected to render a valuable service to delinquent youngsters appear to do so but in practice are known as literally non-functioning. It is important that the professional police officer be aware of the agencies that merit this description so that he can avoid referral to them and thus avoid being deceived into thinking that some realistic action is being taken when in fact it is not, and avoid exposing the youngster to further promise of help that is not received.

At the police level, other dispositions that are made in juvenile matters include counseling sessions at headquarters or at a district station house, hearings before the lieutenant or captain, and the widespread practice of the "emotional whip-saw" in which a youngster is exposed to a "tough" and then to a "soft" or understanding officer with the hope of the desired effect being that the youngster will fear the first and will re-spond to the other and become receptive either to confessing wrongdoing or to responding favorably to the suggestion that he avoid further delinquency. These practices should be care-fully evaluated in the light of the statutes governing the deten-tion of juvenile offenders which require in most places that the youngster be taken "forthwith" or "immediately" to the place of juvenile detention, and that he not be detained even for interrogation or counseling at any other place. (The legal rights of juveniles are covered in detail in later chapters dealing with the constitutional safeguards after apprehension.)

The police officer has at his disposal several methods of getting the juvenile offender to the attention of the juvenile court if the matter is serious enough to warrant such action. These methods usually can be those that do not involve physical arrests, such as referrals or citations in which a youngster is arrested and official paper is processed between the police division and the juvenile court but the child is released in the custody of his parent or guardians until the time of the court hearing.

When the child is physically arrested, he must be taken as soon as possible to the place of juvenile detention and remanded into the care, custody and control of the authorities appointed by the juvenile court to receive the child. Temporary police detention should only rarely be utilized in a juvenile case, and only for very short periods of time and no longer than is necessary for referral to juvenile intake or return to the parents. When juveniles are held in temporary police detention they should not be left unattended nor should they ever be held in the same facility with adults.[3]

Realizing that the law of the several states demands that while society requires protection, juvenile delinquents must not be treated as adult criminals, and while respect for family autonomy and efforts to minimize coercive intervention must be maintained, officers should seek to utilize the least restrictive alternatives consistent with all these considerations.

Finally, because the values and attitudes of any person can only be changed by positive human contact with interested and adequate adults in their lives, the professional police officer, whether he be investigating, arresting or transporting in a juvenile matter, always remains conscious of the conduct he must display in relation to the juvenile offender. And so, he ordinarily has the first opportunity to alter the condition and circumstances of the youngster so that he does not proceed to a life of adult crime.[4]

APPLICATION OF IMPORTANT POINTS EMPHASIZED FOR LAW ENFORCEMENT OFFICERS

1. Attitudes of police administrators and departmental policies can create an atmosphere of professionality within a department.
2. The truest reflection of professionality is the conduct of the individual officer at the level of performance in the course of duty.

[3] Standard 5.9, "Guidelines for Temporary Police Detention Practices," *Juvenile Justice and Delinquency Prevention,* Report of the Task Force on Juvenile Justice and Delinquency Prevention, National Advisory Committee on Criminal Justice Standards and Goals, Washington, D. C., 1976. p. 214-215. (Note: All citations from "Guidelines for Temporary Police Detention Practices" will hereafter be referred to simply as "Standards (1976)").

[4] For complete suggested standards in relation to professional police approach see Standards (1976), Part 3, Chapters 4, 5, 6 and 7.

3. Professionality requires the proper performance of duty as required independently of personal considerations, individual preferences and political pressures.

4. The handling of juvenile cases in a professional way requires that the law be followed as to purpose and method in any course of action.

5. The most desirable course of action in juvenile cases for any professional police officer is that which will be of greatest benefit to the juvenile and the community both now and in the future.

6. A high standard of professional performance in juvenile matters eliminates innumerable abuses and delicate situations before such even have a chance to arise.

7. One of the finest elements in a police effort to professionalize the handling of juveniles is a properly staffed and trained juvenile aid bureau.

8. **Training of all officers in the philosophy and proper methods of handling juvenile cases raises the professional competence level of almost any department.**

9. Professionality does not demand a long list of academic degrees or the ability to use impressive vocabulary; but it does demand that the good police officer approach each case without reacting to the hostility of the offender with hostility of his own. The ability to understand and control his own feelings in relation to the juvenile is the surest mark of professionality.

10. The professional police officer is always aware of the importance of his role as the first and most significant contact in the lives of children in trouble.

Chapter 17

DUE PROCESS AND ITS SPECIAL CONCERNS
RELATING TO JUVENILES

§ 17.1   Due process

"No person shall be . . . compelled in any criminal case to be a witness against himself, nor be deprived of life, liberty, or property, *without due process of law.*" [1] (Fifth Amendment, United States Constitution) (Emphasis added.)

". . . No state shall make or enforce any law which shall abridge the privileges or immunities of citizens of the United States, nor shall any state deprive any person of life, liberty, or property *without due process of law;* nor deny to any person within its jurisdiction the protection of the laws." [2] (Fourteenth Amendment, Section 1, United States Constitution) (Emphasis added.)

Embodied within the above two Amendments to the Constitution, and pervading the concepts of law and law enforcement within the United States of America is the term "due process." In essence these two amendments say that before the state, or any of its agencies, including the police and the court, may deprive any individual of the basic constitutional guarantees of life, liberty, or property, a strict adherence to due process of law must be met at all levels of enforcement, including the judicial process.

The intent of the framers of the Constitution and the purpose they sought to achieve is obvious. Without such restric-

---

[1] Fifth Amendment, United States Constitution. (Emphasis added.)

[2] Fourteenth Amendment, Section 1, United States Constitution. (Emphasis added.)

tions and checks upon government and governmental agencies, as well as upon individual citizens, the citizens would be subject to the arbitrary or capricious acts of the government. These Amendments are designed to guarantee individual liberty and protect the citizen from oppression.

Although the above two sections of the Constitution both use the term "due process," their application is different. The Fifth Amendment states that "no person shall . . . be deprived . . . without due process of law," while the Fourteenth Amendment states that "no state shall . . . deprive any person . . . without due process of law." It should be noted that the original Bill of Rights, which included the Fifth Amendment, came into existence before the Civil War and the Fourteenth Amendment was enacted following that war.

A few years prior to the enactment of the Fourteenth Amendment, in 1855, the United States Supreme Court attempted to define due process. Justice Curtis stated: "The words, 'Due Process of Law' were undoubtedly intended to convey the same meaning as the words, 'By the law of the land' in the Magna Charta." [3]

Another important aspect of due process in most cases, places upon the one seeking to invoke the state's authority, be it the state itself or one of its agencies, the burden of establishing that the one seeking to deprive another of life or liberty has complied with all the procedural requirements, i.e., due process. The importance of this burden of proof cannot be overemphasized. If one seeks to take away the constitutional rights of another, the one so acting must not only have a valid cause, such as a valid arrest, but must comply with the requirements as set forth by the Constitution and the case law interpreting it.

As is the case in many other constitutional areas, due process is not a static, unchanging concept. Time and again the United States Supreme Court, whose decisions control all other inferior or lower courts, both federal and state, has in-

[3] John Den, Ex dem. James B. Murray et al., plaintiff, vs. The Hoboken Land & Improvement Co., 59-60 U.S. 217 at p. 229.

creased, expanded, and redefined the scope and effect of due process.

The purpose of this section will be to discuss due process as it applies to law enforcement in general, and to the juvenile offender in particular.

The problems of the law enforcement officer in dealing with juveniles have not been made easier by recent court decisions. However, procedure must be followed or an otherwise valid case might be dismissed by the officer's failure to follow the law.

In applying due process to juveniles one must examine the juvenile court concept in law. The original theory of the juvenile court was that it would act in the best interest of the child falling within its jurisdiction. However, this brings up the basic issue: who decides what constitutes "best interest"? What might constitute best interest to one judge, to one probation officer, or to one juvenile officer, might be the direct opposite from the interpretation of best interest given by a fellow judge, probation officer or juvenile officer.

Furthermore, such a system demands the utmost of those involved and does not take into account the fact that one might, intentionally or unintentionally, be guilty of indiscretion or simply not have adequate knowledge of what is a particular child's best interest. Therefore, even though one is allegedly acting in the best interest of the child, fair play must be followed and all sides of the case must be weighed. This is true regardless of the authority of the person dealing with the juvenile. This total effort to act within the requirements of the law, for the best interest of the child, in a spirit of fair play in dealing with juveniles, is due process.

Youth is by nature idealistic, and an idealist is quick to sense any injustice. Failure to follow due process in juvenile matters not only threatens the professionality of the law officer's work, but it does great harm to impressionable youngsters who may lose their respect for authority, may increase their hostility, and be convinced that the law is worthless because they have witnessed its violation by police officers.

While we know that laws cannot be "arbitrary," "discriminatory" nor "capricious," no one has ever been able to make a rational argument against the state's power to form rules and regulations, (i.e. statutes and ordinances) to govern the public welfare and needs.

The same applies to the line between the juvenile and adult age levels. Different viewpoints as to what should be a proper cut-off age, age of consent, or age to act without parental consent are constantly argued, but few dispute the question of the basic need for a definite cut-off or for a distinction between juvenile and adult.

For example, there are laws restricting the age at which one may cast a vote in a state or federal election; there are laws specifying at what age one may legally purchase and publicly drink alcoholic beverages; there are laws that state at what age one may legally operate a motor vehicle on the public way; there are curfews; there are laws stating at what age one may, both with and without parental consent, enter into a valid marriage. There are laws limiting the type of labor, work, or employment which those under a certain age, may or may not perform.

There are many laws which treat members of one age class differently than the members of another class. Almost all of the above classifications have, at one time or another, been the subject of not only legislative debate as to what would constitute the proper cut-off age, but they have also been the subject of other legal actions, and the states' right to make such distinctions has always been maintained. Therefore, it is entirely possible to have legislation which treats one group or class of individuals differently than another, and yet have a valid and constitutional piece of legislation.

Let us apply this to the courts. The United States Constitution provides that the Congress may provide for such courts as may be necessary. "The judicial power of the United States shall be vested in one Supreme Court, and such inferior courts as the Congress may from time to time ordain and establish." [4]

State constitutions also establish a corresponding authority for the legislative bodies of their states, e.g. "The Judicial power of the State is vested in a Supreme Court, Courts of Appeals, Courts of Common Pleas, and such other courts inferior to the Supreme Court as may from time to time be established by law." [5]

If the legislative assembly sees fit to create a Court of Domestic Relations, as well as a Municipal Court, a County Court, and/or a Justice of the Peace Court, the legislative assembly may set forth the powers and jurisdiction of each of these individual courts. Because they are limited by law to certain kinds or classifications of cases, (for example, the Court of Domestic Relations involves only marriage and related matters such as custody and support), they become in effect places of non-jurisdiction for other causes of action. The same applies to juvenile courts. They have been assigned a specific function and they are concerned with individuals confined to a particular age classification.

Juvenile courts are "legislative" or "statutory" courts: courts which are created, defined, and in the jurisdictional sense, controlled by the legislative assembly. Consequently, even though they hear only causes involving individuals below a certain age, and as such are in essence "discriminatory" against all other persons and causes of action, they still must comply with all of the procedural requirements of due process.

This was eloquently stated concerning the juvenile courts by former Justice Abe Fortas in the case of *In re Gault*: ". . . it would be extraordinary if our Constitution did not require procedural regularity and the exercise of care implied in the phrase 'due process.' *Under our Constitution, the condition of being a boy does not justify a kangaroo court.*" [6] (Emphasis added.)

---

[4] Article III, Section 1, United States Constitution.

[5] Article IV, Section 1, Constitution of State of Ohio.

[6] 387 U.S. 1, 27-28, 40 OhioOp (2d) 378 (1967).

Justice Harlan, in his concurring in part and dissenting in part position in the same *Gault* case, stated:

"It can scarcely be doubted that it is within the state's competence to adopt measures reasonably calculated to meet more effectively persistent problems of juvenile delinquency: as the opinion of the court makes it abundantly clear, these are among the most vexing and ominous of the concerns which now face communities throughout the country." [7]

If the Appellate Courts are expressing such great concern for due process, how much greater the problem for the legislative assembly which makes the laws which the courts interpret, and the law enforcement officers, who must both enforce the law, and present valid cases to the courts?

Legislative assemblies, whether municipal councils, state legislatures, or the United States Congress, continue to pass legislation which affects the particular group classified by age as juveniles. The police officer should be aware of the laws applicable to the conduct of both adults and juveniles, in his jurisdiction and of his duties with regard to their enforcement.

In enforcing these laws, the law enforcement officer does not need to worry so much about the constitutionality of the particular law, because the courts will, if they have not already, determine those questions; but the law enforcement officer must be more concerned with the constitutionality of *his acts* in enforcing any particular law.

For example, in a 1970 case, *The People of the State of Colorado in the interest of D.H.F., Minor, decided March 17, 1970,* Judge Ted Rubin of the Denver (Colorado) Juvenile Court, reported[8] that a situation arose where juvenile D.H.F. allegedly violated the Denver Municipal Code. The Denver police requested that he report to the police department for interrogation. He did so, at the appointed time, with his mother, his sister, and his attorney. The police officer inquired as to why his attorney was present, and then told the attorney that he was not needed.

---

[7] Id. p. 67.

[8] "Opinion of Trial Judges" in   *Crime and Delinquency,* Volume 16, #3, (July, 1970), pp. 329-331.

Evidently the police officer intended to belittle the constitutionally justifiable appearance of counsel.

Later in the day, the minor was stopped by the police officers and questioned regarding the same offense. The attorney then filed for a temporary restraining order and a permanent injunction to enjoin the police department from speaking with the defendant at all. That is to say, the minor, through his attorney, sought to have a valid court order that would prohibit any member of the city police department from interrogating him about the offense. If the injunctive relief had been granted, and a police officer had then questioned the minor, the police officer could have been held in contempt of court.

In this case, the court found that the Denver police officers had erred, but refused to grant a permanent restraining order and continued the cause for 90 days. If the police officer had respected the right to the presence of D.H.F.'s attorney, as well as the right to have a parent present, the interrogation might not have been as fruitful, but law enforcement would not have stood the risk of being permanently enjoined from continuing with its interrogations and investigations.

In summary, just as juveniles constitute an age group distinct from adults, so there are special laws and orders affecting juveniles. These laws, ordinances, and orders may or may not be valid.

Issues of determining their validity are not to be determined by the individual police officer, but by the appropriate court. The application of the law is the important concern of police officers; and it is in this area that proper action by him is significant with respect to the outcome of the case.

§ 17.2   Investigation and arrest

In the field of criminal law there are numerous rules that apply to making an arrest. These rules cover arrest in general, arrest with a warrant for a felony, arrest without a warrant for a felony, arrest under a warrant for a misdemeanor and arrest without a warrant for a misdemeanor.

While police generally are authorized by the laws of the several states to take into custody all juveniles who violate criminal statutes and/or ordinances of the local, state or federal government, each state is certainly urged to clearly define by statute the authority and guidelines for, and limitations on, taking a juvenile into custody, especially in those "special juvenile situations" where the child is an "endangered child," or when he is from a "family with service needs" and no clear violation of the criminal code is involved.[9]

It must also be noted that in all cases the procedures following the arrest of the child do in fact differ from those relating to the arrest of an adult. When a juvenile is taken into custody the police should:

(1) make an immediate and maximum effort to notify the juvenile's parents or guardians, and

(2) immediately notify the juvenile of his constitutional rights and refrain from any action which would abridge or deny these rights.[10]

Police officers are also urged to issue written citations or summons to appear in lieu of physically arresting juveniles, whenever this is possible and consistent with the demands of public safety and the needs of the child.[11]

Police officers should certainly make investigations of possible law violations by juveniles as quickly as possible and should do just as complete and thorough a job of investigating as in cases of adult offenses. When at all possible, the juvenile unit investigating such allegations should attempt to determine the underlying causes for law violation so that the potential rehabilitation process can be enhanced. Needless to say, during such police investigations, the investigating officers should take every precaution so that the constitutional rights of juveniles being investigated in connection with an alleged offense are not violated.[12]

It has been held that a police officer may take a child into

[9] Standard 5.6, "Guidelines for Taking a Juvenile into Custody," ibid, pp. 206-208.
[10] Ibid.
[11] Standard 5.5, "Guidelines for Issuing Citations," ibid, p. 205.
[12] Standard 5.4, "Guidelines for Police Juvenile Investigations," ibid, p. 203.

protective custody when he has reasonable cause to believe said child to be delinquent or endangered; and it is not necessary, as in the case of an adult, that the child be committing a misdemeanor in his presence or that probable cause exists for the officer to believe that the child has committed a felony.[13]

Investigators must be extremely careful not to allow juveniles to waive the right against self-incrimination without the advice of counsel. There are highly disputed points as to what is required for a valid waiver of the juvenile's rights and as to whether a juvenile can waive his rights alone or whether the advice of a parent or of legal counsel or both is required to fulfill due process requirements.

This issue was addressed directly in the commentary on Standard 5.8, "Guidelines for Interrogation and Waiver of the Right Against Self-Incrimination" of the National Advisory Committee on Criminal Justice Standards and Goals. The commentary states:

"Many courts have concluded that there is no absolute requirement that an attorney and/or parent or guardian be present in order for a youth to make an effective waiver. According to this view, youths are not presumed, for reasons of age alone, to be incapable of waiving their rights. Rather, the effectiveness of the waiver is determined by the traditional test of the totality of the circumstances surrounding the statements.

"Many other courts have rejected this view. For example, a number of recent cases have strongly stressed the importance of a parent's presence in determining the effectiveness of a juvenile's waiver of the right against self-incrimination.

"In general, then, the case law provides no uniform guidance in this difficult and important area of police operations. This report concludes that a juvenile should not be allowed to waive the right against self-incrimination without the advice of counsel. This approach is consistent with the position that no constitutional right of a juvenile may be waived without prior

---

13 Thierry, R. S. v. King, 132 Cal. Rptr., 194 (App. 1976).

consultation with an attorney."[14]

The failure to follow lawful procedures in the case of a juvenile is illustrated by a Missouri case[15] in which a fifteen-year-old boy was picked up for interrogation about a number of burglaries and was taken to the police station instead of to the juvenile court. While under interrogation at the police station he confessed participation in a case involving the stabbing of a woman in her apartment, where she allegedly found him after he had made a forced entry. Following the statement he toured the scene with the police and was then taken to the juvenile detention home.

At his trial, objection was made to the introduction and evidence of the statement he had made to the police on the ground that the juvenile was not taken to the juvenile court as required by law. The court sustained the objection and remanded the case for new trial.

The laws of several states differ as to the arrest of juveniles, but each officer must acquaint himself with the requirements of the law in his jurisdiction. If he fails to do this, he is in danger of denying due process to any juvenile he may arrest.

§ 17.3   Records

The importance of accurate and efficient record-keeping for law enforcement agencies, though not the subject of this book, cannot be over-emphasized. Complete records are an important tool of law enforcement.

However, great harm can result from inaccuracies or over-statement in records, especially regarding juveniles. It is a tragic thing for a law enforcement officer to incorrectly classify or label a juvenile as a particular type of offender and then, years later, have the incorrect record continue to follow the child, who is now an adult.

---

14 Standard 5.8, "Guidelines for Interrogation and Waiver of the Right Against Self-Incrimination," *Juvenile Justice and Delinquency Prevention Report of the Task Force on Juvenile Justice and Delinquency Prevention,* National Advisory Committee on Criminal Justice Standards and Goals, op. cit., pp. 212-213.

15 Missouri v. Arbeiten, (Mo.) 408 S.W. (2d) 26 (1966).

An example of this is reported to have involved a "highly respected and capable police juvenile sergeant." The files indicated that he had been picked up for "child molesting." Investigation indicated that this had occurred when he was fourteen years old and that while walking his 13-year-old girl friend home, he had kissed her while the two were in public view on the street. The local section under which he had been charged dealt "with conduct arousing or tending to arouse the passions of a child under the age of fourteen years."[16]

The paradox of a man charged under law with the enforcement of law and specializing in the area of juveniles, having a record of "child molesting" illustrates the danger of inaccurate record keeping. It is a difficult line to draw. Good law enforcement demands good and accurate records. Good juvenile work deals with rehabilitation. The two, however, should not be in conflict.

The Standards (1976) speak directly to this important matter: "Police records on juveniles should be kept separate from the records of adults. They should not be open to inspection nor should their contents be disclosed except by court order. Criminal Justice agencies should justify their inspection of the records on a need-to-know basis."[17]

Again, as we have stressed throughout, how does this affect the individual police officer?

As we know, practically every police department has a juvenile division or a juvenile bureau or some section, department, or at least an individual officer which, if not devoted exclusively to working with juveniles, does, in fact, spend the majority of its time handling juvenile matters. Logically, all records pertaining to juveniles would be kept by such a division. This fulfills the mandate of keeping them "separate from the records, and files of the arrests of adults."

While tending to disrupt the system of central filing, it has the advantage of maintaining all juvenile records in one area.

16 Aidan R. Gough, "The Expungement of Adjudication Records of Juvenile and Adult Offenders: A Problem of Status," Wash. Univ. L. Q., Vol. 2, (April, 1966), p. 173.

17 Standard 5.14, "Guidelines for Basic Police Records," op. cit., pp. 226-227.

Personnel handling these records are very familiar with local juveniles. They quickly recognize names and description, and they are somewhat specialized in handling juvenile records because this occupies all their record keeping time, since they are not required to work with adult records.

The benefits of such arrangements to law enforcement are obvious. Such a record room clerk or specialist can often furnish correct names, current addresses, and other pertinent information to the police officer out in the field, immediately in many cases. "Alias files," nicknames, family information, neighborhood contacts, and a wealth of other pertinent data are often available due to properly housing juvenile records in one place under one authority with a degree of accuracy and speed that could not otherwise be obtained.

Not only does this aid the field officers in terminating cases, but it provides a maximum amount of information to assist the decision-making process, and in understanding the full circumstances involving the individual juvenile offender.

Such specialized juvenile record-keeping enhances the professionality of the police work with juveniles, protects the confidentiality of the records and enhances compliance with the legal restrictions on the use of such records.

§ 17.4 Fingerprints

Just as we have different statutes pertaining to the arrest of juveniles as opposed to the arrest of adults, we also have different procedures concerning investigation of juveniles allegedly involved in offenses as opposed to investigations involving adults.

For example, a standard practice when an adult is arrested, depending on the jurisdiction, almost always for a felony and often for a misdemeanor, is to have the arresting or transporting officers take the defendant to the identification section in order to have him photographed and fingerprinted. This is often done, not so much for assistance in proving the case for which he has just been arrested, but for aid in clearing other offenses or for future reference.

However, as we know from prior discussion, when a juvenile is arrested or taken into custody, such procedure is not followed. When, if ever, do police officers have the right to photograph and fingerprint a juvenile? The Standards (1976) speak directly to this issue and must be considered.[18]

In essence, the Standards urge that fingerprints of juveniles be taken only for investigative purposes, and only when a juvenile is taken into custody for violation of the law or in cases where the family court has determined that fingerprints must be taken in order to establish the court's jurisdiction. In addition, explicit guidelines are given for the use, retention and destruction of fingerprints in great detail in Standard 5.12, "Guidelines for Fingerprinting, Photographing, and Other Forms of Identification." (The reader is referred to this Standard in the Appendix of this text and is urged to read it carefully because of its importance.)

The statutory law as to fingerprinting of juveniles and the use which can be made of such fingerprints varies in different states. Twenty jurisdictions have statutes on the subject of fingerprinting of juveniles.[19] The law enforcement officer should be thoroughly familiar with the law in his own state and follow its requirements. In a 1969 Mississippi case,[20] the United States Supreme Court reversed the decision of the Mississippi Supreme Court[21] which allowed fingerprints, taken of a fourteen-year-old juvenile being held without charge by police who brought him and numerous other youths in for investigation of a rape, to be used as evidence in a subsequent trial for rape. Davis, the juvenile, was held overnight in jail, (without charge or probable cause for arrest, after the initial fingerprinting), and again fingerprinted. These prints were sent to the FBI for comparison with latent prints and were admitted in evidence at his trial for rape. The United States Supreme Court held that the taking of his fingerprints constituted an unconstitutional search of a

---

[18] Standard 5.12, "Guidelines for Fingerprinting, Photographing, and Other Identification," ibid, pp. 221-223.

[19] Discussion of various state statutes on fingerprinting juveniles is found in Ferster and Courtless, *The*

Beginning of Juvenile Justice, Police Practices, and the Juvenile Offender, 22 Vanderbilt L. Rev. 567, at 600, 601, (March, 1969).

[20] Davis v. Mississippi, 394 US 721, 89 SCt 1394, 22 LEd(2d) 676 (1969).

[21] 204 So(2d) 270.

person without reasonable grounds to believe that he had committed a crime, and that fingerprint evidence is no exception to the rule that all evidence obtained by searches and seizures in violation of the Fourth Amendment to the Federal Constitution is inadmissible in a state court.

The importance of strict adherence by the police officer to the legal requirements concerning fingerprinting of juveniles is illustrated not only by the reversal of the conviction in the *Davis* case of a person who might have been guilty, but by the fact that the other juveniles involved have their fingerprints on record and this may affect their ability to secure employment in the future.

§ 17.5   Photographs

In regard to photographs, the Standards (1976) apply the same principles as in the case of fingerprinting. (Again the reader is urged to read Standard 5.12, "Guidelines for Fingerprinting, Photographing, and Other Forms of Identification" very carefully because of the importance of this matter in investigative work.) The rules for use, retention and destruction of photographs of juveniles, while carefully addressed in the Standards, vary greatly from state to state and so it is essential that the investigative officer acquaint himself thoroughly with the applicable law in his jurisdiction. For example, in some jurisdictions the "consent of the juvenile judge" is required for photographing juveniles. In this circumstance the problem posed for the law enforcement agency is interesting.

If you, as a law enforcement officer, wish to photograph a particular juvenile, you make application to the court following the administrative regulations that it (the court) has established. Depending upon the court, this can be as simple as a telephone call to the judge, or at the other end of the pendulum, a formal written application. If the judge gives permission, you take the photographs, and if he does not authorize the photographs, you do not take them.

However, the application is not so clear cut. Obviously the juvenile judge is going to require that you tell him some reasons why he should authorize you to take photographs. Yet, at some later date, that judge is going to have to sit at trial and determine whether or not you have a valid case. One of the areas that counsel for the juvenile defendant might attack would be the photographs which were permitted by the judge. Your answer is that the juvenile judge authorized it. The juvenile judge is not likely to rule that he was in error in authorizing the taking of the pictures. However, what if the case is appealed?

Therefore, both the requesting officer and the judge granting the permission to photograph must act within the requirements of the law in their jurisdiction. Needless to say, any photographing of juveniles by police officers without complying with the legal restrictions is again not only poor professional police work, but it is an illegal act.

§ 17.6   Sealing and expungement of juvenile records

There is one final category that should be mentioned that deals with the sealing of records and expungement, i.e., destroying or closing the records to make it appear they never existed. If we accept the position that the juvenile court, once it acquires jurisdiction by making a finding on the merits, is interested in rehabilitation, then the idea of sealing records or expungement becomes reasonable.

The juvenile court should not seal records or expunge them if its apparent goal, rehabilitation, has not been achieved. The following quotation is worthy of merit: "what should distinguish the Juvenile from the Criminal Courts is their greater emphasis on rehabilitation, not their exclusive preoccupation with it."[22]

Therefore, if the juvenile court has fulfilled its goal and rehabilitated an individual, why allow the immature mistakes of youth to follow the now law-abiding individual throughout his life? However, if rehabilitation has not been successful, the court should not expunge nor seal records, as they will probably

---

[22] "President's Commission on Law Enforcement and Administration of Justice: Challenge of Crime in a Free Society," 81 (1967).

be needed for future proceedings in the adult court in regard to pre-sentence investigation, etc.

For our purposes, let us assume that an individual has not become involved in further difficulty, but has been living a productive, model life. It does not seem fair that corrected mistakes of his youth should follow him.

A basic understanding of terms is essential. One of the best definitions of the term "expungement" is as follows: "By an expungement statute is meant a legislative provision for the eradication of a record of conviction or adjudication upon fulfillment of prescribed conditions, usually the successful discharge of the offender from probation and the passage of a period of time without further offense. It is not simply the lifting of disabilities attendant upon conviction and a restoration of civil rights, though this is a significant part of its effect. It is rather a redefinition of status, the process of erasing the legal event of conviction or adjudication, and thereby restoring the regenerate offender his status quo ante."[23]

The Standards (1976) tend to favor the use of the word "sealing" over the word "expungement" because an advantage is seen in not actually destroying or eliminating the physical records which are destroyed or lost forever, even for valid research purposes, and certainly the opportunity to read the full account in order to eliminate any misunderstanding is also lost with the destruction of records. Such is not the case when records are sealed and guarded by very careful judicial procedures.

The Standards state very directly that records should be sealed promptly when "due to dismissal of a petition prior to or as a result of adjudication, the rehabilitation of the juvenile, or the passage of time, the adverse consequences that may result from disclosure of such records outweigh the necessity or usefulness of retaining them."[24]

It is strongly recommended that within the legislation relating to the sealing of juvenile records there should be precise procedures for notification of all persons, agencies, or depart-

[23] Washington University L. Q., Vol. 2, at p. 149 (April, 1966).   [24] Standard 28.5, "Sealing of Juvenile Records," op. cit., pp. 781-783.

ments that might have copies of the juvenile's record or notations regarding that record in their files. When so notified,
the agency holding such copies or notations should see to their
deletion or destruction.

The Standard also insists that after a record is sealed only
the juvenile involved or someone authorized as a representative
of that juvenile should be given any access to that record.

The laws in the separate states differ very widely in relation
to this topic, and so the enforcement officer is urged to acquaint
himself thoroughly with the law in his jurisdiction in order to
avoid misunderstanding or conflict with the law governing his
actions in this regard.

If a court orders a record sealed, law enforcement officers
must seal the record or expunge index cards. If in fact an
otherwise valid arrest and conviction of an adult offender can
be shown to have even in part been based upon a "tainted
procedure" of law enforcement, by using information which a
court of competent jurisdiction had previously ordered deleted, the entire conviction would fail, and the defendant
either discharged from custody or a new trial ordered.

There are no short-cuts or "tainted procedures" outside of
the law which are ever conducive to the highest quality of
police professionality. Good police work with juveniles always
starts by meeting the full requirements of the law.

APPLICATION OF IMPORTANT POINTS EMPHASIZED FOR LAW ENFORCEMENT OFFICERS

1. In taking away the life, liberty, or property of an individual, the
   one so acting (police officer, court, etc.) must comply with due
   process.

2. The term "due process" is not an unchanging constant, but depends
   upon the interpretation placed upon it by the review courts.

3. A law enforcement officer follows due process when he adheres to
   the statutes which set forth his authority and the case law defining
   same and their interrelation with the constitutional guarantees and
   freedoms.

4. The fact that a juvenile and not an adult is involved does not relieve law enforcement nor the Juvenile Court from following due process.

5. Arrest of a juvenile usually does not require the existence of a warrant at the time of arrest.

6. An exact compliance with the arrest and procedural statutes is required, if the state statute says that upon arrest a juvenile must be taken "directly" before the juvenile court, he must be so taken or any statements that he gives while being held elsewhere are subject to being suppressed.

7. Records of juveniles should be kept separate from adult records. In certain instances, a juvenile may have his record sealed (or even expunged in some jurisdictions).

8. In relation to the fingerprinting and photographing of juveniles, the law varies widely in various jurisdictions. The professional enforcement officer should acquaint himself well with the applicable law in his area. Failure to do so can not only cause an important case to be handled in a faulty manner, but it can result in the law enforcement officer being in violation of law himself.

9. Modern law enforcement benefits if there is, within each department, a Juvenile Bureau staffed by trained officers dealing exclusively with juveniles.

10. The police officer on the scene is sometimes in a position where he can handle an entire matter without having to bring the case to the attention of the Juvenile Court. In such cases, it is in fact a "police disposition."

Chapter 18

LEGAL DEFINITIONS REQUIRED FOR UNDERSTANDING THE JUVENILE'S RELATIONSHIP TO THE LAW

§ 18.1 Definitions of crime

The legal definition of the word "crime" has over the centuries varied according to the attitude of the times. Each society has proclaimed various acts as being contrary to the then prevailing morals or standards.

A crime is more than a wrong. The purpose of this section is not to discuss public wrongs as opposed to private wrongs. But we should know that a public wrong is a "breach and violation of public rights and duties due to the whole community, considered as such in its social, aggregrate capacity,"[1] while a private wrong is a wrong against an individual.

Of course, it is possible to commit a wrong against an individual and at the same time by the same act commit a public wrong. For example, if one individual strikes another, he has committed a wrong, not only against his victim but, as society through the legislative process has said such acts are prohibited, this same act is also a public wrong. The purpose of this section is to give a basic working definition of the term "crime" and see what are the essential elements of a crime.

[1] C.J.S., Vol. 22 (1961), § 1, p. 7.

A crime has been defined as "a wrong directly or indirectly affecting the public to which the state has annexed certain punishments and penalties, and which it prosecutes in its own name in what is called a criminal proceeding." [2]

Crime has also been defined as: "a violation of, or a neglect to perform, a legal duty of such importance to the protection of society that the state takes notice thereof, and imposes a penalty or punishment for such violation or neglect." [3]

In both of the above definitions, and in the many other valid definitions of the same term, one notes that the term implies injury or wrongdoing, not to oneself, but to society or the public.

Ordinarily, the commission of a crime, unless the legislature has otherwise specified, entails two essential elements: intent and an overt act.

Just as definitions of the term "crime" have changed with prevailing community standards, so has public recognition of the ability of an individual to form the required intent. Even under the common law, persons under seven years of age were conclusively presumed incapable of crime. Minors, ages seven to fourteen years, were presumed incapable of crime, but it was a rebuttable presumption, while minors between the ages of fourteen and twenty-one were presumed capable, but the presumption was rebuttable.[4] Hence, we can see that even under what we would now consider antiquated criminal law standards, the law recognized a difference in the capacity of minors to be held responsible for committing crime.

This distinction carries over into civil law. If an individual commits a civil wrong against another, such actions may be considered to be a "tort." In the law of torts and civil liability, if the tortfeasor or wrongdoer is a minor, the standard of conduct to which he is held in most situations is not that of an adult. The standard is that of other minors of similar ages with similar backgrounds.

2 22 C.J.S., "Criminal Law," § 1, p. 2.

3 Schneider's *Ohio Criminal Code*, The W.H. Anderson Company, Cincinnati, Ohio (1963). § 1.1.

4 21 Am.Jur.(2d), "Criminal Law," § 27, "Infants," p. 112.

Before concluding our discussion of crime from a legal standpoint, we should note the general classification of crimes. Under the common law, as well as under the modern criminal statutes, there were certain specified general classifications. For example, at common law, a crime could either be treason, a felony, or a misdemeanor. In most jurisdictions today the two general classifications are misdemeanors and felonies. "No crime is a felony unless it was so at common law or has been made so by statute. Under most authorities crimes punishable by death, or by imprisonment in the state prison or penitentiary, with or without hard labor, are felonies, whether or not a lesser punishment may be inflicted in the discretion of the court or jury. The fundamental distinction between felonies and misdemeanors rests with the penalty and the power of imprisonment." [5]

Taking all this into consideration, let us look at the practical way in which it affects the juvenile offender and the law. Since the standard as to what constitutes a crime has changed, and there has been a corresponding change in the degree to which minors are held responsible for their acts, persons charged with enforcement or interpretation of the law are faced with the problem of judging standards. Therefore it is important to standardize public wrongs and realistically appraise the degree of culpability to which we hold a minor or a juvenile.

A minor or juvenile, of course, is responsible for his acts to some extent. There is a difference between right and wrong, and a juvenile can distinguish between right and wrong by the standards to which he is held.

However, given the proper facts, it makes sense to hold different individuals to different standards. For example, one expects expert treatment from a qualified physician. By virtue of his education, experience, and reputation, he should be equipped to perform as an expert, and if he fails to perform as such he is held to a high standard. Juveniles, by virtue of their physical, emotional and psychological changes from in-

[5] 22 C.J.S., "Criminal Law," § 6, p. 13.

fancy to mature development, are obviously not on an adult level, and to hold them criminally accountable to the same extent as adults would be unfair.

§ 18.2　Jurisdiction of juvenile courts

a. In general

Courts are classified as being "constitutional courts" or "legislative courts." If the court in question was created by the Constitution, it is a constitutional court while if it was created by a proper enactment of the legislature, it is a legislative court.

A juvenile court is a legislative or statutory court, and as such, its authority is set forth by the legislature in its particular state. As the legislative authority has the power to determine the authority of the juvenile court, it also has the power to determine the types of cases that will appear in juvenile courts within that state.

It would be improper for the legislative authority to provide that all cases involving juveniles must go to the juvenile court. As we shall see from our discussion of jurisdiction, the juvenile court would have no authority over a case involving a juvenile if the object of the suit was damages or enforcement of a contract. This would be a matter for civil court action. Hence, the mere fact that one of the parties, (plaintiff or defendant), in a legal proceeding is a juvenile is not in and of itself sufficient reason to give the juvenile court jurisdiction. Therefore, the legislature has created various classes, classifications, and categories pertaining to children, and has determined which cases shall be heard in juvenile court.

Currently these classifications deal with delinquent children, unruly children (often called status offenders and referred to in the Standards (1976) as "children from families with service needs"),[6] endangered children (often referred to as neglected, dependent or abused) and children alleged to have committed a traffic offense, i.e., the juvenile traffic offender. (In Standard 9.7 "Traffic Offenses"[7] it is urged that most "ordinary" traffic

---

[6] Ibid., Chapter 10, p. 311-334.　　　　[7] Ibid., pp. 308-309.

offenses by juveniles be handled by the adult traffic court, and that only "major traffic offenses" or offenses committed by juveniles who are not old enough to be licensed to drive continue to be handled in the juvenile court. Most jurisdictions, however, continue to handle all traffic offenses by juveniles within the confines of the juvenile court.)

In some states "endangered children" are referred to as "neglected" or "dependent" or "abused" because each legislature has the authority to create and determine the respective categories and to determine the name or designation of each category within that jurisdiction.

b. Age of child

The legislature of each state also has the authority to determine the jurisdictional requirement in regard to maximum and minimum age. The overwhelming majority of the states concur with the maximum age set in the Standards (1976) which state that the family court should have adjudicative jurisdiction over a juvenile only until the age of eighteen. (However, numerous states do have differences, especially in regard to particular categories of jurisdiction. For example, New York sets the age for delinquency jurisdiction as "a person over seven and less than sixteen years of age.")[8]

The Standards urge that the minimum age for exercise of family court delinquency jurisdiction be ten years of age (Standard 9.2, "Minimum Age for Family Court Delinquency Jurisdiction"), but this minimum age of jurisdiction differs as to categories of offenders and certainly differs within the legal framework of the separate states.[9]

Jurisdictional requirements differ widely depending upon the nature of the act involved. This is especially evident in regard to waiver or transfer of jurisdiction to the adult court. In Standard 9.5, "Waiver and Transfer," it is strongly urged that such action take place only when the juvenile was sixteen years or older at the time of the alleged commission of the act,

[8] No. 712, "Definitions," New York Family Court Act, reported in New York Consolidated Laws Service, Cumulative Supplement, Nov. 1976, p. 330.

[9] For example, see New York Family Court Act, ibid.

and it sets rigorous conditions in addition to this age requirement. In actual practice, however, there is a wide discrepancy
in minimum age requirements in regard to waiver, and it
especially varies in relation to the nature of the act involved
and the conditions for waiver.

The relevant age for jurisdiction is the age at the time the
act was committed, or in the event of "endangered children"
(neglected or dependent or abused) the age at the time of the
judicial inquiry into the child's status.

Again, it is important that the reader acquaint himself
thoroughly with the applicable law in his respective jurisdiction.

c. Status offender (also referred to as "unruly child" or "person in need of supervision," and as "children from family in need of service")

The Standards (1976) address this category very directly:
"This report expresses dissatisfaction with the current approach
to status offenders and with recent proposals to abolish judicial
authority over cases of this type. The Standards (in Chapter 10)
authorize jurisdiction over a limited number of well-defined
behaviors: school truancy, repeated disregard for, or misuse of,
lawful parental authority, repeated running away from home,
repeated use of intoxicating beverages, and 'delinquent acts'
by children younger than ten years of age. The Standards focus
on the family as a whole and require findings that all available
voluntary services have been exhausted and that the behavior
requires court jurisdiction to provide services."[10]

The definition of this category in this way by the Standards
differs considerably from similar definitions in the Codes of the
various states (e.g., New York state defines "person in need
of supervision" as "a male less than sixteen years of age and a
female less than eighteen years of age who does not attend
school in accord with the provisions of Part 1 of Art. 65 of
the Educational Law or who is incorrigible, ungovernable, or
habitually disobedient and beyond the lawful control of parent
or other lawful authority").[11]

[10] Standards (1976), Part 4 Judicial
Services, op. cit., p. 268.

[11] Item No. 712, "Definitions,"
Family Court Act, New York, op. cit.,
p. 330.

As can readily be noted by the reader, this New York definition differs to a considerable extent from the definition proposed by the Standards, and the New York definition seems to agree much more closely with traditional definitions found in the laws of many of the states. This is especially true in relation to the proposal in the Standards definition for the inclusion in the status offender category of "children under the age of ten years who commit delinquent acts" and its emphasis that "all available voluntary services have been exhausted."[12]

Consequently, while your author lauds the Standards for the forward looking approach to this category, he reminds the reader to acquaint himself thoroughly with the law in his particular jurisdiction.

In essence, however, the intent of this category is that such a juvenile is not violating any of the statutory laws or municipal ordinances, with the exception of compulsory school attendance, but the juvenile is seen as "getting himself into trouble" either at home, school, or in the community.

Traditionally, in such situations a complaint is filed at the juvenile court alleging that the juvenile is in fact performing in the above manner. In this regard, the Standards suggest a progressive approach in which such a petition may be brought by the parent, the child, or any other individual or agency coming into contact with the parent and/or the child and having reason to believe that the court should exercise such jurisdiction on behalf of the parent and/or the child.[13]

The prayer or formal request of the complaint is that the court inquire as to whether or not the juvenile is in fact engaging in such behaviors, in the traditional process or in the process suggested by the Standards, to determine: (1) that one or more of the specific behaviors under the "families with service needs" jurisdiction have occurred, (2) that all available and appropriate non-coercive alternatives to assist the child and family have been exhausted, and (3) that by virtue of this behavior and the lack of appropriate voluntary alternatives,

[12] Standards (1976), Part 4, op. cit., p. 268.

[13] See Standard 10.1, "Families With Service Needs Petition," (1976), op. cit., pp. 315-316.

the child and/or family is in need of court intervention for services (see Standard 10.2).

The court then must conduct its hearings following the requirements of due process. If the court finds that the juvenile does in fact fit into this category, then it can proceed to make any of the set statutory dispositions as provided by the legislation in its jurisdiction. (Again, Standard 10.3[14] suggests that once jurisdiction has been established, it should extend to the child, his or her parents, and any public institution or agency with a legal responsibility to provide needed service to the child or parents. Your author especially endorses the concept of jurisdiction over agencies with responsibilities to provide needed services, because the deficiency in this area has long been seen as one of the real gaps in the service delivery system in relation to juvenile offenders at all levels.)

d. Endangered child (dependent, neglected, or abused)

The entire concept of the juvenile court is that the court shall act in the best interest of the child. What is the situation if the boy or girl is not violating the law, but is instead a victim of circumstances?

What if the boy or girl is a very small child, an infant, incapable of performing overt acts against anyone, but instead is being abused or beaten by the parents? What if the child, not being emancipated, has been abandoned by his or her parents? These are the children who need immediate care because they do not have proper parental, guardian or custodial guidance.

To meet this responsibility, the legislative assembly has directed that the juvenile court, after a complaint is filed, inquire into the status of such children, and if it finds that they have been battered, neglected, or dependent, make provision for them as set forth in the respective statutes.

In the United States, at the present time, it is estimated that over 200,000 youngsters are currently living apart from their parents since they have been adjudicated, neglected, abused,

14 Ibid., pp. 317-319.

dependent or deprived; and one or more parents of about 140,000 children have been charged with child abuse or neglect. This situation has often caused your author to speak of the "crisis of the unwanted, unloved children" in our society.

While all agree that coercive intervention into families certainly disrupts family ties and can cause real trauma for parents and children, there are situations, all too well known to any practitioner in the field of juvenile justice, in which such coercive intervention is necessary. In Chapter 11, the Standards[15] address themselves very directly to these circumstances where coercive intervention is recommended: (1) a child has no adult with whom he has substantial ties available and willing to care for him or her, (2) a child has suffered or is likely to imminently suffer physical injury of a severe nature, (3) a child has suffered or there is substantial risk that he will imminently suffer severe physical harm as a result of uncorrected conditions or the failure to adequately supervise or protect him, (4) a child is suffering severe emotional damage and parents or guardians are unwilling to permit or cooperate with necessary treatment, (5) a child has been sexually abused by a member of the household, (6) a child is in need of medical treatment to cure or lessen or prevent serious physical harm and parents or guardians are unwilling to permit the treatment, (7) a child is committing delinquent acts as a result of parental pressure, encouragement or approval. (For exact wording of the above, see Chapter 11, "Endangered Children," Standards 11.9 through 11.15.)

e. Juvenile traffic offenders

Another classification exists in regard to the juvenile traffic offender. The state legislature has power to prescribe the requirements for obtaining a driver's license for operating a motor vehicle on the state's highways. Most states set the age at sixteen. As the juvenile court has jurisdiction up to age eighteen, juveniles who commit traffic offenses which are in violation of a state statute or municipal ordinance pertaining to the use and control of motor vehicles, and at the time of the alleged violation are age sixteen and seventeen, fall into the category of the "juvenile traffic offender."

---

[15] Ibid., pp. 335-372.

Traditionally, most state statutes provide that if a juvenile violates a law or local ordinance governing the operation of a motor vehicle upon the streets or highways of the state (or the waterways), subject to certain exceptions (for example, driving while intoxicated), the matter shall be handled as a juvenile traffic offense.

The significance of this for the law enforcement officer is that if the law enforcement officer physically arrests or cites someone for violation of a traffic law, and that person is under age eighteen at the time of the violation, the case will be called on the juvenile court docket, rather than the regular Municipal or County Court docket.

It should be noted that there is a great deal of controversy as to the advisability of having the jurisdiction of traffic offenses for the sixteen to eighteen category vested in the juvenile court. The Standards (1976) urge that all ordinary traffic offenses committed by juveniles be handled by the adult traffic court, and that jurisdiction for traffic offenses in juvenile court be limited to those offenses committed by youngsters not old enough to be licensed to drive, and to major traffic offenses committed by juveniles of any age within the jurisdictional limits, including such offenses as vehicular homicide, hit and run driving, and driving while under the influence of alcohol or drugs.[16]

A legal argument is made that a sixteen or seventeen-year-old is held to the same standard in regard to civil liability as an adult, and as such he should be held accountable for the same violations against the state in the adult courts. If a fourteen-year-old juvenile negligently acts in such a way that another person is injured, and a civil tort action is brought, in most instances the law will impose upon the fourteen-year-old a standard of care that would be required of other fourteen-year-olds of similar background, experience, education, etc., and not the standard that would be applied if an adult had negligently committed the same act.

[16] See Standard 9.7, "Traffic Offenses." Standards (1976), ibid., p. 308-310.

However, if a sixteen or seventeen-year-old motor vehicle operator negligently runs into and injures a party, he or she is not held to the same standard as other sixteen or seventeen-year-olds of similar education, experience, and background, but to the standard normally applied to all motor vehicle operators, regardless of age.

Therefore, the argument is made that if such juveniles are held to the same degree of civil liability, they should be held to face the same sanctions as adults in traffic court. This is the essence of much current dispute concerning the juvenile traffic offender.

f. Special categories: custody, adoption, permission to marry

Developments in the law have created additional categories or classifications of individuals within the juvenile court. Many states have vested in their juvenile courts the authority to determine the custody of a child not a ward of another court of that state.

In Part 4 of the Standards (1976) it is recommended that the jurisdiction of the family court should include such things as adoptions, civil commitments, and in general the consolidation of jurisdictional authority over family related legal matters.[17]

Another area of jurisdiction which many juvenile courts exercise is that pertaining to the court giving consent to the marriage of children in those specific cases where court permission is required. The law differs widely in the various jurisdictions as to this matter, but in general this concept is derived from the idea that the juvenile court acts "in loco parentis" and many states recognize one of its "parental" functions as being the granting of permission to marry when such permission is required.[18]

One other area of jurisdiction should be emphasized even though it is not recognized in all states as being a function of the juvenile court. This concerns the finding of mental illness in children. Normally, questions of this kind, regardless of the age of the individual in question, are determined by the probate

---

[17] See Part 4 "Judicial Process," Standards (1976), ibid., p. 269.

[18] See Rule 42, Ohio Rules of Juvenile Procedure (7173).

court. However, since the juvenile court is a statutory court, the legislature in any state can specify which cases shall be heard in which court within its jurisdiction. In some states, for example Ohio, the legislature has seen fit to have the hearing on a mentally ill child transferred from the probate court to the juvenile court.[19]

g. Delinquency

Many of the cases that appear in the juvenile court, and consequently a number of the cases that law enforcement officers encounter, deal with delinquent acts.

Although most State Codes continue to follow, at least to some degree, the definition of delinquency found in the Uniform Juvenile Court Act[20] as "an act against the criminal laws of the state or the local ordinances, or a violation of a previous lawful order of the juvenile court, in Standard 9.1, "Definition of Delinquency," the jurisdiction of the court in delinquency matters is limited to some extent because it is suggested that such jurisdiction should be only for acts that would be violations of federal or state criminal law or local ordinances if committed by adults. This section excludes those offenses which would not be crimes if committed by adults, and it also excludes all criminal acts committed by youngsters under the age of ten.[21]

As mentioned previously in this text in the discussion of the jurisdiction of the juvenile court, there are disputes as to the maximum age level, but most states agree with the proposal in the Standards that the maximum age for juvenile court jurisdiction be age eighteen, especially in matters of delinquency.

It is important to note that even though many states include such offenses as truancy, running away and other "status offenses" in delinquency actions, the Standards explicitly reject that approach and recommend that the court's delinquency jurisdiction should be exactly the same as its authority over juvenile "criminal" behavior, and that alone. It also points out

---

[19] See § 2151.23 (No. 4), Ohio Revised Code (effective August 26, 1976).

[20] Uniform Juvenile Court Act, Section 2 (No. 2).

[21] See Standards 9.1 and 9.2, Standards (1976), op. cit., pp. 295, 296, 297 and 298.

graphically, and your author concurs entirely, that there are those cases in which the juvenile system's rehabilitative orientation designed for immature delinquents is so inappropriate that there must always remain, within the juvenile court, procedures for waiving jurisdiction and transferring certain youngsters to the adult criminal court in very serious matters.[22]

The Standards specifically allude to this function and also include such matters as domestic legal relations, adoptions, concurrent jurisdiction over intra-family crimes, contributing to the delinquency of a juvenile, criminal non-support, criminal neglect, and the Interstate Compact on Juveniles and Uniform Reciprocal Enforcement of Support Act.[23]

Therefore, if a party under the age of eighteen violates the state's criminal laws by, for example, committing burglary, housebreaking, or robbery, or violates the local municipal ordinances by, for example, committing an assault and battery or being intoxicated in a public place, the case is called in juvenile court and not the adult court. The law enforcement officer cites or arrests the youngster and the case goes to the juvenile court.

h. Cases involving adults

As a law enforcement officer, you will encounter cases in which the party being arrested or named as a party defendant is over the age of eighteen, and yet the case is called in juvenile court. For example, "tending to cause juvenile delinquency," is an offense committed by an adult but heard in the juvenile court.

In most states, if a person over the age of eighteen performs overt acts which would cause someone under the age of eighteen to be delinquent, the case is tried in the juvenile court. Usually, such an offense is a misdemeanor.

Another adult case that would be heard in the juvenile court in some jurisdictions could involve an unmarried woman wishing to have a judicial determination as to the paternity of

---

[22] See Standards, ibid., p. 268.　　　　[23] Ibid., p. 269.

her child. Such a case would be called in the juvenile court as a paternity or "bastardy" case.

Juvenile courts also exercise concurrent jurisdiction along with adult courts in cases of non-support. This means that in some instances a parent who is not supporting his children properly could be arrested and brought either before a juvenile court or one of the adult courts.

If a law enforcement officer charges a parent with abusing his or her child, or abandoning the child, it is also possible to have these criminal-type cases against the parent heard in juvenile court in some jurisdictions.

The laws vary widely in separate jurisdictions, but in all areas the juvenile court does hear cases against adults in some circumstances where their conduct affects children.

§ 18.3   Derivative authority of juvenile court

The juvenile court may also have derivative authority. Many legislative assemblies have said that if another court having jurisdiction sees fit to transfer a case to juvenile court, the jurisdiction is transferred.

For example, if a divorce case originates in the Domestic Relations Court, and the court finds that neither parent is a fit parent, it can certify the question of the custody of the child to the juvenile court.

Some states also have statutes which permit the "transfer of jurisdiction." The effect of these statutes is that a law enforcement officer may arrest an individual for a violation of law in one jurisdiction, but the case and the juvenile will be transferred back to the county from which the juvenile came, or in which he resides, and the matter is handled by the juvenile court of the county of residence.

APPLICATION OF IMPORTANT POINTS EMPHASIZED FOR LAW ENFORCEMENT OFFICERS

1. A crime implies a public wrong. It is a violation of a legal duty. The legal duty directed by the respective legislative body of each state (or the federal government), and so the violations, and the

penalties for such, are set by the legislatures of each state (or the federal government).

2. The culpability of juveniles for their wrong acts has been recognized under both the common law and the statutory law. It has been recognized in both civil and criminal proceedings. However, it is seen as matter for a special court to consider, and not as part of the ordinary criminal proceedings.

3. Juvenile court is a legislative court. The legislative assembly in each state creates it, defines its jurisdiction, and sets forth its powers. Primarily it is established to concern itself with all matters of juvenile care and control.

4. A person that is under the age of eighteen at the time an offense is committed will usually be heard for that alleged violation in juvenile court, although the upper age limit differs in various jurisdictions.

5. Cases of delinquency are heard in juvenile court. Delinquency is an act against the criminal laws of the federal government, or the state or the local ordinances, or a failure by a juvenile to obey a previous lawful order of the juvenile court. (Some jurisdictions include offenses discussed under "children from families in need of services" as delinquent acts also.)

6. Cases of juvenile traffic offenders are heard in juvenile court. A juvenile traffic offender is a juvenile, subject to certain exemptions, who violates a law or local ordinance governing the operation of a motor vehicle upon the streets or highways or waterways of the state. (Some jurisdictions follow the recommendation of the Standards in hearing only those traffic cases of juveniles who are too young to obtain a driving permit or the traffic cases of older juveniles which are deemed "very serious." The "normal traffic cases" of juvenile offenders in such areas are handled by the adult traffic court.)

7. Cases of "endangered children" (also called deprived, dependent, neglected, abused, etc.) are heard in juvenile court. Such children include those who are physically, sexually, or emotionally abused; those who have been abandoned by parents, guardians or custodians; those without an acceptable degree of proper care; and other special categories included by the various state legislatures within particular jurisdictions.

8. Cases of children from "families in need of services" (also called unruly, children in need of supervision, etc.) are heard in juvenile court. Such a child is one that is habitually disobedient, truant, or generally has committed an offense applicable only to a child. (These are the group of children commonly referred to as "status offenders.")

9. There are various other cases that may be heard in a juvenile court. They include custody, paternity, mentally ill children, and

tending to cause juvenile delinquency, as well as nonsupport in some jurisdictions.

10. The professional police officer must acquaint himself thoroughly with the law as it pertains to juvenile matters in his area because of the differences in age limits, areas of legal concern, names of offense categories, and the many other variations in the juvenile law in the several states.

Chapter 19

THE JUVENILE COURT: PHILOSOPHY AND PROCEDURES

§ 19.1   Rights of juveniles prior to and after *Gault* decision

From its inception in Cook County, Illinois in 1899, the juvenile court has been the subject of great controversy; but the differences of opinion and the disputes about its nature and its effectiveness have never been more pronounced than they are today. This fact was most eloquently stated recently by Judge Bertram Polow when he said:

"More than six decades since its birth, the juvenile court is still the subject of brisk controversy. The very humanitarian and rehabilitative goals for which it was conceived constitute the issues of current debate. Increasing delinquency together with concern for the accused's constitutional rights invites attack upon the juvenile court from divergent viewpoints.

"As the United States Supreme Court has been accused of protecting criminals at the expense of law abiding citizens, so the juvenile court has been criticized for 'endangering the public by unleashing young terrorists apprehended at great risk. . . .' Conversely, just as the Supreme Court has been de-

277

fended in imposing stricter safeguards for those accused of crime, so have civil liberties groups demanded similar protection for the juvenile whose freedom, they proclaim, is determined in an atmosphere akin to the benevolence of the Star Chamber. The assault thus comes simultaneously from both sides. And though generated by differing motivations, the varying attacks reach unanimity in concluding that the juvenile court process has failed to provide effective justice." [1]

The idea of a juvenile court hearing, both before and after the *Gault* decision by the U. S. Supreme Court in 1967, discussed in detail later in this chapter, embodies protective and rehabilitation concepts; but before that decision these concepts were often emphasized without full regard to due process.

Once jurisdiction *was* obtained, the primary concern was alleged to be what is in the best interests of the particular juvenile, meaning that the court would determine for the individual juvenile what type of program would keep him or her from repeating the antisocial behavior that brought the juvenile within the court's jurisdiction in the first place. Further, the means of acquiring jurisdiction often failed to meet the basic requirements of due process.

The original concept of the juvenile court was that it always acted in "parens patriae." That is to say, that if the parent failed to assume the responsibility for care, assess the discipline, and assure the development and growth toward maturity of the particular juvenile, then the juvenile court should assume this responsibility. In effect, the juvenile court would act in place of the parent when required to do so.

This was well-intentioned, but assumed a very altruistic attitude and great wisdom on the part of all parties involved. The philosophy was sound but there was historically a great disparity between philosophy and actual practice. Judge Polow graphically pointed this out when he said: "The real dilemma concerns not the philosophy of the juvenile court, but whether

---

[1] Bertram Polow, "The Juvenile Court: Effective Justice or Benevolent Despotism" *Criminological Contro-* *versies*, p. 291. Reprinted from *ABA Journal*, (1967), Appleton Century Crofts, N.Y., N.Y. (1968).

the composite results of its performance justify continued reliance upon the *parens patriae* theory." [2]

Lack of adequate legal counsel, little regard for due process and a large number of judges without legal training deprived many youths of their day in court; while lack of facilities, untrained staff, and inadequate financing of rehabilitative programs combined with the legal deficiencies to make it exceedingly difficult to act in the best interests of the juvenile.

This practical performance lag was commented upon by the U. S. Supreme Court in the *Kent* case in 1966 when it opined that the lack of staff, facilities and techniques prevented some juvenile courts from performing as enlightened parental substitutes.[3]

The Supreme Court took further steps into the controversy in 1967 with the far-reaching *Gault* decision,[4] which was eloquently synopsized by Richard Knudten:

"The appeal of *Gault* v. *Arizona* (1967), the first state juvenile court case to be heard since the creation of the first juvenile court in Chicago in 1899, issued in new protections for the individual juvenile. Gerald Gault was judged a delinquent and sentenced to a potential six-year term in the Arizona reformatory for making obscene telephone calls with a friend, the son of the Globe policeman. Although the other youth was released without charge, Gault, then fifteen years old, was held in custody twelve hours before his mother was notified. The following day a formal petition was filed against him, although it was never served upon his parents. Although the complaining woman neither attended the hearing nor testified against the youth, he was sentenced to the State Industrial School (or reformatory) until the age of twenty-one or until a state board determined his readiness for release in his parents' custody. Although an Arizona adult would have faced a maximum fine of $50 or two months in jail, Gerald Gault served a minimal six-month term. After he had made two

---

2 Ibid., p. 295.

3 Kent v. United States, 383 US 541, 555-556, 40 OhioOp(2d) 270, (1966).

4 In re Gault, 387 US 1, 40 Ohio Op(2d) 378, 18 LEd(2d) 527, 87 SCt 1428 (1967).

unproductive appeals to Gila County and Arizona Supreme Courts, the U. S. Supreme Court reversed Gault's conviction and wrote the contents of the earlier *Escobedo* and *Miranda* decisions into juvenile court philosophy. The landmark decision of May 15, 1967 extended a number of rights guaranteed by the Constitution and Bill of Rights to delinquency hearings including: (1) the right to counsel, whether private or court appointed, in cases which might result in incarceration; (2) the right to confront and cross-examine witnesses; (3) adequate warning of the privilege against self-incrimination; (4) the right to remain silent; and (5) early notice of the charges. . . ." [5]

Prior to the *Gault* decision, each juvenile court functioned as a separate unit. What Juvenile Court "A" determined was best for a particular juvenile in a particular instance, might be entirely different from what Juvenile Court "B" would have determined as best for the same juvenile under the same set of circumstances and whether or not "A" or "B" could supply the resources needed for this purpose was often irrelevant to the decision.

After the *Gault* decision, some juvenile courts found that their procedure prior to *Gault* not only conformed with the specific directives of *Gault*, but exceeded same. However, this was the exception, not the rule in most courts. In most places *Gault* forced the juvenile courts to evaluate and change.

Therefore, this discussion will be based on the idea of *Gault* forcing change. When we mention "before *Gault*" or "since *Gault*," we will use the hypothetical example of a court in which certain changes had to be made to conform with the procedural guarantees as set forth in *Gault*.

§ 19.2   Right of juveniles to jury trial

However, the *Gault* case did not settle all issues which continue to confront the juvenile court and law enforcement. For

---

[5] Richard D. Knudten, "Synthesis," Criminal Controversies, Appleton-Century-Crofts, N.Y. (1968), at 305.

example, in an adult court hearing, in the majority of states, if the defendant is charged with an offense which carries with it a jail sentence, a period of incarceration and/or a fine in excess of a stated amount (for example, in Ohio the amount of $150.00), the defendant is entitled to a trial by jury.[6]

In 1971, the United States Supreme Court, while reaffirming that juveniles are entitled to due process of law, held that due process does not require a jury trial in juvenile court proceedings. This was the decision in the famous "McKeiver case."[7] This case still controls juvenile court policy in relation to jury trials. The idea of a juvenile receiving a jury trial brings up countless possibilities. For example, we know that the defendant is entitled to be tried by "a jury of his peers." Also, the Constitution requires that the trial of a defendant in a criminal case must be open to the public. The question arises as to whether the due process clause of the Constitution affords the same protection to juveniles in Juvenile Court proceedings where the consequences to the juvenile may be as grave or even harsher than those which entitle an adult to a jury trial in a criminal trial, e.g., separation of a child from its parents or even incarceration in a reformatory for the duration of the juvenile's minority.

Prior to *In Re Gault*, wherein the United States Supreme Court held that the due process clause of the United States Constitution was applicable to children, it was uniformly held, absent a statutory requirement, that a jury trial was not required in juvenile court proceedings.

One court, in upholding the view that a juvenile is not entitled to a jury trial, stated:

"A jury trial with all the clash and clamor of the adversary system that necessarily goes with it, would certainly invest a juvenile proceeding with the appearance of a criminal trial, and create in the mind and memory of the child the same effect as if it were. In our opinion there is more to be lost than gained. Certainly we cannot regard a jury as a better, fairer or

---

6 Ohio Revised Code § 2913.02.
7 McKeiver v. Pennsylvania, 29 LEd (2d) 647, 91 Supreme Court . . .

(1971). Justices Douglas, Black, and Marshall dissenting.

more accurate factfinder than a competent and conscientious circuit judge. There may be some judges who do not fit this description, but neither do all juries."[8]

Numerous other courts and cases have dealt with this matter in the recent past and all continue to concur that juvenile court cases shall continue to be heard by judges and not by juries.[9]

§ 19.3   Jurisdiction

It is a well-known legal fact that before a law enforcement officer may make a valid arrest of any person, the person so arrested must fit into a class or classification concerning which the officer has authority to act.[10] For example, subject to certain exceptions, the officer would have a warrant for the person's arrest, the party has committed a misdemeanor in the officer's presence, or the officer has probable cause to believe the party has committed a felony.[11]

Similarly, before any court can make a valid, enforceable order, the matter must be properly before the court and the court must make a finding. This constitutes jurisdiction. A good definition of jurisdiction, as it applies to courts, is as follows: "Jurisdiction of a court is that power conferred upon it by law, by which it is authorized to hear, determine, and render final judgment in an action, and to enforce its judgments by legal process."[12]

In a practical sense, what does this mean? In general, there are two types of jurisdiction. Jurisdiction over the "person," i.e., the defendant or the plaintiff, and jurisdiction over the "thing," i.e., the subject matter of the particular case.

For example, if a husband sues a wife for divorce, the case is not heard in the bankruptcy court. Obviously the Federal Bankruptcy Court has no jurisdiction to hear a domestic problem. Similarly if an offense is against the criminal laws or stat-

---

[8] Dryden v. The Commonwealth (Kentucky), 4 CRL 2253 (1968).

[9] For example, see A "In re F.," 355 New York Supreme Court, (2d) 143 (1974). B "United States v. Doe," 385, F. Supp., 902 (1974).

[10] United States Constitution, Fourth Amendment.

[11] Schneider's Ohio Criminal Code op. cit., pp. 23-27.

[12] 14 OJur(2d), Courts; Section 93.

utes of the state of Ohio, and it is committed within Ohio, the criminal courts of the state of Indiana would have no jurisdiction to hear the offense; and, if the state of Indiana did hear such an action and make an order, or the Federal Bankruptcy Court attempted to hear a domestic problem, the order, decree, or judgment that the court so ordered would be void.

Likewise, before the juvenile court can make an enforceable, binding order, the following prerequisites must have been met:

(1) The subject (person) upon whom the order is made, must fall within one of the categories granted by statute to the juvenile court.

(2) Service of summons in accord with the particular statutory requirements, and the case law interpreting same, must have been had (subject to emergency orders).

(3) After service, a hearing, in accord with the procedures set forth in the *Gault* case must have been had, and the court must have found, not by the civil standard or degree of proof of a mere preponderance of the evidence, nor the equity court standard of clear and convincing evidence, but by the criminal court standard of "beyond a reasonable doubt," that the juvenile has been found to be delinquent or is otherwise within the jurisdiction of the court.[13]

If one seeks to prevent a person from performing a particular act, or in the alternative, seeks to force him to perform some act, there are various remedies at law and in equity available.

In any such case, of course, it would be necessary to file a suit in the proper court, and follow the prescribed procedural aspects. The same applies to controlling juvenile behavior.

Certain legal requirements must be satisfied and procedures followed before the court can make an enforceable

[13] In re Winship, 90 SCt 1068, 51 OhioOp(2d) 323, 25 LEd(2d) 368, 397 US 358 (1970).

order; otherwise, the judgment entry would be void.

Courts should not make unenforceable orders. Within the definition of jurisdiction, we saw that a court has "the ability to enforce its judgment by legal process." [14] Practically applied, this means that a court should not make an order which it cannot "enforce . . . by legal process."

This also applies to law enforcement officers who must exercise their authority within the framework of proper law enforcement, just as courts must follow the law. Youth, always quick to detect hypocrisy, recognizes improper acts and unenforceable orders; and when this occurs respect is undermined for other acts of law enforcement or court orders, no matter how valid and enforceable they may be.

§ 19.4 Intake and detention

As we have previously mentioned, throughout this section, we will be comparing the similarities and noting the differences between cases in which the defendant is an adult, and cases in which the defendant is a juvenile.

If a police officer views an adult committing, for example, a minor traffic offense such as speeding, and if the officer stops the offender, he may if he so desires, issue the errant driver a citation, that is, an affidavit charging the person with the offense. When this is filled out, the person is not actually taken into custody, but he must appear in court. He acknowledges receipt of a copy of the citation, and promises to appear in the Police, County, Municipal, or Mayor's Court at the time stated by the arresting officer.

If the police officer observes an adult commit a more serious offense, for example, driving while intoxicated, he will not issue a citation, but will in accord with the individual state procedures, make a physical arrest and take the allegedly intoxicated driver into custody. That is, he takes him to jail, the police station, or the designated center.

[14] 14 OJur(2d), Courts; Section 93 (op. cit.).

An appearance bond to guarantee the appearance of the defendant is set, usually from a prorated schedule, and the defendant is placed in jail until either the time of his hearing, or the posting of the appearance bond, whichever occurs sooner.

In the same way, if in the judgment of the arresting officer, the facts are such that a juvenile should be given a citation for his minor offense, then the officer does not make a return on a warrant and physically take a minor into custody, but merely releases him or her upon the minor's, and in many instances the parents', promise and signature that the minor will appear in court at either the time stated by the officer, or the time to be set by the court.

Conversely, if in the officer's opinion, the minor should physically be taken into custody, the officer has the authority to do this, and then he must take the minor to the Juvenile Detention Center, or to the holding place designated by the juvenile court, utilizing police detention facilities no longer than is absolutely necessary for such referral to juvenile intake or return to the parents or lawful custodians.[15]

The problems involved in taking a juvenile to the police station instead of directly to the juvenile court have already been discussed.[16] Under present procedure, if a minor is taken to the juvenile court center, or held in temporary police detention, great caution should be taken to avoid the juvenile "waiving his rights" without the presence of legal counsel. Even if parents are present at the time, it is highly possible that a statement taken under such circumstances, in the absence of counsel, might be inadmissible.[17]

However, it is most important to note that this entire area of "under what circumstances a juvenile can waive his rights" is highly controversial. While some courts have concluded that the presence of counsel is required, others have insisted only on the presence of parents, and still others have held to the

---

[15] Standard 5.9, "Guidelines for Temporary Police Detention Practices," Standards, op. cit., p. 214.

[16] Missouri v. Joseph Franz Arbeiten, 408 SW(2d) 26 (1966).

[17] Standard 5.8, "Guidelines for Interrogation and Waiver of the Right Against Self Incrimination," Standards, ibid., pp. 212 and 213.

view that neither are absolutely required in order for a youth to make an effective waiver.[18]

Therefore, it is important for supervisory police personnel, police officers at the Police Academy and the individual officer assigned to the detective division, the juvenile bureau, or the precinct or district to know and follow the state statutory rules. If the officer decides to give a juvenile a citation, he fills out the appropriate affidavit form, has his signature acknowledged by a notary or deputy clerk—in many large departments this is usually a sergeant on his relief—and going through channels, files same with the juvenile court. In this instance, just as in the case involving the previous example of an adult traffic offender, no warrant is returned. The paper work is forwarded to the juvenile court, and the case is placed on its docket according to its own schedule.

However, for the purposes of our current discussion, let us assume that the offense committed by the juvenile, or the circumstances in which the officer finds him, are such as to warrant the officer physically taking the juvenile defendant into custody. The officer takes the juvenile into custody, completes the "on the scene" paper work required, and proceeds to the Juvenile Court Center.

What happens then? What is the responsibility of the police officer at this time? What happens to the juvenile? What follow-through or procedure is required by the arresting officer? These questions will be answered in the following discussion.

Depending upon the statutory language of the given state, the arresting officer should then either "directly" or "forthwith" or in accord with the given statute, take the juvenile in custody before the Juvenile Court judge, or as occurs in virtually all the cases, his agent, the detention home officer.

Let us assume that is now the status of our particular juve-

[18] For discussion of this issue the reader is referred to (A) Samuel M. Davis, *Rights of Juveniles,* Clark Boardman Co., New York, 1974; (B) Commonwealth v. Cain, 279 New England (2d) 706 (Mass., 1972); (C) Connecticut General Statutes. Ann. § 17-66 d (a) (Supp., 1973); (D) Mc-Clintock v. State, 253 Indiana, 333, 253 N.E. (2d) 333 (1969); (E) Okla. Statutes Ann., Title 10, § 1109 (a) (Supp., 1974).

nile. He now finds himself in the Detention Home.

§ 19.5 Detention

We know that in most cases, adults are entitled to be released under bond, pending a hearing on the merits of the case. The question immediately arises, does release pending hearing under bond apply to juveniles?

This is a highly controversial area of contemporary thought. The Standards emphatically oppose the use of bail bonds in any form or the use of any other financial conditions for the release of juveniles.[19]

However, the trend of some cases, and the recommendation of other sources is that juveniles, just as adults, are entitled to be released under bond, pending their appearance for the offense with which they have been charged.[20]

Those who argue in favor of the juvenile's right to bail raise the question as to what constitutional justification exists for depriving those, who by the mere accident of age are under the age jurisdiction of the adult courts, from being released from custody under bond. They cite rather effectively the fact that the law does not exclude from the right to bail arrested defendants who are, for example, between the ages of 30 and 40 or who are, for example, between the ages of 50 and 60; and they pursue the argument by stating that to exclude those "under the age of 18" would be equally as arbitrary as choosing another age group for exclusion.

Those who oppose the use of financial considerations in relation to the release of juveniles from detention, including the Standards, argue very effectively that: "This recommendation is based on the demonstrated inadequacies of the bail system as well as the potential hazards of using financial conditions for juveniles. A juvenile is unlikely to have independent financial resources that could be used to post bail. Even with such resources, he or she could not sign a binding bail bond because a minor is not ordinarily liable on a contract. Consequently, the

[19] Standard 12.12, "Conditions of Release," Standards (1976), op. cit., p. 404.

[20] Smith v. McCravy, *Criminal Law Report*, Vol. 1 2153, May 25, 1967.

youth would have to depend on parents or other interested adults to post bond. If an adult posted a bond, the youth's incentive to appear would arguably be defeated, since he or she would not personally forfeit anything upon non-appearance. On the other hand, a parent might refuse to post bail and force the youth to remain in detention. Finally, financial conditions discriminate against indigent juveniles and their families."[21]

For our present discussion, let us assume that the juvenile does not receive an immediate release on bail. The person charged with the responsibility of maintaining the detention home or place of care should know the reasons why the particular juvenile has been brought to his custody. If a police officer arrests an adult, the adult defendant is taken into custody. If it is a misdemeanor committed in the near presence of the officer, an affidavit is signed, or if it is a misdemeanor arrest under a warrant, or a felony, a "return" is made on the warrant, and the defendant is taken into custody. Likewise, there must be written, properly formulated reasons why a juvenile is brought into custody. And these statements should be weighed carefully against the criteria previously discussed for detaining juveniles in either secure or non-secure custody.

Police procedure manuals are replete with the idea of assurance that after an arrest, an incarcerated defendant is entitled to one telephone call. The Standards address themselves to the problem of communication after detention and are emphatic not only about the need to provide the assistance of legal counsel,[22] but also about the entire matter of phone calls, visits, and letters between delinquents in custody and their families or significant others in their lives.[23]

In effect, all those responsible for custodial care of juveniles as a result of their arrest are strongly encouraged to protect such juveniles' rights to access by counsel in every way possible, and to make no undue prohibitions against phone calls, visits and letters from families and significant others. It is also stressed that phone calls should not be monitored and mail and pack-

[21] Standard 12.12, "Conditions of Release," op. cit., p. 404.

[22] Standard 16.1, "Juvenile's Right to Counsel," Standards (1976), op.

cit., p. 550.

[23] Standard 24.13, "Communications," ibid., p. 722.

ages should not be censored, except when security demands, and then only in the presence of the juvenile involved.

Unfortunately, actual practice varies widely between jurisdictions, and tragically, most jurisdictions continue to house juveniles in the common jail along with adult offenders, in which case they are deprived of many of the protections urged by the Standards.

This means that if you as a duly authorized law enforcement officer deem it advisable that you should take a particular juvenile into custody, and should incarcerate him at the detention center (or the jail in many jurisdictions), he has the protection of the 8th Amendment in regard to communicating with his attorney, having contacts with his parents with "reasonable frequency" and, in some jurisdictions, having the opportunity to be released on reasonable bail.

His legal rights do not cease at the time of his arrest or detention. In fact, as seen above, there are specific rights to which he becomes entitled at those times.

§ 19.6   Physical care

It stands to reason that if one of the goals of a juvenile court is to prevent the juveniles that come before it from becoming hardened criminals, then a Juvenile Court Center should not actively nor passively allow juveniles to become acquainted with the criminal element of society.

Oftentimes juvenile courts do allow, or even force, such situations to come into existence. For example, it is unfortunate, but not uncommon in some states, to find that the juvenile is physically arrested by a police officer and is brought to the Detention Center and finds himself incarcerated in the same holding center or jail, with adults that have been charged with committing a full range of offenses. (In the United States less than one-half of all counties have separate Juvenile Detention Homes or proper facilities.)

Therefore, even though the long-range goal of the juvenile court is to rehabilitate the particular juvenile, it is in fact encouraging him to join the criminal element of society by forcing him through incarceration to associate with hardened criminals. The Standards insist that no juvenile be placed in the common jail with adults.[24] Likewise, many existing statutes provide that juveniles be kept separate and apart from those confined in the county jail. Yet in practice, in many of our nation's cities, as well as our rural areas, juveniles and adults are often confined in not only the same jail range, but often in the same cells. The explanation given is often "overcrowding" despite the mandatory language of the various statutes. For example, "No child under eighteen years of age shall be placed in or committed to any prison, jail or lock up, nor shall such child so brought into any police station, vehicle, or other place where such child can come in contact or communication with any adult convicted of crime or under arrest and charged with crime."[25]

Standard 22.2, "State Standards for Detention and Shelter Care Facilities" very explicitly states that not only should juveniles be kept in a separate place of detention from the jail, but that such a place should meet rigorous conditions as to location, capacity, design, construction, equipment and operation including fire and safety precautions, medical services, qualifications and number of personnel, and the quality of service provided for the juveniles contained therein.[26]

There should also be a distinction made between "secure" and "non-secure" facilities for detaining juveniles. Various state laws and other sources of definitions show some variance in the exact meaning of these terms, but a general concensus exists that the terms should be defined very much as the words themselves sound. For example, New York state defines these terms as follows: (1) Secure detention facility—"A facility characterized by physically restricting construction, hardware and procedures." (2) Non-security detention facility—"A facility characterized by the absence of physically restricting construc-

---

[24] Standard 22.3, "Use of Jails Prohibited," Standards (1976), op. cit., p. 667.

[25] Ohio Revised Code § 2151.34.

[26] Standard 22.2, "State Standards for Detention and Shelter Care Facilities," ibid., p. 665.

tion, hardware and procedures."[27]

In keeping with the recommendations for the use of the "least restrictive alternative" in the placement of juveniles, the non-secure facility should be used at all times for juveniles not requiring a high degree of security, and this includes some adjudicated delinquents along with status offenders, endangered children, etc.

Again, the practical aspects become important. If a county budget provides for only one detention center, how can the same budget provide separate holding centers for adults and juveniles? It is ironical that there are massive expenditures for zoos, dog pounds and libraries, but little funds are available for children in trouble.

This issue has been met in a number of different states by the creation of regional detention centers. In these situations, where the volume and the budget of one particular county does not justify the creation of a juvenile detention center for that county, the statutes authorize the county commissioners or the appropriate administrative agency of that county to enter into a contract with contiguous and adjoining counties, for the creation of a regional center.[28] This has the advantage of offering a true juvenile detention center. It also offers the advantages of sharing the cost, but does present a physical and geographical problem of transporting the juveniles back and forth to their respective counties. However, if one is to weigh the advantages of keeping the juveniles separate from the adults against the mechanics of transportation, the advantages of a regional center become readily apparent.

Once a juvenile has been placed in the detention center, it becomes incumbent upon the restraining authority, the juvenile court, to provide for his physical needs. These necessaries would include such things as adequate shelter, clothing, food, and medical attention. The deplorable condition of many of our nation's jails and incarceration centers has often been brought to the public attention. It is not the purpose of this book to

---

[27] See No. 712 "Definitions," New York Family Court Act, op. cit., p. 330.

[28] Ohio Revised Code § 2151.34.

discuss such evils. Let it suffice to say that in addition to the detention center being secure, it should present as few jail features as possible. For example, the use of closely knit security screening in windows, as opposed to jail bars; the use of trained detention personnel as opposed to armed guards; and the use of effective detention programming, as opposed to mere custodial care.

It should be noted that even a well run and properly staffed detention center will, on occasion, be presented with disciplinary problems presented by some of those incarcerated. A question of reasonableness in the use of proper but not excessive force is the answer. A trained detention officer can often talk with a momentarily disturbed juvenile, and avoid entirely the use of physical force. Just as in making an arrest, force may be required, but restraint is in order. It is always essential that those dealing with juveniles learn not to react to hostility with hostility, and that it is better to restrain an individual than to assault him.

§ 19.7   Psychiatric, psychological clinics and medical examinations

"Following the filing of a petition, the court may order that the child shall be examined by or under the directions of a physician or a psychologist, to aid the court in determining: (1) material allegation in a neglect petition relating to the child's physical or mental condition; (2) the child's competence to participate in the proceedings; (3) the child's legal responsibility for his acts; or (4) the propriety of transferring the case to criminal court under Article III of these rules.

"Following an adjudication, the court may order such an examination to aid it in making the proper disposition concerning the child."[29]

If we look at the above rule, certain things become readily apparent. Mainly, if a child is the victim of an assault or neglect complaint, a medical examination should be completed as quickly as possible to determine the extent of damage to the child. Likewise, if the issue is whether or not the juvenile is

[29] Model Rules for Juvenile Courts, Rule 41.

competent to stand trial, it would be foolish to hold the child, have an adjudicatory hearing, and then have an examination, only to find from the doctor's report that the child was incompetent to stand trial in the first place.

Once the court has acquired jurisdiction to not only hear and determine the matter, but has made an actual finding (adjudication), this makes the child a ward of the court, and the court may then proceed to conduct such physical and mental examinations as may be necessary and proper.[30]

None of these guidlines answers one of the most basic questions concerning the physical and mental examination of juveniles in custody: Does the detention center have a right to conduct a physical or mental examination of a juvenile upon the child's being placed in detention?

A search of the statutory and case law has presented no definite answers. However, certain basic guidelines can be assumed; the superintendent of a detention center should, by the virtue of his office, possess certain inherent powers. He would seem to have the authority to do all things *necessary* and *proper* to fulfill his statutory duties as superintendent. It would appear that one of these would be to regulate the health of those in his charge. Therefore, an examination which would determine the existence of, for example, contagious disease would appear to be such an inherent power.

However, an interesting constitutional problem of search and seizure arises. If, at the time of a physical examination, prior to adjudication, evidence is accumulated which is subsequently used in the adjudicatory hearing of the particular juvenile, it would appear that the normal rules of search and seizure would be necessary.

As we know, search for objects in body cavities are subject to certain limitations. The following statement from the "Manual on the Law of Search and Seizure"[31] sets out the current rules:

---

[30] Ibid.

[31] *Manual on the Law of Search and Seizure,* Criminal Division, Dept. of Justice, p. 20.

"(1) There must be good reason to believe that the person has within his body evidence which should be removed;

(2) The search must be made by a doctor working under sanitary conditions in a medically approved way;

(3) Force may be used only to the extent necessary to make the person submit to the examination."[32]

"Where there is need to prevent the destruction of evidence, as when a person stuffs narcotics in his mouth, an agent can close his arm around the person's neck to prevent him from swallowing the evidence."[33]

The same authority also sets out the current rule for "evidence in body fluids:"[34]

"Under the same limitations (as above), blood, urine, and saliva may be taken from the person and subjected to laboratory analysis to determine the presence of alcohol, narcotics, or dangerous drugs, where there is a clear indication that such evidence will be found."[35]

All of this applies to adults, but it does not answer the still unanswered, and probably unanswerable, question of the authority to touch the body of a minor without the permission of the parent. Nor has the question of civil liability in such matters been determined.

In the absence of a direct answer to these questions by the courts, it would seem that enforcement officers, detention personnel and others must be guided by the dictates of necessity and the limitations imposed by reasonableness.

§ 19.8   Preliminary or detention hearing

Law enforcement officers have long been familiar with preliminary hearings. In essence, when a law enforcement officer thinks of a preliminary hearing in its usual context, he thinks of a hearing before a municipal, county, or a police court judge,

[32] Blackford v. United States, 247 F(2d) 745 (1957).

[33] Espinoza v. United States, 278 F(2d) 802, but see Taglauone v. United States, 291 F(2d) 262 quoted in *Manual on the Law of Search and* *Seizure,* p. 20.

[34] Ibid.

[35] Schmerber v. California, 384 US 757 (1966), quoted in *"Manual on the Law of Search and Seizure,"* p. 20.

in which the particular individual standing before the court is charged with a felony, and in which the state must only show "probable cause" to have the particular defendant bound over to the grand jury.

This is a valid description of preliminary hearings as they apply to adults. However, in Juvenile Courts the context is somewhat different. The Model Rules for Juvenile Courts have in fact provided for three separate and distinct hearings in a juvenile matter.[36] In a number of juvenile courts, these hearings may take place simultaneously. However, in our consideration, we shall deal with them separately so that the purpose and requirements of each might be understood.

If an adult is arrested and charged with a misdemeanor, the usual procedure is to have him appear the morning after arrest or, if not, the following morning at the next regularly scheduled court date, before the police, county, or municipal court judge. Unless a continuance is requested, a hearing is had and disposition rendered. If the offense is a felony, a preliminary hearing is held and the court determines whether or not there is probable cause to believe that this defendant committed the offense. However, as we have seen and will continue to see, in juvenile court before the hearing on the merits, there must be service of summons on not only the particular juvenile defendant, but also upon his parents and/or guardian. Therefore, it is not possible in the ordinary case to fulfill the requirements of service prior to the morning after incarceration or the "next regularly scheduled court date." This is the reason for the detention hearing for juveniles.

A detention hearing has but one issue, and that is whether the particular child who is now incarcerated should: (1) be released from the detention center; or (2) be continued to be held in the detention center, pending the adjudicatory hearing (the hearing trial on the merits).

Standard 12.11, "Detention Hearings" sets the rules for making this determination as follows: "The detention hearings

[36] Model Rules for Juvenile Courts
op. cit., Article VI; Article VII; Article
VIII; Article IX.

should conform to due process requirements. It should commence with the judicial determination of probable cause. If the prosecution establishes by competent evidence probable cause to believe that the juvenile has committed the alleged juvenile act, the court should review the necessity for continued detention. Unless the prosecution demonstrates by clear and convincing evidence that there is a need for continued detention according to detention criteria, the court should release the juvenile upon conditions pending the next judicial proceeding. A court order containing the juvenile's detention should be supported by written reasons and findings of fact.[37]

The criteria for detention mentioned in the above paragraph are those set by Standard 12.7 "Criteria for Pre-Adjudicatory Detention of Juveniles" and they were previously referred to in this text in our discussion of police procedure in arresting and requesting detention of juveniles.[38]

Needless to say, all the pertinent information that the law enforcement officer can present to the court, such as attitude of the child and parents at the time of arrest, unusual factors surrounding the offense, past involvement of the child in offenses which were settled by station-house adjustment, together with the officer's overall knowledge of the child and his family, are of great assistance in determining whether or not the child should be held.

And, as we saw in previous discussion of bail bond, it is possible the court might feel that a particular child should be held, but if it is a court which acts upon the disputed presumption that the child has a constitutional right to release, with financial bond being put up as an assurance, the court might release the child if sufficient surety is posted.

It is the practice in a number of jurisdictions that if a particular juvenile is on probation, is arrested for another offense and is then placed in the detention facility, the probation department, as a matter of course, places a "probation holder" on the particular juvenile. This assures the probation officer that his or her ward will remain in custody. But, if used with-

---

[37] Standards, op. cit., p. 401.   [38] See Standards, op. cit., p. 390.

out discretion, it can also be an effective tool in denying the particular defendant his constitutional guarantees. It is our opinion that a holder should be placed only when the individual probation officer has positive knowledge that the probationer has in fact committed the offense or if the probationer's overall adjustment has been such that the probation officer had begun the process of apprehending him for probation violation.

As we have seen, the whole purpose of bail is to guarantee the appearance of the particular defendant at the hearing on the merits. Likewise, the entire purpose of the detention hearing is to determine whether or not it is necessary to hold the particular juvenile to protect the community, or to assure his presence, and/or his safety, for the hearing on the merits (the adjudicatory hearing).

The detention hearings described above shall be held within forty-eight hours from the time of the admission of the child to the detention facility.[39]

A common problem often arises in locating the boy or girl's parents in time to comply with the above time requirements mandated for the detention hearing.

What are the law enforcement officer's responsibilities at this point? Obviously, if he knows the whereabouts of the parents (e.g., their residence, work, social habits or recreational tastes), he would be assisting the court by advising them of the probable whereabouts of the parents so that they might be served and notified of the matter so that the case might go forward.

§ 19.9   Service, notice (petition and summons)

It is a basic concept of due process that any court, as we saw in our discussion of Jurisdiction, shall have the power to "hear and determine" causes which are properly before it. This concept of *hearing and determining* is the basis of the "Adjudicatory Hearing."

In any court, be it a juvenile court, criminal court, civil

---

[39] Standard 12.11, "Detention Hearings," Standards, op. cit., p. 401; Standard 12.5, "Petition and Summons," Standards, op. cit., p. 385.

court, probate court, domestic relations court, etc., certain pre-requisites must be met before the particular court in question is in a position to hear and determine the particular matter.

For example, in a *civil* action, before the court is in a position to finally hear and determine the matter, and depending upon the statutory rules and the local rules of court, the petition which is the formal proper way of starting a lawsuit and is now often referred to as a complaint, must be filed, and service of summons must be had, that is the defendant is notified that he is defendant. The defendant offers an answer to the complaint or has the opportunity to so act; the plaintiff has the opportunity to "reply" or to answer issues brought up by the defendant in his "answer;" various motions and pretrial orders are taken care of; discovery is fulfilled; and after all of this has been disposed of, the case finally comes on to be heard on its merits. All of the above must be disposed of before the court may hear and determine the particular issue in a *civil court*.

Now let us compare this with an action in the juvenile court. The Standards specify certain procedures for service of summons, that is the formal way in which the child and his parents, and/or guardians or other interested parties, must be notified of the particular charge against the juvenile.

In essence, a copy of the petition alleging the child to be delinquent, etc., must be served personally upon the parents; or there may be service on him by leaving a copy of it at his or her usual place of residence. If the parents have left the jurisdiction, and a diligent search has failed to reveal their whereabouts, it is possible to obtain constructive service upon them through publication. This means that a notice of the hearing is printed in the newspaper. In any event, service of summons must be had upon the parents and/or guardian, as well as upon the child, before the court is in a position to properly hear the matter on the merits.

The importance of this cannot be overstressed. If the court proceeds to make a finding on the merits without complying with the statutory and mandated prerequisites, then its findings will be a nullity, and any order of probation or placement that it will subsequently make would be subject to a motion to have it set aside.

Not only must the notice be given, it must be "timely" given.[40] The idea is to give the juvenile or his parents sufficient time to prepare a defense to the charge.

Finally, notice to the juvenile must contain the elements of the particular charge against him,[41] not the mere conclusion that he is "delinquent." This means that the charge must be made clear and explicit or the actual offense described so that child and parents can understand the reason for the hearing.

§ 19.10   Adjudicatory hearings

Let us assume that the statutory requirements of service and process have been met, and the case now comes up for hearing. What takes place at a juvenile hearing, the degree or quantum of proof, and the role of the law enforcement officer will be the subject of discussion in this section. (Attention is invited to Standards 13.1 through 13.8 which deal explicitly with matters concerning adjudicatory hearings.)[42]

The original concept of the juvenile court was for it to be a "nonadversary" proceeding despite the fact that American jurisprudence has in many cases been based upon the idea that each side shall assume the role of an advocate, adversary proceeding shall take place, and that this will bring out the truth. This concept is seen in the adult criminal courts quite clearly where the state is represented by a prosecutor and the defendant by his defense counsel, a criminal lawyer. This is also seen in civil cases where the plaintiff is represented by his lawyer against the defendant and the defendant's lawyer.

However, the original idea of the juvenile court was that the adversary proceedings should be removed, and without the catalyst of the "other side," the best interest of the child would be met. However, recent court decisions[43] have tended to turn the adjudicatory hearings in the juvenile court to a more or less adversary role. Therefore, it is not uncommon to see the

[40] In re Gault, 387 US 1, at pp. 31-34, 40 OhioOp(2d) 378, 18 LEd (2d) 527, 87 SCt 1428.

[41] Ibid.

[42] See Chapter 13, "Adjudication Processes," (Standards 13.1 through 13.8), Standards, op. cit., p. 407.

[43] In re Gault, U.S. Supreme Court, 387 US 1.

state represented by a prosecutor. As we will see in an ensuing section, the juvenile is also often represented by counsel who, rightfully, assumes the traditional advocate's position. In any event, it becomes incumbent upon the court at the time of the adjudicatory hearing to determine that in fact the matter is properly before the court. "The court shall begin the hearing by determining all parties are present, and that lawful notice of the hearing has been given, and it shall require that these facts be of record."[44]

In the adult courts, a "plea" is always taken. The juvenile courts "after explaining to the child the right to remain silent and finding that he adequately understands this right" will ask the juvenile whether he "admits or denies all or some of the allegations in the petition."[45] This is the juvenile court equivalent of a plea. As we know, in adult courts, if an adult pleads guilty, all the court has left to do is to sentence him. In juvenile court the procedure should follow these guidelines: "Prior to accepting an admission to a delinquency petition, the family court judge should inquire thoroughly into the circumstances of that admission.

"The judge should . . . .determine that the juvenile has the capacity to understand the nature and consequences of the proceeding. . . . The family court judge should also determine whether the admission is knowingly and voluntarily offered. . . . It also should inform the juvenile of the most restrictive disposition that could be imposed in the case. . . . The court should inform the juvenile that negotiated admissions are prohibited and not binding on the court. . . . No admission that is the result of a plea agreement (bargaining) should be accepted by the court."[46]

Let us now assume that the particular juvenile has denied involvement in the complaint. It now becomes incumbent upon the state to prove its case. The immediate issue is how far the state will have to go in proving its case. This is of great importance to law enforcement officers.

---

[44] Model Rules for Juvenile Courts, Rule 23.

[45] Ibid.

[46] Standard 13.2, "Acceptance of an Admission to a Delinquency Petition," Standards, op. cit., p. 414.

As we noted under the section on Jurisdiction, there are three degrees or standards of proof which have been recognized at law. In an ordinary civil case, the plaintiff or the one bringing the suit must prove his case by only "a mere preponderance" of the evidence. In the ordinary criminal case, the state must prove its case not by a "mere preponderance" of the evidence, but must prove it "beyond a reasonable doubt."

What constitutes "a reasonable doubt"? It has been defined as follows:

"It is not a mere possible doubt, because everything relating to human affairs or depending upon moral evidence is open to some possible or imaginary doubt. It is that state of the case which, after the entire comparison and consideration of all the evidence, leaves the minds of the jurors in that condition that they cannot say they feel an abiding conviction to a moral certainty of the truth of the charge."[47]

Somewhere in between the standard of a mere "preponderance of the evidence," and the above much higher standard of "beyond a reasonable doubt" falls the traditional equity standard of "clear and convincing" evidence.

Historically, equity cases in which there was no adequate remedy under the common law, required this standard of proof of "clear and convincing" evidence. As there were no provisions for juvenile courts and they arose somewhat outside the common law courts, the standard of proof which has long been associated with them is the equity standard, i.e., clear and convincing evidence. Indeed, this standard is set forth in Rule 26, "Standard of Proof" wherein it is said: "The facts alleged in the petition shall be proved by clear and convincing evidence."[48]

However, a case decided by the United States Supreme Court in 1970 changed this standard and stated that cases involving juveniles must be proven "beyond a reasonable doubt." In the recent case In re Winship,[49] the highest court in the land settled this question emphatically; and it is the opinion of your

---

[47] Ohio Revised Code § 2945.04.
[48] Model Rules for Juvenile Courts op. cit., Rule 26.

[49] In re Winship, 397 US 358, 51 OhioOp(2d) 232, 25 LEd(2d) 368, 90 SCt 1068 (1970).

author that this is in keeping with sound legal thinking.[50]

§ 19.11 Right to counsel

One of the most basic constitutional rights which any defendant, any accused, or any party has at any time is the right to counsel. It has not always been this way. For example, we know from history that back in the days of the "Star Chamber," a defendant did not have the right to be present at his own hearing. He was merely informed of the order and sentence of the court. None of the constitutional guarantees, which all of us, and all defendants in court enjoy in the United States in this day and age, were known.

In this country, the right to counsel, while not in accord with the old "Star Chamber" philosophy, has not always been recognized. For example, just within the past fifty years, cases have gone to the United States Supreme Court on whether or not appointed counsel is necessary for an indigent defendant in cases where the charge was a capital one (death sentence), a felony, or a guilty plea.[51]

The review courts have frequently made a distinction between one's right to retained counsel, as opposed to appointed counsel. For example, for years there has been no question in the American courts that a defendant charged with a felony, even if he pleads guilty, is entitled to counsel at the time of his hearings. However, not until the 1960's did the United States Supreme Court mandate that appointed counsel be present for a guilty plea for all indigent defendants in felony cases.[52]

What effect, if any, does all of this have upon law enforcement officers in juvenile cases? The *Gault* case mandated upon all juvenile courts the fact that counsel be present, unless knowingly and intelligently waived in all cases in which a

---

[50] (See for example: "The Standard of Proof and Juvenile Proceedings; Gault Beyond a Reasonable Doubt" by James H. Cohen, 68 MichLRev 567, January, 1970.) See also Standard 13.5, "Adjudication of Delinquency—Standard of Proof," Standards (1976), op. cit., p. 422.

[51] See Powell v. Alabama, 287 US 45 (1932); Betts v. Brady, 316 US 455 (1942); Gideon v. Wainwright, 372 US 335 (1963).

[52] Gideon v. Wainwright, 372 US 335 (1963).

juvenile, convicted (adjudicated), might as a result thereof be incarcerated.[53]

The Standards state in essence that the juvenile is entitled to representation by legal counsel at every stage of the court process.[54] It also provides for the appointment of counsel for all indigents.[55] Within the same paragraph it also provides that juveniles can be represented by counsel retained by them and that the juvenile court should not accept a waiver of counsel unless the court determines that the juvenile has conferred at least once with a lawyer and is waiving the right competently, voluntarily and with full understanding of the consequences.[56]

An interesting situation may arise. What if the parent waives the right to counsel, but the child refuses? Or, in the alternative, what if the child waives the right to counsel, but the parent refuses?[57] Or, what if the parent is in fact the prosecuting witness which is the case when a parent charges his child with being incorrigible, and in fact the parent is appearing as a witness for the prosecution? Finally, what happens if the parent is not present, or has in fact abandoned the child?

Again, the Standards provide for such matters.[58] In essence, when it appears that the interest of the child and the parent are adverse, a "guardian ad litem" shall be appointed to represent the interest of the child. This guardian ad litem is often also the child's attorney.

An interesting problem and cause of great dispute arises around the question of how, or even if, juveniles (even when assisted by their parents) may "competently and intelligently waive the right to counsel." Justice Douglas of the United States Supreme Court said in the case of *Gallegos* v. *Colorado*, that a "14 year old boy does not know his constitutional rights, let

---

[53] In re Gault op. cit.

[54] Standard 16.7, "Stages of Representation in Family Court Proceedings," Standards, op. cit., p. 565.

[55] Standard 16.5, "Representation for Children in Family Court Proceedings," ibid., p. 559.

[56] Standard 16.1, "Juvenile's Right to Counsel," ibid., p. 550.

[57] Model Rules for Juvenile Courts, Rule 39.

[58] Standard 16.4, "The Role of Counsel Appointed Guardian Ad Litem," op. cit., p. 557.

alone how to assert them."[59] Conversely, how can a 14-year-old boy, or for that matter, a 15, 16, or 17-year-old, know what the right to counsel means when many adults do not?

The Standards make it very clear that in the opinion of the learned members of the committee compiling their recommendations, it is simply impossible for a juvenile to waive this right without consulting at least once with counsel.

And, as has been stated by one authority: "of all the rights an accused has, the right to be represented by counsel is by far the most pervasive for it affects his ability to assert any other right he may have had."[60]

Law enforcement officers know from case law that at the proper time one must be advised of certain rights, including the right to counsel, and the right to remain silent, and that the accused defendant must "voluntarily, knowingly and intelligently" waive these rights before any statement made by him in a custodial interrogation may be admissible over objections at a hearing on the merits.[61]

The moral is clear. The mere acknowledgment, admission, or confession of a defendant is not enough to sustain a conviction. When we forget this, we jeopardize our effectiveness and we risk operating outside of the law.

We have just seen that this presents an enormous problem for law enforcement officers, as it is almost impossible to get a "knowing and intelligent" waiver from a juvenile. Again, from criminal law we realize that the best cases in this day and age are ones based upon investigative work and real or demonstrative evidence, and not on confessions.

Convictions in the criminal court today based solely and exclusively to any measurable degree upon an admission by the defendant, are on shaky grounds at best. If this is true in adult courts, it is more so in juvenile court where the defendant is by definition a juvenile.

[59] Gallegos v. Colorado, 370 US 49, 8 LEd(2d) 325, 82 SCt 1209, 87 ALR (2d) 614 (1962).

[60] "Federalism and State Criminal Procedure," 70 Harv. L. Rev. 8.

[61] Miranda v. Arizona, 384 US 436.

§ 19.12   Hearings for mentally ill and retarded

The law has long taken the position that every man is "presumed to be sane" and so liable at law for his voluntary acts. However, historically, the law has also recognized that if an individual is insane, he is not fully responsible. Even under the old common law, there was some recognition of mental illness. Today, mental illness may, under certain standards and conditions, excuse behavior that would otherwise be criminal.

As we know from criminal law, with certain exceptions every crime requires two elements, a "guilty mind" and an "overt act." The basis of this guilty mind is what the law refers to as the "mens rea." Obviously, if there is something mentally wrong with the defendant and by virtue thereof he cannot form the "mens rea," he cannot be guilty of a crime even if he has performed an overt criminal act.

A further distinction must be made, and that is, the difference between "present sanity" and the "defense of insanity." The former refers to the mental state of the defendant "before, during or after his trial."[62] The latter refers to his state of mental being "at the time the offense was committed."[63]

In recent times, the law has recognized several tests for determining whether or not one is "legally insane." We must stress again that we are talking about insanity from a legal viewpoint, and not from a medical viewpoint.

A leading case was decided by the House of Lords in 1843. In the *Daniel McNaughten* case[64] the issue of insanity was before the English court. In the facts, Danny McNaughten had shot and killed one Edward Drumond. The defense evidence was that at the time of the act Danny McNaughten was of "unsound mind." In the opinion, which was written by Lord Chief Justice Tindal, the following rule, which has become known as the "McNaughten Rule," was stated: "A defendant is not entitled to a defense on the grounds of insanity unless at the time of the crime he was laboring under such a defect of reason, from disease of the mind, as not to know the nature

62 Schneider's Ohio Criminal Code op. cit., p. 171.

63 Ibid., p. 172.

64 Daniel McNaughten, 10 Cl. and F. 200, 8 Ng Reprint 718.

and quality of the act he was doing; or, if he did know it, that he did not know he was doing what was wrong."[65] This McNaughten Rule has been followed in a majority of jurisdictions.

A modification of the above rule was introduced in 1954 in the case of *Durham* v. *United States*,[66] which was decided by the United States Court of Appeals for the District of Columbia Circuit. The defendant, Monty Durham, had past convictions for murder, theft, bad checks, and had also been a parole violator. At one point he had attempted suicide. In this particular case, he had been involved in a house-breaking. After waiving a jury, he was found guilty by the court. In essence, the only defense that Durham offered was that he was of unsound mind at the time of the offense. His lawyers argued that the previously mentioned, discussed and defined "McNaughten Rule" should be changed.

The trial court found Mr. Durham guilty and the case was appealed. In the above cited case in the Court of Appeals, the Court found errors and reversed and remanded for a new trial. In so doing, the court, through Circuit Judge Bazelon, set forth the following rule, which has become known as the "Durham Rule." It is simply that "an accused is not criminally responsible if his unlawful act was the product of mental disease, or mental defect."[67] This case is not followed in the vast majority of jurisdictions, but it is noteworthy.

The *Durham* case also introduced another important principle. This principle, although again noteworthy, is also not followed in the majority of jurisdictions. It was held that if the defendant offers some evidence of an unsound mind on the date of the act set forth in the indictment, the burden of proving that he was in fact sane, shifts to the prosecutor. As we saw before, every man is presumed by the law to be sane. However, under this *Durham* holding, if the defendant introduces some evidence that he was in fact not sane, then the state must prove that he was.[68] This becomes an essential element in proving the case, just as venue and the elements of the particular

---

[65] Ibid.

[66] Durham v. United States, 94 US App D.C. 228; 214 F(2d) 862 (1954).

[67] Ibid.

[68] Ibid.

charge are essential to the case.

What effect, if any, does all of this have on the law enforcement officers' relationship with juveniles? The effect is considerable because the courts recognize that a mature adult may, in a given factual situation, be held to a lesser degree of responsibility due to mental impairment. The standard of responsibility for immature juveniles should be less stringent than the standard for adults.

The Standards specifically deal with this issue of procedures related to disposition of mentally ill or mentally retarded juveniles by providing for the court to hold a hearing to determine the validity of allegations of mental illness or retardation, providing for institutional or agency study of the juvenile if such hearing finds that such a condition does exist, and if at such hearing the court finds that the desired study cannot be made on an outpatient basis, the Standards provide for temporary placement of the juvenile in a diagnostic facility for not more than thirty days with the condition that the facility submit a comprehensive report as to the juvenile's condition and an opinion as to whether the juvenile is committable within that time frame. It is further provided that if upon receipt of such a report it appears probable that the juvenile is so mentally retarded or ill as to be committable under the laws of that state, then the court should initiate proceedings under the law within that state relating to the commitment of the mentally ill or mentally retarded juvenile.[69]

In some states, such as under certain circumstances in Ohio, jurisdiction for the mentally ill child falls in the juvenile court.[70] In these hearings, which are similar to the hearings conducted for adults in probate court, an affidavit is filed in the juvenile court, stating that the juvenile in question is mentally incompetent. The following procedure outlining the appropriate Ohio Revised Code sections[71] is then followed.

After a service of summons is had in accordance with the

[69] Standard 14.18, "Procedures for Disposition of Mentally Ill or Mentally Retarded Juveniles," op. cit., p. 468.

[70] Ohio Revised Code, § 2151.23.

[71] Ohio Revised Code, Chap. 5122.

established statutory procedures, the case is called before a judge or referee of the juvenile court. Sitting with the judge or referee is a psychiatrist who has been appointed by the court. The psychiatrist, in fact, conducts the examination and makes a medical inquiry into the alleged mental impairment of the child. The petitioner (the person who signed the affidavit alleging the child to be mentally ill) is questioned as to why he believes the child is mentally ill.

At this time, (and this hearing is held within a statutory set period of time, which is usually one to two weeks after the petition is filed and the warrant returned), a determination is made as to whether or not the particular child shall be returned to the mental institution for further studies. If the examining psychiatrist finds that the child is not mentally ill, the child is discharged from custody forthwith. If the doctor feels that possible further study or hospitalization is indicated, the child is returned to the mental institution for such studies. Statutes, again varying from jurisdiction to jurisdiction, require that the child be brought back for further hearing within a short period of time, for example, in Ohio, a period not to exceed ninety days.

During the next ninety days, the child is studied by the doctors. At the end of that time their report is submitted to the court, and the court's examining psychiatrist. At this hearing, determination is made as to whether the child should be committed to the hospital indefinitely (I/H) or should be discharged.

§ 19.13   Dispositions

If the state, as we have seen in our previous discussions, fails to prove the allegations contained in the complaint beyond a reasonable doubt, the complaint should be dismissed and unless detained for another reason, the juvenile discharged from custody or from bond.

However, for purposes of this section let us assume that the above is not the case and the juvenile involved has been found to have been involved in the acts alleged in the petition. It is at this point that an important distinction between the adult

courts and the juvenile courts comes into play. In many instances, in the adult courts sentencing by the courts is "pro
forma," and merely a perfunctory act. In other words, if the
adult is convicted of offense "A," the court has no alternative
but to impose that sentence. For example, in the state of Ohio
in a first degree murder case, if the jury finds the defendant
guilty and fails to recommend mercy, the judge must sentence
the defendant to death in the electric chair. This is due to the
fact that the legislative assembly has so written the law.[72]

However, the whole concept of the juvenile court is that the
court acts in the best interest of the child. Once we have overcome, through due process, the problem of acquiring jurisdiction in the sense of a finding or adjudication, the juvenile court
is not bound to assess a set penalty but can truly act in the
best interest of the child. Of course, here again there are certain
statutory limitations upon what the court may or may not do.
For example, the dispositions it can impose upon a finding
of "delinquency" are different from those that may be imposed
upon a finding of "endangered."[73]

This distinction becomes necessary to avoid extremes. For
example, it would not be just to place a young man who has
only been illegally absent from school in a state industrial
school, although his absence has been a frequent occurrence.
The truancy would constitute an act which would be an "unruly" complaint, and as such the case should be handled and
disposed of in the manner provided for unruly children. However, if while truant from school the young man had burglar-
ized a home, stolen a car, and committed other delinquent
offenses, placement in a state institution is legally authorized.

It cannot be over-emphasized that the juvenile court is dealing with children, and it must make its dispositions accordingly.
The proper court should not fail to impose discipline, but it
should not over-react. One of the basic ideas of juvenile court
is to change the attitude and factors which caused the particular juvenile to become unruly and/or delinquent and, hope-

---

[72] Ohio Revised Code, § 2929.23.

[73] Standard Chapter 14, "Dispositions," Standards (1976), op. cit., pp.
431-501.

fully, prevent him or her from committing illegal or antisocial acts in the future.

Factors which cause a particular individual to commit a delinquent act might be entirely different from those which influence another juvenile at another time to go out and commit exactly the same act. This brings in the importance of individualized justice. If the juvenile court through its dispositions can act in such a manner as to change the factors which caused the delinquent act in the first place, and at the same time, if indicated, restore the victim of the delinquent act to his original position, then the juvenile court would be fulfilling its stated and statutory goal.

The Standards call[74] for a social study to be prepared by the probation department and presented to the court prior to actual disposition of the case. This study is in many ways similar to the pre-sentence investigation in the adult court. In both instances, the idea is to give the court proper perspective and the necessary tools before imposing sentence or disposition. Past record, family structure, school record, psychological studies, friends and associates, police contacts not reported to the court, past placements, if any, in foster homes or in more structured institutions, intelligence tests, marital status, children, if any, education, work record, general attitude, and outlook, all of these are important in determining the proper disposition.

Obviously, if a youngster has not eaten in three days and steals food because he is hungry, the motivation is different than that of a juvenile who wants an exciting experience and steals food he does not need. Consequently, the disposition should be different. Likewise, if a juvenile breaks into a building to have a warm place to sleep at night, his disposition should be different from that of a party who breaks into the same building with the intent to steal property which he in turn will sell to support his drug habit.

Explicitly, Standard 14.23 urges the prohibition of institutional commitment of status offenders. It states "In no event

[74] Standard 14.5, "Dispositional Information" Standards, op. cit., p. 442.

shall the family court disposition confine the child in an institution to which delinquents are committed."[75] Such a boy or girl should be allowed to remain in residence in his present location, but with one form or another of court supervision or assistance. In the case of a delinquent child, placement in a state institution is authorized (although it certainly is not always indicated).[76]

However, this practice was abolished by the United States Supreme Court in the case of *Kent* v. *United States*.[77] This case stands for the proposition that before a case involving a juvenile can be transferred from the juvenile court to the adult court, a hearing *must* be had in the juvenile court.

The Standards[78] are even more specific in this regard. The requirements outlined therein for transfer to adult court are as follows:

(1) The juvenile is charged with a delinquent act.

(2) The juvenile was sixteen years or over at the time of the alleged commission of the act.

(3) The alleged delinquent act is:
    (a) Aggravated or heinous in nature, or
    (b) Part of a pattern of repeated delinquent acts

(4) There is probable cause to believe the juvenile committed acts which are to be the subject of the adult criminal proceedings if waiver and transfer are approved.

(5) The juvenile is not amenable, by virtue of his maturity, criminal sophistication, or past experience in the juvenile justice system, to services provided through the family court.

(6) The juvenile has been given a waiver and transfer hearing that comports with due process. . . .[79]

How does this affect law enforcement officers? If you have arrested a child who is sixteen or over (age may vary from state to state), it is entirely possible that you would be required to

---

[75] Standard 14.23, "Families with Service Needs—Dispositional Alternatives," Standards, op. cit., p. 480.

[76] Standard 14.14, "Limitations on Type and Duration of Dispositions," ibid., p. 461.

[77] Kent v. United States, 383 US 541, 40 OhioOp(2d) 270, 86 SCt 1045, 16 LEd(2d) 84 (1967).

[78] Standard 9.5, "Waiver and Transfer," op. cit., p. 303.

[79] Ibid.

appear and testify in juvenile court just as you would in the adult or municipal court. "Probable cause must be shown."

If the court then finds that the above items are present, you, as the law enforcement officer, will be summoned before the grand jury, where with the assistance of the prosecuting attorney, you will present your evidence.

After indictment, arraignment, and if a plea of not guilty is entered, then you would be required to appear and testify in the adult court, where the case would be tried, just as if the juvenile defendant had in fact been an adult. This means that if the juvenile and his defense counsel so desire, a jury trial and all the other formalities surrounding a regular criminal proceeding must be met.

The reasoning in these instances is that a juvenile court has found that the particular juvenile involved, due to the particular circumstances, should be tried as an adult. Once this finding has been made, and the appropriate entries are placed on record, the matter is handled as any other routine adult criminal proceeding.

In the ordinary run of cases, those handled by juvenile court and not referred to the adult courts, the matters are often heard and disposed of without the police officer or law enforcement officer actually appearing. This leads to a lot of criticism of the juvenile courts, in that the officer, once he has made the arrest, has no more contact with the case and never learns the outcome. Then while he is out on the beat, he sees the boy or girl and does not know if the case was dismissed, or if in fact at that very time the boy or girl is in violation of some court order by, for example, being out late at night. This type of criticism is not unique to the juvenile court, as the same criticism is often heard in adult cases in courts in which an arraignment system is used and the police officer's attendance is not required at the first call.

Looking at it from the position of the juvenile court, the court would like to have the law enforcement officer advised of the disposition because the law enforcement officer will often have continuing contact with the boys or girls; and if he in fact knows the order of the court or the terms of probation, he is in a better position to determine whether or not a violation is being committed.

Hence the importance of communication, the need for a positive relationship between the law enforcement officer and the courts cannot be over-stressed. While it is true that records in juvenile court are considered confidential and are not made available to the general public, it would appear reasonable that the police officer should know the disposition rendered in the case in which he started. Unfortunately, in actual practice this information frequently does not reach the officer.

Returning to our discussion of dispositions, frequently a fine or imposition of court costs are authorized under the particular state statutes. The constitutionality of the use of incarceration in lieu of payment of a fine or court cost, although it has been challenged in the courts, is not the subject matter of this article. Our only concern is in regard to whether or not the juvenile court can constitutionally incarcerate a juvenile for nonpayment of a fine or court cost. It is one attorney general's opinion that a juvenile judge may not so act.[80]

In some instances it is apparent that the proper disposition must include removing the child from his or her home. This involves commitment to the state or to an appropriate agency.

Standard 14.14 places limits on the type and duration of dispositions which can be exercised by the court and they include four classes in increasing grades of severity, with class four including placement for a period up to the juvenile's twenty-first birthday.[81]

It is also possible for the court to terminate the parental rights to some extent in special cases. The law in this regard differs from state to state, but the Standards suggest that this should require hearings finding the children to be endangered or finding that the child has reached "responsible self sufficiency."[82]

[80] Ohio Attorney General Opinion, No. 70-143, October 15 ,1970.

[81] Standard 14.14, "Limitations on Type and Duration of Dispositions," Standards (1976), op. cit., p. 461.

[82] See Standards 14.27, "Endangered Children—Removal of the Child from the Home," ibid., p. 488, and Standard 14.24, "Responsible Self Sufficiency," ibid., p. 482.

Oftentimes in reaching a disposition, it becomes important to place the child in the home of a relative or friend in another state. In such an instance it is customary to place the child on probation and have the supervision carried out by probation officers not in the state where the particular child was tried, but in the state where he is placed. Again, the Standards[83] provide authority for such actions. That is to say, if a child is tried and found delinquent in state "A," and the court, due to the personal dynamics or circumstances of the particular individual, feels that the best disposition is to place him in a home in state "B," the court has the authority to so act, and can also, at the same time, place the child under the supervision of the probation department in the receiving state, state "B." Therefore, it is entirely possible for an individual to live in a jurisdiction and be under the supervision of a probation department without having been found to be delinquent in the local court in the area where he is living and supervised.

The importance of the proper use of the authority of probation officers cannot be over-stressed. By looking at the duties of the probation officer, we can immediately see the interrelationship between the probation officer and the police officer. The probation officer shall:

"(1) make investigations; reports and recommendations to the Juvenile Court; (2) receive and examine the complaints and charges of delinquency, unruly conduct, deprivation of the child; (3) supervise and assist the child placed on probation or protective supervision or care by order of the court or other authority of law; (4) make appropriate referrals to private or other agencies in the community if their assistance appears to be needed or desirable; (5) take into custody and detain a child who is under his supervision and care as a delinquent, unruly, or deprived child. . . . Except as provided by this Act a probation officer does not have the authority of a law enforcement officer. He may not conduct accusatory proceedings under this

---

[83] Standard 23.10, "Dual Jurisdiction and Interstate Compact," ibid., p. 694, and see also Commentary on Standard 19.6, "Limitations on Authority," ibid., p. 623.

Act against a child . . . under his care or supervision. . . ."[84] (See Section 6(a) "Duties of Probation Officers," Uniform Juvenile Court Act.)

Therefore, while a police officer is not a probation officer, and a probation officer is not a police officer, it is readily apparent that both have a proper and related position in working with the children who come to the attention of the juvenile court.

§ 19.14   Summary

A brief review of the decisions regarding rights of juveniles will be helpful to the law officer, who is oftentimes the first person to confront a juvenile suspected of delinquent behavior or fitting into one of the categories designated in the Standards as "endangered" or as a child from a "family in need of services."

A brief review of the decisions regarding rights of juveniles will be helpful to the law officer, who is the first person to confront a juvenile suspected of delinquent behavior or fitting one of the categories designated as unruly or deprived by the Uniform Juvenile Court Act. (See Appendix C.)

The decisions of the United States Supreme Court in *Kent v. United States*, 383 U.S. 541, 40 OhioOp.(2d) 270, 86 S.Ct. 1045, 16 L.Ed.(2d) 84 (1967) and *In re Gault*, 387 U.S. 1, 40 OhioOp.(2d) 378, 87 S.Ct. 1428, 18 L.Ed.(2d) 527 (1967) answered questions as to whether proceedings in juvenile court must meet certain requirements of due process applicable to adults. *Kent* held that before a case involving a juvenile can be transferred from juvenile court for trial as if he were an adult, a hearing must be held at which counsel for the child must be given an opportunity to examine and present witnesses and the judge must state his reasons for the transfer so that his decision may be reviewed. *In re Gault* held that in proceedings to determine delinquency which may result in commitment to an in-

---

[84] See Section 6(a) "Duties of Probation Officers," Uniform Juvenile Court Act, op. cit. Also, see Standard 17.4, "Non-Judicial Support Personnel," Standards (1976), op. cit., p. 586, and Standard 18.1, "The Court's Relationship with Law Enforcement Agencies," ibid., p. 593.

stitution, the child and his parents are entitled to notice of the specific charges and an opportunity to refute them, to be advised of right to counsel, including the right to appointment of counsel if unable to afford one, to confrontation and examination of witnesses, and that the constitutional privilege against self-incrimination is applicable to juveniles. The question of whether *Miranda* warnings must be given to a juvenile at the pre-judicial stages was left open in *Gault*, but it would seem wiser for a police officer to give such a warning, particularly in a serious case where the juvenile might be transferred to adult criminal court. Some states apply *Miranda* restrictions to juvenile interrogations generally. Waiver of right to be silent must be made knowingly and intelligently, and in view of questions regarding a juvenile's understanding of the warning, great care should be taken in accepting the waiver without presence of counsel.

In re Winship, 397 U.S. 358, 51 OhioOp.(2d) 323, 25 L.Ed.(2d) 368, 90 S.Ct. 1068 (1970), held that to justify a court finding of delinquency against a juvenile, the proof must be beyond a reasonable doubt that the juvenile committed the alleged delinquent act. Prior to this case the requirement was that the judge should be persuaded by a preponderance of the evidence. Contemplating *Winship* and the danger of an invalid confession, thorough investigation by the police officer is indicated.

In view of a trend toward applying to juveniles the Fourth Amendment guarantee against unreasonable searches and seizures, and the provision in the Uniform Juvenile Court Act, Sec. 27(b), that "Evidence illegally seized or obtained shall not be received over objection to establish the allegations made against him (the child), . . ." caution should be observed in making a search for evidence when taking a juvenile into custody. Even when the child is taken into custody for his own welfare, there may be a question as to using the fruits of a search as evidence to substantiate allegations that he has committed an unlawful act. Another problem is determining the validity of a juvenile's consent to search and seizure, involving the maturity and judgment of a juvenile to intelligently waive his rights by consenting to a search.[85]

In all such matters, the best trained and most professional officers will always thoroughly acquaint themselves with the controlling law and its interpretation in their jurisdiction in order to avoid violation of rights or any other acts which might impede the justice process.

APPLICATION OF IMPORTANT POINTS EMPHASIZED FOR LAW ENFORCEMENT OFFICERS

1. Juvenile court hearings, in some jurisdictions, were changed by the Rules set forth by the U. S. Supreme Court on May 15, 1967 in the case, *In re Gault*, 387 U.S. 1. This is, as of today, the most important case involving juvenile courts that has been decided.

2. The *Gault* case said that juveniles in juvenile court are entitled to:
   a. Timely notice of the charge against them.
   b. Confrontation and cross-examination of witnesses.
   c. The privilege against self-incrimination.
   d. The right to council.

3. Both the United States Supreme Court and several state courts have continued to reject the motion that juveniles have a right to a jury trial.

4. Jurisdiction of a court is: "That power conferred upon it by law, by which it is authorized to hear, determine, and render final judgment in an action, and to enforce its judgments by legal process."[86]

5. A law enforcement officer, just as with an adult defendant, makes the original decision as to whether to incarcerate a juvenile defendant or in the alternative, to issue to him a citation or notice to appear. If a juvenile is taken into custody, he should be taken directly to the juvenile court. (If there is any delay in transferring into the custody of the juvenile court, even a limited stay in police detention must be governed by strict rules so that due process is not violated. Exact wording of the state laws in these matters differs widely from state to state.)

6. There is considerable dispute in various jurisdictions as to whether a juvenile, just as an adult, has a right to be released under bond pending hearing on the merits. While the Standards recommend against the use of financial conditions of any kind for the release of

---

[85] Ferster and Courtless, *The Beginning of Juvenile Justice, Police Practices and the Juvenile Offender*, 22 Vanderbilt L. Rev. 568, 588 et seq.

[86] 14 OJur(2d), "Courts," Section 93.

juveniles, the practice continues in many jurisdictions. However, there is uniformity to the requirement that when incarcerated juveniles must be kept separate and apart from adults in custody.

7. There are provisions for three (3) separate and distinct hearings for juveniles in juvenile court:

   a. The *Detention Hearing* where the issue is whether or not the juvenile should be held in custody pending a hearing on the merits.

   b. The *Adjudicatory Hearing*, i.e., the hearing on the merits.

   c. The *Dispositional Hearing*.

8. Before the adjudicatory hearing there must be some form of service (i.e., notice of the charge) upon not only the juvenile but the juvenile's parent or guardian. If a juvenile denies the offense, the case against him must be proven "beyond a reasonable doubt."

9. Dispositions in juvenile court are made with the idea of correcting the juvenile's behavior and protecting society. Depending upon individual circumstances, the particular offense, background, etc., if the juvenile is found to have been involved in the complaint, dispositions can vary from admonishment and release all the way through long term institutional placement. The court can also, under proper conditions, waive its right to hear certain juvenile cases and hand the matter over to the adult court for trial of the juvenile as an adult.

10. Probation officers are not police officers and police officers are not probation officers. However, their two positions are not incompatible but complementary, as they both should be working for the best interests of the juveniles with whom they have contact.

Chapter 20

THE JUVENILE COURT: CONCEPT VERSUS PRACTICE

§ 20.1 Juvenile court dilemma

a. Denial of due process

In the recent past we have seen the punitive "Junior Criminal Courts" fail both the youngsters before them and the communities they were intended to safeguard. On the other hand, those courts which permitted themselves to degenerate into merely social agencies where decisions and sentences were given out arbitrarily as a result of casework conferences or hearings without full legal safeguards, have met with equal lack of success and can justly be termed no longer operable.

However, a review of the failure of these two types of juvenile courts leads us to present the thesis that the juvenile court concept, as originally planned, is not dead; it has simply in most instances never been tried. In those few enlightened places where the real principles and philosophy of the juvenile court have been given some opportunity to develop, it would seem that the juvenile court is not yet dead, it is simply being strangled by many factors outside of itself over which it has little control; or it is being destroyed from within by conditions over which it seems to have the right of control but very little real ability to remedy.

Outstanding scholars in the field of juvenile court law long ago told us that the original premises on which the entire legal structure of the juvenile court system is based, require that a contract be entered into between those responsible for establishing juvenile courts and those who come before such bars of justice. This contract very simply contains the agreement that the juvenile and his family would surrender many of their most basic and fundamental rights to the court in return for the court's promise to act "on behalf of the child" and in a way befitting "an enlightened parent." It contains the promise that there would be nothing done "to" the child, but that all actions would be motivated "for" the child. The further promise was extended that the child would be cared for in his home as far as possible, and that only when absolutely necessary would he be removed from his natural habitat to be cared for in a setting as closely resembling a good home as possible. All this was pledged to be accomplished in a setting that was not a criminal court, but a court of equity, from which no criminal stigma or civil disability would result. Although reduced to an almost oversimplified form, these statements represent the essence of the contract developed with the establishment of the juvenile court in Cook County, Illinois in 1899 and in all of the other fifty states in subsequent years.

That this contract has been violated, negated, forgotten and, in many instances, almost openly denied, seems to be a historical fact. There has been incarceration without explanation of formal charge; denial of legal counsel; commitment to maximum-security-type state correctional facilities without benefit of due process; sentencing of the offender based upon the nature of the offense regardless of his personality structure and character; dehumanizing conditions in institutions where juveniles are held; over half of the nation's counties not even possessing a special place of juvenile detention, and a host of other abuses which are vivid testimony to the failure of the juvenile courts in many cases to live up to the contractual promises.

The widespread geographical and numerical extent of these failures is well known to those of us whose careers have placed us in contact with the field of juvenile corrections. Complaints and investigations on the part of bar associations and individual members thereof throughout the country, the expressed concern of various federal and state agencies, a quick tour of juvenile correctional facilities in any or all of the fifty states, or the recent heightened interest of the United States Supreme Court in rendering decisions to assure the elimination of some of the more crass inequities—any one of these methods of analysis very quickly paints a vivid and almost embarrassing picture of the real and frequent existence of the fact that many juvenile courts fail to honor their contract.

b. Failure of juvenile courts to serve best interests of children

In looking at some of the underlying causes, foremost in our thinking is the fact that most certainly all of these conditions do not exist in all courts or even at all times in any one particular court, just as a listing of the many problems within families or within any other social unit certainly are not meant to apply to all families, all schools or all neighborhood groups. We must keep in mind that there are many good courts when evaluated from a standpoint of the positive intentions of the personnel involved, and the intensity of the effort to operate in a beneficial way in the face of the many obstacles that exist.

Underlying most of the problems confronted by the juvenile courts of this country is public apathy. This is a manifestation of the same syndrome that is so visible in many of the problems that exist in our mental hospitals, penitentiaries, workhouses, slum housing, neglect of the aged, and most of the other major social problems confronting contemporary society. In general, this lack of public concern about the human problems among us can be illustrated by a comparison of the amounts of money spent on sports stadia, tourist attractions and other pleasure or profit-making facilities as compared with all money spent on helping problem human beings in mental health, housing, corrections or any other human services. A second example of apathy can be seen in the fact that there is usually great public clamor and furor created over the proposed loss of a facility for pleasure or convenience and practically no outcry over the death of a human being from improper care or malnutrition

The juvenile court does not escape the ravages of such imbalance in the public value system. The overcrowding or total lack of juvenile detention facilities in many cities, the overloaded caseloads of most probation officers, the obvious lack of training for those who will assume the tremendous responsibilities for supervising the conduct and general well-being of thousands of youngsters with problems, the lack of practically all the necessary supportive tools such as sufficient clerical and office space, sufficient equipment, medical and psychiatric clinic requirements, and a whole list of other physical items that should be a necessary part of any juvenile court center—all of these lacks indicate very clearly the public apathy which has been the lot of the juvenile courts in most communities since their foundation.

The tremendous volume of new cases, combined with the lack of qualified referees and untrained intake staff in many juvenile courts causes the hurried or inadequate screening of cases at the intake level. The unprepared and quickly disposed preliminary hearings and the lack of case evaluations too frequently lend themselves to the result that those needing help are sent away from a court building with only a confused experience of rejection, while in many cases those who could not possibly profit from casework services are ushered into the already over-burdened probation officers' caseload. Faulty diagnoses, improper treatment plans, and non-implemented treatment programs are often present and are the direct result of too little money for staff, for services and for programs.

When applied to the establishment and maintenance of treatment facilities, the unwillingness of the public to concern itself personally with the problems of the juvenile court is even more evident. The deplorable lack of facilities at state and local levels has been one of the single most responsible factors for the "non-treatment" of offenders and the resulting high recidivism rate. We have too often witnessed the institutional housing of all kinds of offenders, and in some cases adult offenders, along with delinquent youngsters, in large "catch-all" institutions where the mentally ill, the intellectually retarded, and sociopathic, the situational reaction, the casual or accidental offender and the hardened habitual criminal are commonly treated; in many cases they are housed in an atmosphere not only inadequate to do any real good for any one single type, but totally unable to service the needs of all of the types that are cramped together.

This "un-care" treatment is even more tragic when it is observed in a so-called enlightened community where some money is available to establish diagnostic facilities in the courts and a good diagnosis and treatment plan could be developed, but where no varied facilities exist to treat the real problem as diagnosed.

This unfortunate situation has been compounded in some cases by the professional worker who is trained in a specific discipline but who finds his way by default into the vacuum which exists in many places in the field of corrections. This kind of "highly trained" worker only reinforces the problem by viewing diagnosis itself as practically identified with treatment. Consequently, one of the great tragedies takes place in many places where some limited resources are available but treatment never progresses any further than the diagnostic aspect.

It seems that we can never repeat too often that diagnosis is *not* treatment. No matter how profound, accurate, or professional our diagnostic insights, we must remember that hunger must still be fed, undetected physical abnormalities must still be corrected, those without internal controls must be helped to develop them, and those who have been left out of all of the fundamental positive ingredients of child growth and development must have these needs somehow supplied in their lives. The finest diagnosis does not provide these treatment elements; and if it culminates in placement in a mass-custody setting along with the undiagnosed and untreated, it accomplishes nothing.

At the root of most of these difficulties is the manifest lack of public interest, and consequently the lack of proper funds to provide the juvenile court with the kind of resources and service-complex that it needs to function effectively in any community. This reveals itself graphically in the small low-income communities where there are absolutely no resources of any type available, as well as in the larger, wealthier, and presumably more enlightened metropolitan areas where budget for operation extends itself to some staff, perhaps multiple judges and maybe even an elaborate diagnostic facility, but then tapers off to a mere fraction of the kinds of placement and programming facilities necessary to service the needs of the tremendous number of troubled young people walking through its often very attractive buildings. The child who is sent to a state school for truancy or "stealing an apple" in a small rural community, because there is no probation service and no diagnostic facilities available, is not really much worse off than the child from a community with a court possessed of an outstanding reputation for its diagnostic services, but where the child receives only a tremendous amount of social investigation, psychological and psychiatric testing and observation in a modern detention facility in order to be diagnosed accurately, and then is disposed of by being sent to the same massive antiquated custodial facility where his needs are undifferentiated from the many others, and where the treatment often consists of everything except what he really needs in order to be helped along the road to rehabilitation.

This tragic condition recently prompted one observer to note that "We are a funny country. We are willing to spend $10,000 to keep criminals behind bars for every dollar that we are willing to spend on the kind of child-care services which would keep youngsters from joining the criminal ranks in an ever-increasing number in the first place."

A lack of community knowledge, involvement and willingness to pay the expense of good juvenile court programs can also be seen in many places in the fact that oftentimes the person elected to the juvenile court bench is a successful local politician who has no real experience in the problems of children, but is simply temporarily placed in this office as a stepping-stone to further political opportunities. This is not to say that there are not dedicated juvenile judges throughout the country who have devoted their entire professional lives to properly handling the children in front of them and to the development of community facilities to meet their needs; but in all too many cases, community apathy has permitted the juvenile court bench to be just a secondary office to be routinely filled through ordinary political channels, or to be handled as a mere part of another court's work.

To further complicate this problem, it is also apparent that in many cases a dedicated judge, especially in a large jurisdiction, who accepts a juvenile court judgeship to do the best possible job, suddenly finds himself overwhelmed by the countless duties showered upon him as the ex-officio administrator of the court. These duties include budget control, personnel problems, public relations, the supervision of the probation department and countless other tasks that, for all his goodwill and many talents, render him totally unable to devote his full attention to the cases before him or to the kinds of legal research that is becoming ever more necessary in our complex society.

Worse, in many courts when the administrative overload is lifted from the shoulders of the harassed judiciary, by default it becomes the responsibility of "administrators" who have neither the training for, nor personal abilities to cope with the multi-faceted problems of administration in a large community. Because of this haphazard development of administration in many communities, the chief administrator of the court facilities frequently is simply the one having a greater skill at working with problem youngsters on a one-to-one basis, or many times he is chosen by simple seniority as a reward for length of service, or even by political considerations. In all of these cases, the complex problems of personnel recruitment and training, departmental administration, budget control, public relations and the many other tasks of the administrator are handled in a way that is to the detriment of the court operation, the community it is supposed to serve, and especially to the clients who are so dependent on the court for assistance during a most troubled period of their young lives.

The situation is worsened in many communities by the fact that the overwhelming number of youngsters constantly being referred to the court for its services continues to increase because there is little or no screening provided at the community level to keep those youngsters who do not need its services out of court, as well as for making absolutely certain that those being referred to the court are really in need of the service which only the court can provide. Many youngsters in almost every community in this country could have, or perhaps should have, been screened out of the juvenile court caseload and handled through the instrumentality of more sensitive and responsive police services, school services, or public and private agencies. For example, the "irresponsible" delinquent, one becoming involved in delinquency because of chronic health conditions which have remained uncorrected, because of organic brain damage, because of mental retardation and a whole host of other causes, continues to overload the juvenile court caseloads, and in many cases finds his way into the probation department of the juvenile court when his real needs could have been met far sooner and better through other arms of an enlightened and resourceful community.

The failure of most communities to understand the real role of the juvenile court and the area in which it can be most singularly effective, as well as the unwillingness or inability of these communities to provide the kinds of resources needed for the court to really service the right kind of youngster when he is referred, are perhaps the most sweeping and intensive causes of the over-burdening of the court caseloads and the inability of even dedicated judges and staff to keep abreast of the multiplicity of problems constantly thrust before them.

As a result, the overloading of the courts with the "wrong type" of youngsters contributes to and increases the problems of the hasty and arbitrary hearings that are customary in many juvenile courts. The cursory supervision of children on probation, the commitment of too many and often the wrong children to already inadequate state schools, the lack of proper time for diagnosis and treatment planning, and the quick recidivism of many youngsters who could have been assisted by the proper services, are the result of the fact that the juvenile court by default is seen as a solution for all community problems related to youngsters.

If for no other reason, the very fact that the juvenile court is often seen as a panacea for all problems confronting young people or caused by their behavior, should demand that a community be concerned about the quality of a man and his training and interest before assigning to him by election the responsibility of sitting on the juvenile court bench. And yet, history seems to indicate that too many communities do not face even this fundamental responsibility. In even more cases, when a competent and dedicated individual is selected for this responsible task, it is then thought that he has inherited the entire problem of all child and adolescent behavior, and that the community can rest assured that he and he alone can solve them without any further involvement and help from his fellow citizens.

Also, in those courts where the judge does not have access to professional staff and the assistance of those trained in the behavioral sciences, there are often many more subtle problems that quickly arise. Jurisdictional disputes between the court, the schools, the police department, family agencies and a whole host of other sources of friction arising from "vested interest" on the part of "professionals," constantly present obstacles to the smooth operation and proper functioning of the juvenile court. Within the court itself, a misunderstanding of the role of many of the professional staff in relation to other agencies, their inability to interpret their role in the community at large, further complicate the problem. The lack of communication and effective cooperation which results from these circumstances greatly inhibits the ability of the court to adequately serve its clients at the most realistic and helpful levels.

The many lines of demarcation between governmental agencies have not helped children in many circumstances. Charges of "encroachment" have been hurled in enlightened states which have a program of community development at the state level for youngsters, when individual communities feel that their proper area of responsibility is being invaded.

At the same time, in all too many instances, the constant public demand for action concerning the problem presented by individuals or groups of youngsters encourages those who would make personal gain from the exploitation of panaceas or "cure-all" approaches to the problem of the juvenile delinquent. This happens unwittingly and without malice on the part of the perpetrator many times because he has found a certain approach succeeds with a certain percentage of the youngsters known to him; and in his enthusiasm he recommends his solution to those who are looking for a simple solution to the many and complex problems presented by the deviant behavior of the youngsters in our troubled society. Regardless of the motives of the advocate of a simplistic solution, this approach is always harmful.

In a desire to classify problems, children have been grouped together indiscriminately so that effective treatment can be made available and thousands of youngsters have been labeled with the term "delinquent" in a legal and professional sense, or with such designations as "unsuitable for adoption," "borderline feebleminded," "sex problems," and many other equally undesirable titles. Considering the lack of knowledge of the individual and the lack of full exploration of his total living circumstances, in many cases these titles are premature or richly undeserved; but they can follow the child in his contacts with the professionals, perhaps for a lifetime.

Areas of legitimate concern at the national level seem to have been overlooked, also. The need to remove the inequities in the hearing and consequent treatment of problem youngsters based on the accident of where and in what jurisdiction they happen to have been born or reside, certainly requires attention. There is great need for the codification of juvenile court law and for the equalization of diagnostic and treatment facilities throughout the fifty states and within each state. And yet, in this sophisticated and "enlightened" day and age we still find circumstances like those existing in one midwestern county where if the youngster happens to be born on one side of a main street he belongs to one jurisdiction, and if he happens to reside across the street he belongs to another where there are far less diagnostic or treatment resources available, and his entire handling at the court level takes on a generically different description.

There is need for a "model juvenile court" established, funded and propelled to successful fruition by the Federal Government with all of its great resources. There are many responsible persons, well acquainted with the problems previously discussed, who have long advocated that such a federal exemplar be established so that less prosperous and enlightened communities could look to it for guidance and motivation. However, this experiment has not been undertaken because citizens at large have assigned a low priority to the juvenile court and to the children with problems.

The primary thesis of this chapter is that the above-named problems certainly indicate the reason for much of the disillusionment, frustration and even hostility which exists in the minds of many citizens, and especially in many of the families of clients who have had experience with the juvenile courts in America. This is a sufficiently weighty indictment to question whether we should begin to fulfill the promise originally made by the establishment of the juvenile courts, or abandon the surface appearances by making the juvenile courts part of the larger system of criminal justice to be sure that some of the greater inequities are corrected, or so that we at least cease to build the false hope that the juvenile court is "different" and somehow better for children.

§ 20.2   Necessary steps to correct present conditions in juvenile courts

The juvenile court concept seems to be under attack from two extremely polarized positions at opposite ends of the spectrum currently: 1. Those who hold that the juvenile court system has historically deprived youngsters of their constitutional rights and that countless numbers of children appearing in these courts, especially the poor, have been denied due process.

The second group, holding that the juvenile court has been much too "lenient" and that because all fear of punishment has been taken out of the process, the juvenile court has indeed failed to protect society from the hostile impulses and resulting behavior of countless young persons in our society.

Those who would hold the first mentioned views would see the primary area of reform being increased emphasis on the availability of due process at every step of the juvenile system.

(Your author would suggest that while due process certainly should be required, just the provision of constitutional rights in the absence of provision of necessary services and programs will never address itself totally successfully to the needs and the consequent correction of the behavior of millions of youngsters in our society. For example, a child who steals because of hunger certainly needs more than "the right to remain silent," etc.)

Those who would hold the second point of view, advocate at best that the juvenile court adopt a punitive stance and conduct itself as a "junior criminal court"; extreme advocates of such a position would suggest, as many currently are, that the juvenile court be abolished and youngsters be handled in the criminal courts. (Your author would suggest that in relation to this second point of view, we should consider the historical failure of the adult correctional system to control behavior of large numbers of persons, even at the present. And furthermore it is suggested that we keep in mind that it seems relatively simplistic to suggest that those youngsters raised in the total absence of all that is required to train someone in good citizenship or even in being good human beings can suddenly after sixteen or eighteen years be "frightened" or "punished" into good citizenship or genuine concern for the rights of their fellow man. While there is certainly a place for effective discipline in the life of all youngsters, this must be part and parcel of their entire educative process, and it is not simply a "pill" or "magic wand" which can be inserted into their lives quickly and much too late and be expected to produce "miraculous results" in terms of behavioral control.)

The beguiling statement that "the juvenile court concept is the greatest advancement in law since the signing of the Magna Charta," should not deter us from a close scrutiny of the necessity of examining the underlying causes which lead to ever-increasing problems relating to the behavior of juveniles. To make a reality of the juvenile court dream, in our opinion there are five necessary steps, besides the obvious one of keeping a specialized court to deal with the unique problems of children in trouble.

a. Preventive treatment prior to assumption of jurisdiction

One, we must equip communities at all levels with the

necessary tools of diagnosis and treatment, so that they can keep *out* of the juvenile courts the countless thousands that are being sent there by default. This means more realistic and practical medical, casework, job placement and other services housed in schools, public agencies, government and private facilities. The effective Juvenile Aid Bureau within the police departments is essential in this effort and needs considerably increased support. Also, the youth service bureaus and the other newly developed diversionary programs should be encouraged in their development and utilized heavily at this point, at the very beginning of the process, in order to keep countless numbers of youngsters from penetrating more deeply into the juvenile justice system.

b. Selection of qualified judges

Two, it would seem that sufficient community education must be undertaken so that the necessary interest and concern is focused on the juvenile court to insure that the proper persons are appointed or elected to the juvenile court benches, and that when so selected, they receive the benefit of the proper training, consultation, guidance and professional assistance to adequately perform their tasks.

c. Establishment of diagnostic and treatment facilities available to juvenile courts

Three, juvenile court diagnostic and treatment facilities should be established in all communities to enable the court to fulfill its assigned task and its pledge to alter the conditions and circumstances of each child before it, so that the child will be able to make a better adjustment to the demands of responsible citizenship. The court must be supplied with the proper programs to deal with each child in his home as far as possible, and only when necessary to remove him and place him in a setting, whether it be a foster home, group home, half-way house, treatment center, detoxification unit or any other necessary facility where his real needs would actually be met in an attempt to save him from a life of adult crime. When necessary, this should be done by combining resources into regional centers in sparsely populated areas—and this can only be accomplished by abandoning political interests and short-sighted possessiveness.

d. Restriction of use of state institutions to juveniles who must be removed from community; decentralization of institutions

Four, those state institutions that receive the "hard-core offenders" would receive only those juveniles who *cannot* be treated in their own home or in local facilities and would be geared to the treatment of the real needs of the youngsters placed therein. This would require dissolving the mammoth facilities where all offenders are placed together and the establishment of smaller, differentiated treatment units throughout each state. Needless to say, in keeping with the current legislative trends and the best available correctional thinking, status offenders (those whose offenses would not be criminal if committed by adults) would find no place in these state institutions, and only those truly delinquent youngsters who could not be handled because of demands of community safety or their personal needs in any less restrictive environment would be institutionalized at this level.

Your author calls attention to his previously developed "strainer theory"[1] which, when briefly summarized, states simply that the selection process for juvenile institutionalization should be much like a skilled housewife shaking a kitchen strainer. All particles are permitted to filter through the strainer and only those large particles which simply find it impossible to fit are retained in the net. Applying this to placement considerations, every conceivable program, residential and non-residential, short of secure institutionalization, is utilized, and state institutions are employed only for those youngsters who absolutely require secure placement, and where there is no less restrictive alternative available in keeping with the needs of community safety or the demands of their individual behavioral difficulties.

e. Proper treatment of juveniles returning from institutions

Finally, the group of youngsters with problems returning to society from care in state institutions must be properly handled by those who know and understand their needs, so that the entire professional community receives them back in a

[1] Paul H. Hahn, *Community-based Corrections and the Criminal Justice System,* Davis Publishing Co., Santa Cruz, California (1975), pp. 23-24.

community-wide "treatment milieu." This would include the cooperation of schools, private agencies, job placement resources and all other arms of the community that can be opened to receive the rehabilitated offender.

Each of these five phases are so general that they would demand very sweeping changes in order to implement them properly. For example, in order to properly screen away from the juvenile court the kinds of offenders that do not belong there may require in many jurisdictions a tremendously upgraded program of training in the police departments. In other jurisdictions it may demand establishment or vast enlargement of existing police juvenile aid bureau facilities. In some areas, perhaps in most, it would require the establishment of a third community-wide agency to deal with the problems of children who need supervision, such as simple runaways, school problems and incorrigibles. In almost every area, it would require great enlightenment on the part of the citizenry, as well as the surrendering of jurisdictional claims and vested interests on the part of professionals and agencies.

§ 20.3   Implementation of five steps

The requirements to implement the other treatise suggestions are so vast and so beyond the real scope of this limited treatise that we must simply state the need for awakened public interest and the expenditure of large sums of money. However, it is our belief that these things can be accomplished with a re-focusing of interest, more dedication and the kind of determination that has made America so successful in meeting so many other problems in the past. The choice remains very simple. We have seen the tremendous increase in all crime in the past decade. The crime cost has risen from staggering to unbelievable. We are aware of the rate of juvenile suicide, drug addiction, alcoholism, venereal disease and problems in every area of social concern. We have seen the failure of many of the old methods, and especially the tremendous cost to us and to our children of the neglect that we have exhibited toward this problem up until now. Do we want these conditions to endure and to intensify, or are we willing to pay the cost in terms of economics and our personal concern, to change them radically for the better? We must remember that every nation, and each of its communities, has as much juvenile crime as it deserves.

APPLICATION OF IMPORTANT POINTS EMPHASIZED FOR LAW ENFORCEMENT OFFICERS

1. Much of our concern with the failure of juvenile courts to control delinquency is caused by the lack of staff and funding of particular courts, not by a failure in the idea of having a special court for children.

2. The juvenile court should not function merely as a "criminal court for children," nor should it function merely as a social agency. It is neither, because by statute it has a particular task to perform as a court in order to protect society and exercise maximum concern for the care and correction of the juvenile offender.

3. No court can perform this important task without staff and facilities. The provision of these depends on community understanding and cooperation; and enforcement officers can help to educate the community and gain its support; or they can further the apathy by their own negative attitudes and expressions of hostility toward the court.

4. Unnecessary arrests and referrals increase the inability of already overburdened courts to service the cases which need their help.

5. The success of a juvenile court can be judged much more effectively by the amount and kinds of services it really delivers to children than by the number it incarcerates or by the amount of diagnostic work it performs.

6. Police officers should utilize all community services on behalf of children who do not need to be referred to the juvenile court. Proper use of other facilities for medical and social services is of great benefit in certain cases.

7. Good working relationships with schools, churches and neighborhood groups often make it possible to obtain services when needed.

8. Adequate communication with juvenile court personnel is essential if children and the community are going to benefit; therefore, professional criticism or personal feelings must never prevent the good enforcement officer from maintaining communications with court staff.

9. Knowing from personal experience the complexities underlying juvenile delinquency, the truly professional police officer should be the very last person to advocate simple solutions or one cure for all offenders. The police attitude influences the public.

10. The dedicated police officer who is really interested in controlling delinquency and seeing juvenile offenders rehabilitated should promote efforts to recruit, train and pay competent court personnel with the same zeal with which he supports these efforts in law enforcement.

Chapter 21

THE PHILOSOPHY AND GOAL OF JUVENILE CORRECTIONS

Section

§ 21.1   Conflict between theories and purpose of corrections

When discussing the philosophies and goals of any correctional system, it is necessary to state in the beginning that we must protect the larger society from the impulses and unbridled behavior of those individuals who might be dangerous to it. Society has a right to protect itself, and dangerous antisocial behavior must be contained. However, in our zeal to protect the larger society oftentimes we fall into the error of believing that imprisonment or brutal punishment is a certain way of insuring that that protection takes place.

The error in this position can clearly be seen from the high rates of recidivism among offenders of all categories who return from inadequate mass-custody institutions unprepared for normal living in society. It is especially tragic in the field of juvenile corrections, where an opportunity to change the values and attitudes that cause dangerous delinquent behavior oftentimes is forfeited in order to incarcerate the offenders, despite the realization that several months of custodial care is not the answer in general or even in a particular case.

It is essential in considering juvenile corrections to remember that the juvenile offender, unless he happens to die of disease or by accident while in an institution, always returns to the community from which he was committed, or to another community, no matter what offense he has committed. Juveniles, as such, are not subject to the death penalty when their cases are heard in juvenile courts. No state law permits life imprisonment of juveniles, nor is there any institution prepared to keep a juvenile in custody for life. In most circumstances he is kept only several months, and at the very longest until he reaches the age of maturity.

Consequently, any society which is truly interested in protecting itself, as well as attempting to assist the juvenile in trouble, must necessarily be concerned with what happens to him while he is in the custody of the court or institutions. The argument very clearly is not to decide whether or not we wish to protect the community, but the most effective way to accomplish the goal of protection.

Historically speaking, the belief that pure punishment or harsh treatment or long terms of institutionalization in mass-custody settings protect society, simply does not stand in the face of sophisticated evidence gathered in countless ways over a large number of years. This is not to say that society does not need to temporarily institutionalize those whose inner controls have broken down to the point where they are unable at the present time to control their behavior.

Such individuals must be institutionalized, not only for the protection of society, but in order to enable the offender to receive the assistance he needs to develop personal control. But what is done with this impulsive, aggressive juvenile offender while he is institutionalized is of paramount importance both to his future behavior and to the protection of society.

The field of juvenile corrections historically has been beset by serious conflicts between two extreme positions. On the one hand there have been those who, not understanding the complex nature of the causal factors in juvenile crime, have taken the simplistic, punitive approach and insisted that more and longer mass-custody institutionalization or the "return to the whipping-post" would be a great step forward toward controlling juvenile offenders.

Advocates of this position, who insist that "nothing works," who think that the simple prescription of "just deserts" to each offender will solve the crime problem, who among other things advocate "post punishment incapacitation" in which offenders would be contained even up until their thirty-fifth birthday because of predictions of possible offenses,* are currently shouting the so-called "new penology" which your author believes is really the old brutalization and repression which has never effectively controlled human behavior throughout the history of mankind.

On the other hand, an extremely permissive position has been taken for many years by many, largely because of emphasis given to such a position through the rise of the "child-guidance" approach and the application of traditional psychoanalytic theories to delinquent behavior. The prophets of that persuasion have insisted that all juvenile delinquents are frustrated or sick, and oftentimes they have refused to recognize the need for the control of much undesirable behavior. Their ranks have recently been joined by those who feel that all law and all discipline are simply outmoded, and seem to feel that anyone "doing their own thing" should be left totally free to do so even if it infringes on the rights of others, and that no one under any circumstances should ever be locked up. This simplistic position certainly presents great dangers from a criminal justice planning standpoint because it seems to deny the existence of the very obvious "dangerous offenders," who, although small in number, do realistically exist.

In the opinion of your author, every community has the right of self-protection from their impulsive actions and destructive behavior.

In the middle of these two extreme positions, the field of corrections has been a battleground of complicated and often conflicting philosophies or goals of corrections which Conrad referred to as the "patchwork quilt" of operating correctional philosophies in this country.[1]

In many discussions of correctional goals, especially as directed toward the juvenile offender, one readily finds authors

*These advocates admit that there would be a margin of error of about 40% (meaning that they seem to be willing to lock up 40% of a large number of individuals just because of the possibility that they might do something further which would offend society).

[1] John P. Conrad, *Crime and Its Correction*, University of California Press, Berkeley and Los Angeles, Calif., (1965), p. 2.

and practitioners discussing the need for control of behavior, change in values and attitudes, deterrence of the commission of similar offenses by others, the protection of society, punishment, containment, neutralization, rehabilitation, resocialization, treatment, correction, and even elements that can be described only as retribution, vindication, revenge, retaliation, and other words and phrases embracing a combination of any or most of the previous listed terms. Unfortunately, in practice, the correctional system of many states seems to embrace a combination of many or even all of these complex ideas within the framework of the confused and confusing approach that is taken in handling the juvenile offender.

In many jurisdictions, we recognize theoretically that there are innumerable kinds of offenders committing countless offenses for innumerable kinds of individual, personal reasons. And yet, in the large, mass-custody institutions of most of these states, we find the lumping together of many or all of these types in a program allegedly designed to "treat," "resocialize," or "rehabilitate" the young offender in a setting which is primarily custodial.

In some more enlightened communities, individual juvenile offenders receive expert diagnosis which indicates special treatment, but are then placed in mass-custody institutions where all the offenders, diagnosed and undiagnosed, receive the same regimented and dehumanizing treatment.

§ 21.2   Meeting needs of juveniles: diagnosis and treatment

This result caused one learned and dedicated public official to say that we are guilty, even in the best settings, of doing "five thousand dollars worth of diagnosis and only five dollars worth of treatment" of the juvenile offender.[2]

In many places, of course, this is due to the problem of lack of budget and consequent lack of staff and facilities. However, much of this paradox is due to the confusion in philosophies

2 Judge Donald Young, U. S. Court of Appeals, Toledo, Ohio (lectures and private conversations).

and goals in the field of juvenile corrections.

We often do not do what is required in the case of an individual offender simply because we are not certain as to what we are really supposed to be accomplishing with him. One researchist recently said, "It must be said that at best we have been inefficient, and at worst we have been inhumane, and at all times we have been confused. We need to lessen the confusion by being more specific about our objectives and agreeing upon them."[3]

But while most enlightened and interested parties concur that agreement upon correctional goals for the juvenile offender must be reached, in practice, our antiquated methods fall far short of any legitimate, professional expectancy.

While effective discipline is certainly a necessity in the growth and development of every youngster, and while the protection of society demands that we take strong measures to make certain that the violent and dangerous are not permitted to vent their rage and aggression upon innocent citizens, it must be remembered that in those settings, where pure punishment is seen as the sole purpose of juvenile corrections, intelligent planning cannot be directed toward the needs of the juvenile offenders marching through the courts. Punishment for its own sake relies completely on the notion of fear. Even amateur observers of human behavior quickly note that fear is often cancelled by a variety of emotional factors.

Crime committed in the heat of passion, delinquent acts caused by severe deprivation and dire need, confused behavior resulting from emotional conflict and ambivalence, calculated behavior rooted in a confidence of not being detected or convicted, and the neurotic behavior of those who are seeking punishment itself because of their delinquent acts all give eloquent testimony to the fact that punishment cannot prevent the commission of all offenses.

When we add to this list the offenses committed by those

[3] Don M. Goltfredson, quoted in "Correctional Briefings," #8, published by Joint Commission on Correctional Manpower and Training, Washington, D.C.

who have suffered organic brain damage and by the severely mentally retarded, it is easy to see that no amount of punishment or threat of the harshest retribution will deter delinquent activities in these circumstances because the penalties and threats cannot even be understood, and the behavior at best can be called irresponsible.

This is not to say that punishment does not act as a deterrent upon some potential offenders. For example, most normal citizens are deterred from parking beside a fire plug by the threat of a considerable financial loss if they are detected and convicted.

Most respectable citizens are deterred from many kinds of activities because of the great deterrent effect of public shame, disgrace to family and loss of social status which would come from swift detection, arrest, conviction, and sentencing process. However, these by and large are not the persons who make up the daily bulk of the juvenile correctional system; and so, in discussing the handling of those who are marching by the millions through the courts and agencies of this country, we must speak more particularly about methods suited to their needs.

§ 21.3   Effect of punitive methods: deterrent or detriment?

There are also those who feel that severe and even brutal methods are of great value in the field of juvenile correction because they deter the adjudicated offender from committing further offenses upon his release from incarceration. But we must recognize in considering this argument, that neither history nor the current recidivism rates tend to confirm that any change in the attitudes and values which cause deviant behavioral manifestations take place as a result of purely negative experiences. In fact, history tends to indicate that brutality begets more brutality, and that a person dehumanized in a setting of over-severity tends to have his control of hostility weakened and his self-concept lowered; and this, of course, reinforces the delinquent pattern instead of causing beneficial change.

On the other hand, it is equally ridiculous to deny that any offender is deterred from committing a further offense because of the penalties that the law might invoke. We know that some people are deterred by the fear of penalty or by having had experienced the consequences of their acts previously. So deterrence does seem to be effective in preventing repeat offenses by some offenders.

However, we must also remember that while some are deterred from committing offenses because of the threat of punishment or because of having previously experienced penalties, for the great mass of delinquents who are acting out severe deprivation or who commit acts of delinquency in fits of passion, or because of medical reasons, or for a whole host of other causal factors, pure punishment is not the answer. There must be something done to change the attitudes and values that have caused the delinquent behavior in all cases, and in most situations this requires more than simply punishment.

In many correctional systems, unfortunately, we still see such motives operating as retaliation, pure repression, retribution and revenge. These motives certainly do not seem, in the ideal order, worthy as major goals in the treatment of the youth of this country; nor do they seem practical when applied; but, because of what has been so accurately referred to as "inertia aided and abetted by tradition," [4] much thinking prompted by these motives still survives in the correctional planning and institutional programming for juvenile offenders.

The demand for punishment heard so frequently from an enraged public after the commission of a particularly heinous offense is ample indication of the extent to which these motives still operate among the public at large.

In a recent murder case with which your author was associated in terms of its court handling, letters were received not only asking that the "whipping-post" be restored to a public place in this community, but even suggesting that we "set fire to his hair so that he might know what pain feels like." These concepts, rooted so obviously in vengeance and ignorance, would be tragic enough if they remained the idle ramblings of a bitter and disgruntled segment of the non-professional population. But these comments and the type of thinking that prompts

---

[4] Conrad, op. cit., p. 1.

them, carry great weight with the sensitive politicians who are responsive to mass thinking. Consequently, in many of the politically dominated areas of corrections these impractical and harmful ideas are operative and influential in the planning of corrections for youngsters in large numbers.

While we see no legitimate place in juvenile corrections for the kinds of vengeful motives mentioned above, we must not forget that confinement for the protection of society or in order to enable an offender to have sufficient time, in a structured situation, to develop inner behavioral controls is necessary for some offenders.

Even the most permissive of thinkers in the correctional field do concede society's right to its own protection, and most concede that there are times when certain offenders can be helped only by removal from the open society to a more structured situation. But it is of the greatest importance to recognize that confinement does not have to include the condition of dehumanization, regimentation and brutality that are so often associated with it because of antiquated, overcrowded and understaffed facilities.

Again, from a practical standpoint, most lawyers, and many from the field of law enforcement, will quickly agree that if laws are too punitive, or if a particular setting is known for its excessive severity, convictions in the courts and sentences to such institutions are much harder to obtain; and, consequently, instead of such severe laws or brutal treatment actually serving to protect society, they work against that purpose by permitting many who really need confinement to remain at large because of the reluctance of juries and judges to be a party to such primitive or excessively severe measures.

Finally, it would seem that within the word "corrections" itself, we see contained a statement of meaningful philosophy and practical goals for the field. In this notion of corrections, it seems that one can readily find the intent of the model juvenile code to so alter the conditions and circumstances of the child that he does not go on to a life of adult crime. This term seems to lend itself quite readily to the inclusion of the notions of rehabilitation, treatment, re-socialization or even, as many practitioners now find in dealing with the severely deprived and alienated youth of our complex society, that we must socialize or provide habilitation for the very first time in many young lives.

These terms, while there are technical differences of some concern to treatment specialists, basically contain the same notions, and that is that an atmosphere be created in which a change in the values and attitudes of the child can take place. This is best done in the child's home or a setting as closely resembling his home as possible; but where institutionalization is necessary, the institutional atmosphere and program should be so designed as to reinforce acceptable behavioral values and standards, and the reintroduction to normal community living, not to provide an oppressive, alien atmosphere dominated by a delinquent sub-culture and devoid of all normal social experiences.

It is well known to most observers that some youngsters, especially first offenders, do undergo the necessary attitude change simply by the shock of arrest, adjudication, perhaps placement in a detention facility, and the legal process itself.

It is also equally evident that there are others who, despite our best efforts, never really are capable of effecting such inner change or improvement in their overt behavior. These are the small minority of offenders who have traditionally been referred to as psychopathic, sociopathic or, in very recent times, anti-social disorders. There are still others including some of the severely retarded and those grouped under the label "organic brain syndrome," who do not have the capacity to function under the stress and complicated circumstances of community living. (However, it must be remembered that with proper educational methods many of this latter group are able to live surprisingly free and productive lives.)

There is also a large group that comes to the attention of law enforcement and finds its way into the court and correctional system who really do not need the treatment process at all. These are the so-called "casual" or "accidental" or "one-shot" offenders who in very unusual circumstances or, perhaps, under a great passing environmental stress do become involved in an illegal act, but certainly are not likely to reappear before the bar of justice. Most police officers are well acquainted with this kind of offender as a "casual weekend offender," a misguided conventioner, an over-enthusiastic prankster or, perhaps, a teenage sex offender whose controls were thoroughly tempted by the opportunity provided by a willing partner, and his activities happened to have been seen by an over-zealous citizen who reported the incident to a police officer.

The great majority of juvenile offenders in the correctional system do very definitely need treatment, whether it be treatment for their home environment, their neighborhood, their total community, or themselves; and, of course, this treatment requires people and programs in order that it might be achieved.

This treatment may require in some instances a longer term of confinement than a purely punitive or repressive approach might indicate. For example, it might be required that a youngster spend at least two years in an open-type setting in order to develop proper controls of his aggressive tendencies or in order to learn normal living habits, whereas the particular offense that brought this youngster to the attention of law enforcement would carry only a thirty day sentence in a very punitive setting.

On the other hand, it is possible that the protection of society or the neutralization of the offender can better be achieved in certain circumstances by probation than by confinement. A case in point would be a youngster who is not at all dangerous to others, but who has a low self-concept and who would be readily destroyed in an institutional setting.

There are other youngsters who require a "work therapy" experience culminating in job placement, while others need limits set for their behavior by a trained probation officer who might even act as a parent-substitute. Thousands of youngsters are in need of foster homes, others require residential treatment centers; others half-way houses; and still others, would profit best from a job and an increased sense of accomplishment and responsibility.

The secret of success in planning treatment programs is the ability to distinguish between juveniles requiring institutionalization and those who can function in the community. There must necessarily be adequate diagnostic facilities to determine who needs the satisfaction of dependency needs and who needs strict limit-setting.

The secret of successful treatment lies in providing all kinds of care for those who need it, reserving the highly structured institutional setting only for the ones who need that kind of facility, and only for the length of time for which it is absolutely necessary. Proper program elements and proper staff to make them functional must be part of the institutional setting.

If, in the name of treatment, we provide only the antiquated, punitive, repressive mass-custody type of institutions with no adequate programs, we have accomplished nothing. At the same time, if we are blindly permissive and do nothing when a youngster is crying out for control of his behavior, we have failed the community and the child as well.

If under the name of treatment we permit ourselves to be manipulated so that we are permissive with the psychopath, while at the same time placing a very dependent, deprived youngster in a program of psychiatric treatment, when what he needs is the satisfaction of basic survival needs, we have accomplished nothing.

There is no "short-cut" to the treatment of juvenile offenders. Its total success depends upon the knowledge of the offender related to his offense in the light of the particular subculture in which he lives, and in relation to the expectancy of the total community.

§ 21.4   Legislative, judicial and administrative changes needed

To create programs based on this philosophy of juvenile corrections, it is necessary that we approach all the problems on three levels.

Legislatively, there must be the creation of laws and systems that recognize the need for individualized justice for the juvenile offender and provide the ingredients necessary to reach him in terms of altering his attitudes and values and, assisting him to change his behavior.

Judicially, enlightenment is required so that the real needs of the offender are taken into consideration in the true spirit of the juvenile code. The juvenile court should be concerned with the offense to a sufficient degree to provide protection for society, but it should also be concerned with the offender; and all dispositions should be concerned with providing the necessary elements in order to reach his individual needs and thus fulfill the dual role of protecting society and giving the offender opportunity for change.

Administratively, the methods and aims provided for by legislation and proper judicial handling must be effectively carried out despite community pressures, lack of budget, and the resistance to method changes.

APPLICATION OF IMPORTANT POINTS EMPHASIZED FOR LAW ENFORCEMENT OFFICERS

1. Enlightened programs of juvenile corrections or treatment do *not* disregard or oppose society's right to protect itself from aggressive antisocial behavior of young offenders.

2. Harsh punishments and brutality do *not* protect society as well as a sound program of enlightened juvenile corrections which always considers the long term protection of society as well as immediate danger.

3. Because all juvenile offenders return to the community in a relatively short time, incarceration for a given period does *not* insure the protection of society.

4. In situations where police find that a youngster steals because of hunger, runs away because of incest in the family home, or is chronically "out late" because no one cares, much more than routine handling is indicated.

5. If we succeed in changing the factors that cause delinquent behavior, the behavior itself will change. This is not only good for the child, but it is the best protection of society. Oftentimes, the police officer is the first to uncover, or at least suspect, the real causes in a particular offense situation.

6. It certainly should not be seen as a failure or a personal affront by an arresting officer when a juvenile offender is not incarcerated.

7. The officer's contribution of his knowledge of the causes of a particular offender's behavior is very valuable to courts and agencies who have to determine what to do with the offender. (When this information is not requested or seems unappreciated when given, the

officer has real cause to question the adequacy of the service being rendered to the community by the particular court or agency.)

8. Enlightened corrections or treament of the juvenile offender does not mean simply "psychiatric treatment" or "insight therapy." Corrections should embrace every conceivable service that links a child with the satisfaction of his real needs, from counseling and discipline through food, clothing and shelter (depending entirely on what the individual offender requires in each case).

9. Brutality, excessive force and personal abuse of an offender never help—they always do harm by either generating more hostility, lower self-concept or further reinforcing delinquent attitudes.

10. The truly professional officer learns to individualize his techniques more and more, and he carefully avoids generalizations and "snap judgments" as to the dynamics of individual offenders. For example, he would never say: "This boy is one of the Jones family and he's no good because they are all no good!"

Chapter 22

TREATMENT OF THE JUVENILE OFFENDER

§ 22.1 Purpose of juvenile correction

Certainly the most pressing issue connected with treatment of the juvenile offender within the past several years has been the wholesale attack upon treatment by those who hold the opinion that "nothing works" and that behavior can't really be changed or the only way to truly protect society is through punitive and regressive programs abolishing the juvenile court, eliminating probation and parole in the adult courts, and in general adopting a certain "lock-em-up" philosophy of crime control and juvenile justice.

The writings and public pronouncements of men like Robert Martinson, Ernst Van denHaag, James Q. Wilson, Andrew VonHirsch, and others from the academic world have been adopted and popularized by politicians and columnists such as Ronald Reagan and William Buckley with the result that large segments of the community at large have come to really believe that there is a sound scientific base which "proves" that "nothing works," and that all attempts to intervene positively in the lives of those who misbehave in our society have been futile. And even more unfortunate, many political leaders and criminal justice professionals have adopted this same position, relying heavily on the findings of the aforementioned academic-types to support a trend which sees a total reliance on pure punishment rapidly replacing sound treatment programming in many places, as though punishment alone could answer all the complex problems which are represented by the vast amount of juvenile delinquency currently rampant in our society.

349

Your author has always defended the right of any society to protect itself from the hostile impulses of those who would prey upon others; even in this text, consistent discipline within the family, the schools, and the larger society itself has been promoted and expounded as one of the chief means of delinquency prevention. However, these common-sense axioms have no kinship with the currently prevailing trend toward "social revenge" and the mistaken simplistic notion that punishment alone can control juvenile delinquency in our society and give us "safety on the streets."

In response to the "nothing works" critics and the "lock-em-up" advocates, your author would like to make the following points which hopefully the thoughtful reader will use to analyze the complexity of the situation to which such over-simplified solutions are suggested: 1. No one has ever proven scientifically that "nothing works." A survey of the literature in the field, an analysis of the works of the current researchists or any other source of investigation has never established that positive programs have no meaningful effect on behavior. The only thing which has been developed consistently is the already acknowledged fact that we simply do not have the instruments to effectively measure what does work under such circumstances, and especially to get at the important question of why it works when it does. 2. Professionals within the juvenile justice system have often been guilty of not really doing the things or implementing the programs which do work when properly resourced and carried out. Many professionals look at "half-hearted" efforts, only to conclude that such concepts have been truly implemented and are not working, when, in fact, the concepts have never been truly implemented. As a result, we fall into the trap of trying to "re-invent the wheel" when we have not really ever fully utilized the many "wheels" which are lying around for lack of proper resources or participation. 3. Those who see a "get tough policy" as the answer to juvenile delinquency in our society seem to be reacting much more to their own fear, frustration and anger because previous inadequate commitments to productive approaches have not succeeded. "Kids" in this sophisticated day and age simply will not play the game of "being good" if, at the same time that we give lip-service to certain ideals or programs, we refuse to pay the cost of real involvement in their world and in their lives. In the face of this social failure, the "hardliners" turn to the simplistic solution of prison because it sounds good to the public and because it hits a very responsive note within the frightened public ear, even though such an approach historically has never worked, even though it falls short of being able to work in the face of today's complex problems, even though it misleads the public into thinking there are still easy answers, and above all, in spite of the fact that it caters to the most base human emotions of revenge, hatred, prejudice, and fear. 4. The juvenile justice system is constantly asked to do things far beyond its scope or ability, and then is damned for not achieving unrealistic expectancies. For example, in the face of the massive breakdown of controls, both internal and external, in our society and in the face of the failure of all existing social units which historically have controlled the amount of crime among our young people, (i.e., the family, neighborhood, schools, churches, etc.), the juvenile court is expected to do the entire job of behavioral control. It is not unrealistic or intellectually dishonest to say that if we could deal with the problems of family breakdown, neighborhood decay, religious revolution, excessive affluence side-by-side with degrading poverty, a pleasure-crazy culture, the loss of confidence in high officials and perhaps in government itself, rampant racial prejudice, and many of the other social ills which are literally gnawing at the vital areas of our society, we could much more effectively control juvenile behavior than by the complete overhaul or doubling of all police, juvenile courts and correctional facilities in this country. Behavioral control starts "at the mother's knee" and it is reinforced through all the socializing experiences throughout the child's development. To remove all of the positive influences from the lives of many youngsters who live with more rats and roaches than with benevolent human beings, and who are exposed to more criminal activity at an early age than they are to "good examples," and who live in the total absence of everything that goes into making a good citizen and a good human being, and then sixteen years later to simply say to this child that we will now threaten you or punish you into "being good" and into loving and respecting your neighbor and his property, is so totally unrealistic, simplistic and full of the dangers of the establishment of totalitarian kinds of control mechanisms that it amazes your author that so many professionals and other allegedly "thinking persons" can espouse this position in this enlightened day and age in our highly sophisticated nation.

Two points that your author definitely wishes to clarify are the following: 1. Your author certainly does not hold that no one ever needs to be locked up, because there are certainly those who do require secure custody for the protection of others or for their own safety. This has been made abundantly clear in many places in this current text and in the other writings of the author. However, this very fact does not justify the two abuses which so easily develop in a "lock-em-up" kind of philosophy of juvenile justice where on the one hand we "lock up" numerous youngsters who do not meet the criteria for the use of secure custody; and on the other, where we permit abusive, totally punitive and degrading conditions to exist in those settings where we do provide secure custody.

2. Your author certainly admits that there have been some intolerable abuses of the juvenile justice concept, and these certainly do need to be remedied in those juvenile courts which have adopted a "totally social agency stance" and where, as a result, the juvenile justice system has been exploited to permit dangerous offenders to go in and out like a "revolving door," serious adjustments do need to be made; those changes can be made and safeguards built in to truly protect society within the present juvenile court concept, without creating a "junior criminal court" within the juvenile court itself.

The law pertaining to juveniles makes it very clear that the purpose of juvenile correction is to alter the conditions and circumstances of juvenile delinquents so that they are able to change behavior patterns and not go on to a life of adult crime. For this reason, if for no other, it is necessary to evaluate constantly how we can best help youngsters to cope with the problems of complex community living and to learn to control their own impulses more effectively.

Common sense and experience clearly indicate that any person, not just a child, can only learn adequate community-living habits by living in the community or in a setting as closely resembling it as possible.

Conversely, it is difficult to teach people to make the proper choices, to accept responsibility, and to engage in healthy emotional exchange with countless other human beings in a wide variety of situations, if they are placed in a setting where all of their decisions are made for them; where there is no opportunity for the exercise of the responsibility of free choice; and where normal, healthy emotional experience is rendered impossible. For this reason, and many others, institutionalization of youngsters must never be seen as the solution in planning their treatment; and it should be utilized only as a last resort when the protection of society from their hostile impulses absolutely demands it.

Unfortunately, this has not been the operating philosophy upon which the juvenile corrections system in this country has been based until now. Despite much rhetoric to the contrary, the mass-custody institution is still the basis of America's system, and efforts to avoid it are still seen as novel and innovative.

Whenever a youngster gets into serious difficulty, the first question seems to be "Where can we send him?" This kind of thinking seems to represent part of a more general problem-solving idea that has prevailed for many years in America, and which has been applied not only to delinquents, but to the mentally ill, the retarded, the aged and the chronically infirm. It seems to reflect the notion that if we can only remove them from society, the problems which they present to us will cease to exist. For this reason, massive state mental hospitals, large publicly operated institutions for the "chronically sick poor," and various other facilities have been established, and their existence perpetuated for people who temporarily or permanently are not able to function in normal society.

§ 22.2   Institutionalization: demand and effect on juveniles

This "away syndrome," along with a misguided notion of what really contributes best to public safety, has caused the mass-custody institution to become the principal ingredient of the juvenile correction system for many years despite the fact that we were told decades ago that "Prisons are only a stop-gap—not a cure. A plumber can bury the leaky pipe deeper, but it will still leak."[1]

It seems that society wishes first to have its juvenile problems put away: and then wishes that they be kept securely away, in an atmosphere where possibility of escape and illegal return to the community is made very difficult; and finally, all this is expected to be done with as little expense as possible. Therefore, after the offenders are put securely and cheaply away, there seems to be little concern as to what happens to them while institutionalized and little effort made to alter their conditions and circumstances so that at the time of their return to the community, they might be able to function as more productive, law-abiding members of society.

In principle, there are few who would deny the need for effective programming and good personnel in corrections; but in fact, the major emphasis seems to be on institutionalization with secure custody as the paramount objective, and very little concern for the other elements in the program. This is affirmed by the fact that far more than one-half of the counties in America have not even bothered to build detention facilities in order to keep our children out of jail while awaiting trial.

Another contributory factor to this kind of correctional approach seems to have been caused by our industrialized and systematized problem-solving techniques that have been so successful in other areas of life. The carry-over of this thinking into corrections has caused us to feel that if we have a correctional system through which we process a large number of offenders, they will turn out as a "finished product," in this case "rehabilitated persons," whether or not there is real intervention of a meaningful nature in their lives.

We tend to think about the correctional system very much as we view the process by which license-plates are manufactured in some of our penal institutions. We establish a mechanical apparatus into which we insert an unfinished piece of metal and at the proper point it is shaped, painted, then stamped and finally it emerges from the apparatus as the desired finished product—a completed license-plate.

[1] Jesse O. Stutsman, *Curing the Criminal*, (1926), p. 29.

Should the end-product of our system not be of the quality desired, we simply re-insert it into the system and on the second or third or fourth time around, it emerges exactly the way we desire.

There are many real parallels to be drawn from this example and applied to our correctional thinking. But the irony is that we find more and more that we must keep re-inserting the incomplete product back into the system because the delinquency rates tell us, and the recidivism figures glaringly proclaim, that we are not producing the desired effect. We are not correcting delinquents.

The real tragedy of this philosophy of corrections needs no explanation in this volume, as it is so well known. Human beings, especially the sensitive young and very complicated adolescents, are not simply pieces of metal; and any system which does not provide for personal intervention in the solving of real life problems cannot possibly change their values and attitudes, or help them to control their behavior.

Since it is not the purpose of this discussion to attempt to make highly trained correctional experts out of the readers, it is not necessary to get into a detailed and scientific exploration of all of the problems which arise in attempting to do enlightened treatment of juvenile offenders within the mass-custody institutional framework. However, it is necessary to point out that delinquent values and attitudes are often reinforced and strengthened by the very nature of the institutional life-style.

The existence of the delinquent sub-culture within large institutions enhances the opportunity for dominance of the strong over the weak; gives impetus to the exploitation of the simple and the unsophisticated by the crafty and more knowledgeable; lowers self-concept because of regimentation and loss of identity; isolates from home and community and normal experiences; reinforces a feeling of deprivation and alienation; and when prolonged, promotes a feeling of real helplessness and encourages complete dependency.

These observations must be kept in mind so that institutions are not looked upon as a panacea or as the best solution to the problems of the juvenile offender.

At the same time, we must constantly remember that the protection of society demands that we do remove certain offenders who cannot control their impulses, who are venting their rage, or in other ways injuring or exploiting the larger society. The protection of society demands that dangerous offenders be placed in a highly structured environment until such time as they have developed better impulse control. This is also necessary for the treatment of such offenders because it is impossible to help anyone to improve his behavior when he acknowledgedly cannot control his impulses in free society. There are some who must be temporarily contained for their own good, as well as for society's benefit.

§ 22.3　Community-based treatment

a. Preventive services

The important thing to remember is that while such offenders must be removed and incarcerated, their removal is only temporary, and every effort must be made to understand and treat the real causal problems in their situation so that their behavior is changed when they return to society. It is also important to note that contrary to public opinion, the majority of delinquents are not dangerous; most offenders can be effectively controlled and much more adequately treated outside of large institutional programs.

This, of course, brings us immediately to the notion of "community-based treatment." As the name implies, this concept requires that the offender be dealt with, if possible, within the community; and that the community with all of its wealth of resources and services becomes involved in the treatment of the offender.

All problem behavior can best be handled at the earliest level at which it is recognized, and before the pattern becomes set. For this reason, good preventive services in the schools, at the neighborhood level, and through public and private agencies are absolutely essential in order to prevent the ever-increasing number of youngsters from making their first appearance as delinquents at the official level.

Tragically, the major emphasis in the past has not been on early detection and treatment, but has been concentrated on punishment after the transgression. We have been willing in this country to spend ten thousand dollars on the cost of crime and keeping criminals behind bars, for every dollar that we have been willing to expend on community services to needy children. There are countless communities which have beautiful air conditioned libraries, but no juvenile facilities. In other places there are modern dog pounds, but children are kept in antiquated jails; and some jurisdictions provide more and better paid gameskeepers than child care personnel.

As the delinquency rates continue to soar, and when public outcry becomes sufficiently loud, we usually have an emergency building program of a new institution, or perhaps a larger detention home, but we seldom think of spending dollars, time and energy at the prevention level where it is most effective.

b. Probation

Within the correctional process itself, we continue to apply this same ineffective planning and improper allocation of money at other levels. We permit probation to be constantly criticized as unsuccessful, even though we have never provided the full range of services and adequate staff necessary to implement the kinds of probation programs that can succeed. Overworked and underpaid probation staffs are the rule throughout the country. One veteran officer with a caseload of over two hundred offenders recently stated that "All I can do is have them line up by my window and wave at them." Yet we know, in theory and in practice, that when the opportunity is given to really try probation with relationship therapy, environmental manipulation, and the use of auxiliary services, offenders have the opportunity to improve while on probation, and real results can be obtained.

Probation implies a contract with the community and with the offender. This contract promises to the community that we can protect it from delinquent acts on the part of the probationer while permitting him to remain outside of institutional walls. To the offender, it promises that we have the time and the skill to understand his difficulties, and the resources to do something realistic about assisting him to cope with them, and thus to control his behavior.

For example, if an offender only steals when he is hungry, or if another only assaults when he is drinking, the behavior of these two individuals will not be controlled unless we do something about the hunger and the drinking problem respectively. If we do not do this, probation will fail to protect the community or to assist the offender to really become more law-abiding.

Society can only be protected, and the offender can only be helped, if we have the time, the staff and the resources to intervene realistically in the real problem areas. To provide only token supervision, or simply have routine periodic reporting for a neurotic offender, for a person overwhelmed with family problems, or an offender whose delinquency is rooted in degrading poverty and severe deprivation, is neither realistic nor helpful.

Services which can and do alter the conditions and circumstances of juvenile offenders and provide an opportunity to change behavior patterns include foster home care for an abused or deprived child, psychiatric treatment for the severely emotionally damaged and vocational training and a job for an economically deprived offender.

Successful treatment, therefore, demands the existence and utilization of a wide variety of services in the community. Detoxification units, residential treatment centers, programs for the narcotic abusers, half-way houses, and the mobilization of all existing medical and social services are absolutely necessary if successful community-centered treatment is to be provided.

When such facilities are unavailable and probation is confined merely to surveillance or a legal-type supervision, successful results cannot be anticipated and the recidivism rate will continue to soar.

c. Use of volunteers and paraprofessionals

Even the most enlightened programs for rehabilitation are doomed to failure without the opportunity for contacts with positive human beings. There must be time for the formation of meaningful human relationships somewhere in the correctional process. When high caseloads prohibit relating to the probationer, the lack can be supplemented by the intelligent use of paraprofessionals, indigenous workers and volunteers. Many fine programs are being operated throughout the country on a limited scale which provide offenders with the opportunity to relate to vocational counselors, community-center leaders and detached workers of many types. Failure to provide meaningful human relationships in corrections is simply a perpetuation of one of the basic problems that cause delinquency in the first place.

The use of ex-offenders, when properly screened and supervised, can be extremely helpful because of the ease of communication and ready identification-potential which exists between the offender and such a worker.

The use of volunteers drawn from all segments of community life is becoming much more widespread and is perhaps the only solution for the lack of professional personnel who can take time to relate to those entrusted to their care. It is estimated that there are currently well over one thousand courts and agencies making considerable use of volunteers in every role from big-brother type to volunteer psychiatrist, volunteer counselors, and even volunteer probation officers.[2]

§ 22.4   Decentralization of mass-custody institutions

When institutionalization is absolutely necessary, and some youngsters do require such placement, the program should be geared to meet the real life-needs of the offender as far as possible. To accomplish this we must decentralize the large mass-custody type institution. We must bring it from its remote and unrelated location to as close to the offender's community as possible. Its program must contain as many ingredients closely resembling normal life situations as can possibly be arranged; and every opportunity for positive human contacts with persons and programs inside the community should be

---

[2] N. C. V. T. P. Publication #1, (October, 1969), Boulder, Colorado, "Suggestions Toward a Curriculum in the Management of Volunteer Programs in Courts."

eagerly pursued. Needless regimentation, idle time and an atmosphere of hostility and futility must be totally eliminated if the program is to be of any real value in rehabilitation.

It seems ironic that in this advanced day and age, with all of the highly sophisticated technical knowledge at our disposal in so many fields, and with all that we have been able to determine about the causes of delinquency and the needs of the offenders in order to be rehabilitated, that we are still committed to a policy of undifferentiated treatment in so many places, without regard to the problems of the particular offender.

We know that the delinquent population includes the deprived, the rebellious, the retarded, the brain-damaged, the inadequate, situational reactions, thrill seekers, neurotics, psychotics, psychopaths; and we know that the delinquent acts of some were caused by individual motives of escape from problems, adolescent confusion, child neglect, the desire for revenge or to have unrequited guilt punished; but we delude ourselves into believing that we can handle all of these individual situations and reverse all of these causal patterns simply by placing large numbers of such individuals together in a program where they have little individual attention.

Literature in the correctional field makes us well aware of the dangers existing within mass-institutional placement because of possible contamination of less sophisticated youngsters by older, more hardened offenders, dehumanization by mass methods, educational retardation by being removed from normal school situations, introduction to poor living habits, the increase of hostility because of insensitive handling, lowering of self-concept because of degrading experiences, the further diminution of the already damaged concept of authority, and the possibility of sexual abuse at the hands of the perverted or the deranged; and yet all too often we do not let this knowledge influence us in doing individual treatment-planning at the time of adjudication.

The question is simply, if the mass-custody institutions meet the individual needs of such a few offenders, and if there are so many dangers of further contamination and reinforcement of delinquent values and attitudes in such an institutional setting, why is the practice still so prevalent in the field of juvenile corrections?

When one analyzes the question carefully, it seems that the need to incarcerate youngsters, rather than to properly control their behavior in the kind of community-based facilities that are required, tends to satisfy certain of society's needs, even though it disregards the demands of sound treatment policy.

For example, institutionalization seems to appease the anger of the community and satisfy the desire for revenge upon the offender. It is also functional in passifying an irate public who might be quite vociferous about expressing their desire that the child be sent away because of a particular offense. It certainly seems to fulfill society's need to separate "them" from "us," and thus to perpetuate the "away syndrome" in which we tend to feel comfortable when we have succeeded in isolating our problems rather than facing them. Finally, it seems to prevent us from having to face the real issues involved in confronting the causes of the offender's misdeeds.

The tragedy is that we seem to be guided in our actions of institutionalization by the need to feel that most offenders must be placed in an extremely secure situation in order for society to be protected. This, of course, would be a valid reason if it were true, but most offenders can be controlled and better assisted to avoid further recidivism by the use of smaller treatment units in their own community. The mistaken notion that most offenders require maximum security in order to protect society, can be seen in the practice of placing juvenile delinquents in jails with adult criminals. This is a widespread practice in this country despite the fact that most persons would answer in the affirmative if they were asked whether they believe that juveniles should be separated from hardened adult offenders at all times. The difference between what we say and what we do in juvenile corrections is never more obvious than in the area of the jailing of children.

It is estimated that in the United States far more areas do not have separate juvenile facilities than actually do have such detention homes, and some observers have indicated that five out of six counties in this country utilize jails as the place of detention for children.

The defense of the practice of jailing children is always that society would be in danger if they were not taken into secure custody and held there, and that most places cannot afford separate detention facilities for juvenile offenders. An examination of actual conditions will demonstrate the fallacy of this defense. In a recent survey taken by the Children's Bureau of the Department of Health, Education and Welfare in Washington, D.C., concerning eleven thousand, three hundred ninety-seven children being held in jail, in a random sampling of a large number of jails throughout the country, over nine thousand of the eleven thousand children were sent home after hearing.[3] These children certainly were not great risks to the community in the first place, or if they were, they certainly should not have been returned to their homes after just a few days in jail; and as to expense, the cost of security is always greater than the cost of housing.

In a similar study by the same agency, of nine thousand one hundred seventy-seven children in jail at the time of another sampling, three thousand, eight hundred eighteen of those children were languishing in jails for having committed acts which would not have been crimes if committed by an adult.[4] Such acts as truancy, runaway from home and late hours were the offenses for which almost four thousand of the children were being held in jail with criminal offenders. And more revealing is the fact that only three hundred forty-eight of the youngsters surveyed had committed an offense of any kind against another person.[5] Nevertheless, we constantly use the defense that our lives would be in danger if these children were not held in jail.

When we consider the fact that the placement of impressionable and confused children with sophisticated adult offenders, and the delinquent status which comes from having

[3] "Why Children are in Jail and How to Keep Them Out," Office of Juvenile Delinquency and Youth Development, HEW, Washington, D.C., (1970), p. 5.

[4] Ibid, p. 4.

[5] Ibid, p. 4.

familiarity with jail and adult criminals tends to strengthen delinquent values and attitudes and thus increase the likelihood of repeated delinquent offenses by the juveniles when released, the argument that jailing protects society does not stand the test of reality. In fact, the late Warden of Central Prison in Canada, J. T. Gilmore, said emphatically that "twenty-four hours in some jails can ruin a man." [6] How much more must this apply to children?

§ 22.5   Role of law enforcement officer

This damaging practice of jailing children can be remedied in several ways; and here the enlightened law enforcement officer can be of great service. The arresting officer and his superiors can work to establish truly effective criteria for physically arresting and detaining any child. These criteria should be based on four principles:

(1) the protection of persons or property in the community (in cases where such protection cannot be insured by the use of a less restrictive alternative)

(2) the certainty that the child will leave the jurisdiction before a hearing can be arranged

(3) the child's need for protection

(4) the lack of any other place for the child to go[7]

In exercising these four principles, it must be kept in mind that three other governing principles must be enforced:

(1) under no circumstance should the child who is physically arrested, in keeping with the four principles above, be placed in an adult jail. (Unfortunately, there are far more counties in the United States which have only the common adult jail as a place of detention for children than those which have a separate place; however, the principle remains very clear that this process is not in the best interest of the child nor does it provide any lasting protection of the community)

(2) when the child requires secure custody as in numbers (1) and (2) above, then placement in the separate juvenile

---

[6] Quoted in Jesse O. Stutsman, op. cit., p. 354.

[7] See also Standard 12.7, "Criteria for Preadjudicating Detention in Delinquency Cases," pp. 390-392.

detention facility should be made

(3) when the child does not require secure custody, as in numbers (3) and (4) above, he should certainly be placed in a "non-secure" facility, such as "attention homes," volunteer homes, open temporary shelters, runaway houses, etc. (Those offenders committing "status offenses" can be considered in this category in most instances)[8]

This will remove the needless incarceration of large numbers of juveniles who, unfortunately, are placed in jails because their communities have not provided properly for them.

Law enforcement officials and correctional workers should be in the forefront of the battle to demand that there be separate facilities for juvenile offenders in every community, and that these facilities contain a proper program and staff.

Adequate distinction must be made between dependent and delinquent youngsters; and especially at all levels, between those who are in need of a security facility and those who simply need temporary shelter. The insistence on this vital separation can be of great service in eliminating the abuse resulting from jails and secure detention facilities being utilized for the homeless and destitute.

The enlightened police officer should always locate parents and release a child to them unless detention is absolutely necessary. The juvenile courts must be equipped to review each case at the intake level as to the necessity of detention, and this necessarily requires a 24-hour program of screening at the court or place of detention.

It should not be necessary to emphasize that a child without a severe personality disturbance, or without a sophisticated delinquent pattern of behavior, who is subjected to detention in adult jail, and then processed into a mass-custody institution, is in grave danger of reaching a level of delinquent values and attitudes far beyond what normally would be the case if he could be treated as a "child with problems," and surrounded

[8] See also Standard 12.9, "Endangered Children . . . Temporary Custody . . ., etc." pp. 396-398.

with an atmosphere of community concern for his future behavior rather than fear of his present delinquent act.

With a reminder of the importance of understanding the behavioral dynamics of delinquent children in mind, it is necessary to raise the important question of the difficulty encountered in a given offense situation in trying to protect society by conducting a proper investigation, and by completing the formalities of arrest and court action, without seriously contributing to a further aggravation of the very real problems of a totally deprived or extremely aggressive child. This question and this conflict can only be answered and resolved by enforcement officers and court officials functioning at the highest degree of professionality and remaining keenly aware of their dual responsibility to the community and to the child in their custody. Questions must be asked, information must be probed and verified, charges must be filed, and custody must be taken all within an atmosphere of professional competence and efficiency, but without in any way further degrading and humiliating the troubled youngster who sees himself as being helpless. In such situations great harm can be done by further lowering the self-concept of increasing the alienation of the young offender by reacting to his hostility with hostility.

It should be carefully noted that great gain in reaching "children who hate" can be made by not being abusive when they are apprehended and are tense. Severely delinquent children can cope with further rejection, and even with brutality, because they are familiar with it and prepared for it; but kindness, concern, and even professional efficiency force them to challenge their well-developed "justification for hate." This can well be the beginning of treatment; and the first opportunity is usually given to the police officer.

APPLICATION OF IMPORTANT POINTS EMPHASIZED FOR LAW ENFORCEMENT OFFICERS

1. The law requires the treatment of the juvenile offender, as far as possible, in a way that will assist him to change his behavior. This is a legal requirement.

2. The best place to teach good community living habits is in the community itself, so whenever possible, sound programs of effective

probation, halfway houses and the like should be utilized.

3. Treatment does *not* mean permissiveness or freeing the offender to prey upon society. Children need discipline, and sound treatment programs do not overlook this need. Consistent limit-setting is a necessary part of juvenile correction.

4. Institutional placement is not the only way to discipline or to set limits for children, and it is the most difficult setting in which to teach the skills and habits required for effective community living. Therefore, such placement should be the last, not the first solution proposed.

5. The most important influence on children for behavioral change is people. "Significant others" do influence values and attitudes of youngsters, and all buildings and programs are ineffective without positive personal intervention.

6. A person does not have to be a psychiatrist, or have any professional training, to exert great influence in the lives of some youngsters. Enlightened treatment programs are utilizing more and more paraprofessionals, indigenous workers, volunteers and a whole host of untrained personnel to relate to children with problems on an individualized basis.

7. The effective police officer can be a positive contact at the point of arrest and be the beginning of treatment for the juvenile offender.

8. The attitude and conduct of the arresting or transporting officer, even when seemingly unappreciated by a hostile juvenile offender, is never unnoticed, and the officer is always a plus or a minus depending on how he conducts himself officially and as a person.

9. Truly professional enforcement attitudes never conflict with truly professional treatment methods. It is only when enforcement degenerates into some abuse such as personal vindictiveness, or when professional treatment methods are used to promote pseudo-professional snobbishness or deteriorate into unrealistic permissiveness that conflicts arise.

10. The professional police officer must be also interested in correcting the causes of juvenile misbehavior; and the professional "treatment specialist" must be also interested in the protection of society. The two roles should not be in opposition to each other.

APPENDIX

A. Constitutional Rights of Juveniles
B. National Advisory Committee on Criminal Justice Standards and
    Goals
C. Juvenile Justice and Delinquency Prevention Act of 1974

Appendix A

CONSTITUTIONAL RIGHTS OF JUVENILES
WAIVER OF JUVENILE COURT JURISDICTION

The case of *Kent* v. *United States*, 383 U.S. 541, 40 OhioOp.(2d) 270, 86 S.Ct. 1045, 11 L.Ed.(2d) 84 (1966), concerned the limitations on a juvenile court's exercise of its statutory power to relinquish its jurisdiction so that certain minors may be tried as adult criminals.

Kent presented the issue of whether a sixteen-year-old boy charged with housebreaking, robbery, and rape was properly transferred from the exclusive jurisdiction of the District of Columbia's juvenile court to the United States District Court, where he was found guilty on six counts of housebreaking and robbery, and was sentenced to a total of thirty to ninety years in prison. In cases of what would involve felonies if committed by adults, the District's juvenile act permitted the juvenile court, after "full investigation" to waive its "exclusive jurisdiction" with respect to children aged sixteen and seventeen. Kent was represented by counsel who, when informed of the possibility of waiver, requested a hearing on that issue. Counsel requested also that he be given access to his client's social service file on the ground that the information therein would have considerable bearing on the juvenile judge's decision whether to retain or relinquish jurisdiction. The judge, without ruling on the motions and without notifying Kent, his parents, or his lawyer, entered an order reciting that "after full investigation, I do hereby waive" jurisdiction. Five years later the case reached the United States Supreme Court. The Court held that "read in the context of constitutional principles relating to due process and the assistance of counsel," the District of Columbia Juvenile Court Act did not permit the "critically important" waiver decision to be made: (1) without hearing; (2) without effective assistance of counsel; (3) that effective assistance of counsel required that counsel be given access to the child's social service file;

and (4) that for purposes of review, any waiver order must be accompanied by statement of reasons for that decision considerably more enlightening than the recitation of "full investigation." Implicit in the express holding of the Court is the requirement that the child, and probably his parents, must be given adequate notice of any hearing that is to be held to determine whether the juvenile court will retain jurisdiction.[1]

PROCEEDINGS WITH POSSIBILITY OF COMMITMENT TO INSTITUTION

Careful Supreme Court scrutiny of juvenile court procedures was carried further in *In re Gault*, 387 U.S. 1, 40 OhioOp.(2d) 378, 87 S.Ct. 1428, 18 L.Ed.(2d) 527 (1967). The Court held that Fourteenth Amendment due process requires that in juvenile court proceedings which may result in the juvenile's commitment to an institution, the child and his parents or guardian must be: (1) given notice sufficient to permit preparation of defense to charges, (2) notified of the child's right to be represented by counsel (including assigned counsel), and (3) the child must be afforded the privilege against self-incrimination and the rights of confrontation and cross-examination.

The case grew out of the following facts: As a result of a verbal complaint by a woman neighbor about lewd and indecent phone calls made to her, Gerald Gault, a fifteen-year-old boy, was placed in the Children's Detention Home. A probation officer filed a petition with the juvenile court praying for a hearing regarding the care and custody of Gault. The petition gave no factual basis for the judicial action it initiated, but recited only that "said minor is a delinquent minor" and "in need of the protection" of the court. Gault's parents were neither served nor saw the petition. No one was sworn at this hearing or at a second one held a week later. No transcript or recording was made of either hearing. There was a conflict as to whether, at these hearings, the boy admitted making the lewd phone calls. The complaining witness did not attend either hearing. A "referral report" made by the probation officer was filed with the court but not shown to Gault or his parents. The judge committed the boy as a juvenile delinquent to the state industrial school "for the period of his minor-

---

[1] Schornhorst, *The Waiver of Juvenile Court Jurisdiction: Kent Revisited,* 43 Ind. L. J. 583, 584 (1967-68). (Footnotes omitted.)

ity," which was six years. If Gault had been eighteen the maximum penalty for making "vulgar, abusive or obscene" phone calls would have been a $50 fine or two months imprisonment.

Speaking for five members of the Court, Justice Fortas confronted "the reality of that portion of the juvenile court process with which we deal in this case":

"A boy is charged with misconduct. The boy is committed to an institution where he may be restrained of liberty for years. It is of no constitutional consequence—and of limited practical meaning—that the institution to which he is committed is called an Industrial School. The fact of the matter is that, however euphemistic the title, a 'receiving home' or an 'industrial school' for juveniles is an institution of confinement in which the child is incarcerated for a greater or lesser time. * * * In view of this, it would be extraordinary if our Constitution did not require the procedural regularity and the exercise of care implied in the phrase 'due process.' Under our Constitution, the condition of being a boy does not justify a kangaroo court. * * * The essential difference between Gerald's case and a normal criminal case is that safeguards available to adults were discarded in Gerald's case. The summary procedure as well as the long commitment were possible because Gerald was 15 years of age instead of over 18."[2]

There were four additional opinions, but only one dissenter, Justice Stewart, from the judgment of reversal. The Court did not deal with the right to a transcript of the proceedings or the right to appellate review.

DEGREE OF PROOF REQUIRED

The degree of proof required when a juvenile is charge with an act which would be a crime if committed by an adult was laid down by the Supreme Court in *In re Winship*, 397 U.S. 358, 51 OhioOp.(2d) 323, 25 L.Ed.(2d) 368, 90 S.Ct. 1068 (1970). In that case a 5-3 majority held that "proof beyond a reasonable doubt is among the 'essentials of due process and fair treatment' required during the adjudicatory stage when a juvenile is charged with an act which would constitute a crime if committeed by an adult." The juvenile had been charged

2 Lockhart, Kamisar and Choper, *Constitutional Law, Cases-Comments-Questions,* 3rd ed., at p. 703, American   Casebook series, West Publishing Co., St. Paul, Minn. (1970).

with delinquency for an act of stealing which rendered him liable to confinement for six years. The judge acknowledged that the juvenile's guilt was not established beyond a reasonable doubt, but relied on a statute which provided that a determination at the conclusion of an adjudicatory hearing that a juvenile did an act or acts must be based on a preponderance of the evidence. The majority opinion stated: "Lest there remain any doubt about the constitutional stature of the reasonable-doubt standard, we explicity hold that the Due Process Clause protects the accused against conviction except upon proof beyond a reasonable doubt of every fact necessary to constitute the crime with which he is charged."[3]

ESCOBEDO AND MIRANDA DECISIONS

As stated in the summary in Chapter 19, The Juvenile Court: Philosophy and Procedures, the issue of whether *Miranda* warnings must be given at the stage of interrogation of juveniles has not yet been decided by the Supreme Court. A brief statement of the holdings in *Escobedo* v. *Illinois*,[4] and *Miranda* v. *Arizona*,[5] appears here for the guidance of police officers.

Escobedo held that where a police investigation is no longer a general inquiry into an unsolved crime but has begun to focus on a particular suspect, the suspect has been taken into policy custody, the police carry out interrogations which lend themselves to eliciting incriminating statements, the suspect has requested and been denied an opportunity to consult with his lawyer, and the police have not effectively warned him of his absolute constitutional right to remain silent, the accused has been denied the assistance of counsel in violation of the Sixth Amendment to the Constitution as made obligatory upon the states by the Fourteenth Amendment.

Miranda held that when a person is taken into custody or deprived of his freedom in any significant way, prior to questioning him the police must warn him of his right to remain silent, that any statement he makes may be used in evidence against him, and that he has a right to counsel, either retained or appointed. These rights can be waived, but the waiver must be made voluntarily, knowingly and intelligently.

[3] *Id.*, at 707.
[4] 378 U.S. 478, 84 S.Ct. 1758, 12 L.Ed.(2d) 977 (1964).
[5] 384 U.S. 436, 86 S.Ct. 1602, 16 L.Ed.(2d) 694 (1966).

Unless these requirements are fulfilled, any statement taken from a defendant questioned while in custody and deprived of his freedom of action is inadmissible in evidence against him.

Appendix B

STANDARDS AND GOALS
1976
NATIONAL ADVISORY COMMITTEE ON CRIMINAL JUSTICE

STANDARD 1.1

Developing a Comprehensive Delinquency Prevention Plan

A comprehensive delinquency prevention plan should be developed by an appropriate level of general purpose government. The comprehensive plan should include the following components:

1. A detailed analysis of the delinquency problem in the community;

2. An inventory of current programs and resources available for delinquency prevention;

3. A clear statement of institutional and agency responsibilities for delinquency prevention;

4. A mechanism for institutionalizing coordination of delinquency prevention programs and efforts; and

5. A planned strategy for reducing the incidence of delinquency through prevention.

STANDARD 1.2

Collecting Delinquency Data

Every unit responsible for the construction of a comprehensive plan should develop a system for obtaining adequate data for delinquency prevention planning. Information sources should be continually evaluated and updated and new sources of data should be sought out and included in prevention planning.

STANDARD 1.3

Profiling the Nature of the Delinquency Problem

Every unit responsible for the construction of a comprehensive delinquency prevention plan should develop a more descriptive and accurate picture of the delinquency problems in the surrounding community. A more specific description of delinquent behavior should be used to reanalyze official statistics about delinquency to determine which children are being served and which children are not being served by current programs.

STANDARD 1.4

Clarifying Delinquency Prevention Goals

A statement of the goals to be achieved by a delinquency prevention effort should be formulated during the initial stages of a community's planning process. Determination of goals should be attempted only after participants in the planning process have a clear understanding of their assumptions about prevention. A self-assessment survey should be utilized for this purpose.

STANDARD 1.5

Inventorying Community Resources

Participants in the prevention planning process should be aware of existing community resources that may contribute to a comprehensive delinquency prevention effort. When making decisions, planners should have at their disposal a resource book that summarizes the prevention functions of community institutions. The information compiled should be made available for easy dissemination.

STANDARD 1.6

Integrating Individual Prevention Programs Into the Community Comprehensive Plan

The merits of an individual agency's prevention program should be compared with the overall community plan. Planners should appraise a program in terms of the following criteria:

1. The purpose and policy assumptions of the program proposal;

2. The nature of the target population for which the program is intended;

3. The goals of the comprehensive community prevention plan that are satisfied by the program;

4. Alternative methods of accomplishing these goals; and

5. Information about the experiences and results of similar programs in other communities.

STANDARD 1.7

Evaluation

All delinquency prevention programs should be carefully evaluated and the results should be used to refine and improve the community's comprehensive delinquency prevention plan.

STANDARD 2.1

The Local Role in Delinquency Prevention

Localities should be responsible for

the operation of direct service programs for delinquency prevention. This responsibility should include identifying local needs and resources, developing programs to resolve the needs, and delivering the services needed.

STANDARD 2.2

Office of Delinquency Prevention Planning

An Office of Delinquency Prevention Planning should be established within appropriate units of local general purpose government. This office should be responsible for coordination of local prevention efforts on an ongoing and permanent basis.

STANDARD 2.3

The State's Role in Delinquency Prevention

States should create a single agency to coordinate delinquency prevention programs. The role of the State agency should include the following:

1. Coordination of services to children and youth on a statewide basis;

2. Encouragement of the development of relevant services in localities;

3. Emphasis on and financial support for the prevention of delinquency and diversion from the justice system;

4. Administration and granting of subsidy funds for all youth service agencies, along with the establishment of standards for both quality and quantity of services offered;

5. Encouragement and arrangement of training programs that would include training for volunteers, paraprofessionals, and anyone connected with the services being offered to children and youth;

6. Advocacy on behalf of the well-being of children and youth; and

7. Leadership in a statewide strat-

egy and plan for delinquency prevention.

Where a statewide juvenile services department exists, and it is to perform the function required by this standard, the department should also be authorized to provide direct services to children and youth.

STANDARD 2.4

The Federal Role in Delinquency Prevention

The role of the Federal Government in assisting local and State delinquency prevention efforts should be to:

1. Identify needs and problems;

2. Recommend standards related to meeting those needs and problems;

3. Support research and evaluation designed to expand the base of knowledge about delinquency and methods for its prevention; and

4. Provide resources, technical assistance, and consultation for prevention programs.

STANDARD 2.5

Organizational Capacity to Act

States and local units of government should establish delinquency prevention coordinating bodies, such as interagency councils or intergovernmental standing committees, with the capacity to provide people, money and support for delinquency prevention. This capacity should be derived through the active participation of persons who serve on these bodies and represent general purpose government, statutory agencies, the private sector, citizen representatives of the community to be served, policy advisory groups, and technical support units.

STANDARD 2.6

Achieving Coordination and Cooperation of Delinquency Prevention Programs

All agencies affecting youth in any community should cooperate and coordinate with others in the delivery of services to insure that each agency:

1. Clarifies its interdependent relationship with others;

2. Standardizes its exchanges of communication;

3. Has a complete description of the volume and frequency of linkages and exchanges with other agencies; and

4. Is aware of which of its goals are competitive with those of other organizations and which are facilitative.

STANDARD 2.7

Youth Participation

Youth should be included in the membership of all commissions and organizations concerned with the planning, implementation, and evaluation of programmatic and policy decisions relating to delinquency prevention.

STANDARD 2.8

Financing Delinquency Prevention Programs

Delinquency prevention should become a high priority for public support. State government and units of local government should develop methods of insuring continuous levels of adequate funding for delinquency prevention programming.

The Federal Government also has a significant funding responsibility for delinquency prevention. Funds earmarked for prevention should be provided on a block grant basis to States.

Allocation of funds from all levels of government should be based on knowledge of the problems associated with delinquency in a particular area rather than solely on population factors.

STANDARD 2.9

Resource Allocation

Federal, State, and local governments should insure adequate resources for juvenile justice and delinquency prevention programs. Each level of government should recognize that:

1. Resource allocations should be of a stable, ongoing character. Erratic efforts that generate unfulfilled expectations are seriously counterproductive.

2. Adequate resource allocation requires the concerted efforts of all levels of government. Expectations of Federal assistance should not deter State, local, and private authorities from energetic efforts to procure adequate resources.

3. Juveniles currently account for nearly half of the arrests for serious crimes in the United States and the ratio of resources allocated to the adult/juvenile systems should conform to these findings.

4. Adequate resource allocation requires the continuing support of major efforts to employ empirical means to identify resource needs, plan for maximum utilization of available resources, and assure competent evaluation of juvenile programs.

STANDARD 3.1

Health—Providing Health Services

Comprehensive public health services should be made available to youth. Health services should include preventive health care services, low-cost medical and dental care and programs to assist parents during prenatal and post partum periods.

STANDARD 3.2

Health—Mental Health Services

States and units of local government should provide a full range of community mental health services to all children and their families.

STANDARD 3.3

Family—Parent Training

States and units of local government should provide parent training programs to strengthen family cohesion.

STANDARD 3.4

Family—Family Counseling

States and units of local government should provide adequate family counseling services to promote family cohesion.

STANDARD 3.5

Family—Protective Services

States and units of local government should establish or expand protective services to children and families to facilitate the raising of all children in permanent, stable family environments. Crisis centers for families with potentially Endangered Children should be maintained with personnel trained in problem-solving on a 24-hour basis. The objective of protective services should be to strengthen the family unit and prevent the severance of family ties whenever feasible. Family ties should be severed only in accordance with the standards regarding coercive intervention on behalf of Endangered Children. If the parent-child relationship is terminated, services should be provided to insure provision of a new, permanent, stable family home for the child at the earliest time practicable.

STANDARD 3.6

Family—Nutritional Services

Each State and local government unit should insure that all children and their families receive adequate and proper nutrition.

STANDARD 3.7

Family—Assistance in Meeting Basic Needs of the Family

Units of State and local government should provide informational services to help families better meet their basic housing, food, clothing, and social service needs.

STANDARD 3.8

Family—Day Care

Each community should establish day care and drop-in child care centers for appropriate children of all ages and for children with special needs. The centers should utilize community residents and other qualified personnel as staff members, and rely on community residents for direction in running the centers.

STANDARD 3.9

Education—Integrating Schools Into the Community

Schools should expand their efforts to foster learning and education throughout the community. Interested groups and individuals from the community should participate actively in all aspects of school functioning.

STANDARD 3.10

Education—Developing Comprehensive Programs for Learning

Schools should assume the responsibility for working with families to coordinate all efforts to assist students in achieving agreed-upon objectives of academic proficiency at each stage of their educational careers.

STANDARD 3.11

Education—Survival Education

Schools should institute reality-based curricula that enable students to respond successfully to the demands of living in contemporary society. Instruction in basic skills such as reading, verbal and written expression, and mathematics should be an integral part of this "survival education" program.

STANDARD 3.12

Education—Alternative Education

Schools should provide for alternative educational experiences that encourage experimentation and diversity in curriculum, instructional methods, and administrative organization of the learning process.

STANDARD 3.13

Education—The Home as a Learning Environment

Schools should initiate methods and techniques for enriching the potential of the home as a learning environment; children, parents, and school staff all should participate.

STANDARD 3.14

Education—Bilingual and Bicultural Education

Schools should develop bilingual and bicultural educational programs to improve ethnic relations and provide relevant instruction for those students who speak English as a second language.

STANDARD 3.15

Education—Supportive Services

Schools should provide a full range of supportive services for all students, and particularly for those students experiencing adjustment problems within the regular school program and structure.

STANDARD 3.16

Education—Problems in Learning

Schools should develop programs to diagnose and provide appropriate programs to deal with learning problems in children. Teachers should be given training in early identification of specific learning problems.

STANDARD 3.17

Education—Learning Disabilities

Schools should develop special education programs for children exhibiting learning disabilities. States should review and, if necessary, amend their State educational codes to permit more flexibility for providing necessary resources and services for children with learning disabilities. States also should establish commissions to review and update the classification schemes of their special education programs.

STANDARD 3.18

Education—Teacher Training

School authorities should develop or improve methods of teacher training, certification, periodic recertification, and accountability. Closer cooperation with universities, colleges, and other school districts is crucial to upgrading the quality of classroom instruction.

STANDARD 3.19

Education—Utilization of School Facilities

School officials should strive to develop a community school concept by promoting total utilization of school facilities and resources.

STANDARD 3.20

Education—The School as a Model of Justice

Schools should serve as models of justice by adopting policies that reflect democratic principles in their organization and fairness in the rules and regulations governing conduct.

STANDARD 3.21

Education—Career Education

Schools should provide the basic components of career education for all students.

STANDARD 3.22

Employment—Expansion of Job Opportunities

All levels of government should initiate or expand programs that develop job opportunities for youth. A comprehensive employment and manpower strategy should be employed that includes maintaining a larger number of available jobs, job training, and the elimination of discriminatory hiring practices.

STANDARD 3.23

Employment—Community Job Placement and Information Centers

Each community should have at its disposal highly visible and easily accessible job placement and information centers. Each center should have staff who are familiar with special employment problems faced by youth who may not be in school. Where feasible, existing public agencies should be required to provide these services.

STANDARD 3.24

Employment—Employment Counseling and Work-Study Programs

Each high school should have counselors trained in employment counseling. Counselors should develop with local employers opportunities for meaningful employment during a student's nonclassroom hours. Public financing should be provided for high school work-study programs.

STANDARD 3.25

Employment—Summer Programs

Each community should expand summer employment opportunities available to youth. Agencies coordinating efforts to place youths in summer jobs should be staffed on a year-round basis. In addition to placement activities, agencies should provide counseling and guidance services.

STANDARD 3.26

Employment—Job Opportunities for Youths With a History of Delinquency

Employment services and correctional officials should work together to develop and/or expand job opportunities for youths with a history of delinquency.

STANDARD 3.27

Employment—Confidentiality of Juvenile Records

Each State should enact legislation making the records of all juvenile proceedings inaccessible to potential employers. This legislation should make illegal the questioning of a youth by an employer as to the existence or content of the youth's juvenile record.

STANDARD 3.28

Employment—Age and Wage Restrictions

The Federal Government and each State should examine thoroughly their legislation that affects youth employment. Laws that restrict youth employment opportunities without real risks to health or development should be removed or revised.

STANDARD 3.29

Justice System—Diversion

States and units of local government should develop programs that divert children from the juvenile justice system.

STANDARD 3.30

Justice System—Citizen Efforts to Prevent Delinquency

Persons who administer the juvenile

justice system should both encourage and assist citizen efforts to prevent and control juvenile delinquency.

STANDARD 3.31

Justice System—Information on Deterrence

Police agencies should systematically disseminate crime prevention information to citizens, particularly to those people who are victimized most frequently by delinquent acts. Such information should suggest practical and proven steps that such individuals can take to safeguard themselves and their property.

STANDARD 3.32

Justice System—School Programs

Juvenile justice system personnel should take an active role in school programs that educate youngsters about the purposes and functions of the juvenile justice system.

STANDARD 3.33

Justice System—Handgun Control

The Federal Government and each State should enact legislation prohibiting the manufacture and sale of handguns to anyone other than law enforcement and private security personnel and Federal and State governments for military purposes. In addition, each State should prohibit private ownership and possession of handguns by persons not included in the above categories.

STANDARD 3.34

Recreation—Providing Recreational Opportunities

Municipal recreation programs should provide recreational opportunities for all youths in the community. Recreational programming should emphasize outreach services in order to recruit youths who otherwise might not be reached and for whom recreational opportunities may be an alternative to delinquency.

STANDARD 3.35

Recreation—Utilization of Recreational Facilities

Maximum use should be made of existing recreational facilities, especially within the schools, during the afternoons and evenings, on weekends, and throughout the summer. Where existing recreational facilities are inadequate, other community agencies should be encouraged to provide facilities at minimum cost or at no cost, where feasible.

STANDARD 3.36

Recreation—Meeting Individual Needs

Individual needs should be considered in planning recreational programming.

STANDARD 3.37

Recreation—Increased Opportunities in Cultural Programs

All levels of government should initiate programs that expose young people to the arts and develop their interests in the arts. Communities should increase opportunities for all young artists to perform, create new works, and present their talents to the public.

STANDARD 3.38

Recreation—Selection of Staff

Local recreational programs should strive to select staff who are genuinely interested in youth, able to serve as resource persons, and capable of helping people find personally satisfying experiences.

STANDARD 3.39

Housing—Adequate Housing

Housing and urban development agencies at all levels of government should promote decent and adequate housing for low-income families through increased construction of new housing units and recycling existing housing. Potential residents should be involved in the planning and design of all new housing developments. Special priorities should be placed on programs that reclaim existing housing through rehabilitation, reasonable code enforcement, and tax incentives to reduce abandonment.

STANDARD 3.40

Housing—Street Safety

Local government agencies should insure the security of the citizenry by improving the environmental design of urban areas. This requires designing and utilizing public areas in such a manner as to discourage delinquent and criminal activity; encouraging frequent use of streets, sidewalks, parks, and other public areas enhances continuous public surveillance.

STANDARD 3.41

Housing—Security Codes

Each community should develop building security codes designed to prevent or reduce the likelihood of criminal or delinquent activity in any new structure, public or private.

STANDARD 3.42

Religion—Contributions to Delinquency Prevention

Religious organizations should contribute to the delinquency prevention effort by providing counseling services, educating their constituencies about delinquency problems, offering their facilities for youth services, and developing their own delinquency prevention programs.

STANDARD 3.43

Media—Media as an Educational Force

The mass media should accept responsibility for being a positive educational influence on youth. Media activities should include development of policies to regulate the nature and extent of articles and programs designed to develop positive images for minority groups and greater internal regulation of advertising directed toward the youth market. All avenues for youth and citizen involvement in media productions should be explored.

STANDARD 3.44

Media—Television Violence

Federal regulatory agencies and the television industry should as promptly as possible promulgate rules and regulations to immediately reduce and eventually to eliminate the dramatization of contemporary violence and dehumanization.

STANDARD 4.1

Police Policy as an Expression of Community Standards

The police role in juvenile justice and delinquency prevention should be responsive to community needs. The police should function in both an enforcement and prevention capacity, emphasizing neither role at the expense of the other.

STANDARD 4.2

Police Responsibility in Protecting Integrity of the Law

The police objective in protecting the integrity of the law should be twofold: (1) to enforce the law and maintain order; and (2) to insure impartiality in enforcement.

STANDARD 4.3

Use of Least Coercive Alternative

To respect family autonomy and minimize coercive State intervention, law enforcement officers dealing with juveniles should be authorized and encouraged to use the least coercive among reasonable alternatives, consistent with preserving public safety, order, and individual liberty.

STANDARD 4.4

Guidelines on Use of Police Discretion

To stimulate the development of appropriate administrative guidance and control over police discretion in juvenile operations, legislatures and courts should actively encourage or require police administrative rulemaking.

Police chief executives should establish administrative procedures to structure and control the use of discretion. These should include policy guidelines on the use of discretionary judgment when dealing with juveniles and training programs to acquaint officers with situations where discretion may be exercised.

STANDARD 4.5

Procedural Differences for Handling Juveniles

There should be some procedural differences in police agency operations when handling juveniles. These differences should be based upon sound legal, social and constitutional principles. For example:

1. In handling juveniles, the police should be provided with dispositional alternatives such as referral of the child to social service and youth service agencies;

2. To the maximum extent feasible, the police should be required to notify parents or guardians when a juvenile is taken into custody;

3. The police should not detain juveniles in facilities which are utilized to detain adults; and

4. Police should exercise all due caution in complying with constitutional standards in the custodial interrogation of juveniles and should not accept an attempt by the juvenile to waive the right against self-incrimination without the advice of counsel.

STANDARD 4.6

Participation in Policy Formulation Efforts

Police chief executives should broaden the scope of participation in police policy formulation affecting juveniles. Those who should participate include laypersons, other juvenile justice system personnel, community youth service groups, educators, and other community groups working in a youth-serving capacity.

STANDARD 5.1

Guidelines for Preventive Patrols and Early Identification of Juveniles With Problems

The police department should direct its efforts to help create an environment in the community that will serve to prevent crime and delinquency. The prevention program should include the following elements:

1. The Patrol Division should conduct a roving surveillance designed to prevent juvenile delinquency, frequently checking places where juveniles may become involved in delinquent acts and easily become victims of crimes. Patrol personnel should maintain continuous and conspicuous operations in such areas;

2. For minor law violations, police patrol officers should be required to complete contact cards after each incident in which a full report is not submitted. The parents or guardians of the juvenile should be notified that a contact card has been filed and should be given an opportunity to question and discuss the information contained in the report;

3. The importance of maintaining positive, open communication with juveniles should be stressed to all officers.

STANDARD 5.2

Guidelines for Patrol Officers

The duties and responsibilities of patrol officers should include:

1. Taking appropriate action when observing delinquent acts in progress; responding to all dispatches and appropriately processing all requests for service in juvenile matters; and completely investigating all cases. These duties include preserving evidence and, when warranted, taking juveniles into custody, except in those cases that require the attention of specialists;

2. Responding to family disturbance calls in an expeditious and safe manner and, where necessary, taking appropriate action in accordance with the Standard on Guidelines for Police Intercession for the Protection of Endangered Children (Standard 5.3);

3. Securing emergency medical treatment, according to procedures established by specific legislative directives, for children needing immediate attention, and immediately reporting cases of Endangered (Neglected or Abused) Children to the appropriate State agency;

4. Keeping order on streets and highways, enforcing all moving traffic violations involving juveniles and investigating traffic accidents, unless instructed to do otherwise by traffic division investigators;

5. Providing for the safety of children attending school by surveilling for persons who loiter on or near school property, and intervening immediately when observing potential or inprogress criminal or delinquent activities or dangerous situations on or near school property; and

6. Apprehending and protecting juveniles from homes of Families With Service Needs when requested to do so by police-juvenile officers.

STANDARD 5.3

Guidelines for Police Intercession to Protect Endangered Children

Police should have clear statutory authority to intercede and provide necessary protection for children whose health or safety is endangered. Statutes should specify the following:

1. When a child is endangered in an environment other than the home, police should remove the child from danger and make maximum possible efforts to return him or her to the home;

2. When a child is endangered in the home, police should make maximum possible efforts to protect the child without resorting to removal from the home;

3. When the child is endangered in the home and removal is necessary to prevent bodily injury, police should be authorized to remove the child according to the procedures established by Standard 12.9 on emergency removal of endangered children from the home.

STANDARD 5.4

Guidelines for Police Juvenile Investigations

Investigations of law violations by juveniles should be made as quickly as possible and should be as thorough and complete as the investigations of adult offenses. Equally important, the juvenile unit investigator should attempt to determine the underlying causes for the law violation, in order to assist in the rehabilitation process. Police investigators must also take every necessary precaution to safeguard the constitutional rights of juveniles being investigated in connection with a criminal offense or delinquent act.

STANDARD 5.5

Guidelines for Issuing Citations

Police departments should make maximum effective use of State statutes permitting police agencies to issue a written citation and summons to ap-

pear at intake in lieu of taking a juvenile into custody. A copy of each citation and summons should also be forwarded to the juvenile's parents or guardians.

STANDARD 5.6

Guidelines for Taking a Juvenile Into Custody

The police are authorized to take into custody all juveniles who violate criminal statutes and/or ordinances of the local, State, or Federal Government.

In addition, every State should clearly define by statute the authority and guidelines for, and limitations on, taking a juvenile into custody in Families With Service Needs cases and Endangered Child cases.

Whenever a juvenile is taken into custody the police should:

1. To the maximum extent possible take immediate affirmative action to notify the juvenile's parents or guardians; and

2. Immediately notify the juvenile of his constitutional rights and refrain from any action that would abridge or deny these rights.

STANDARD 5.7

Guidelines for Counseling and Releasing

When taking a juvenile into custody for an alleged delinquent act, the police should emphasize delinquency prevention and seek alternatives to court referral.

When the delinquent act is not serious, a record check shows no prior delinquency, and an informal adjustment is agreeable to the complainant and the youth's parents or guardians, the police juvenile officer should consider a community or station adjustment. This procedure involves settling the matter at the police level, without referral to juvenile court.

Community adjustment should be limited to release and referral. It should not include the imposition of sanctions by the police, nor should the police be permitted to place juveniles on police probation.

If at any stage in community adjustment proceedings, juveniles begin to volunteer information that could lead to a more serious charge on another criminal offense or delinquent act, they and their parents should be advised immediately of the youth's constitutional rights, which should not be abridged or denied in any way by the police.

STANDARD 5.8

Guidelines for Interrogation and Waiver of the Right Against Self-Incrimination

When police are conducting a custodial investigation of an individual who is legally a juvenile, they should take care not to allow that juvenile to waive the right against self-incrimination without the advice of counsel. During interviews or interrogations, as in all police procedures, police officers must be sensitive to and respect the basic constitutional rights and personal dignity of both juveniles and adults. Police officers must scrupulously avoid practices that could be described as inherently coercive in the sense that a person may cooperate or confess to unlawful conduct as a result of induced fear.

STANDARD 5.9

Guidelines for Temporary Police Detention Practices

The temporary detention of juveniles by the police should be protective in nature, not punitive. A juvenile should be held in police detention facilities no longer than is necessary for referral to juvenile intake or return to the parents. Juveniles being held in temporary detention should be under observation at all times. Under no circumstances should these juveniles be held in the same detention facilities with adults.

STANDARD 5.10

Guidelines for Diversion or Referral to Community Resources

Where permitted by law, every police agency should immediately divert from the juvenile justice system any juvenile for whom formal proceedings would be inappropriate or other resources more effective. All such police diversion decisions should be made pursuant to written agency policy that insures fairness and uniformity of treatment.

Police chief executives should develop written policies and procedures that allow juveniles to be diverted from formal proceedings in appropriate cases. Such policies and procedures should be prepared in cooperation with other elements of the juvenile justice system.

STANDARD 5.11

Guidelines for Referral to Juvenile Intake

Police referral of alleged delinquents to juvenile intake should be restricted to those cases involving serious delinquent or criminal conduct or repeated law violations of a more than trivial nature.

STANDARD 5.12

Guidelines for Fingerprinting, Photographing, and Other Forms of Identification

Fingerprints and photographs of juveniles should be taken for investigative purposes only. Juveniles should not be subjected to these procedures unless they are taken into custody for a violation of the law, or the family court has determined there is probable cause to believe that the fingerprints or photographs must be taken to establish the court's jurisdiction.

Police policies for identifying juveniles should conform to the following guidelines:

1. The police should be authorized to fingerprint a juvenile taken into custody in connection with a crime or delinquent act in which fingerprints have been found or may be expected to be found on yet undiscovered evidence. Fingerprints should be taken only for the purpose of verifying or disproving the juvenile's personal contact with objects pertinent to the defense. If the comparison is negative, the fingerprint card and other copies of the fingerprints taken should be destroyed immediately. If the comparison is positive and the juvenile is referred to the court, the fingerprint card and other copies should be delivered to the court for disposition. If the juvenile is not referred to the court, the fingerprints should be destroyed immediately.

2. All fingerprints and photographs of juveniles should be filed and coded for restricted use only. Fingerprint and photograph files of juveniles should be kept separate from those of adults and should be maintained on a local basis only. Copies of fingerprints and photographs should not be sent to a central State or Federal depository unless the juvenile authorizes such transmission for the purpose of obtaining a national security clearance.

3. Fingerprint and photograph files of juveniles may be inspected by law enforcement officers when necessary for the discharge of their official duties. Other inspections may be authorized by the court in individual cases, upon a showing that such inspections are in the public interest.

4. Fingerprints and photographs of a juvenile should be removed from the file and destroyed if the following occurs:

    a. No petition alleging delinquency is filed, or the proceedings are dismissed after a petition is filed or after the case is transferred to the family court from the criminal court;

    b. The juvenile is adjudicated not to be a delinquent; or

    c. The juvenile reaches 21 years of age and there is no record of a delinquent act after the age of 16.

STANDARD 5.13

Guidelines for Regulation of the Release of Information and Photographs to the News Media

Each State should enact legislation to require confidential police handling of identifying information about juveniles. With the exception of dangerous fugitives, law enforcement agencies should not release the names or photographs of juvenile law violators to the news media.

STANDARD 5.14

Guidelines for Basic Police Records

Police records on juveniles should be kept separate from the records of adults. They should not be open to inspection nor should their contents be disclosed except by court order. Criminal justice agencies should justify their inspection of the records on a need-to-know basis.

STANDARD 6.1

Participation in Community Planning Organizations

Police departments should encourage the development of interdisciplinary juvenile justice coordinating councils at the community level (city/county/regional). These councils should work to prevent crime and delinquency by doing the following:

1. Aiding systemwide planning for service delivery to juveniles, while avoiding duplication of those services;

2. Providing for the distribution of local, State, and Federal monies to insure a maximum return;

3. Communicating with State and Federal criminal justice and juvenile justice planners;

4. Eliminating interpersonal conflicts among those in the juvenile justice field;

5. Evaluating programs; and

6. Sharing information on innovative efforts with juvenile justice specialists throughout the Nation.

STANDARD 6.2

Developing and Maintaining Relationships With Other Juvenile Justice Agencies

To prevent delinquent behavior and combat juvenile crime, police should cooperate actively with other agencies and organizations, public and private, in order to employ all available resources. Police should also provide initiative and leadership in forming needed youth service organizations in communities where needs exist.

STANDARD 6.3

Relationships With Youth Service Bureaus

Police departments should make full use of the diagnostic and coordinating services of youth service bureaus for the referral of juveniles and, where appropriate, should also take an active role in their organization and policy deliberations.

STANDARD 6.4

Police-School Liaison

Police should make every effort to develop effective delinquency prevention programs in the schools through collaborative planning with school administrators and student leaders. All junior and senior high schools should seek to implement a school liaison officer program with their local police department, with the specification that the police officer involved be trained and qualified to serve in an educational and counseling role. Police chiefs, school administrators, and student leaders also should develop guidelines for police-school liaison.

STANDARD 6.5

Participation in Recreation Programs

Police departments should take an active leadership role in developing community recreational programs for juveniles, but the police should not operate those programs. A supplemental police role should encourage community support of recreational activities with officers volunteering to participate during their offduty hours as other citizens do.

STANDARD 7.1

Organization of Police Juvenile Operations

Every police agency having more than 75 sworn officers should establish a juvenile investigation unit, and every smaller police agency should establish such a unit if community conditions warrant.

This unit should be functionally centralized to the most effective command level; and should be assigned responsibility for conducting as many juvenile investigations as possible, assisting field officers in juvenile cases, and maintaining liaison with other agencies and organizations interested in juvenile matters.

Police administrators with existing juvenile units should improve the status of those units if necessary, to insure that all members of the department recognize that juvenile-related activity is a necessary and valuable component of the police organization.

STANDARD 7.2

Planning Commitment

All police departments should establish a planning function and staff it with personnel who can help the department plan for the administration and management of police delinquency prevention and control services. Continuous planning should be carried on in order to cope effectively with tactical and strategic problems involving juveniles.

STANDARD 7.3

Evaluations Commitment

Periodic evaluations and assessments of police juvenile operations should be performed to insure that those operations are accomplishing their goals, objectives, and stated missions.

STANDARD 7.4

Citizen Involvement in Evaluation of Juvenile Operations

All police departments should establish citizen participation programs to aid in assessing effectiveness of police management of juvenile operations.

STANDARD 7.5

Planning Resource Allocation for Police Juvenile Operations

State criminal justice and law enforcement planning agencies (SPA's) should do the following:

1. Determine actual expenditures by law enforcement agencies for those functions directly related to juvenile delinquency prevention and control; and

2. Through consultation and participation with local agencies and citizens, recommend expenditure levels according to type of jurisdiction and the population served so realistic statewide planning in the juvenile area can proceed.

STANDARD 7.6

Personnel Selection and Development

Police juvenile officers should be assigned by chief executives on the basis of a departmental written and oral examination, rather than being appointed by a civil service or merit commission. Juvenile officers should, if possible, be selected from among the department's experienced line officers. Selection boards established to interview candidates for the position of police juvenile officer should include police department command officers and selected individuals from the juvenile justice system and public youth service agencies.

Police chief executives should allow qualified officers to pursue careers as police juvenile specialists, with the same opportunities for promotion and advancement as are available to other officers in the department. Police departments also should provide juvenile officers with salary increases that are commensurate with their duties and responsibilities.

STANDARD 7.7

Personnel Training

State law enforcement training commissions should establish statewide standards governing the amount and type of training in juvenile matters given to police recruits and to pre-service and inservice juvenile officers. Training programs should include the following elements:

1. All police recruits should receive at least 40 hours of mandatory training in juvenile matters;

2. Every police department and/or State or regional police training academy should train all officers and administrators in personal and family crisis intervention techniques and ethnic, cultural, and minority relations;

3. All officers selected for assignment to juvenile units should receive at least 80 hours of training in juvenile matters either before beginning their assignment or within a 1-year period;

4. All police juvenile officers should be required to participate in at least one 40-hour inservice training program each year, either within the department or at regional, State and/or national schools and work shops;

5. Where feasible, cities should ex-

change police juvenile officers for brief periods of time so those officers can observe procedures in other jurisdictions; and

6. Community, regional, or State juvenile justice agencies should periodically conduct interdisciplinary inservice training programs for system personnel, and police juvenile officers should actively participate in such programs. Community juvenile justice agencies also should exchange personnel on an interdisciplinary basis for brief periods of time, to enable such personnel to familiarize themselves with the operational procedures of other agencies.

STANDARD 7.8

Participation in Juvenile Justice Higher Education Programs

Police departments should encourage all officers to pursue college and university education in juvenile problems and related disciplines. Where feasible, departments should provide leaves of absence with pay to allow the achievement of academic objectives that can contribute significantly to the employee's professional growth and capacity for current and future assignments.

STANDARD 7.9

Controls and Disciplinary Procedures

The police chief executive should develop written policy guidelines to measure the performance of police juvenile personnel and insure that those individuals perform their duties in a professional manner.

STANDARD 8.1

Level and Position of Court Handling Juvenile Matters

The court having jurisdiction over juvenile matters should be at the level of the highest court of general trial jurisdiction and should be a division of that court. This court also should have authority to assume jurisdiction over all family-related legal matters (see Standard 8.2., Family Court Structure).

STANDARD 8.2

Family Court Structure

Each State's judicial system should include a family court. Family court jurisdiction should include: juvenile delinquency, domestic legal relations, adoptions, civil commitments, Families With Service Needs, Endangered (Neglected or Abused) Children, concurrent jurisdiction over intrafamily crimes, contributing to the delinquency of a juvenile, criminal nonsupport, and the Interstate Compact on Juveniles and Uniform Reciprocal Enforcement of Support Act.

STANDARD 8.3

Judicial Proceedings Heard by a Judge

All judicial proceedings relating to juveniles, including but not limited to detention, shelter care, waiver, arraignment, adjudicatory, and dispositional hearings should be heard only by a judge.

STANDARD 8.4

Family Court Judges

Family court judges should be lawyers who possess a keen and demonstrated interest in the needs and problems of children and families. Service in the family court should be a permanent assignment. Family court judges should participate in professional training programs.

STANDARD 8.5

Supervising Judge

Where the presiding judge of the general trial court determines the need for a supervising judge of the family court division, the family court judges should be requested to submit two names to the presiding judge from whom the designation shall then be made.

The individual designated supervising judge of the family court should then serve for a term of 2 years with reappointment being permitted for one additional 1-year term.

The criteria for appointment, duties, and responsibilities of the supervising judge should be established by a written court policy.

STANDARD 8.6

Family Court Rules

Comprehensive rules governing family court practice and procedure should be adopted and published to insure regularity and promote efficiency in family court proceedings. The rules should provide in detail for pretrial discovery procedures appropriate for family court proceedings.

STANDARD 9.1

Definition of Delinquency

Family court delinquency jurisdiction should be exercised only for acts that would be violations of Federal or State criminal law or of local ordinance if committed by adults.

STANDARD 9.2

Minimum Age for Family Court Delinquency Jurisdiction

The minimum age for exercise of family court delinquency jurisdiction over a juvenile who is charged with delinquent conduct should be 10 years of age.

STANDARD 9.3

Maximum Age for Family Court Adjudicative Jurisdiction

The family court should have adjudicative jurisdiction over a juvenile only until the juvenile reaches the age of 18.

STANDARD 9.4

Time at Which Jurisdiction Attaches

Subject to any applicable statute of limitations, the jurisdiction of the family court should be determined by the age of the juvenile at the time of the delinquent act and not by the juvenile's age at the time of apprehension or adjudication.

STANDARD 9.5

Waiver and Transfer

The family court should have the authority to waive jurisdiction and transfer a juvenile for trial in adult criminal court if:

1. The juvenile is charged with a delinquent act as defined in Standard 9.1.

2. The juvenile was 16 years or older at the time of the alleged commission of the delinquent act.

3. The alleged delinquent act is:

a. aggravated or heinous in nature or

b. part of a pattern of repeated delinquent acts.

4. There is probable cause to believe the juvenile committed acts that are to be the subject of the adult criminal proceedings if waiver and transfer are approved.

5. The juvenile is not amenable, by virtue of his maturity, criminal sophistication, or past experience in the juvenile justice system, to services provided through the family court.

6. The juvenile has been given a waiver and transfer hearing that comports with due process including but not limited to the right to counsel and a decision rendered in accord with specific criteria promulgated by either the court or the legislature. The *Kent v. United States,* 383 U.S. 541 (1966), criteria should be the minimum specific criteria on which these decisions are based.

STANDARD 9.6

Venue

The family court that has jurisdiction within the city, county, or other political subdivision where the delinquent act was allegedly committed should be the court that adjudicates the act, unless, on the motion of the juvenile or the prosecution or on its own motion, the court decides to transfer the case to the jurisdiction of the juvenile's residence.

STANDARD 9.7

Traffic Offenses

The family court's jurisdiction over traffic offenses should be limited to:

1. Traffic offenses committed by juveniles who are not old enough to be licensed to drive, and

2. Major traffic offenses committed

by all juveniles. These offenses should include vehicular homicide, hit-and-run driving, and driving under the influence of alcohol or drugs.

All other traffic offenses committed by juveniles should be handled by the adult traffic court.

STANDARD 10.1

Families With Service Needs Petition

The Families With Service Needs jurisdiction should be invoked by a petition that is a formal request for family court intervention to provide appropriate services.

The petition may be brought by the parent, child or any other individual or agency coming in contact with the parent and/or child and having reason to believe that the Families With Service Needs jurisdiction should be exercised on behalf of the parent and/or child.

STANDARD 10.2

Allegations Contained in the Families With Service Needs Petition

The Families With Service Needs petition should allege:

1. That one or more of the specific behaviors under the Families With Service Needs jurisdiction has occurred;

2. That all available and appropriate noncoercive alternatives to assist the child and family have been exhausted; and

3. That by virtue of this behavior and the lack of appropriate voluntary alternatives, the child and/or family is in need of court intervention for services. The family court should determine whether each of the facts alleged in the petition is true. However, there should be no designation of fault at-

tached to these determinations.

STANDARD 10.3

Scope of Jurisdiction

In the Families With Service Needs proceedings, once jurisdiction is established, it should extend to the child, his or her parents, and any public institution or agency with a legal responsibility to provide needed service to the child or parents.

STANDARD 10.4

Running Away

The Families With Service Needs jurisdiction should include jurisdiction over juveniles who repeatedly run away from home. Running away should be defined as a juvenile's unauthorized absence from home for more than 24 hours.

STANDARD 10.5

Truancy

The Families With Service Needs jurisdiction should include jurisdiction over truancy. Truancy should be defined as a pattern of repeated, unauthorized absences or habitual absence from school by any juvenile subject to the compulsory education laws of the State.

STANDARD 10.6

Disregard for or Misuse of Parental Authority

The Families With Service Needs jurisdiction should include jurisdiction over the repeated disregard for or misuse of lawful parental authority.

STANDARD 10.7

Use of Intoxicating Beverages

The Families With Service Needs jurisdiction should include jurisdiction over the repeated possession or consumption of intoxicating beverages by juveniles.

STANDARD 10.8

"Delinquent Acts" by Child Younger Than 10

The Families With Service Needs jurisdiction should include jurisdiction over juveniles younger than 10 who commit repeated "delinquent acts" or a "delinquent act" of a serious nature.

STANDARD 11.1

Respect for Parental Autonomy

Statutes authorizing coercive State intervention should be based on a strong presumption for parental autonomy in childrearing.

STANDARD 11.2

Focus on Serious, Specifically Defined Harms to the Child

The statutory grounds for coercive State intervention should be:

1. Defined as specifically as possible;
2. Drafted in terms of specific harms that the child has suffered or may suffer, not in terms of parental behavior; and
3. Limited to those cases where a child is suffering serious harm or there is a substantial likelihood that he or she will imminently suffer serious harm.

STANDARD 11.3

Elimination of Fault as a Basis for Coercive Intervention

Fault concepts should not be con-

sidered in determining the need for, or type of, coercive State intervention.

STANDARD 11.4

Consideration of Cultural Values

Standards for coercive State intervention should take into account cultural differences in child rearing. Decisionmakers should examine the child's needs in light of his or her cultural background and values and should take cognizance of the child's needs for continuity of cultural identity at every phase of the intervention process.

STANDARD 11.5

Protection of Child's Interests

Although coercive State intervention should promote family autonomy and strengthen family life whenever feasible, in cases where a child's needs as defined in these standards conflict with parents' interests, the child's needs should be protected.

STANDARD 11.6

Promotion of Continuous, Stable Living Environments

The entire system of coercive State intervention should be designed to provide children, to the maximum degree possible, with continuous, stable living environments. Decisionmakers should take cognizance of this objective at every phase of the intervention process, from initial coercive involvement to proceedings for termination of parental rights.

STANDARD 11.7

Encouraging Accountability

The entire system of coercive State intervention should be designed to insure that all agencies and branches of government including courts, participating in the intervention process, are accountable for all of their actions. Decisionmakers should be required to specify the bases for their actions and mechanisms should be established to review important decisions.

STANDARD 11.8

Statutory Bases for Coercive Intervention

Courts should be authorized to assume jurisdiction, in order to condition custody upon the parents accepting supervision or to remove a child from the home, only when the child is endangered in a manner specified in Standards 11.9 through 11.15.

STANDARD 11.9

No Caretaking Adult

Coercive State intervention should be authorized when a child has no parent or guardian or other adult, to whom the child has substantial ties, available and willing to care for him or her.

STANDARD 11.10

Nonaccidental Physical Injury

Coercive State intervention should be authorized when a child has suffered or is likely imminently to suffer a physical injury, inflicted nonaccidentally upon him or her by his or her parent, that causes or creates a substantial risk of disfigurement, impairment of bodily functioning, or severe bodily harm.

STANDARD 11.11

Physical Injury From Inadequate Supervision or Protection

Coercive State intervention should be authorized when a child has suffered or there is a substantial risk that the child will imminently suffer disfigurement, impairment of bodily functioning or severe bodily harm as a result of conditions uncorrected by the parents or by the failure of the parents to adequately supervise or protect the child.

STANDARD 11.12

Emotional Damage

Coercive State intervention should be authorized when a child is suffering serious emotional damage, evidenced by severe anxiety, depression or withdrawal, or untoward aggressive behavior toward self or others, and the parents are unwilling to permit and cooperate with necessary treatment for the child.

STANDARD 11.13

Sexual Abuse

Coercive State intervention should be authorized when a child has been sexually abused by a member of the household.

STANDARD 11.14

Need for Medical Care

Coercive State intervention should be authorized when a child is in need of medical treatment to cure, alleviate, or prevent serious physical harm that may result in death, disfigurement, substantial impairment of bodily functions, or severe bodily harm and the parents are unwilling to permit the medical treatment.

STANDARD 11.15

Delinquent Acts as a Result of Parental Encouragement or Approval

Coercive State intervention should be authorized when a child is committing delinquent acts as a result of parental pressure, encouragement or approval.

STANDARD 11.16

Intervention Under These Standards

The fact that a child is endangered in a manner specified in Standards 11.9 through 11.15 is a necessary but not a sufficient reason for a court to authorize coercive intervention. In every case a court also should find that the proposed intervention will prove to be a less detrimental alternative for the child than abstaining from intervention.

STANDARD 11.17

Parties

The following should be parties to all proceedings regarding a child alleged to be or adjudicated endangered:
1. The child;
2. The child's parents, guardians, and if relevant any other adult to whom the child has substantial ties who has been performing the caretaking role; and,
3. The appropriate agency.

STANDARD 12.1

Case Processing Time Frames

Each State juvenile code should set forth the time frame standards for juvenile case processing. Those should include:
1. For juveniles in detention or shelter care:
   a. From admission to detention or shelter care to filing of petition, arraignment, detention, or shelter care hearing and probable cause hearing if continued detention has been ordered: 48 hours.
   b. From arraignment hearing to adjudicatory hearing: 20 calendar days.
2. For juveniles not in detention or shelter care:
   a. From referral to filing of petition: 30 calendar days.
   b. From referral to filing of petition when the juvenile has been referred by the intake department to a service program: 90 calendar days.
   c. From filing of petition to arraignment hearing: 5 calendar days.
   d. From arraignment hearing to adjudicatory hearing: 60 calendar days.
3. For all juveniles:
   a. From adjudicatory hearing to dispositional hearing: 15 calendar days.
   b. From submission of any issue taken under advisement to trial court decision: 30 calendar days.
   c. From trial court decision to appellate decision when interlocutory appeal is taken: 30 calendar days.
   d. From trial court decision to appellate decision on appeal of the adjudicatory finding: 90 calendar days.
4. For detained juveniles:
   A review detention hearing each 10 judicial days.
Failure to comply with these time frames should result in appropriate sanctions upon the individual(s) within the juvenile justice system respon-

sible for the delay. The court should be able to grant reasonable continuances for demonstrably justifiable reasons. Case dismissal should occur only when failure to comply with statutory time frames results in prejudice to the particular juvenile.

STANDARD 12.2

Motion Practice

Each jurisdiction should develop rules for the regulation of motion practice in family court, requiring motions normally to be made in writing and, when appropriate, to be supported by affidavit. The rules should specify time limits for filing motions and serving them on opposing parties, and should prescribe procedures for securing motion hearings.

The rules governing motions should provide for extrajudicial conferences between the parties before motions are argued whenever discovery motions are filed and in other appropriate circumstances.

Requests for continuances should be made in the usual course of motion practice. Untimely motions for continuances should not be granted except for exigent reasons.

STANDARD 12.3

Court Proceedings Before Adjudication in Delinquency Cases

Court procedures in delinquency cases prior to adjudication should conform to due process requirements. Except for the right to bail, grand jury indictment, and trial by jury, the juvenile should have all the procedural rights given a criminal defendant.

The juvenile should have the following rights in addition to the right to counsel:

1. An impartial judge;
2. Upon request by the juvenile, a proceeding open to the public or, with the court's permission, to specified members of the public;
3. Timely written notice of the proceeding, and of the juvenile's legal rights;
4. The presence of parent or guardian;
5. The assistance of an interpreter when necessary;
6. The right to avoid self-incrimination;
7. The right to avoid waiving his or her constitutional rights without prior consultation with an attorney; and
8. The right to the keeping of a verbatim record of the proceedings.

STANDARD 12.4

Juvenile's Initial Appearance in Court

Promptly after a delinquency petition is filed, the juvenile should be required to appear in court to be arraigned. Juveniles in custody should be arraigned at the start of the detention hearing. Juveniles who are not detained should be required to appear for arraignment within 72 hours of the time that the summons or citation is served upon them. The juvenile's parent or guardian also should be required to attend the arraignment.

At the arraignment the court should orally inform the juvenile of his or her legal rights, and of the allegations and possible consequences of the delinquency petition. The court also should appoint counsel if appropriate, and set the date for trial.

STANDARD 12.5

Petition and Summons

A delinquency petition should set

forth in plain and concise language and with reasonable particularity the time, place, and manner of the acts alleged, and should cite the Federal or State statute or local ordinance that is alleged to have been violated.

A summons should be issued that provides notice to the juvenile and his or her parents of their required appearance in court on a designated date, their right to representation by counsel, and the available procedures for obtaining counsel.

The summons and petition should be served on a juvenile and on his or her parents. The form and contents of the petition and summons should be determined by the Supreme Court, the judicial counsel, or other rulemaking body and should be uniform throughout a State.

STANDARD 12.6

Search and Seizure

Evidence that is illegally seized or obtained should not be received to establish the allegations of a juvenile delinquency petition.

STANDARD 12.7

Criteria for Preadjudicatory Detention of Juveniles in Delinquency Cases

A juvenile should not be detained in any residential facility, whether secure or open, prior to a delinquency adjudication unless detention is necessary for the following reasons:

1. To insure the presence of the juvenile at subsequent court proceedings;

2. To provide physical care for a juvenile who cannot return home because there is no parent or other suitable person able and willing to

supervise and care for him or her adequately;

3. To prevent the juvenile from harming or intimidating any witness, or otherwise threatening the orderly progress of the court proceedings;

4. To prevent the juvenile from inflicting bodily harm on others; or

5. To protect the juvenile from bodily harm.

A detained juvenile should be placed in the least restrictive residential setting that will adequately serve the purposes of detention.

STANDARD 12.8

Families With Service Needs— Preadjudicatory Shelter Care

Preadjudicatory shelter care should not be used in any Families With Service Needs proceedings unless such shelter care is clearly necessary to protect the juvenile from bodily harm and all available alternative means for adequately providing such protection have been exhausted.

When it is necessary to provide temporary custody for a juvenile pending a Families With Service Needs proceeding, every effort should be made to provide such custody in the least restrictive setting possible, and to assure that the juvenile does not come into contact with juveniles detained pending delinquency proceedings or adjudicated delinquents awaiting disposition.

STANDARD 12.9

Endangered Children: Preadjudicatory Temporary Custody—Emergency Removal From the Home

Statutes governing emergency removal of Endangered Children from the home should:

1. Specifically enumerate the types of personnel authorized to undertake removal;

2. Allow removal only when it is necessary to protect the child from bodily injury and the child's parents or other adult caretakers are unwilling or unable to protect the child from such injury; and,

3. Authorize removal without prior court approval only if there is not enough time to secure such approval.

Emergency caretaking services should be established to reduce the incidence of removal.

When removal does occur, the child should be delivered immediately to a State agency that:

1. Has been previously inspected and certified as adequate to protect the physical and emotional well-being of children it receives;

2. Is authorized to provide emergency medical care in accordance with specific legislative directives; and,

3. Is required to assure the opportunity for daily visitation by the parents or other adult caretakers.

Within 24 hours of the time the child is removed, the agency responsible for filing petitions should either file a petition alleging that the child is endangered or return the child to the home. If a petition is filed, the court should immediately convene a hearing to determine if emergency temporary custody is necessary to protect the child from bodily injury.

STANDARD 12.10

Endangered Children: Preadjudicatory Temporary Custody—Emergency Removal From an Environment Other Than the Home

A child who is endangered in an environment other than the home should not be taken into preadjudicatory temporary custody unless such temporary custody is clearly necessary to protect the child from bodily injury and no other satisfactory means is available for providing such protection. When temporary custody occurs, the child should be delivered immediately to the State agency authorized to receive children in cases of emergency removal from the home.

Within 24 hours the agency responsible for filing endangered child petitions should either file a petition alleging that the child is endangered or return the child to the home. If a petition is filed, the court should immediately convene a hearing to determine if temporary custody is necessary to protect the child from bodily injury.

STANDARD 12.11

Detention Hearings

Unless a juvenile who has been taken into custody has been released, a judicial hearing to review the necessity for continued detention should be held within 48 hours from the time he or she was taken into custody.

The detention hearing should conform to due process requirements. It should commence with a judicial determination of probable cause. If the prosecution establishes by competent evidence probable cause to believe that the juvenile has committed the allegedly delinquent act, the court should review the necessity for continued detention. Unless the prosecution demonstrates by clear and convincing evidence that there is a need for continued detention according to detention criteria, the court should release the juvenile upon conditions pending the next judicial proceeding. A court order continuing the juvenile's detention should be supported by written reasons and findings of fact.

If the juvenile's detention continues, a new detention hearing should be held promptly upon motion by the respondent asserting the existence of new or additional evidence. Absent such motions, the court should review the case of each juvenile held in secure detention no less frequently than every 10 court days. Each jurisdiction should provide for an expedited appellate procedure to permit speedy review of allegedly wrongful detention orders. The same judge who sits at a detention hearing should not sit at the adjudicatory hearing without the respondent's consent.

STANDARD 12.12

Conditions of Release

The release of a juvenile from detention should be conditioned upon his or her own promise to appear for subsequent court proceedings. If a juvenile cannot appropriately be released on this basis, release should be based on the least onerous other condition(s) necessary to assure appearance. These may include:

1. Release on the written promise of parent or guardian to produce him or her in court for subsequent proceedings;

2. Release into the care of a responsible person or organization;

3. Release conditioned on restrictions on activities, associations, residence or travel if reasonably related to securing the juvenile's presence in court; and

4. Any other conditions reasonably related to securing the juvenile's presence in court.

The use of bail bonds in any form or any other financial conditions should be prohibited.

STANDARD 13.1

Plea Negotiations Prohibited

Plea bargaining in all forms should be eliminated from the delinquency adjudication process. Under no circumstances should the parties engage in discussions for the purpose of agreeing to exchange concessions by the prosecutor for the juvenile's admission to the petition.

STANDARD 13.2

Acceptance of an Admission to a Delinquency Petition

Prior to accepting an admission to a delinquency petition, the family court judge should inquire thoroughly into the circumstances of that admission.

The judge should, in the first instance, determine that the juvenile has the capacity to understand the nature and consequences of the proceeding. If a guardian ad litem has been appointed for the juvenile, no admission should be accepted without independent proof of the acts alleged.

The family court judge also should determine whether the admission is knowingly and voluntarily offered. In making such an inquiry, the court should address the youth personally, in simple language, and determine that he or she understands the nature of the allegations in the petition. The court should then satisfy itself that the juvenile understands the nature of those rights waived by an entry of an admission, as well as the consequences of waiving them. It also should inform the juvenile of the most restrictive disposition that could be imposed in the case. By inquiry of the juvenile, the court should then determine that the allegations in the petition are true.

The court should inform the juvenile that negotiated admissions are prohibited and not binding on the court. It should inquire of the juvenile, the juvenile's counsel, and the people's representatives whether any plea agreements have been discussed or concluded. The statements of counsel that no such agreements have been made should appear on the record. No admission that is the result of a plea agreement should be accepted by the court.

By examining the juvenile and the attorney, the court should determine that the juvenile has been fully and effectively represented. No juvenile should receive harsher treatment at any stage of the proceedings for the reason that he or she has contested the delinquency petition.

STANDARD 13.3
Withdrawal of Admissions

The family court should allow a juvenile to withdraw an admission for any fair and just reason prior to final disposition of the case. After final disposition, the family court should allow withdrawal of an admission whenever the juvenile proves that the admission was not competent, voluntary, or intelligent; that he or she did not receive the effective assistance of counsel and did not properly waive counsel; or that withdrawal of the plea is necessary to correct any other manifest injustice.

An admission to a delinquency petition that is not accepted or is withdrawn should not be admissible in any subsequent proceeding against the juvenile.

STANDARD 13.4
Contested Adjudications

Adjudications of delinquency petitions should conform to due process requirements. The hearing to determine whether the juvenile is delinquent should be distinct and separate from the proceedings at which—assuming an adjudication of delinquency—a decision is made as to what disposition should be made concerning the juvenile. At the adjudicatory hearing, the juvenile alleged to be delinquent should have all the rights given a criminal defendant except for the right to trial by jury. In addition to the rights specified in Standards 16.1 (Juvenile's Right to Counsel) and 12.3 (Court Proceedings Before Adjudication in Delinquency Cases), the juvenile should have the following rights:

1. To confront and cross-examine witnesses for the State;

2. To compel the attendance of witnesses in his favor;

3. To require the State to prove the allegations of delinquency beyond a reasonable doubt;

4. To have applied the rules of evidence that apply in criminal cases; and

5. Protection against double jeopardy.

STANDARD 13.5
Adjudication of Delinquency— Standard of Proof

Adjudication of delinquency should be made only when a juvenile has been found beyond a reasonable doubt to have committed an act that would be a crime if committed by an adult.

STANDARD 13.6

Endangered Children—
Rules of Evidence

The adjudicatory phase of Endangered Child proceedings should be conducted in accordance with the general rules of evidence applicable to the trial of civil cases in the courts of general jurisdiction where the petition is filed.

STANDARD 13.7

Endangered Children—
Standard of Proof

In the adjudicatory phase of Endangered Child proceedings, the burden should rest on the petitioner to prove by clear and convincing evidence that the child is endangered as defined in Standards 11.9 through 11.15.

STANDARD 13.8

Appeals

Any juvenile aggrieved by a final order or judgment should be entitled to appeal to the appropriate appellate court. The appeal should be heard upon the files, records and transcript of the evidence of the family court. If the juvenile is financially unable to purchase a transcript of the family court proceedings, a transcript should be furnished, or as much of it as requested, upon filing of a motion stating financial incapacity. To avoid publication, the name of the juvenile should not appear in the record on appeal.

STANDARD 14.1

Purpose of Dispositions

The purpose of a juvenile delinquency disposition should be to determine that course of action which will develop individual responsibility for lawful behavior through programs of reeducation. This purpose should be pursued through means that are fair and just; recognize the unique physical, psychological, and social characteristics and needs of juveniles; and give juveniles access to opportunities for normal growth and development, while insuring that such dispositions will:

1. Protect society;

2. Deter conduct that unjustifiably and without excuse inflicts or risks substantial harm to individual or public interests;

3. Maintain the integrity of the substantive law proscribing certain behavior; and

4. Contribute to the proper socialization of the juvenile.

STANDARD 14.2

Duration of Dispositional Authority

The family court dispositional authority over a juvenile who has been adjudicated a delinquent should not exceed the juvenile's 21st birthday.

STANDARD 14.3

Requirements for Postadjudicative Juvenile Delinquency Dispositions

A disposition is coercive when it limits the freedom of action of the adjudicated juvenile in any way that is distinguishable from that of a nonadjudicated juvenile and when failure or refusal to comply with the disposition may result in further enforcement action.

A disposition is noncoercive when it in no way limits the freedom of action of the adjudicated juvenile and no further enforcement action can result out of the disposition. A noncoercive disposition always must include unconditional release.

The imposition of any coercive disposition by the State imposes the obligation to act with fairness and to avoid arbitrariness. This obligation includes the following requirements:

1. Adjudicated Violation of Substantive Law. No disposition may be imposed unless there has been an adjudicated violation of the substantive law.

2. Specification of Disposition by Statute. No disposition may be imposed unless pursuant to a statute that proscribes the particular disposition with reasonable specificity.

3. Procedural Regularity and Fairness. The disposition and implementation of all dispositions should conform to standards governing procedural regularity and fairness.

4. Information Concerning Obligations. Juveniles should be given adequate information concerning the obligation imposed on them by all coercive dispositions and the consequences of failure to meet such obligations.

5. Legislatively Determined Maximum Dispositions. The maximum severity and duration of all coercive dispositions should be determined by the legislature, which should limit them according to the seriousness of the offense for which the juvenile has been adjudicated and the degree to which the juvenile has previously been involved in delinquent activities.

6. Judicially Determined Dispositions. The nature and duration of all coercive dispositions should be determined by the family court at the time of disposition within the limitations established by the legislature.

7. Availability of Resources. No coercive disposition should be imposed unless the resources necessary to carry out the disposition are shown to exist. If services required as part of a disposition are not available, an alternative disposition no more severe should be employed.

8. Physical Safety. No coercive disposition should subject the juvenile to unreasonable risk of physical harm.

STANDARD 14.4

Selection of Least Restrictive Alternative

In choosing among statutorily permissible dispositions, the court should employ the least coercive category and duration of disposition that are appropriate to the seriousness of the delinquent act, as modified by the degree of culpability indicated by the circumstances of the particular case, age and prior record of the juvenile. The imposition of a particular disposition should be accompanied by a statement of the facts relied on in support of the disposition and the reasons for selecting the disposition and rejecting less restrictive alternatives.

STANDARD 14.5

Dispositional Information

Information that is relevant and material to disposition should be gathered by representative of the state acting on behalf of the family court. The sources of dispositional information, the techniques for obtaining it, and the conditions of its use should be subject to legal rules.

Copies of the predispositional report should be supplied to the attorney for the juvenile and the family court prosecutor in sufficient time prior to the dispositional hearing to permit careful review and verification if necessary.

Dispositional information should be shared with those charged with correctional or custodial responsibilities, but it should not be considered a public record.

The handling of dispositional information matters should be governed by the following principles:

1. Investigation: Timing. Investigation by representatives of the state for the purpose of gathering dispositional information may be undertaken whenever it is convenient to the correctional agency responsible, but under no circumstances should it be turned over to the court until the adjudicatory proceedings have been completed and the petition sustained.

2. Questioning the Juvenile. The juvenile may be questioned by representatives of the state concerning dispositional information but the juvenile should first be informed of the purpose of the questioning, the intended uses of the information, and the possible dispositional consequences which may ensue. The juvenile should have access to counsel or an adult parent or guardian upon whom he or she relies prior to any such questioning in order to insure voluntariness and an informed judgment concerning the providing of information.

3. Information Base.

a. The information essential to a disposition should consist of all details, whether in aggravation or mitigation, concerning the present offense; the juvenile's age and identity; and any prior record of adjudicated delinquency and the disposition thereof.

b. Information concerning the social situation or personal characteristics of the juvenile, including the results of psychological testing, psychiatric evaluations, and intelligence testing may be considered as relevant to the disposition.

c. The social history report should indicate clearly the sources of information, number of contacts with such sources and when made, and the total time expended on investigation and preparation.

d. The juvenile's feelings and attitudes concerning his or her present situation as well as any victim's statements also should be included.

4. Diagnostic Commitments. If diagnostic information is sought, then any form of confinement or institutionalization should be used only as a last resort. A hearing should be held to indicate why such confinement or institutionalization is necessary and what nonconfining alternatives were explored and with what result.

An order for confinement and examination should be of limited duration with a maximum of 30 days allowed. The orders should specify the nature and objectives of the proposed examination as well as the place where such examination is to be conducted.

STANDARD 14.6

Sharing and Disclosing of Information

No dispositional decision should be made on the basis of a fact or opinion not previously disclosed to the lawyer for the juvenile and any lawyer representing the State. In unusual circumstances, the judge may elect to caution the attorney not to disclose information to the juvenile if it appears that such information may prove harmful to the juvenile.

STANDARD 14.7

Formal Dispositional Hearing

After adjudication, a full dispositional hearing with a record made and preserved should be held. A dispositional hearing may be conducted immediately after the adjudication hearing but not later than 30 days in the discretion of the court. The court should provide written notice to the proper parties as to the date, time, and place of such hearing and do so sufficiently in advance of the hearing to allow adequate time for preparation.

The parties should be entitled to compulsory process for the appearance of any persons, including character witnesses and persons who have prepared any report to be utilized by the judge, to testify at the hearing.

The court should first be advised concerning any stipulations or disagreements on dispositional facts and then allow the representative for the State and then the attorney for the juvenile to present evidence concerning the appropriate disposition.

The attorney for the juvenile and the representative for the State may question any documents and examine and cross-examine witnesses including any person who prepares a report concerning the juvenile which is before the court.

STANDARD 14.8

Imposition and Order of Disposition

The judge should determine the appropriate disposition as expeditiously as possible after the hearing. When the disposition is imposed, the judge should:

1. Make specific findings on all controverted issues of fact and note the weight attached to all significant facts in arriving at the disposition;

2. State for the record, in the presence of the juvenile, the reasons for selecting the particular disposition and the objective or objectives to be achieved thereby, pursuant to Standard 14.1;

3. Where the disposition is other than a reprimand and release, state for the record those alternative dispositions, including particular places and programs, which were explored and the reasons for their rejection; and

4. State with particularity, both orally and in the written order of disposition, the precise terms of the disposition which is imposed, including the nature and duration of the disposition and the person or agency in whom custody is vested and who is responsible for carrying out the disposition.

STANDARD 14.9

Dispositions Available to the Court for Juveniles Adjudicated Delinquent

There should be three types of dispositions that a family court may impose upon a juvenile adjudicated to have committed a delinquent act. Ranked from least to most severe, they are:

1. Nominal. In which the juvenile is reprimanded, warned, or otherwise reproved and unconditionally released;

2. Conditional. In which the juvenile is required to comply with one or more conditions, none of which involves removal from the juvenile's home; and

3. Custodial. In which the juvenile is removed from his or her home.

STANDARD 14.10

Nominal Disposition

In a nominal disposition, the family court should specifically set forth in writing its warning or reprimand to the juvenile and its unconditional release of the case.

STANDARD 14.11

Conditional Disposition

In a conditional disposition, the family court should specifically set forth in writing the condition or conditions of its order and assign responsibility to a person or agency for carrying out the disposition. Conditions should not involve removal from the juvenile's home nor interfere with the juvenile's schooling, regular employment, or other activities necessary for normal growth and development. Conditional dispositions should fall within the following general categories:

1. Financial
   a. Restitution
      i. Restitution should be directly related to the delinquent act, the actual harm caused, and the juvenile's ability to pay.
      ii. The means to carry out a restitution order should be available.
      iii. Either full or partial restitution may be ordered. Repayment may be requested in a lump sum or in installments.
      iv. Consultation with victims may be encouraged but not required. Payments may be made directly to victims or indirectly through the court.
      v. The juvenile's duty for repayment should be limited in duration. In no event should the time necessary for repayment exceed the maximum jurisdiction permissible

for the delinquent act.
   b. Fine
      i. Imposition of a fine is most appropriate in cases in which the juvenile has derived monetary gain from the delinquent act.
      ii. The amount of the fine should be directly related to the seriousness of the delinquent act and the juvenile's ability to pay.
      iii. Payments of a fine may be required in a lump sum or installments.
      iv. The juvenile's duty of payment should be limited in duration. In no event should the time necessary for payment exceed the maximum term permissible for the delinquent act.
2. Community Service
   a. If the court orders a juvenile to perform community service, the judge should specify the nature of the work and the number of hours required.
   b. The amount of work required should be related to the seriousness of the juvenile's delinquent act.
   c. The juvenile's duty to perform community service should be limited in duration. In no event should the duty to work exceed the maximum duration permissible for the delinquent act.
3. Community Supervision
   a. The court may order the juvenile to a program of community supervision, requiring him or her to report at specific intervals to a community supervision officer or other designated individual and to comply with any reasonable conditions that are designed to facilitate supervision.
   b. The court may order the juvenile to a program of day custody, requiring him or her to be present at

a specified place for all or part of every day or of certain days.

c. The court may order the juvenile to a community program of academic or vocational education or counseling, requiring attendance at sessions designed to afford access to opportunities for normal growth and development.

d. The duration of community supervision should not exceed the maximum permissible for the delinquent act.

e. This standard does not permit the coercive imposition of any program that may have harmful effects.

4. Suspended Disposition

a. The court may suspend imposition or execution of a more severe, statutorily permissible disposition with the provision that the juvenile meet certain conditions agreed to by him or her and specified in the dispositional order.

b. Such conditions should not exceed, in severity or duration, the maximum sanction permissible for the delinquent act.

STANDARD 14.12

Custodial Disposition

In a custodial disposition, the family court should specifically set forth in writing the condition or conditions under which a juvenile will be removed from his or her home and assign responsibility to a person or agency for carrying out the disposition. The court may order whether the placement should be within or outside of the juvenile's community and the level of custody (secure-nonsecure) that must be maintained.

In making a custodial disposition, the family court should utilize the following criteria:

1. There should be a presumption against coercively removing a juvenile from his or her home, and this category of sanction should be reserved for the more serious or repeated delinquent acts. It should not be used as a substitute for a judicial finding of Families With Service Needs or Endangered Child. These findings should conform to the standards for those two categories of cases.

2. A custodial disposition normally should not be used simultaneously with other sanctions. However, this does not prevent the imposition of a custodial disposition for a specified period of time to be followed by a conditional disposition for a specified period of time, provided that the total duration of the disposition does not exceed the maximum duration permissible for the delinquent act.

3. Custodial confinement may be imposed on a continuous or an intermittent basis, not to exceed the maximum period permissible for the delinquent act. Intermittent confinement includes: night custody, weekend custody, and custody during school vacation periods.

4. Levels of custody include but are not limited to nonsecure residences including foster homes, group homes, halfway houses, camps, ranches, schools; and secure facilities.

STANDARD 14.13

Classes of Delinquent Acts for Dispositional Purposes

All conduct included within the delinquency jurisdiction of the family court should be classified for the purpose of disposition into categories which reflect substantial differences in the seriousness of offenses. Such categories should be few in number. The maximum term which may be imposed for conduct falling within each category should be specified.

Acts within the juvenile delinquency jurisdiction of the family court should be classified as Class I through Class IV delinquent acts.

1. Class I Delinquent Acts—Delinquent acts that would be misdemeanors if committed by an adult;

2. Class II Delinquent Acts—Delinquent acts that would be property felonies if committed by an adult;

3. Class III Delinquent Acts—Delinquent acts against persons that would be crimes if committed by an adult or a Class II Delinquent Act with a prior adjudication of a Class II Delinquent Act; and

4. Class IV Delinquent Acts—Delinquent acts that if committed by an adult would under criminal statute authorize death or imprisonment for life or for a term in excess of 20 years.

STANDARD 14.14

Limitations on Type and Duration of Dispositions

The family court should not impose dispositions more severe than the following:

1. For a Class I Delinquent Act: Nominal, conditional, and/or custodial placement for a period up to 8 months. If, at the completion of the 8 months' disposition, the correctional agency responsible for the case and supervision of the juvenile can with clear and convincing evidence demonstrate to the family court that additional community supervision is required for the protection of the public, the court may authorize an extension of jurisdiction not to exceed 4 months. In no event

shall the total jurisdiction exceed 12 months. Under no circumstances can this extension be used for a further custodial sanction.

2. For a Class II Delinquent Act: Nominal, conditional, and/or custodial placement for a period up to 24 months. If, at the completion of the 24-month disposition, the correctional agency responsible for the case and supervision of the juvenile can with clear and convincing evidence demonstrate to the family court that additional community supervision is required for the protection of the public, the court may authorize an extension of jurisdiction not to exceed 6 months. In no event shall the total jurisdiction exceed 30 months. Under no circumstances can this extension be used for a further custodial sanction.

3. For a Class III Delinquent Act: Nominal, conditional, and/or custodial placement for a period up to 36 months. If, at the completion of a 36-month disposition, the correctional agency responsible for the case and supervision of the juvenile can with clear and convincing evidence demonstrate to the family court that additional community supervision is required for the protection of the public, the court may authorize an extension of jurisdiction not to exceed 12 months. In no event shall the total jurisdiction exceed 48 months or the juvenile's 21st birthday, whichever occurs first. Under no circumstances can this extension be used for a further custodial sanction.

4. For a Class IV Delinquent Act: Nominal, conditional, and/or custodial placement for a period not to exceed beyond the juvenile's 21st birthday. There can be no extension of a Class IV delinquent act beyond the 21st birthday.

STANDARD 14.15

Criteria for Dispositional Decision

In determining the type of disposition to be imposed and its duration within the statutorily prescribed maximum, the family court should base its decision on the following:

1. Category of delinquent act committed;
2. Age and culpability of the juvenile;
3. Prior record;
4. Least restrictive category that is appropriate to the delinquent act; and
5. Needs, interests, and motivations of the juvenile.

STANDARD 14.16

Limitations on Dispositions— General

In making dispositions of juvenile delinquency petitions, the court should be prohibited from:

1. Making a coercive disposition prior to an adjudicative finding of delinquency;
2. Making an order of disposition, other than outright release, without an additional finding that the youth is in need of supervision, care, or training or that the disposition is for the purpose of deterrence or for victim restitution;
3. Committing or authorizing a transfer to any penal institution or other facility used for pretrail detention of adults charged with crimes or for the execution of sentences of persons convicted of crimes;
4. Committing or authorizing the transfer of any juvenile to a facility for the mentally retarded or mentally ill for the purpose of long-time care or treatment;
5. Imposing any unreasonable condition which would expose the juvenile to public ridicule;
6. Imposing any unreasonable conditions which would be beyond the juvenile's physical or financial capacity to discharge;
7. Imposing any unreasonable condition which would interfere with the juvenile's schooling or employment obligation when the disposition is a conditional one;
8. Imposing any condition upon a juvenile which would be a form of exploitation and
9. Imposing any fine or order of restitution upon the parents of a juvenile before the court on the basis of the juvenile's behavior.

STANDARD 14.17

Multiple Delinquent Acts

When a juvenile is found to have committed two or more delinquent acts during the same transaction or episode or during separate transactions or episodes, the family court should not impose a disposition more severe than the maximum disposition authorized by Standard 14.14 for the most serious delinquent act.

STANDARD 14.18

Procedures for Disposition of Mentally Ill or Mentally Retarded Juveniles

If at any time after the filing of a delinquency petition it is brought to the attention of the court, juvenile's counsel, the family court prosecutor, or the parents, guardian, or other legal custodian of the juvenile that there is evidence that the juvenile may be mentally ill or mentally retarded, upon motion by the juvenile's counsel or the family court prosecutor, the court should hold a hearing (see Standard 14.7) to determine the validity of such allegations.

If at such hearing there is evidence indicating that the juvenile may be suffering from mental illness or mental retardation, the court should direct an appropriate individual, agency, or institution to study the juvenile's condition and submit, within a certain time, a comprehensive report as to such condition and an opinion as to whether the juvenile appears to be committable.

If at such hearing the court finds that such study cannot be made on an outpatient basis, the court should order the temporary placement of the juvenile in a diagnostic facility for not more than 30 days, with the facility to submit a comprehensive report within that time as to the juvenile's condition and an opinion as to whether the juvenile is committable.

If upon receipt of such report it appears probable that the juvenile is so mentally retarded or mentally ill as to be committable under the laws of that State, the court should order the initiation of proceedings under the laws relating to the commitment of mentally retarded or mentally ill juveniles.

If the juvenile is ultimately committed as a mentally retarded or mentally ill juvenile, the case should be kept open in the family court and, when the juvenile is discharged, the case should be referred to court intake for review and appropriate action.

STANDARD 14.19

Provision of Dispositional Services

In both conditional and custodial dispositions, the administration of correctional programs and assignment and reassignment of juveniles to activities, programs, and services within the category and duration ordered by the court should be the responsibility of the State's correctional agency.

1. Purchase of Services. Services may be provided directly to the State correctional agency or obtained by that agency through purchase of services from other public or private agencies. Whichever method is employed, the correctional agency should set standards governing the provision of services and establish monitoring procedures to insure compliance with such standards.

2. Prohibition Against Increased Dispositions. Neither the severity nor the duration of a disposition should be increased in order to insure access to services.

3. Obligation of Correctional Agency and Family Court. If access to all required services is not being provided to a juvenile under the supervision of the correctional agency, the agency has the obligation to so inform the family court. In addition, the juvenile, his or her parents, or any other interested party may inform the court of the failure to provide the services. The court may act on its own initiative.

If the court determines that access to all required services in fact is not being provided, it should do the following:

a. The family court may order the correctional agency or other public agency to make the required services available.

b. Unless the court can insure that the required services are provided, it should reduce the nature of the juvenile's disposition to a less severe disposition that will insure the juvenile access to the required services or discharge the juvenile.

STANDARD 14.20

Right to Services

All publicly funded services to which nonadjudicated juveniles have access should be made available to adjudicated delinquents. In addition, juveniles adjudicated delinquent should have access to all services necessary for their normal growth and development.

STANDARD 14.21

Modification of Dispositional Orders

Dispositional orders may be modified as follows:

1. Reduction Because Disposition Is Inequitable. A juvenile, his or her parents, the correctional agency with responsibility for the juvenile, or the family court on its own motion may petition the family court at any time during the course of the disposition to reduce the nature or the duration of the disposition on the basis that:

    a. It exceeds the statutory maximum;

    b. It was imposed in an illegal manner;

    c. It is inappropriate in light of newly discovered evidence;

    d. It is unduly severe with reference to the dispositions given by the same or other courts to juveniles convicted of similar offenses;

    e. It appears at the time of the application that by doing so it can prevent an unduly harsh or inequitable result;

    f. Changes have occurred in the juvenile's home situation; and

    g. The objective or objectives of the original order have been achieved.

2. Reduction Because Services Not Provided. The family court should reduce a disposition or discharge the juvenile when it appears that access to required services is not being provided.

3. Reduction for Good Behavior. The correctional agency with responsibility for a juvenile may reduce the duration of the juvenile's disposition by an amount not to exceed 10 percent of the original disposition if the juvenile has refrained from major infraction of the dispositional order or of the reasonable regulation governing any facility or program to which the juvenile is assigned.

4. Reduction Based on Delegated Discretion. At the time of the disposition order, the court may authorize the correctional agency responsible for carrying out the order to modify, at the agency's discretion, the disposition to a less severe sanction or to a shorter duration. Unless such an authorization is given, all changes in the court's dispositional order must be returned to the court for its action. Under no circumstances can the correctional agency increase the severity or duration of the disposition.

STANDARD 14.22

Enforcement of Dispositional Order When Juvenile Fails to Comply

The correctional agency with responsibility for a juvenile may petition the family court if it appears that the juvenile has willfully failed to comply with any part of the dispositional order. Compliance is defined in terms of attendance at and participation in the specified program and not in terms of performance.

If after a hearing it is determined that the juvenile, in fact, has not complied with the order and that there is no excuse for the noncompliance, the court may do one of the following:

1. Warning and Order to Comply. The court may warn the juvenile of the consequences of failure to comply and order him or her to make up any missed time (in the case of supervisory, remedial, or custodial dispositions) or missed payment (in the case of restitution or fines).

2. Modification of Conditions and/or Imposition of Additional Conditions. If it appears that a warning will be insufficient to induce compliance, the court may modify existing conditions or impose additional conditions calculated to induce compliance, provided the conditions do not exceed the maximum sanctions permissible for the offense. The duration of the disposition should remain the same, with the addition of any missed time or payments ordered to be made up.

3. Imposition of a More Severe Disposition. If it appears that there are no permissible conditions reasonably calculated to induce compliance, the court may sentence the juvenile to the next most severe category of disposition. The duration of the disposition should remain the same, except that the court may add some or all of the missed time to the remainder of the disposition.

4. Commission of a New Offense. When conduct is alleged that constitutes a willful failure to comply with the dispositional order and also constitutes a separate delinquent act, prosecution for the new delinquent act is preferable to modification of the original order. The preference for separate prosecution in no way precludes the imposition of concurrent dispositions.

STANDARD 14.23

Families With Service Needs — Dispositional Alternatives

In the Families With Service Needs proceedings, family court dispositions may order the provision of services, the cooperation with offered services, continuation or discontinuation of behaviors by any party, or placement of the child in alternative care. In no event shall the family court disposition confine the child in an institution to which delinquents are committed.

STANDARD 14.24

Responsible Self-Sufficiency

The family court should have the power to enter an order of responsible self-sufficiency in favor of any juvenile. Before making such an order, the court must determine:

1. That the juvenile wishes to be free from parental control;

2. That he or she understands the consequences of being free from parental control; and

3. That he or she has an acceptable plan for independent living and self-support and the apparent ability and maturity to implement such a plan.

The legal effect of an order of responsible self-sufficiency is the complete emancipation of the minor child.

STANDARD 14.25

Endangered Children — Dispositional Resources

Upon finding a child endangered, a court should have available at least the following dispositional resources:

1. Casework supervision;

2. Day care services;

3. Individual, group or family counseling, therapy, or medical treatment;

4. Homemaker services; and

5. Placement of the child with a relative, in a foster family or group home, or in a residential treatment center.

STANDARD 14.26

Endangered Children — Dispositions Other Than Removal

In ordering a disposition other than removal of the child from the home, the court should select services designed to alleviate the immediate danger to the child, to mitigate or cure any harm the child has already suffered, and to aid the parents so that the child will not be endangered in the future. The court should choose those services which least interfere with family autonomy, provided that the services are adequate to protect the child.

STANDARD 14.27

Endangered Children — Removal of the Child From the Home

In the dispositional phase of Endangered Child proceedings, the child should not be removed from the home unless the court finds that:

1. The child has been endangered in the manner specified in Standard 11.10 and there is a preponderance of the evidence that removal is necessary in order to protect the child from further nonaccidental physical injury; or

2. The child has been endangered in a manner specified in Standard 11.9 or Standards 11.11 through 11.15 and there is clear and convincing evidence that removal is necessary in order to protect the child from further harm of the type precipitating intervention; and,

3. There is a placement available in which the child's physical and emotional well-being can be adequately protected.

Those advocating that the child be removed should bear the burden of proof on these issues.

STANDARD 14.28

Endangered Children — Initial Agency Plans — In-Home Treatment Programs

Whenever the child is left in the home, the agency should develop with the parents a specific plan, detailing the changes which must be made in order for the child not to be endangered, the services which will be provided to the parents and/or the child, and the agency's expectations regarding parental conduct. This plan should serve as a basis for future court review of agency and parent performance.

STANDARD 14.29

Endangered Children —Initial Agency Plans — Removal

Whenever the child is ordered removed from the home, the agency should develop with the parents a specific plan as to where the child will be placed, what steps will be taken to return the child home, and what actions the agency will take to maintain parent-child ties. The plan should specify what services the parents will receive in order to enable them to resume custody and what actions the parents must take in order to resume custody. This plan should serve as a basis for future court review of agency and parent performance.

The child should usually be placed as close to his or her home as possible, preferably in the same neighborhood, and, the agency should be required to facilitate maximum parent-child contact, including visitation and participation by the parent in the care of the child while in placement, unless otherwise ordered by the family court.

The agency also should be responsible for assuring that all ordered services are provided. It should report to the court if it is unable to provide such services, for whatever reasons. The agency may perform services other than those ordered, as necessitated by the case situation.

STANDARD 14.30

Postdispositional Monitoring of Endangered Children — Periodic Review Hearings

The court should conduct a hearing to review the status of each child in placement at least every 6 months.

STANDARD 14.31

Postdispositional Monitoring of Endangered Children — Return

A child should be returned to the home when the court finds by a preponderance of the evidence that, if returned home, the child will not be endangered by the harm which precipitated intervention.

STANDARD 14.32

Postdispositional Monitoring of Endangered Children — Termination of Parental Rights

Statutes governing termination of parental rights should be premised on the child's need for a permanent, stable family home, not on principles related to parental fault. Therefore, termination should be required if the child cannot be returned home within 6 months to 1 year after placement, depending on the child's age, unless:

1. Termination would be harmful to the child because of the strength of the child's family ties;

2. The child is placed with a relative who does not wish to adopt the child;

3. The child is placed in a residential treatment program and termination is not necessary to provide a permanent family home; or

4. There is a substantial likelihood that a permanent placement cannot be found and that the failure to terminate will not jeopardize the child's chances of obtaining a permanent placement.

STANDARD 15.1

Family Court Prosecution Services — Organization

In each local prosecutor's office in which there are at least six attorneys, there should be a specialized division or attorney devoted to representing the State in family court. The attorney in charge of this unit should be known as the family court prosecutor.

STANDARD 15.2

Family Court Prosecution Services — Full-Time Function; Salary

If possible, the family court prosecutor, assistant family court prosecutors, and clerical staff should be employed on a full-time basis. Paralegal workers and law student interns may be employed on a part time basis. Salaries of the family court prosecutor and his attorney staff should be comparable to those of attorneys in other public agencies.

STANDARD 15.3

Family Court Prosecution Services — Selection Criteria

Family court prosecutors should be attorneys admitted to practice before the highest court in the State, and should be selected on the basis of interest, education, experience, and competence. They should have prior criminal prosecution or other trial experience.

STANDARD 15.4

Family Court Prosecution Services — Separate and Adequate Staff

Family court prosecutors should have professional staffs adequate to handle all family court cases in their jurisdiction, as well as clerical and paralegal workers, law student interns, investigators, and police liaison officers. Where practicable, such staff should be in an organizational unit that is separate and distinct from those prosecutors who handle adult criminal cases.

STANDARD 15.5

Family Court Prosecution Services — Selection of Staff

The Family Court Prosecutor's staff should be selected under the same general criteria as the family court prosecutor. This staff should represent, as much as possible, a cross-section of the community, including minority groups.

STANDARD 15.6

Family Court Prosecution Services — Staff Training

An orientation and training program is needed for the family court prosecutor and every new assistant before they assume their offices or duties. Also needed is an interdisciplinary program that provides ongoing, inservice training for both professional and nonprofessional staff in the philosophy and intent of the family court; problems of young people; and community problems, conflicts, and resources.

STANDARD 15.7

Presence of the Family Court Prosecutor at Family Court Proceedings

As attorney for the State, the Family Court Prosecutor may participate in every proceeding of every case that is subject to the jurisdiction of the family court and in which the State has an interest. Family court prosecutors should participate in all contested delinquency cases. In uncontested delinquency cases and other matters, they may determine when to appear. However, the family court, in exercising its discretion, may order the prosecutor to participate in any case or proceeding.

STANDARD 15.8

The Role of Family Court Prosecutor

The primary duty of the family court prosecutor is to seek justice by fully and faithfully representing the State's interests without losing sight of the philosophy and purpose of the family court. The family court prosecutor shall function as an adversary, but shall avoid the typical role of an adult crime prosecutor.

STANDARD 15.9

Conflicts of Interest

Family court prosecutors should avoid the appearance or reality of a conflict of interest with respect to their official duties. In some instances failure to do so will constitute unprofessional conduct.

STANDARD 15.10

Public Statements of Family Court Prosecutor

The family court prosecutor should

avoid exploiting his office by means of personal publicity connected with a case before, during, or after trial.

STANDARD 15.11

Leadership Responsibility of Family Court Prosecutor

The family court prosecutor should take an active community role in preventing delinquency and protecting the rights of young people, and should work to help others initiate and improve existing programs designed to prevent delinquency.

STANDARD 15.12

Relationships of Family Court Prosecutor With Other Participants in the Juvenile Justice System

With Counsel for the Youth and with the Court

An atmosphere of detachment between the family court prosecutor and counsel for the youth and with the court should be maintained at all times. The appearance as well as reality of collusion should be zealously avoided.

With Prospective Nonexpert Witnesses

The family court prosecutor must not compensate a nonexpert witness. He may, however, request permission from the family court to reimburse a nonexpert witness for the reasonable expenses of attending court, including transportation and loss of income.

In interviewing an adult prospective witness, it is proper but not mandatory for the family court prosecutor or his investigator to caution the witness concerning possible self-incrimination and his possible need for counsel. However, if the prospective witness is a juvenile, such cautions are mandatory and

should be extended in the presence of the juvenile's parents or guardian. Where a parent or guardian is not available, the family court may, in the exercise of its discretion, appoint a guardian ad litem or independent counsel for the juvenile witness to be present at the giving of such cautions (see Standard 16.1, Juvenile's Right to Counsel).

With Expert Witnesses

A family court prosecutor who engages an expert for an opinion should respect the independence of the expert's opinion on the subject. To the extent necessary, the prosecutors should explain to the expert his role as an impartial expert called to aid the fact finder, and the manner in which witnesses are examined.

The family court prosecutor must not pay an excessive witness fee to influence the expert's testimony or make the fee contingent upon the testimony the witness will give or the case results.

With the Police

There should be at all times an atmosphere of mutual respect and cooperation between the family court prosecutor's office and the police. The family court prosecutor should strive to establish an effective line of communication with the police.

The family court prosecutor should provide legal advice to police concerning functions and duties in juvenile matters and cooperate with police in providing services of the prosecutor's staff to aid in training them on their duties in juvenile matters.

With Intake Officers, Probation Officers and Social Workers

An atmosphere of mutual respect and trust should exist between the family court prosecutor and intake officers, probation officers, and social workers.

The prosecutor should be available to advise those individuals as to their functions.

STANDARD 15.13

Responsibilities of Family Court Prosecutor at Intake Stage of Family Court Proceedings

Family court prosecutors should be available to advise intake officers of the appropriate State agencies to whether the facts alleged by a complainant are legally sufficient to file a petition of delinquency.

All petitions should be prepared, signed, and filed by the family court prosecutor. Filing should be done as expeditiously as possible. Where a juvenile is in custody, the petition should be filed within 48 hours of the initiation of custody.

Upon receiving a complainant's request for review, the Family Court Prosecutor should consider the facts presented by the complainant, consult with the intake officer who made the initial decision, and make a determination as to whether a petition should be filed. In the event that a petition is not filed by the family court prosecutor, any aggrieved party may ask that family court proceedings be initiated by a verified petition to the court.

STANDARD 15.14

Form and Content of the Complaint

The intake officer of the appropriate State agency should receive complaints from persons wishing to initiate the intake process. Any complaint that serves as the basis of an intake officer's report to the family court prosecutor requesting the filing of a petition should be in writing. The complaint also should be sworn to and signed by one who has personal knowledge of the facts or is informed of them and believes that they are true.

The complaint should set forth specifically the essential facts describing the juvenile's acts or omissions that form the basis of the complaint. Finally, no petition should be filed by the family court prosecutor unless a complaint has first been filed with the intake agency and appropriate procedures have been followed.

STANDARD 15.15

Form and Content of Petition Filed With Family Court by Family Court Prosecutor

Petitions filed by family court prosecutors with the family courts to initiate formal adjudicatory processes should be in writing and signed by the family court prosecutors, to certify that they have read the petition and that, to the best of their knowledge, information, and belief, the petition is true.

The petition should set forth facts sufficient to allege the subject matter and establish the jurisdiction of the court; where the basis of the proceeding is a law violation, the document should set forth the specific law allegedly violated by the juvenile. The petition also should describe facts sufficient to inform juveniles of the acts or omissions they are alleged to have committed.

The petition should contain the following separate parts:

1. The name, address, and date of birth of the juvenile;

2. The name and address of the juvenile's parents or guardian;

3. The date, time, manner, and place of the acts alleged as the basis of the court's jurisdiction;

4. The citation to the section of the Family Court Act relied upon for jurisdiction;

5. The citation of the Federal, State, or local law or ordinance, if any, alleged to have been violated by the juvenile; and

6. A brief statement of the adjudicatory relief sought.

STANDARD 15.16

Dismissal of Petition Upon a Subsequent Finding of Lack of Legal Sufficiency

If subsequent to the filing of a petition, the family court prosecutor determines there is an insufficient quantum of evidence, admissible in a court of law under the rules of evidence, to establish the legal sufficiency of the petition, the prosecutor should move to dismiss the petition.

STANDARD 15.17

Disclosure of Evidence Favorable to Juvenile

The family court prosecutor has the same obligation to disclose evidence favorable to a youth in family court proceedings as does the prosecuting attorney in adult criminal proceedings.

STANDARD 15.18

Family Court Prosecutor's Role in Plea Negotiations

After the initial contact of a complainant with the intake office of the appropriate State agency, the family court prosecutor should not engage in plea negotiations or plea agreements with any person at any stage of juvenile proceedings. Proscribed plea negotiations and plea agreements are those actions of a family court prosecutor that lead to the following:

1. Reduction in seriousness of a charge originally filed;

2. Dismissal of individual counts or number of charges; or

3. Recommendations on action or inaction with regard to the ultimate disposition of a case.

STANDARD 15.19

Dispositions — Requirement of Taking an Active Role

Family court prosecutors should take active roles in dispositional hearings, making independent recommendations after reviewing reports prepared by their staff, the probation department, and others. While the safety and welfare of the community are a paramount concern, family court prosecutors should consider alternative modes of disposition that more closely satisfy the interests and needs of juveniles without jeopardizing public safety.

STANDARD 16.1

Juvenile's Right to Counsel

A juvenile should be represented by a lawyer at every stage of delinquency proceedings. If a juvenile who has not consulted a lawyer indicates intent to waive assistance of counsel, a lawyer should be provided to consult with the juvenile and his or her parents on the wisdom of such waiver. The court should not accept a waiver of counsel unless it determines after thorough inquiry that the juvenile has conferred at least once with a lawyer, and is waiving the right competently, voluntarily, and with full understanding of the consequences.

STANDARD 16.2

The Role of Counsel in the Family Court

The principal duty of an attorney in family court matters is to represent zealously a client's legitimate interests under the law. In doing so, it is appropriate and desirable that the lawyer advise the client of the legal and social consequences of any decision the client might make, as well as to advise the client to seek the counsel of parents or others in making that decision. However, the ultimate responsibility for making any decision that determines the client's interests within the bounds of the law remains with the client.

STANDARD 16.3

The Role of Counsel for the Incompetent Client

If an attorney finds, after interview and other investigation, that the client cannot understand the nature and consequences of the proceedings affecting him and is, therefore, unable to determine rationally his or her own interests in that proceeding, the attorney should promptly bring that circumstance to the court's attention and ask that a guardian ad litem be appointed on the client's behalf.

STANDARD 16.4

The Role of Counsel Appointed Guardian Ad Litem

A lawyer appointed to serve as guardian ad litem for a person subject to family court proceedings should inquire thoroughly into all circumstances that a careful and competent person in the ward's position would consider in determining his or her interests in the proceeding. When the client is the respondent, the guardian ordinarily should require proof of the facts necessary to sustain jurisdiction, and, if jurisdiction is sustained, take the position requiring the least intrusive intervention justified by the child's circumstances. In representing a child in Endangered Child, custody, or adoption proceedings, the guardian may limit his or her activity to presentation and examination of material evidence or may adopt the position requiring the least intrusive intervention justified by the child's circumstances.

STANDARD 16.5

Representation for Children in Family Court Proceedings

Legal representation should be made available, without cost if necessary, to any child whose liberty, custody, or status may be affected by delinquency, Families With Service Needs, Endangered Child, child custody, termination of parental rights, or civil commitment proceedings.

STANDARD 16.6

Representation for Parents in Family Court Proceedings

The parent, guardian, or custodian of a child alleged to be endangered should have the right to legal assistance, without cost if necessary, throughout those proceedings. The parent, guardian, or custodian of a child alleged to be delinquent or the parent, guardian, or custodian involved in a Families With Service Needs proceeding should have the right to legal counsel, without cost if necessary, at the dispositional stage of those proceedings when it appears that their affirmative participation will be required in the dispositional order or plan.

STANDARD 16.7

Stages of Representation in Family Court Proceedings

Except as provided in Standard 16.6, legal representation should be made available at the earliest feasible stage of family court proceedings. Each State at least should adopt procedures whereby counsel can be appointed:

1. At the intake stage where the juvenile is not detained; and

2. At the judicial detention hearing stage where the child has been removed from the home.

Legal representation should continue throughout the family court proceedings and, if necessary, through postdispositional matters that may change the level of deprivation of liberty or the kind or amount of treatment the juvenile receives, such as proceedings to determine or change the place or course of treatment or to revoke probation or parole.

STANDARD 16.8

Training and Qualification of Lawyers for Family Court Practice

Adequate training of lawyers for family court representation is mandatory for the proper functioning of family courts. All members of the legal community, including courts, legal aid and defender agencies, educational institutions, and private practitioners share the responsibility for insuring that attorneys are competent to provide legal assistance in this forum and that competent attorneys are made available to persons subject to family court proceedings.

1. Educational institutions, bar associations, and other legal professional groups should provide suitable undergraduate and postgraduate curricula relating to representation in family court matters. These programs should include both legal and nonlegal courses relevant to family court representation. Other methods for training lawyers, such as apprenticeship programs with experienced counsel, also should be devised and encouraged.

2. In selecting attorneys for appointment in family court proceedings, the responsible authority should carefully evaluate each lawyer's competence, taking into account his or her educational background and experience in family court or related practice.

STANDARD 16.9

Organization of Defense Services

Where possible, a coordinated plan for providing representation that combines public defender and assigned counsel systems should be adopted.

STANDARD 16.10

Procedures for Assignment and Compensation of Appointed Counsel

Where possible, the public defender office or a State bar association committee should have the responsibility for compiling and maintaining a panel of attorneys eligible for appointment in family court matters. The trial court should have the right to add attorneys not placed on the panel by the public defender office or bar committee. Appointments should be made from this panel according to a systematic and well-publicized plan.

STANDARD 16.11

Adequacy of Compensation for Attorneys in Family Court Matters

Lawyers appearing in family court matters, however engaged, should receive reasonable compensation for their time and services according to prevailing professional rates and full reimbursement for expenses reasonably necessary to provide competent and thorough representation. Public defender attorneys should be paid a salary equivalent to that paid other government attorneys with similar qualifications, experience, and responsibility.

STANDARD 16.12

Communications with Youthful Clients and Witnesses

In communicating with a youthful client or witness, lawyers should accommodate their expectations to the age and background of their client. It is proper for lawyers to question the credibility of their client's statements or those of any other witness. However, they may not suggest, expressly or by implication, that their client or other witness prepare or give, on oath or to the lawyer, a version of the facts that is in any respect untruthful, nor may they intimate that the client should be less than candid in revealing material facts to the attorney.

STANDARD 17.1

Selection of Judges

The selection of judges for the family court should be governed by the following procedures:

1. Where the selection entails an assignment to the family court as a matter of internal trial court policy, the assignment should be made by the presiding judge without regard to seniority or any other factors that may detract from the objective evaluation of an individual's competence to serve on the family court; and

2. Where the selection involves a vacancy that can only be filled by the election or appointment of a new judge, the merit plan of judicial selection should be used. The judicial nominating commission should include representatives from the judiciary, the general public, and the legal profession who have experience in juvenile justice.

STANDARD 17.2

Training and Compensation of Judges

Each State should require all new judges to attend training programs and also should require attendance by other judges in continuing judicial educational programs, with emphasis on specialized training in areas relevant to juvenile and family matters.

In a related matter, family court judges should be compensated at the same level as other judges of the highest court of general jurisdiction.

STANDARD 17.3

Interim Use of Other Judicial Officers

Where commissioners and/or referees continue to be used to hear family court cases, they should meet the same qualifications as a judge of the family court, and should be subject to the same standards on discipline and removal, training and education, demeanor, and assignment.

Secondly, plans for phasing out commissioners and referees should be developed consistent with the maintenance of an adequate level of service in the family court.

STANDARD 17.4

Nonjudicial Support Personnel

The family court division should be provided with adequate administrative support staff to meet all the nonjudicial administrative needs of that division. Each jurisdiction should develop staffing standards to assure the provision of such support, written standards delineating the responsibilities of the division's administrative personnel, and clear lines of authority to maintain coordination with the administrative structure of the general trial court.

STANDARD 17.5

Training and Compensation of Nonjudicial Support Personnel

Every State and local jurisdiction should coordinate the development and maintenance of ongoing education and training programs and materials for the administrative support staff of the family court.

Compensation of nonjudicial personnel should be adequate to attract and retain qualified personnel for the specialized duties inherent in the family court structure.

STANDARD 18.1

The Court's Relationship With Law Enforcement Agencies

Family court divisions and law enforcement agencies should develop effective working relationships while retaining the integrity of their unique responsibilities and functions. Written court procedures and rules, reviewed with law enforcement agencies prior to adoption, should clarify the judicial system's requirements and responsibili-

ties for case processing. Similarly, law enforcement agencies should adopt written policies and procedures, following court review, concerning police practices with juveniles.

STANDARD 18.2

The Court's Relationship With Probation Services

State judicial rules should be promulgated to govern court requirements for the probation agency at the local level; intake guidelines and practices should be reviewed with the presiding judge of the family court division. In no event should a judge participate in intake decisions concerning individual case referrals. Judges and intake and probation officers should not discuss cases in the absence of counsel for the State and the child.

The general format, content, and presentation of social study reports should receive the approval of the presiding judge of the family court division.

Judges of this court should meet regularly with senior probation officials to review probation procedures and services to youth under supervision.

STANDARD 18.3

The Court's Relationship With Public and Private Social Service Agencies

Family court divisions should maintain effective working relationships with public and private social service agencies in assisting individuals and families. The respective procedures and responsibilities of the court and social service agencies should be clarified through written agreements. These agreements should be reviewed on the basis of experience, and modified as needed.

Court personnel should develop systems to monitor external agency services. Such agencies should comply with the court's need for social reports, for direct testimony at hearings, and for information about serious problems in implementing the court's objectives in individual cases. The court should provide prompt hearings in making decisions relevant to agency provision for necessary services to children.

STANDARD 18.4

The Court's Relationship With the Public

Family court divisions should implement organized programs of public information and education to advise the public of the progress and problems in achieving court objectives. The court should encourage citizen and media observation of court proceedings within statutory constraints.

A representative family court division citizens' advisory committee, appointed by the presiding judge of the general trial court, should provide advice and critiques to the family court.

STANDARD 18.5

The Leadership Role of the Family Court Judge

Judges of family courts should provide strong leadership to citizen, agency, and government efforts in developing services and solutions to the problems presented by parties to court actions that cannot be addressed sufficiently by the court alone.

Advocacy to achieve sharply expanded external agency services, as alternatives to court intervention for juvenile noncriminal misbehavior, should be an immediate priority.

Judicial leadership should be exerted to encourage and support programs for the prevention of delinquency, child endangerment, and family breakdown. Judges should perform an educational role in communicating their knowledge of law and insights derived from court experience to the public at large.

STANDARD 19.1

Purposes of Juvenile Corrections

The purposes of juvenile corrections are to protect society, carry out the dispositional orders of the family court, and plan, develop, and operationalize the necessary correctional programs and services.

These purposes should be carried out through means that are fair and just; that recognize the unique physical, psychological, and social characteristics and needs of juveniles; and that give juveniles access to opportunities for normal growth and development.

STANDARD 19.2

Creation of a State Agency for Juvenile Intake and Corrections

There should be a strong preference for a single statewide agency with responsibility for the administration of all juvenile intake and corrections. This State agency should be located within the executive branch of government, and its chief administrator should report directly to the governor or a cabinet level official. The State agency should be a separate administrative entity but may be under an umbrella organization in which a number of people-serving agencies are brought together for coordination purposes.

STANDARD 19.3

Provision of Services

The State agency should be responsible for providing or assuring the provision of all services required to carry out the predispositional and post-dispositional orders of the family court. It also should be responsible for overall planning, policy development, fiscal management, monitoring, and evaluation of service programs.

The provision of direct services to juveniles should be decentralized to the smallest geographic entities consistent with retaining the juvenile in his or her home community and providing services at a reasonable cost. Specific direct services to be provided should include, but not be limited to:

1. A statewide system of intake and diagnostic study;

2. A statewide system of secure and nonsecure facilities for juveniles awaiting family court action or implementation of the family court's order;

3. A statewide system of community supervision;

4. A statewide system of institutions, camps, and group homes for the care of adjudicated juveniles; and

5. Acting as agent for the State in the operation of the Interstate Compact for Juveniles.

The State agency may directly provide all services or it may contract with the private sector or with other public agencies to provide such services. When services are contracted for, the State agency should retain responsibility for monitoring and enforcing program standards in the same manner prescribed for State-operated programs.

STANDARD 19.4

General Authority and Responsibility for Services

The State agency should provide services pursuant to a valid order of the family court and act on authority delegated to it by the family court to carry out such orders.

STANDARD 19.5

Specific Responsibilities

The State agency's specific responsibilities should include the following:

1. To accept legal custody of all adjudicated delinquents committed to it and to exercise supervision and custody and provide necessary services for adjudicated delinquents as ordered by the family court;

2. As soon as possible after an adjudicated delinquent is committed to its custody, to conduct an investigation of the juvenile, including the juvenile's life and behavior and that of the juvenile's family. In so doing the State agency may make use of any previous studies if they are sufficiently current and pertinent;

3. On the basis of its investigation, to provide the juvenile with a program of supervision, care, counseling, and/or placement that complies with the dispositional order of the family court and will best meet the juvenile's normal personal growth and development needs;

4. To inform the family court if it determines, as a result of its investigation, that it cannot provide access to all services required by the juvenile;

5. To periodically (every 90 days) review the case of each juvenile committed to its custody. This review should include an evaluation of the progress made by the juvenile since the previous review and should determine whether existing plans for the juvenile should be modified or continued. A written summary of the periodic review should be sent to the juvenile's parents or guardians and to the family court;

6. Whenever the State agency learns that any juvenile in its custody does not have a parent or legal guardian capable of exercising effective guardianship of

the juvenile, to petition the family court for the appointment of a guardian and/or conservatorship;

7. To provide or contract with mental health agencies for diagnosis and short-term (90-day) care of those juveniles in need of short-term mental health services;

8. Whenever the State agency has reasonable grounds to believe that a juvenile under its legal custody or supervision is mentally ill or mentally retarded, to petition the family court for a review and rescission of the order vesting legal custody or supervision in the agency and for the initiation of proceedings for the civil commitment of such juvenile as mentally ill or mentally retarded; and,

9. To maintain complete written records of all studies and examinations of juvenile commitments and the resulting conclusions and recommendations and of all major decisions and orders affecting juvenile commitments. Such records should be maintained in a manner that will facilitate administrative decisions, planning, and evaluation (see Standard 25.4).

STANDARD 19.6

Limitations on Authority

The State agency's authority to take action with respect to the juvenile commitment should be limited. Some activities should be specifically prohibited. For example, the State agency should not:

1. Place a juvenile in or transfer a juvenile to any institution or facility designated for the temporary or long-time incarceration of adults; any mental hospital for the purpose of extended care or treatment; or any public or private institution or facility outside of the State without court approval.

2. Consent to the juvenile's marriage, adoption, enlistment in the armed forces, or any other action that would have a serious impact upon the juvenile that is included within the authority of the legal custodian and for which the consent of the parents or guardians is required.

3. Subject the juvenile to any medical care or treatment that is other than routine or preventive without the express written permission of the parents or guardians or to any care or treatment that is contrary to the religious tenets of the juvenile or the parents or guardians.

4. Subject the juvenile to any medical experimentation or administer any drugs or chemical restraints to control the juvenile's behavior, unless such drugs or chemical restraints are necessary to prevent the juvenile's injury or sustain the juvenile's health.

The State agency should not delegate important decisions to low-echelon personnel. Important decisions such as the initial placement of the juvenile, the transfer of the juvenile from one type of foster care to another, or the release of the juvenile should be made by the regional director or a designated deputy in consultation with the appropriate program and staff.

STANDARD 19.7

Right to Refuse Services

Although all juveniles committed to the State agency should be expected to participate in any programs or services set forth in the family court's dispositional order, the concept of the right of the juvenile to refuse rehabilitative services should be respected.

Rehabilitative services are counseling, religious programs, student government, and other activities in which nonadjudicated juveniles would not be required to participate.

STANDARD 19.8

Duties of the State Agency — General

The State agency should exercise leadership in working with other public and private agencies and citizens' organizations to develop and implement comprehensive programs to provide needed services for juveniles who have been adjudicated delinquent. The State agency should assure that these services are provided equally throughout the State. In addition, the agency should:

1. Develop, maintain, and revise a long-range plan for its operations;

2. Collect, evaluate, and disseminate statistics and information regarding the nature, extent, and causes of juvenile delinquency, and conduct research and evaluation including studies and demonstration projects on all aspects of juvenile delinquency;

3. Encourage and assist in the development of innovative programs for the diversion of juveniles from the juvenile justice system, taking into consideration the safety of the community and the best interests of the juveniles involved;

4. Develop written instructional and standard-setting materials with respect to the State agency's programs and consult with other public and private agencies regarding its programs;

5. Establish an advisory citizens' committee to assist the State agency in assessing the effectiveness of juvenile corrections programs; and

6. Enter into contracts and agreements with the Federal Government with respect to the receipt of Federal funds for delinquency programs and for the care of juveniles found to be delinquent by the Federal courts and committed for care and treatment.

STANDARD 19.9

Personnel

The State agency should adopt personnel policies, practices and procedures that provide that all employees of the State agency who are employed in programs for the care and rehabilitation of delinquents will come within the provisions of a merit system.

There should be a strong commitment to the recruitment and employment of staff at all levels on an affirmative action basis. This commitment should include an affirmative action policy and plan for implementation including, but not limited to, the elimination of discrimination against the employment of women in juvenile corrections and the elimination of policies that bar the employment of capable, qualified exoffenders.

The State agency should also develop:

1. A grievance procedure to be used as the principal vehicle for the resolution of conflicts between employees and the State agency's policies and practices. Information on this procedure should be disseminated to all employees.

2. A code of conduct for all employees. This code should become part of the employment contract entered into by the State agency with each of its employees and should also be a part of any contract for purchase of services.

3. Policies and procedures for communicating with its employees concerning wages, hours, and working conditions.

STANDARD 19.10

Training

The State agency should provide or assure the provision of comprehensive training programs for employees of the State agency and for the employees of other public and private agencies engaged in activities related to its programs.

STANDARD 19.11

Volunteers

The State agency should develop a strong volunteer program to enrich and supplement all services to juveniles.

STANDARD 20.1

Grievance Procedures — Hearings and Representation

The State agency should develop and implement grievance procedures to provide a means for juveniles to challenge the substance or application of any policy, behavior, or action directed toward the juvenile by the State agency or any of its program units. Complaints about the policy, behavior, or action of other organizations that exercise jurisdiction over juveniles pursuant to contractual relationships with the State agency should be covered by the grievance procedures.

A full hearing should be conducted promptly and all parties to the grievance should be given an opportunity to be present and to participate in the hearing.

The juvenile should be entitled to select a representative from among other juveniles, staff, or volunteers regularly participating in the program. Representatives should be entitled to attend and participate in any informal conferences, hearings, or reviews in which the juvenile participates.

STANDARD 20.2

Grievance Procedures — Appeal and Review

The grievance procedures should provide for levels of review, which should be kept to a minimum. These levels should coincide with the major decisionmaking levels of the organization.

Any party to a grievance, juvenile or staff, should be authorized to appeal a decision to the next level of review. Time limits should be established for the receipt of responses at each level of review and for any action that must be taken to put a response into effect.

The final level of advisory review should be made by an independent party or parties outside the State agency.

STANDARD 20.3

Purposes of Disciplinary Procedures

The purposes of the State agency's disciplinary procedures should be to insure the orderly protection of the facility, staff, and juvenile clients and to encourage the development of self-discipline by the juveniles. Such procedures should treat juveniles fairly and should assure that:

1. Procedural safeguards are provided to juveniles accused of major institutional role violations;

2. Cruel and unusual punishment is prohibited within juvenile correctional facilities; and

3. Juveniles in correctional facilities who are victims of criminal or delinquent acts have the same rights to file legal complaints as juveniles outside of such facilities.

STANDARD 20.4

Orientation to Rules and Regulations

Juveniles should be assured of prior knowledge of rules through orientation and by posting of written regulations. Juveniles admitted to secure facilities should be given such orientation within 24 hours of their arrival.

Such rules and regulations should include the following:

1. Corporal punishment should be prohibited;

2. Restriction to secure quarters (discipline unit) should not be employed unless a juvenile detained in an institution:

    a. constitutes a danger to himself or others;

    b. is in danger from others; or

    c. is likely to escape;

3. All reasonable alternatives to restriction to secure quarters (discipline unit) should be considered before the determination is made to institute or continue such restriction. Any juvenile who is restricted should have access to an appeal procedure regarding the reasons for and/or the length of the restriction; and

4. Restriction to secure quarters (discipline unit) should not exceed 5 consecutive days.

STANDARD 20.5

Hearing Rights of the Accused Juvenile

The rights of an accused juvenile should include the following:

1. The right to an impartial and objective fact finding hearing when accused of a major rule violation that might result in a deprivation greater than 24 hours restriction to secure quarters (discipline unit);

2. The right to a written notice of the allegations against him or her and the evidence upon which the allegations are based 48 hours in advance of the factfinding hearing;

3. The right to request a substitute counsel to represent him or her during the disciplinary proceedings. A substitute counsel may be a staff member, another juvenile (subject to the reasonable approval of the program director), or a volunteer who is a member of a regular volunteer program at the institution. Factfinders should assure that juveniles who do not comprehend the proceedings due to a lack of maturity or intellectual ability or because of the complexity of the factual questions at issue are provided with a substitute counsel. And translators should be provided when the juvenile does not speak English.

4. The right to confront accusers, call witnesses, and present written documents and other evidence at the factfinding hearing; and

5. The right to receive a written record of any true findings and the evidence relied upon. This should include a statement of the disposition and the reasons for the disposition.

STANDARD 20.6

Appeal Rights of the Accused Juvenile

An accused juvenile should have the right to appeal disciplinary proceedings to an independent and impartial hearing officer within the State agency on any one of the following grounds:

1. The procedural safeguards provided for in the State agency's disciplinary system were not met;

2. New evidence is now available that would be relevant and material to the findings; or,

3. The disposition was disproportionate in relation to the finding.

STANDARD 21.1

State Agency Responsibility for Intake Services

Intake services should be the responsibility of the State agency. These services should be designed to serve three functions:

1. To act for the family court in screening applications for petitions;

2. To act for the family court in developing the necessary information to make a dispositional order; and,

3. To act as the intake apparatus for the State agency in the cases of children or families for which the State agency has responsibilities for carrying out dispositional orders.

STANDARD 21.2

Processing Applications for Petitions to the Family Court

The State agency's intake services unit should process all applications for petitions to the family court alleging that a juvenile is delinquent.

1. Within 48 hours if the juvenile is in detention or shelter care; or,

2. Within 30 calendar days if the juvenile is not in detention or shelter care.

Intake personnel should have the authority and responsibility to:

1. Refer the case to the family court prosecutor for court action;

2. Refer the juvenile and/or the juvenile's family for noncourt services;

3. Defer the decision on filing a petition for up to 90 days after the receipt of the application where a juvenile, not in detention or shelter care, has been referred by the intake unit to a non-court service program; or,

4. Dismiss an application that is not substantiated by the available facts.

STANDARD 21.3

Dispositional Report

The dispositional report should be prepared by the State agency's intake personnel. This report should comply with the guidelines set forth for such reports in Standard 14.5. The recommendations contained in the report should be consistent with the criteria and limitations on dispositional decisions described in the standards in Chapter 14.

STANDARD 22.1

Development of a Statewide System of Detention and Shelter Care

The State juvenile intake and corrections agency should be responsible for the development of a statewide system of detention care facilities and approved shelter care facilities for juveniles referred to or under the jurisdiction of the family court or who are in the legal custody of the State agency or under community supervision.

The State agency should be authorized to purchase detention and shelter care services from other public agencies or from private organizations, provided that the agency's standards are met in the provision of such services.

Where it determines that adequate shelter care cannot otherwise be provided, the State agency should construct shelter care facilities and operate these facilities in accordance with its promulgated standards.

STANDARD 22.2

State Standards for Detention and Shelter Care Facilities

The State juvenile intake and corrections agency should develop and promulgate standards for detention and shelter care facilities. These standards should govern such matters as the capacity of the facility, its location, design, construction, equipment and operation, fire and safety precautions, medical services, qualifications and number of personnel, and the quality of services provided to the juveniles.

The use of any detention or shelter care facility not operated by the State agency should be subject to the agency's approval. The agency should notify the appropriate public officals whether:

1. The facility meets its standards and is suitable for the detention or shelter care of juveniles;

2. The facility is in substantial compliance with the standards and their general purpose and intent, with deficiencies noted; or,

3. The facility is disapproved and will be declared unsuitable for the detention or shelter care of juveniles 60 days thereafter, with the reasons noted. Provision should be made for opportunity to correct the deficiencies and approve the facility upon reinspection.

The State agency should conduct an annual inspection of each detention and shelter care facility. It also should require monthly written reports from these facilities, containing such information as the State agency may need to set and enforce its standards.

STANDARD 22.3

Use of Jails Prohibited

Jails should not be used for the detention of juveniles.

STANDARD 22.4

Preadjudicatory Detention Review

An investigation and review of the need for preadjudicatory detention should be completed by intake personnel within 48 hours of a juvenile's being placed in custody.

Whenever a juvenile is taken into custody, the juvenile should be released with a citation or to a parent or guardian, unless detention is necessary:

1. To insure the presence of the juvenile at subsequent family court proceedings;

2. To provide physical care for a juvenile who cannot return home because there is no parent or other suitable person able and willing to supervise and care for the juvenile adequately;

3. To prevent the juvenile from harming or intimidating any witness, or otherwise threatening the orderly process of the family court proceedings;

4. To prevent the juvenile from inflicting bodily harm on others; or

5. To protect the juvenile from bodily harm.

STANDARD 23.1

Organization

The State agency should have responsibility for developing a statewide network of community supervision that will provide implementation of the family court's dispositional order, supervision, counseling, and other services for juvenile delinquents. These services should be made available on a decentralized basis by workers located as close to the community and the family court as feasible.

STANDARD 23.2

Nature of Services

The primary responsibility of the community supervision division of the State agency should be the implementation of the conditional dispositions of the family court. Such dispositions should not interfere with the juvenile's schooling, regular employment, or other activities necessary for normal growth and development.

STANDARD 23.3

Formulation of Services Plan

A services plan should be developed for each juvenile ordered to community supervision by the family court. The components of the plan should be derived from all available information including: the diagnostic and dispositional reports, the comprehensive community assessment, the input of significant others in the delinquent's life, and the wishes of the delinquent himself. The plan should be developed by the worker with the assistance of other resources available at the time the case is assigned. Its objectives should be clearly stated and in keeping with the needs outlined in the dispositional order.

The adjudicated juvenile referred for services should be given full opportunity to participate in creating the services plan and have a voice in setting his own goals. He should be present when possible at case staffings and should participate as a member of the staffing team. Significant others, including parents, spouse, or others, also should be included in these staffings whenever possible.

STANDARD 23.4

Level of Services

All adjudicated delinquents should receive the level of supervision and services identified in the services plan. Where specific services ordered by the family court are not available, it should be the responsibility of the community supervision staff to return the case to the family court for further dispositional consideration pursuant to Standard 14.19.

STANDARD 23.5

Caseload Ratio

The State agency should establish a maximum caseload ratio for community supervision workers.

STANDARD 23.6

Authority of Community Supervision Workers

The authority of community supervision workers to enforce conditions, provide services, purchase services, or recommend modification of the dispositional order is derived from the family court. Neither the worker nor the State agency should modify, substitute, or escalate any condition of the dispositional order without the specific authorization of the family court.

In their capacity as officers of the court, the community supervision workers should have peace officer powers, including the powers of arrest, search, and seizure of contraband items. These peace officer powers should not, however, extend to the carrying of firearms.

STANDARD 23.7

Noncompliance With Court Orders

Community supervision workers

should petition the family court in cases involving alleged noncompliance with the conditions of the court's dispositional order. However, the petition should not request that the juvenile be taken into custody prior to a hearing unless there are reasonable grounds for believing that:

1. The juvenile poses an imminent threat of physical harm to another person;

2. The juvenile is in danger of physical harm from another and requests protection; or

3. The juvenile is in imminent danger of causing physical harm to himself.

STANDARD 23.8

Investigation of New Law Violations

The community supervision workers should refer cases involving the commission of a new law violation by the delinquent to the juvenile intake unit for full investigation. Upon completion of the investigation, intake personnel should either petition the court for modification of the disposition in accordance with Standard 14.22 or refer the case to the family court prosecutor for adjudication of the new law violation.

STANDARD 23.9

Education and Training

Community supervision staff should possess the necessary educational background to enable them to implement effectively the dispositional orders of the family court. They should possess a minimum of a bachelor's degree in one of the helping sciences, e.g., psychology, social work, counseling or criminal justice. In addition, they should receive 40 hours of initial and 80 hours of ongoing training each year

in the subject areas in which they will be required to provide services.

STANDARD 23.10

Dual Jurisdiction and Interstate Compact

Whenever an adjudicated delinquent is found to be under the jurisdiction of more than one court, the matter should be returned to the family court of original jurisdiction with a recommendation as to whether the jurisdiction of one or more of the courts should be terminated. However, nothing in this standard should be construed to interfere in any way with the provisions of the Interstate Compact or with the provision of services to a minor in one State by the community supervision staff of another State.

STANDARD 24.1

Development of a Statewide System

The State agency should establish a statewide network of coeducational residential facilities for the care and training of adjudicated delinquents committed to its custody. These facilities should be of a wide variety, ranging from secure facilities to camps, ranches, and residential schools. They may be operated by the State agency under a division of residential services or by local public or private organizations.

STANDARD 24.2

Secure Residential Facilities

A secure residential facility is one that is used exclusively for the placement of adjudicated delinquents where the staff controls the rights of the delinquents to enter or leave the facility. As a part of its network of residential facilities, the State agency should maintain a number of these facilities. The precise number of secure facilities should be based on need and should be kept to an absolute minimum.

Secure residential facilities should comply with the following guidelines:

1. They should not exceed a bed capacity of 100. The State agency should develop a plan with specific time limits to remodel existing facilities to meet this requirement or to discontinue the use of present facilities that have a population in excess of 100. No new facilities should be constructed unless it can be demonstrated that there is a need for them and that this need cannot be met by any other means.

2. They should be located in or near the community from which they draw their population insofar as geography and demographic constraints permit.

3. The living units' capacity in secure facilities should not exceed 20 beds and should provide an individual room for each delinquent. Design should also provide space for recreation, offices for staff, and an area for quiet games and study.

4. They should be staffed with an adequate number of trained professionals from the various disciplines necessary to provide specialized program services as well as basic care. Staffing ratios should be developed on the basis of the 20-bed living unit.

STANDARD 24.3
Security

It should be the responsibility of the administrator of each secure residential facility to assure the safety of both residents and staff and to prevent juveniles from escaping.

At a minimum, each secure facility should relate its security policies and procedures to the following areas: relationship between staff and juveniles, written policies and procedures, classification system, staff training, staffing ratios, structure of the facility, and security equipment.

STANDARD 24.4
Nonsecure Residential Facilities

A nonsecure residential facility is one in which a small number of adjudicated delinquents reside where the delinquents can enter or leave the facility under staff supervision or, if authorized, without staff supervision. As a part of its network of residential facilities, the State agency should maintain a variety of these facilities for those delinquents who do not need a secure facility but are unable to remain in their own homes.

STANDARD 24.5
Educational and Vocational Training

Each facility that is responsible for the care and treatment of adjudicated delinquents should examine its educational and vocational training programs to insure that they meet the individual needs of its clientele. Such programs should be geared directly to the reintegration of youth into the community and should have provisions for continuing support within the community supervision program.

Appropriate opportunities for work or educational furloughs should be provided. Where possible, the juvenile should receive education within the community. Where this is not possible, the juvenile should receive academic credit for education in the facility that can be transferred to schools in the community. Appropriate professionally trained educational staff should be employed or contracted to provide the needed educational and vocational programs.

STANDARD 24.6

Educational Assessment and Diagnosis

Each adjudicated delinquent should be assessed in terms of academic, vocational, and personal needs. The assessment should be accomplished through acquisition of relevant information both of record and by interview at such community resources as public and private schools and agencies, places of employment, known associates, and parents or guardians.

The assessment should cover those factors that are pertinent to the development of an appropriate educational plan. These factors should include, but not be limited to: attitude toward education, achieved academic levels, developed vocational skills and expressed interests, level of cognitive development, most efficient or disabled communication modality, learning style, functional level of vision and hearing, significant physical abnormalities or disabilities, and feelings related to self-worth and such neurotic traits as might be causal factors in emotional impediments to learning.

STANDARD 24.7

Educational Programs

Each facility should have a comprehensive academic educational program. Such a program should include, but not be limited to, instruction in the following broad categories: developmental education, remedial education, special education, multicultural education, bilingual education, tutorial

services, and higher education (community college program).

STANDARD 24.8

Prevocational and Vocational Programs

Each institution should have prevocational and vocational training programs to enhance the juveniles' marketable skills. Such programs should include, but not be limited to: prevocational orientation, world-of-work education, vocational instruction and counseling, related remedial instruction, career education and counseling, and employability plans and work experience.

STANDARD 24.9

Educational Program Staffing

Each facility should provide a professionally trained educational staff. This staff should be differentially placed in each facility to meet the academic and vocational needs and interests of the clientele.

STANDARD 24.10

Medical/Dental and Mental Health Services

Every adjudicated delinquent committed to the State agency should have available comprehensive medical, dental, and mental health care services. Medical and dental services should provide for both diagnostic and treatment needs. Mental health services should provide for diagnosis and short-term treatment.

Delinquents assessed to be mentally ill or mentally retarded should be returned to the family court to determine the validity of such an assessment in accordance with the procedures established in the Standard on Disposition of Mentally Ill or Mentally Retarded Juveniles.

STANDARD 24.11

Rehabilitative Services

The State agency should provide or assure the provision of an array of rehabilitative services available on a voluntary basis to all delinquents placed in residential settings. These services should include, but not be limited to: individual counseling, small group counseling, community group counseling, drug abuse programs, religious services, and student government.

STANDARD 24.12

Recreation and Leisure Time Activities

The State agency should provide or assure the provision of a wide range of recreation and leisure time activities for delinquents committed to its custody. These activities should be balanced between individual and team activities.

STANDARD 24.13

Communications

The State agency should encourage and make no undue prohibitions against communications, including visits, phone calls, and letters, between delinquents in its custody and their families or significant others in their lives.

The State agency should not censor mail other than to open envelopes or packages in the presence of the delinquent to inspect for contraband materials, such as drugs or weapons. The State agency should not monitor telephone calls between the delinquent and his family or significant others.

STANDARD 24.14

Work Assignments and Work Release Programs

Work assignments for delinquents in the State agency's facilities should be limited to normal housekeeping and yardkeeping tasks in the living area and work directly related to vocational training to which the delinquent has been assigned. Any other productive work that contributes to the maintenance of the facility should be remunerative. Repetitious, nonfunctional, degrading, or unnecessary tasks should be prohibited as work assignments.

Facilities housing older delinquents of an employable age should provide work release programs.

Wages paid a delinquent should be used for payments of restitution to the victim of the instant offense or for purposes of contributing to the support of the delinquent's family only if so ordered by the family court as part of the disposition.

STANDARD 24.15

Health, Safety, and Sanitation

All residential facilities in which delinquents committed to the State agency are placed should conform to existing health, safety, and sanitation codes, both in facility structure and program operation. The State agency and other agencies responsible for administering such codes should inspect each facility at least once a year.

STANDARD 24.16

Food Services

All delinquents in facilities of the State agency should be provided a nutritionally adequate diet that offers choices and is varied enough to be acceptable to the ethnic and religious groups represented in the facility's population. The measure of adequacy should be the recommended daily dietary allowance established by the Food and Nutritional Board of the National Academy of Sciences' National Research Council.

STANDARD 25.1

State and Local Responsibility for Planning and Evaluation

Each State should designate by statute the governmental unit(s) responsible for juvenile justice and delinquency prevention planning and evaluation at the State and local level.

STANDARD 25.2

Adequate Operational Funds for Planning and Evaluation

Each State should adopt legislation stipulating that an adequate portion of the funds for juvenile justice and delinquency prevention programs must be devoted to planning and evaluation.

STANDARD 25.3

Interjurisdictional and Community Participation in Decisionmaking Bodies Concerned With Planning and Evaluation

A fair sample of the community and its juvenile-related agencies must participate in the decisions of the governmental body that plans and evaluates juvenile justice and delinquency prevention activities.

STANDARD 25.4

Data Requirements

Data must be made available to support administrative decisions, planning, and evaluation.

STANDARD 26.1

Analyze the Present Situation

Each governmental unit with responsibility for juvenile justice and delinquency prevention planning should complete a detailed analysis of the community's delinquency problem and current efforts to control delinquency.

STANDARD 26.2

Develop Goals

Each governmental unit responsible for juvenile justice and delinquency prevention should develop a 5-year plan of community goals aimed at juvenile delinquency prevention and/or system improvements goals for their community.

STANDARD 26.3

Developing Problem Statements

Each governmental unit responsible for juvenile justice and delinquency prevention planning should identify the gap between its goals and its present accomplishments. Specific problem statements should then be developed to explain that gap. These statements should provide a basis for program and project development.

STANDARD 26.4

Program Development

Each governmental unit responsible for juvenile justice and delinquency prevention planning should develop programs on the basis of problems and goals statements.

STANDARD 26.5

Program Implementation

Each governmental unit responsible for juvenile justice and delinquency prevention planning should develop a specific program implementation plan.

STANDARD 27.1

Setting Evaluation Goals and Developing an Evaluation Strategy

Goals for an evaluation system should be developed prior to creating or improving an evaluation capability. These goals should be based on an analysis of local evaluation needs.

STANDARD 27.2

Developing or Improving Evaluation Capability

Present evaluation processes and products should be reviewed in terms of their utility in reaching evaluation goals. Evaluation capability should then be developed or improved in order to meet evaluation goals.

STANDARD 27.3

Developing a Standardized Evaluation System

Each governmental unit having responsibility for an evaluation system should develop a standardized monitoring system with the capability of assessing juvenile justice and delinquency prevention activities within its jurisdiction.

STANDARD 27.4

Developing an Evaluation Research Capability

In order to evaluate selected projects, programs or systems in depth, each governmental unit with a responsibility for conducting an evaluation program should develop the capability to conduct or sponsor evaluation research.

STANDARD 28.1

Collection and Retention of Information on Juveniles

Each State should enact laws governing the collection and retention of information pertaining to juveniles. Rules and regulations should be promulgated to provide for reasonable safeguards to protect against the misuse, misinterpretation, and improper dissemination of the information and for periodic evaluations of information collection and retention practices within the State to determine whether information is being collected, retained, and utilized properly.

STANDARD 28.2

Access to Juvenile Records

Juvenile records should not be made public. Access to and use of these records should be strictly controlled to limit the risk that disclosure will result in the misuse or misinterpretation of information, the unnecessary denial of opportunities and benefits to children or an interference with the purposes of official intervention.

STANDARD 28.3

Children's Privacy Committee

Each State should establish by statute at least one Children's Privacy Committee. In some States the geography or diversity of population concentrations may make it necessary for this committee to include regional committees or subcommittees. Those States with a Security and Privacy Council on adult information systems could establish a Children's Privacy Committee as a subcommittee of the council. Committee members should include persons with expertise in child advocacy, delivery of youth services, information systems, and juvenile justice activities.

The purpose of the Children's Privacy Committee is to institutionalize a concern for juvenile records, to promote consistency in recordkeeping practices, and insure visibility in recordkeeping decisions. The Committee should have the authority to examine, evaluate, and make recommendations on privacy, juvenile records, and information practices and policies pertaining to children. The Committee also should be able to apply civil remedies and administrative, civil, and criminal sanctions for the improper maintenance and use of juvenile records.

STANDARD 28.4

Computers in the Juvenile Justice System

Any computerized system used by a juvenile justice system to store information pertaining to juveniles should be designed to assure compliance with Standard 28.1, Collection and Retention of Information on Juveniles; Standard 28.2, Access to Juvenile Records; and Standard 28.5, Sealing of Juvenile Records. The data included in the computerized system should be objective and factual rather than subjective, predictive, or diagnostic.

A computerized system should be adopted only if the ability of the juvenile justice system to deliver services to children and families will be substantially enhanced by automation, and if the economic and privacy costs of auto-

mation are less than the benefits it offers.

STANDARD 28.5

Sealing of Juvenile Records

Each State should enact legislation providing for the prompt sealing of juvenile records when, due to dismissal of a petition prior to or as a result of adjudication, the rehabilitation of the juvenile, or the passage of time, the adverse consequences that may result from disclosure of such records outweigh the necessity or usefulness of retaining them.

Included within the legislation relating to the sealing of juvenile records should be precise procedures for notification of all persons, agencies, or departments that may have copies of the juvenile's record or notations regarding that record in their files, that the juvenile record has been sealed by the family court and that any such copies or notations should be destroyed or deleted.

Whenever a juvenile's record is ordered sealed, the family court proceedings should be deemed never to have occurred and the juvenile who is the subject of the record may inform any person or organization that, with respect to the matter in which the record was sealed, he or she was not arrested and never appeared before a family court.

Once a juvenile record is sealed, only the juvenile involved or an authorized representative should have access to that record.

Appendix C

JUVENILE JUSTICE AND DELINQUENCY PREVENTION ACT OF 1974
SUBCHAPTER I—GENERALLY

§ 5601. Congressional statement of findings

(a) The Congress hereby finds that—

(1) juveniles account for almost half the arrests for serious crimes in the United States today;

(2) understaffed, overcrowded juvenile courts, probation services, and correctional facilities are not able to provide individualized justice or effective help;

(3) present juvenile courts, foster and protective care programs, and shelter facilities are inadequate to meet the needs of the countless, abandoned, and dependent children, who, because of this failure to provide effective services, may become delinquents;

(4) existing programs have not adequately responded to the particular problems of the increasing numbers of young people who are addicted to or who abuse drugs, particularly nonopiate or polydrug abusers;

(5) juvenile delinquency can be prevented through programs designed to keep students in elementary and secondary schools through the prevention of unwarranted and arbitrary suspensions and expulsions;

(6) State and local communities which experience directly the devastating failures of the juvenile justice system do not presently have sufficient technical expertise or adequate resources to deal comprehensively with the problems of juvenile delinquency; and

(7) existing Federal programs have not provided the direction, coordination, resources, and leadership required to meet the crisis of delinqency.

(b) Congress finds further that the high incidence of delinquency in the United States today results in enormous annual cost and immeasurable loss of human life, personal security, and wasted human resources and that juvenile delinquency constitutes a growing threat to the national welfare requiring immediate and comprehensive action by the Federal Government to reduce and prevent delinquency.

Historical Note

Effective Date. Section 263 of Pub.L. 93–415, as amended by Pub.L. 94–273. § 32(a), Apr. 21, 1976, 90 Stat. 380, provided that:

"(a) Except as provided by subsection (b), the foregoing provisions of this Act [enacting subchapters I and II of this chapter and amending section 5108 of Title 5 Government Organization and Employees] shall take effect on the date of enactment of this Act [Sept. 7, 1974].

"(b) Section 204(b)(5) and 204(b)(6) [section 5614(b)(5) and 5614(b)(6) of this title] shall become effective at the close of the thirty-first day of the twelfth calendar month of 1974. Section 204 (*l*) [section 5614 (*l*) of this title] shall become effective at the close of the thirtieth day of the eleventh month of 1976."

Short Title. Section 100 of Pub.L. 93–415 provided: "That this Act [enacting this chapter and sections 3772 to 3774, and 3821 of this title, and sections 4351 to 4353, 5038 to 5042 of Title 18, amending sections 3701, 3723, 3733, 3768, 3811 to 3814, 3882, 3883 and 3888 of this title, section 5108 of Title 5, and sections 5031 to 5037 of Title 18, and repealing section 3889 of this title] may be cited as the 'Juvenile Justice and Delinquency Prevention Act of 1974'."

Legislative History. For legislative history and purpose of Pub.L. 93–415, see 1974 U.S.Code Cong. and Adm.News, p. 5283.

Library References

Infants (West) 13, 16.

C.J.S. Infants §§ 11 et seq., 93 et seq.

§ 5602. Congressional declaration of purpose and policy

(a) It is the purpose of this chapter—

(1) to provide for the thorough and prompt evaluation of all federally assisted juvenile delinquency programs;

(2) to provide technical assistance to public and private agencies, institutions, and individuals in developing and implementing juvenile delinquency programs;

(3) to establish training programs for persons, including professionals, paraprofessionals, and volunteers, who work with delinquents or potential delinquents or whose work or activities relate to juvenile delinquency programs;

(4) to establish a centralized research effort on the problems of juvenile delinquency, including an information clearinghouse to disseminate the findings of such research and all data related to juvenile delinquency;

(5) to develop and encourage the implementation of national standards for the administration of juvenile justice, including recommendations for administrative, budgetary, and legislative action at the Federal, State, and local level to facilitate the adoption of such standards;

(6) to assist States and local communities with resources to develop and implement programs to keep students in elementary

and secondary schools and to prevent unwarranted and arbitrary suspensions and expulsions; and

(7) to establish a Federal assistance program to deal with the problems of runaway youth.

(b) It is therefore the further declared policy of Congress to provide the necessary resources, leadership, and coordination (1) to develop and implement effective methods of preventing and reducing juvenile delinquency; (2) to develop and conduct effective programs to prevent delinquency, to divert juveniles from the traditional juvenile justice system and to provide critically needed alternatives to institutionalization; (3) to improve the quality of juvenile justice in the United States; and (4) to increase the capacity of State and local governments and public and private agencies to conduct effective juvenile justice and delinquency prevention and rehabilitation programs and to provide research, evaluation, and training services in the field of juvenile delinquency prevention.

Pub.L. 93–415, Title I, § 102, Sept. 7, 1974, 88 Stat. 1110.

Historical Note

References in Text. "This chapter", referred to in subsec. (a), was in the original "this Act", meaning Pub.L. 93–415, Sept. 7, 1974, 88 Stat. 1109. For complete classification of Pub.L. 93–415, see Short Title note under section 5601 of this title.

Effective Date. Section effective Sept. 7, 1974, see section 263 of Pub.L. 93–415, set

out as a note under section 5601 of this title.

Legislative History. For legislative history and purpose of Pub.L. 93–415, see 1974 U.S.Code Cong. and Adm.News, p. 5283.

Notes of Decisions

Construction with other laws   1
Dismissal   2

_____

1. Construction with other laws

This chapter was applicable to juvenile, who was 16 years old at time of incident in national park giving rise to first-degree murder charge, where indictment had not been tried by date of approval of this chapter; exposure of juvenile to mandatory treatment as an adult for offenses punishable by death or life imprisonment was not

a liability saved by section 109 of Title 1, the general savings provision. U. S. v. Azevedo, D.C. Hawaii 1975, 394 F.Supp. 852.

2. Dismissal

Although this chapter applied to defendant, who was 16 years old at time of incident in national park giving rise to first-degree murder charge and who had not been tried prior to approval of this chapter, proper remedy was not necessarily dismissal. U. S. v. Azevedo, D.C.Hawaii 1975, 394 F.Supp. 852.

§ 5603.   Definitions

For purposes of this chapter—

(1) the term "community based" facility, program, or service means a small, open group home or other suitable place located

near the juvenile's home or family and programs of community supervision and service which maintain community and consumer participation in the planning operation, and evaluation of their programs which may include, but are not limited to, medical, educational, vocational, social, and psychological guidance, training, counseling, alcoholism treatment, drug treatment, and other rehabilitative services;

(2) the term "Federal juvenile delinquency program" means any juvenile delinquency program which is conducted, directly, or indirectly, or is assisted by any Federal department or agency, including any program funded under this chapter;

(3) the term "juvenile delinquency program" means any program or activity related to juvenile delinquency prevention, control, diversion, treatment, rehabilitation, planning, education, training, and research, including drug and alcohol abuse programs; the improvement of the juvenile justice system; and any program or activity for neglected, abandoned, or dependent youth and other youth who are in danger of becoming delinquent;

(4) the term "Law Enforcement Assistance Administration" means the agency established by section 3711(a) of this title;

(5) the term "Administrator" means the agency head designated by section 3711(b) of this title;

(6) the term "law enforcement and criminal justice" means any activity pertaining to crime prevention, control, or reduction or the enforcement of the criminal law, including, but not limited to police efforts to prevent, control, or reduce crime or to apprehend criminals, activities of courts having criminal jurisdiction and related agencies (including prosecutorial and defender services, activities of corrections, probation, or parole authorities, and programs relating to the prevention, control, or reduction of juvenile delinquency or narcotic addiction;

(7) the term "State" means any State of the United States, the District of Columbia, the Commonwealth of Puerto Rico, the Trust Territory of the Pacific Islands, and any territory or possession of the United States;

(8) the term "unit of general local government" means any city, county, township, town, borough, parish, village, or other general purpose political subdivision of a State, an Indian tribe which performs law enforcement functions as determined by the Secretary of the Interior, or, for the purpose of assistance eligi-

bility, any agency of the District of Columbia government performing law enforcement functions in and for the District of Columbia and funds appropriated by the Congress for the activities of such agency may be used to provide the non-Federal share of the cost of programs or projects funded under this subchapter;

(9) the term "combination" as applied to States or units of general local government means any grouping or joining together of such States or units for the purpose of preparing, developing, or implementing a law enforcement plan;

(10) the term "construction" means acquistion, expansion, remodeling, and alteration of existing buildings, and initial equipment of any such buildings, or any combination of such activities (including architects' fees but not the cost of acquisition of land for buildings);

(11) the term "public agency" means any State, unit of local government, combination of such States or units, or any department, agency, or instrumentality of any of the foregoing;

(12) the term "correctional institution or facility" means any place for the confinement or rehabilitation of juvenile offenders or individuals charged with or convicted of criminal offenses; and

(13) the term "treatment" includes but is not limited to medical, educational, social, psychological, and vocational services, corrective and preventive guidance and training, and other rehabilitative services designed to protect the public and benefit the addict or other user by eliminating his dependence on addicting or other drugs or by controlling his dependence, and his susceptibility to addiction or use.

Pub.L. 93—415, Title I, § 103, Sept. 7, 1974, 88 Stat. 1111.

Historical Note

References in Text. "This chapter", referred to in text, was in the original "this Act", meaning Pub.L. 93—415, Sept. 7, 1974, 88 Stat. 1109. For complete classification of Pub.L. 93—415, see Short Title note under section 5601 of this title.

Effective Date. Section effective Sept. 7, 1974, see section 263 of Pub.L. 93—415, set out as a note under section 5601 of this title.

Legislative History. For legislative history and purpose of Pub.L. 93—415, see 1974 U.S.Code Cong. and Adm.News, p. 5283.

SUBCHAPTER II—PROGRAMS AND OFFICES

PART A—JUVENILE JUSTICE AND DELINQUENCY PREVENTION OFFICE

§ 5611. Establishment

Placement within Law Enforcement Assistance Administration, Department of Justice

(a) There is hereby created within the Department of Justice, Law Enforcement Assistance Administration, the Office of Juvenile Justice and Delinquency Prevention (referred to in this chapter as the "Office").

Administration of programs

(b) The programs authorized pursuant to this chapter unless otherwise specified in this chapter shall be administered by the Office established under this section.

Assistant Administrator; nomination by President

(c) There shall be at the head of the Office an Assistant Administrator who shall be nominated by the President by and with the advice and consent of the Senate.

Powers of Assistant Administrator

(d) The Assistant Administrator shall exercise all necessary powers, subject to the direction of the Administrator of the Law Enforcement Assistance Administration.

Deputy Assistant Administrator; appointment; general functions

(e) There shall be in the Office a Deputy Assistant Administrator who shall be appointed by the Administrator of the Law Enforcement Assistance Administration. The Deputy Assistant Administrator shall perform such functions as the Assistant Administrator from time to time assigns or delegates, and shall act as Assistant Administrator during the absence or disability of the Assistant Administrator or in the event of a vacancy in the Office of the Assistant Administrator.

Supervision of National Institute for Juvenile Justice and Delinquency Prevention

(f) There shall be established in the Office a Deputy Assistant Administrator who shall be appointed by the Administrator whose function shall be to supervise and direct the National Institute for Juvenile Justice and Delinquency Prevention established under section 5651 of this title.

Pub.L. 93—415, Title II, § 201(a)—(f), Sept. 7, 1974, 88 Stats. 1112, 1113.

Historical Note

References in Text. "This chapter", referred to in subsecs. (a) and (b), was in the original "this Act", meaning Pub.L. 93—415, Sept. 7, 1974, 88 Stat. 1109. For complete classification of Pub.L. 93—415, see Short Title note under section 5601 of this title.

Effective Date. Section effective Sept. 7, 1974, see section 263 of Pub.L. 93—415, set out as a note under section 5601 of this title.

Legislative History. For legislative history and purpose of Pub.L. 93—415, see 1974 U.S.Code Cong. and Adm.News, p. 5283.

Library References

Infants (West) 17.

C.J.S. Infants §§ 17, 18.

§ 5612. Personnel

Selection; employment; compensation

(a) The Administrator is authorized to select, employ, and fix the compensation of such officers and employees, including attorneys, as are necessary to perform the functions vested in him and to prescribe their functions.

Special personnel

(b) The Administrator is authorized to select, appoint, and employ not to exceed three officers and to fix their compensation at rates not to exceed the rate now or hereafter prescribed for GS-18 of the General Schedule by section 5332 of Title 5.

Personnel from other agencies

(c) Upon the request of the Administrator, the head of any Federal agency is authorized to detail, on a reimbursable basis, any of its personnel to the Assistant Administrator to assist him in carrying out his functions under this chapter.

Experts and consultants

(d) The Administrator may obtain services as authorized by section 3109 of Title 5, at rates not to exceed the rate now or hereafter prescribed for GS-18 of the General Schedule by section 5332 of Title 5.
Pub.L. 93—415, Title II, § 202, Sept. 7, 1974, 88 Stat. 1113.

Historical Note

References in Text. "This chapter", referred to in subsec. (c), was in the original "this Act", meaning Pub.L. 93—415, Sept. 7, 1974, 88 Stat. 1109. For complete classification of Pub.L. 93—415, see Short Title note under section 5601 of this title.

Codification. "Section 5332 of Title 5", referred to in subsec. (d), was, in the original "section 5332 of Title I" and has been editorially changed to conform to the apparent intent of Congress.

Effective Date. Section effective Sept. 7, 1974, see section 263 of Pub.L. 93–415, set out as a note under section 5601 of this title.

Legislative History. For legislative history and purpose of Pub.L. 93–415, see 1974 U.S.Code Cong. and Adm.News, p. 5283.

§ 5613.   Voluntary and uncompensated services

The Administrator is authorized to accept and employ, in carrying out the provisions of this chapter, voluntary and uncompensated services notwithstanding the provisions of section 665(b) of Title 31. Pub.L. 93–415, Title II, § 203, Sept. 7, 1974, 88 Stat. 1113.

Historical Note

References in Text. "This chapter", referred to in text, was in the original "this Act", meaning Pub.L. 93–415, Sept. 7, 1974, 88 Stat. 1109. For complete classification of Pub.L. 93–415, see Short Title note under section 5601 of this title.

Effective Date. Section effective Sept. 7, 1974, see section 263 of Pub.L. 93–415, set out as a note under section 5601 of this title.

Legislative History. For legislative history and purpose of Pub.L. 93–415, see 1974 U.S.Code Cong. and Adm.News, p. 5283.

§ 5614.   Concentration of federal efforts

Implementation of policy by Administrator; consultation with Council and Advisory Committee

(a) The Administrator shall implement overall policy and develop objectives and priorities for all Federal juvenile delinquency programs and activities relating to prevention, diversion, training, treatment, rehabilitation, evaluation, research, and improvement of the juvenile justice system in the United States. In carrying out his functions, the Administrator shall consult with the Council and the National Advisory Committee for Juvenile Justice and Delinquency Prevention.

Duties of Administrator

(b) In carrying out the purposes of this chapter, the Administrator shall—

(1) advise the President through the Attorney General as to all matters relating to federally assisted juvenile delinquency programs and Federal policies regarding juvenile delinquency;

(2) assist operating agencies which have direct responsibilities for the prevention and treatment of juvenile delinquency in

the development and promulgation of regulations, guidelines, requirements, criteria, standards, procedures, and budget requests in accordance with the policies, priorities, and objectives he establishes;

(3) conduct and support evaluations and studies of the performance and results achieved by Federal juvenile delinquency programs and activities and of the prospective performance and results that might be achieved by alternative programs and activities supplementary to or in lieu of those currently being administered;

(4) implement Federal juvenile delinquency programs and activities among Federal departments and agencies and between Federal juvenile delinquency programs and activities and other Federal programs and activities which he determines may have an important bearing on the success of the entire Federal juvenile delinquency effort;

(5) develop annually with the assistance of the Advisory Committee and submit to the President and the Congress, after the first year the legislation is enacted, prior to December 31 an analysis and evaluation of Federal juvenile delinquency programs conducted and assisted by Federal departments and agencies, the expenditures made, the results achieved, the plans developed, and problems in the operations and coordination of such programs. The report shall include recommendations for modifications in organization, management, personnel, standards, budget requests, and implementation plans necessary to increase the effectiveness of these programs;

(6) develop annually with the assistance of the Advisory Committee and submit to the President and the Congress, after the first year the legislation is enacted, prior to June 1, a comprehensive plan for Federal juvenile delinquency programs, with particular emphasis on the prevention of juvenile delinquency and the development of programs and services which will encourage increased diversion of juveniles from the traditional juvenile justice system; and

(7) provide technical assistance to Federal, State, and local governments, courts, public and private agencies, institutions, and individuals, in the planning, establishment, funding, operation, or evaluation of juvenile delinquency programs.

Report by President to Congress and Council; time for report

(c) The President shall, no later than ninety days after receiving each annual report under subsection (b)(5) of this section, submit a report to the Congress and to the Council containing a detailed statement of any action taken or anticipated with respect to recommendations made by each such annual report.

First and second annual reports of Administrator; contents

(d)(1) The first annual report submitted to the President and the Congress by the Administrator under subsection (b)(5) of this section shall contain, in addition to information required by subsection (b)(5) of this section, a detailed statement of criteria developed by the Administrator for identifying the characteristics of juvenile delinquency, juvenile delinquency prevention, diversion of youths from the juvenile justice system, and the training, treatment, and rehabilitation of juvenile delinquents.

(2) The second such annual report shall contain, in addition to information required by subsection (b)(5) of this section, an identification of Federal programs which are related to juvenile delinquency prevention or treatment, together with a statement of the moneys expended for each such program during the most recent complete fiscal year. Such identification shall be made by the Administrator through the use of criteria developed under paragraph (1).

Third annual report of Administrator; contents

(e) The third such annual report submitted to the President and the Congress by the Administrator under subsection (b)(6) of this section shall contain, in addition to the comprehensive plan required by subsection (b)(6) of this section, a detailed statement of procedures to be used with respect to the submission of juvenile delinquency development statements to the Administrator by Federal agencies under subsection ("l") of this section. Such statement submitted by the Administrator shall include a description of information, data, and analyses which shall be contained in each such development statement.

Information, reports, studies, and surveys from other agencies

(f) The Administrator may require, through appropriate authority, departments and agencies engaged in any activity involving any Federal juvenile delinquency program to provide him with such information and reports, and to conduct such studies and surveys, as he may deem to be necessary to carry out the purposes of this part.

Delegation of functions

(g) The Administrator may delegate any of his functions under this part, except the making of regulations, to any officer or employee of the Administration.

Utilization of services and facilities of other agencies; reimbursement

(h) The Administrator is authorized to utilize the services and facilities of any agency of the Federal Government and of any other public agency or institution in accordance with appropriate agreements, and to pay for such services either in advance or by way of reimbursement as may be agreed upon.

Transfer of funds to other agencies

(i) The Administrator is authorized to transfer funds appropriated under this subchapter to any agency of the Federal Government to develop or demonstrate new methods in juvenile delinquency prevention and rehabilitation and to supplement existing delinquency prevention and rehabilitation programs which the Assistant Administrator finds to be exceptionally effective or for which he finds there exists exceptional need.

Grants and contracts to other agencies, institutions and individuals

(j) The Administrator is authorized to make grants to, or enter into contracts with, any public or private agency, institution, or individual to carry out the purposes of this part.

Coordination of functions of Administrator and Secretary of Health, Education, and Welfare

(k) All functions of the Administrator under this part shall be coordinated as appropriate with the functions of the Secretary of the Department of Health, Education, and Welfare under the Juvenile Delinquency Prevention Act.

Annual juvenile delinquency development statements of other agencies; procedure; contents; review by Administrator

(l)(1) The Administrator shall require through appropriate authority each Federal agency which administers a Federal juvenile delinquency program which meets any criterion developed by the Administrator under subsection (d)(1) of this section to submit annually to the Council a juvenile delinquency development statement. Such statement shall be in addition to any information, report, study, or survey which the Administrator may require under subsection (f) of this section.

(2) Each juvenile delinquency development statement submitted to the Administrator under this subsection shall be submitted in accordance with procedures established by the Administrator under subsection (e) of this section and shall contain such information, data, and analyses as the Administrator may require under subsection (e) of this section. Such analyses shall include an analysis of the extent to which the juvenile delinquency program of the Federal agency submitting such development statement conforms with and furthers Federal juvenile delinquency prevention and treatment goals and policies.

(3) The Administrator shall review and comment upon each juvenile delinquency development statement transmitted to him under this subsection. Such development statement, together with the comments of the Administrator, shall be included by the Federal agency involved in every recommendation or request made by such agency for Federal legislation which significantly affects juvenile delinquency prevention and treatment.

Pub.L. 93–415, Title II, § 204, Sept. 7, 1974, 88 Stat. 1113; Pub.L. 94–273, §§ 8(3), 12(3), Apr. 21, 1976, 90 Stat. 378.

Historical Note

References in Text. "This chapter", referred to in subsec. (b), was in the original "this Act", meaning Pub.L. 93–415, Sept. 7, 1974, 88 Stat. 1109. For complete classification of Pub.L. 93–415, see Short Title note under section 5601 of this title.

The Juvenile Delinquency Prevention Act, referred to in subsec. (k), is classified to chapter 47 (section 3801 et seq.) of this title.

1976 Amendment. Subsec. (b)(5). Pub. L. 94–273, § 8(3), substituted "December 31" for "September 30".

Subsec. (b)(6). Pub.L. 94–273, § 12(3), substituted "June" for "March".

Effective Date. Section effective Sept. 7, 1974, except that subsecs. (b)(5) and (b)(6) effective at the close of the thirty-first day of the twelfth calendar month of 1974, and subsec. (l) effective at the close of the thirtieth day of the eleventh calendar month of 1976, see section 263 of Pub.L. 93–415, set out as a note under section 5601 of this title.

Legislative History. For legislative history and purpose of Pub.L. 93–415, see 1974 U.S.Code Cong. and Adm.News, p. 5283. See, also, Pub.L. 94–273, 1976 U.S. Code Cong. and Adm.News, p. 690.

§ 5615. Joint funding; non-Federal share requirements

Notwithstanding any other provision of law, where funds are made available by more than one Federal agency to be used by any agency, organization, institution, or individual to carry out a Federal juvenile delinquency program or activity, any one of the Federal agencies providing funds may be requested by the Administrator to act for all in administering the funds advanced. In such cases, a single non-Federal share requirement may be established according to the proportion of funds advanced by each Federal agency, and the Administrator may order any such agency to waive any technical grant or contract requirement (as defined in such regulations) which is inconsistent with the similar requirement of the administering agency or which the administering agency does not impose.

Pub.L. 93–415, Title II, § 205, Sept. 7, 1974, 88 Stat. 1116.

Historical Note

Effective Date. Section effective Sept. 7, 1974, see section 263 of Pub.L. 93–415, set out as a note under section 5601 of this title.

Legislative History. For legislative history and purpose of Pub.L. 93–415, see 1974 U.S.Code Cong. and Adm.News, p. 5283.

§ 5616.   Coordinating Council on Juvenile Justice and Delinquency Prevention

Establishment; membership

(a)(1) There is hereby established, as an independent organization in the executive branch of the Federal Government a Coordinating Council on Juvenile Justice and Delinquency Prevention (hereinafter referred to as the "Council") composed of the Attorney General, the Secretary of Health, Education, and Welfare, the Secretary of Labor, the Director of the Office of Drug Abuse Policy, the Secretary of Housing and Urban Development, or their respective designees, the Assistant Administrator of the Office of Juvenile Justice and Delinquency Prevention, the Deputy Assistant Administrator of the Institute for Juvenile Justice and Delinquency Prevention, and representatives of such other agencies as the President shall designate.

(2) Any individual designated under this section shall be selected from individuals who exercise significant decisionmaking authority in the Federal agency involved.

Chairman and Vice Chairman

(b) The Attorney General shall serve as Chairman of the Council. The Assistant Administrator of the Office of Juvenile Justice and Delinquency Prevention shall serve as Vice Chairman of the Council. The Vice Chairman shall act as Chairman in the absence of the Chairman.

Functions

(c) The function of the Council shall be to coordinate all Federal juvenile delinquency programs. The Council shall make recommendations to the Attorney General and the President at least annually with respect to the coordination of overall policy and development of objectives and priorities for all Federal juvenile delinquency programs and activities.

Meetings

(d) The Council shall meet a minimum of six times per year and a description of the activities of the Council shall be included in the annual report required by section 5614(b)(5) of this title.

Executive Secretary of Council; appointment; responsibilities

(e)(1) The Chairman shall, with the approval of the Council, appoint an Executive Secretary of the Council.

(2) The Executive Secretary shall be responsible for the day-to-day administration of the Council.

(3) The Executive Secretary may, with the approval of the Council, appoint such personnel as he considers necessary to carry out the purposes of this subchapter.

Expenses of Council members; reimbursement

(f) Members of the Council who are employed by the Federal Government full time shall be reimbursed for travel, subsistence, and other necessary expenses incurred by them in carrying out the duties of the Council.

Authorization of appropriations

(g) To carry out the purposes of this section there is authorized to be appropriated such sums as may be necessary.

Pub.L. 93–415, Title II, § 206, Sept. 7, 1974, 88 Stat. 1116; Pub.L. 94–237, § 4(c)(5)(D), Mar. 19, 1976, 90 Stat. 244.

Historical Note

1976 Amendment. Subsec. (a)(1). Pub. L. 94–237 substituted "Office of Drug Abuse Policy" for "Special Action Office for Drug Abuse Prevention".

Legislative History. For legislative history and purpose of Pub.L. 93–415, see 1974 U.S.Code Cong. and Adm.News, p. 5283. See, also, Pub.L. 94–273, 1976 U.S. Code Cong. and Adm.News, p. 690.

§ 5617.　National Advisory Committee for Juvenile Justice and Delinquency Prevention

Membership

(a) There is hereby established a National Advisory Committee for Juvenile Justice and Delinquency Prevention (hereinafter referred to as the "Advisory Committee") which shall consist of twenty-one members.

Members of Coordinating Council as ex officio members

(b) The members of the Coordinating Council or their respective designees shall be ex officio members of the Committee.

Regular members; appointment; qualifications

(c) The regular members of the Advisory Committee shall be appointed by the President from persons who by virtue of their training or experience have special knowledge concerning the prevention and treatment of juvenile delinquency or the administration of juvenile justice, such as juvenile or family court judges; probation, correctional, or law enforcement personnel; and representatives of private voluntary organizations and community-based programs. The President shall designate the Chairman. A majority of the members of the Advisory Committee, including the Chairman, shall not be full-time employees of Federal, State, or local governments. At least seven members shall not have attained twenty-six years of age on the date of their appointment.

Term of office; time of appointment; reappointment; vacancies

(d) Members appointed by the President to the Committee shall serve for terms of four years and shall be eligible for reappointment except that for the first composition of the Advisory Committee, one-third of these members shall be appointed to one-year terms, one-third to two-year terms, and one-third to three-year terms; thereafter each term shall be four years. Such members shall be appointed within ninety days after September 7, 1974. Any members appointed to fill a vacancy occurring prior to the expiration of the term for which his predecessor was appointed, shall be appointed for the remainder of such term.

Pub.L. 93–415, Title II, § 207, Sept. 7, 1974, 88 Stat. 1117.

Historical Note

Effective Date. Section effective Sept. 7, 1974, see section 263 of Pub.L. 93–415, set out as a note under section 5601 of this title.

Legislative History. For legislative history and purpose of Pub.L. 93–415, see 1974 U.S.Code Cong. and Adm.News, p. 5283.

§ 5618. Duties of Advisory Committee

Meetings

(a) The Advisory Committee shall meet at the call of the Chairman, but not less than four times a year.

Recommendations to Administrator

(b) The Advisory Committee shall make recommendations to the Administrator at least annually with respect to planning, policy, priorities, operations, and management of all Federal juvenile delinquency programs.

Subcommittee for advice on particular functions

(c) The Chairman may designate a subcommittee of the members of the Advisory Committee to advise the Administrator on particular functions or aspects of the work of the Administration.

Subcommittee to serve on Advisory Committee for National Institute for Juvenile Justice and Delinquency Prevention

(d) The Chairman shall designate a subcommittee of five members of the Committee to serve, together with the Director of the National Institute of Corrections, as members of an Advisory Committee for the National Institute for Juvenile Justice and Delinquency Prevention to perform the functions set forth in section 5655 of this title.

Subcommittee to serve as Advisory Committee to Administrator on Standards for Administration of Juvenile Justice

(e) The Chairman shall designate a subcommittee of five members of the Committee to serve as an Advisory Committee to the Administrator on Standards for the Administration of Juvenile Justice to perform the functions set forth in section 5657 of this title.

Appointment of personnel

(f) The Chairman, with the approval of the Committee, shall appoint such personnel as are necessary to carry out the duties of the Advisory Committee.

Pub.L. 93–415, Title II, § 208, Sept. 7, 1974, 88 Stat. 1117.

Historical Note

Effective Date. Section effective Sept. 7, 1974, see section 263 of Pub.L. 93–415, set out as a note under section 5601 of this title.

Legislative History. For legislative history and purpose of Pub.L. 93–415, see 1974 U.S.Code Cong. and Adm.News, p. 5283.

§ 5619. Compensation and expenses

(a) Members of the Advisory Committee who are employed by the Federal Government full time shall serve without compensation but shall be reimbursed for travel, subsistence, and other necessary expenses incurred by them in carrying out the duties of the Advisory Committee.

(b) Members of the Advisory Committee not employed full time by the Federal Government shall receive compensation at a rate not to exceed the rate now or hereafter prescribed for GS-18 of the General Schedule by section 5332 of Title 5, including traveltime for each day they are engaged in the performance of their duties as members of the Advisory Committee. Members shall be entitled to reimbursement for travel, subsistence, and other necessary expenses incurred by them in carrying out the duties of the Advisory Committee.

Pub.L. 93–415, Title II, § 209, Sept. 7, 1974, 88 Stat. 1118.

Historical Note

Effective Date. Section effective Sept. 7, 1974, see section 263 of Pub.L. 93–415, set out as a note under section 5601 of this title.

Legislative History. For legislative history and purpose of Pub.L. 93–415, see 1974 U.S.Code Cong. and Adm.News, p. 5283.

PART B—FEDERAL ASSISTANCE FOR STATE AND LOCAL PROGRAMS
Subpart I—Formula Grants

§ 5631. Grants to States and local governments

The Administrator is authorized to make grants to States and local governments to assist them in planning, establishing, operating, coordinating, and evaluating projects directly or through contracts with public and private agencies for the development of more effective education, training, research, prevention, diversion, treatment, and rehabilitation programs in the area of juvenile delinquency and programs to improve the juvenile justice system.

Pub.L. 93–415, Title II, § 221, Sept. 7, 1974, 88 Stat. 1118.

Historical Note

Effective Date. Section effective Sept. 7, 1974, see section 263 of Pub.L. 93–415, set out as a note under section 5601 of this title.

Legislative History. For legislative history and purpose of Pub.L. 93–415, see 1974 U.S.Code Cong. and Adm.News, p. 5283.

Library References

United States (West) 82.

C.J.S. United States § 122.

§ 5632. Allocation of funds

Time; basis; amounts

(a) In accordance with regulations promulgated under this part, funds shall be allocated annually among the States on the basis of relative population of people under age eighteen. No such allotment to any State shall be less than $200,000, except that for the Virgin Islands, Guam, American Samoa, and the Trust Territory of the Pacific Islands no allotment shall be less than $50,000.

Reallocation of unobligated funds

(b) Except for funds appropriated for fiscal year 1975, if any amount so allotted remains unobligated at the end of the fiscal year, such funds shall be reallocated in a manner equitable and consistent with the purpose of this part. Funds appropriated for fiscal year 1975 may be obligated in accordance with subsection (a) of this section until June 30, 1976, after which time they may be reallocated. Any amount so reallocated shall be in addition to the amounts already allotted and available to the State, the Virgin Islands, American Samoa, Guam, and the Trust Territory of the Pacific Islands for the same period.

Use of allotted funds for development of state plans; limitations

(c) In accordance with regulations promulgated under this part, a portion of any allotment to any State under this part shall be available to develop a State plan and to pay that portion of the expenditures which are necessary for efficient administration. Not more than 15 per centum of the total annual allotment of such State shall be available for such purposes. The State shall make available needed funds for planning and administration to local governments within the State on an equitable basis.

Limitations on financial assistance

(d) Financial assistance extended under the provisions of this section shall not exceed 90 per centum of the approved costs of any assisted programs or activities. The non-Federal share shall be made in cash or kind consistent with the maintenance of programs required by section 5671 of this title.

Pub.L. 93–415, Title II, § 222, Sept. 7, 1974, 88 Stat. 1118.

Historical Note

Effective Date. Section effective Sept. 7, 1974, see section 263 of Pub.L. 93–415, set out as a note under section 5601 of this title.

Legislative History. For legislative history and purpose of Pub.L. 93–415, se 1974 U.S.Code Cong. and Adm.News, p. 5283.

§ 5633.   State plans

Requirements

(a) In order to receive formula grants under this part, a State shall submit a plan for carrying out its purposes consistent with the provisions of section 3733(a)(1), (3), (5), (6), (8), (10), (11), (12), (15), and (17) of this title. In accordance with regulations established under this subchapter, such plan must—

(1) designate the State planning agency established by the State under section 3723 of this title as the sole agency for supervising the preparation and administration of the plan;

(2) contain satisfactory evidence that the State agency designated in accordance with paragraph (1) (hereafter referred to in this part as the "State planning agency") has or will have authority, by legislation if necessary, to implement such plan in conformity with this part;

(3) provide for an advisory group appointed by the chief executive of the State to advise the State planning agency and its supervisory board (A) which shall consist of not less than twenty-one and not more than thirty-three persons who have training, experience, or special knowledge concerning the prevention and treatment of juvenile delinquency or the administration of juvenile justice, (B) which shall include representation of units of local government, law enforcement and juvenile justice agencies such as law enforcement, correction or probation personnel, and juvenile or family court judges, and public agencies concerned with delinquency prevention or treatment such as welfare, social services, mental health, education, or youth services departments, (C) which shall include representatives of private organizations concerned with delinquency prevention or treatment; concerned with neglected or dependent children; concerned with the qual-

ity of juvenile justice, education, or social services for children; which utilize volunteers to work with delinquents or potential delinquents; community-based delinquency prevention or treatment programs; and organizations which represent employees affected by this chapter, (D) a majority of whose members (including the chairman) shall not be full-time employees of the Federal, State, or local government, and (E) at least one-third of whose members shall be under the age of twenty-six at the time of appointment;

(4) provide for the active consultation with and participation of local governments in the development of a State plan which adequately takes into account the needs and requests of local governments;

(5) provide that at least 66⅔ per centum of the funds received by the State under section 5632 of this title shall be expended through programs of local government insofar as they are consistent with the State plan, except that this provision may be waived at the discretion of the Administrator for any State if the services for delinquent or potentially delinquent youth are organized primarily on a statewide basis;

(6) provide that the chief executive officer of the local government shall assign responsibility for the preparation and administration of the local government's part of a State plan, or for the supervision of the preparation and administration of the local government's part of the State plan, to that agency within the local government's structure (hereinafter in this part referred to as the "local agency") which can most effectively carry out the purposes of this part and shall provide for supervision of the programs funded under this part by that local agency;

(7) provide for an equitable distribution of the assistance received under section 5632 of this title within the State;

(8) set forth a detailed study of the State needs for an effective, comprehensive, coordinated approach to juvenile delinquency prevention and treatment and the improvement of the juvenile justice system. This plan shall include itemized estimated costs for the development and implementation of such programs;

(9) provide for the active consultation with and participation of private agencies in the development and execution of the State plan; and provide for coordination and maximum utilization of existing juvenile delinquency programs and other related pro-

grams, such as education, health, and welfare within the State;

(10) provide that not less than 75 per centum of the funds available to such State under section 5632 of this title, whether expended directly by the State or by the local government or through contracts with public or private agencies, shall be used for advanced techniques in developing, maintaining, and expanding programs and services designed to prevent juvenile delinquency, to divert juveniles from the juvenile justice system, and to provide community-based alternatives to juvenile detention and correctional facilities. That advanced techniques include—

(A) community-based programs and services for the prevention and treatment of juvenile delinquency through the development of foster-care and shelter-care homes, group homes, halfway houses, homemaker and home health services, and any other designated community-based diagnostic, treatment, or rehabilitative service;

(B) community-based programs and services to work with parents and other family members to maintain and strengthen the family unit so that the juvenile may be retained in his home;

(C) youth service bureaus and other community-based programs to divert youth from the juvenile court or to support, counsel, or provide work and recreational opportunities for delinquents and youth in danger of becoming delinquent;

(D) comprehensive programs of drug and alcohol abuse education and prevention and programs for the treatment and rehabilitation of drug addicted youth, and "drug dependent" youth (as defined in section 201(q) of this title);

(E) educational programs or supportive services designed to keep delinquents and to encourage other youth to remain in elementary and secondary schools or in alternative learning situations;

(F) expanded use of probation and recruitment and training of probation officers, other professional and paraprofessional personnel and volunteers to work effectively with youth;

(G) youth initiated programs and outreach programs designed to assist youth who otherwise would not be reached by assistance programs;

(H) provides for a statewide program through the use of

probation subsidies, other subsidies, other financial incentives or disincentives to units of local government, or other effective means, that may include but are not limited to programs designed to—

(i) reduce the number of commitments of juveniles to any form of juvenile facility as a percentage of the State juvenile population;

(ii) increase the use of nonsecure community-based facilities as a percentage of total commitments to juvenile facilities; and

(iii) discourage the use of secure incarceration and detention;

(11) provides for the development of an adequate research, training, and evaluation capacity within the State;

(12) provide within two years after submission of the plan that juveniles who are charged with or who have committed offenses that would not be criminal if committed by an adult, shall not be placed in juvenile detention or correctional facilities, but must be placed in shelter facilities;

(13) provide that juveniles alleged to be or found to be delinquent shall not be detained or confined in any institution in which they have regular contact with adult persons incarcerated because they have been convicted of a crime or are awaiting trial on criminal charges;

(14) provide for an adequate system of monitoring jails, detention facilities, and correctional facilities to insure that the requirements of paragraphs (12) and (13) are met, and for annual reporting of the results of such monitoring to the Administrator;

(15) provide assurance that assistance will be available on an equitable basis to deal with all disadvantaged youth including, but not limited to, females, minority youth, and mentally retarded and emotionally or physically handicapped youth;

(16) provide for procedures to be established for protecting the rights of recipients of services and for assuring appropriate privacy with regard to records relating to such services provided to any individual under the State plan;

(17) provide that fair and equitable arrangements are made to protect the interests of employees affected by assistance under this chapter. Such protective arrangements shall, to the maximum extent feasible, include, without being limited to, such pro-

visions as may be necessary for—

(A) the preservation or rights, privileges, and benefits (including continuation of pension rights and benefits) under existing collective-bargaining agreements or otherwise;

(B) the continuation of collective-bargaining rights;

(C) the protection of individual employees against a worsening of their positions with respect to their employment;

(D) assurances of employment to employees of any State or political subdivision thereof who will be affected by any program funded in whole or in part under provisions of this chapter;

(E) training or retraining programs.

The State plan shall provide for the terms and conditions of the protection arrangements established pursuant to this section;

(18) provide for such fiscal control and fund accounting procedures necessary to assure prudent use, proper disbursement, and accurate accounting of funds received under this subchapter;

(19) provide reasonable assurance that Federal funds made available under this part for any period will be so used as to supplement and increase (but not supplant), to the extent feasible and practical, the level of the State, local, and other non-Federal funds that would in the absence of such Federal funds be made available for the programs described in this part, and will in no event replace such State, local, and other non-Federal funds;

(20) provide that the State planning agency will from time to time, but not less often then annually, review its plan and submit to the Administrator an analysis and evaluation of the effectiveness of the programs and activities carried out under the plan, and any modifications in the plan, including the survey of State and local needs, which it considers necessary; and

(21) contain such other terms and conditions as the Administrator may reasonably prescribe to assure the effectiveness of the programs assisted under this subchapter.

Such plan may at the discretion of the Administrator be incorporated into the plan specified in section 3733(a) of this title.

Approval by State planning agency

(b) The State planning agency designated pursuant to subsection (a) of this section, after consultation with the advisory group referred to in subsection (a) of this section, shall approve the State plan and any modification thereof prior to submission to the Administrator.

Approval by Administrator

(c) The Administrator shall approve any State plan and any modification thereof that meets the requirements of this section.

Failure to submit or qualify plan; expenditure of allotted funds

(d) In the event that any State fails to submit a plan, or submits a plan or any modification thereof, which the Administrator, after reasonable notice and opportunity for hearing, in accordance with sections 3757, 3758, and 3759 of this title, determines does not meet the requirements of this section, the Administrator shall make that State's allotment under the provisions of section 5632(a) of this title available to public and private agencies for special emphasis prevention and treatment programs as defined in section 5634 of this title.

Disqualification of plan by neglect or oversight; expenditure of allotted funds

(e) In the event the plan does not meet the requirements of this section due to oversight or neglect, rather than explicit and conscious decision, the Administrator shall endeavor to make that State's allotment under the provisions of section 5632(a) of this title available to public and private agencies in that State for special emphasis prevention and treatment programs as defined in section 5634 of this title. Pub.L. 93–415, Title II, § 223, Sept. 7, 1974, 88 Stat. 1119; Pub.L. 94–503, Title I, § 130(b), Oct. 15, 1976, 90 Stat. 2425.

Historical Note

References in Text. "This chapter", referred to in subsec. (a)(17)(D), was in the original "this Act", meaning Pub.L. 93–415, Sept. 7, 1974, 88 Stat. 1109. For complete classification of Pub.L. 93–415, see short Title note under section 5601 of this title.

1976 Amendment. Subsec. (a). Pub.L. 94–503, substituted "(15), and (17)" for "and (15)" in the provisions preceding par. (1).

Effective Date. Section effective Sept. 7, 1974, see section 263 of Pub.L. 93–415, set out as a note under section 5601 of this title.

Legislative History. For legislative history and purpose of Pub.L. 93–415, see 1974 U.S.Code Cong. and Adm.News, p. 5283. See, also, Pub.L. 94–503, 1976 U.S. Code Cong. and Adm.News, p. 5374.

Subpart II—Special Emphasis Prevention and Treatment Programs

§ 5634. Funding

Grants and contracts to public and private agencies, organizations, etc.; purpose

(a) The Administrator is authorized to make grants to and enter into contracts with public and private agencies, organizations, institutions, or individuals to—

    (1) develop and implement new approaches, techniques, and methods with respect to juvenile delinquency programs;

    (2) develop and maintain community-based alternatives to traditional forms of institutionalization;

    (3) develop and implement effective means of diverting juveniles from the traditional juvenile justice and correctional system;

    (4) improve the capability of public and private agencies and organizations to provide services for delinquents and youths in danger of becoming delinquent;

    (5) facilitate the adoption of the recommendations of the Advisory Committee on Standards for Juvenile Justice and the Institute as set forth pursuant to section 5657 of this title; and

    (6) develop and implement model programs and methods to keep students in elementary and secondary schools and to prevent unwarranted and arbitrary suspensions and expulsions.

Limitations on availability of appropriated funds

(b) Not less than 25 per centum or more than 50 per centum of the funds appropriated for each fiscal year pursuant to this part shall be available only for special emphasis prevention and treatment grants and contracts made pursuant to this section.

Availability of funds for private agencies, etc.

(c) At least 20 per centum of the funds available for grants and contracts made pursuant to this section shall be available for grants and contracts to private nonprofit agencies, organizations, or institutions who have had experience in dealing with youth.

Pub.L. 93–415, Title II, § 224, Sept. 7, 1974, 88 Stat. 1122.

Historical Note

Effective Date. Section effective Sept. 7, 1974, see section 263 of Pub.L. 93–415, set out as a note under section 5601 of this title.

Legislative History. For legislative history and purpose of Pub.L. 93–415, see 1974 U.S.Code Cong. and Adm.News, p. 5283.

§ 5635. Applications for grants and contracts

Time and manner prescribed by Administrator

(a) Any agency, institution, or individual desiring to receive a grant, or enter into any contract under section 5634 of this title, shall submit an application at such time, in such manner, and containing or accompanied by such information as the Administrator may prescribe.

Contents

(b) In accordance with guidelines established by the Administrator, each such application shall—

(1) provide that the program for which assistance is sought will be administered by or under the supervision of the applicant;

(2) set forth a program for carrying out one or more of the purposes set forth in section 5634 of this title;

(3) provide for the proper and efficient administration of such program;

(4) provide for regular evaluation of the program.

(5) indicate that the applicant has requested the review of the application from the State planning agency and local agency designated in section 5633 of this title, when appropriate, and indicate the response of such agency to the request for review and comment on the application;

(6) provide that regular reports on the program shall be sent to the Administrator and to the State planning agency and local agency, when appropriate;

(7) provide for such fiscal control and fund accounting procedures as may be necessary to assure prudent use, proper disbursement, and accurate accounting of funds received under this subchapter; and

(8) indicate the response of the State agency or the local agency to the request for review and comment on the application.

Approval by Administrator; criteria

(c) In determining whether or not to approve applications for grants under section 5634 of this title, the Administrator shall consider—

(1) the relative cost and effectiveness of the proposed pro-

gram in effectuating the purposes of this part;

(2) the extent to which the proposed program will incorporate new or innovative techniques;

(3) the extent to which the proposed program meets the objectives and priorities of the State plan, when a State plan has been approved by the Administrator under section 5633(c) of this title and when the location and scope of the program makes such consideration appropriate;

(4) the increase in capacity of the public and private agency, institution, or individual to provide services to delinquents or youths in danger of becoming delinquents;

(5) the extent to which the proposed project serves communities which have high rates of youth unemployment, school dropout, and delinquency; and

(6) the extent to which the proposed program facilitates the implementation of the recommendations of the Advisory Committee on Standards for Juvenile Justice as set forth pursuant to section 5657 of this title.[1]

(7) the adverse impact that may result from the restriction of eligibility, based upon population, for cities with a population greater than forty thousand, located within States which have not[2] city with a population over two hundred and fifty thousand.

Application by city

(d) No city should be denied an application solely on the basis of its population.

Pub.L. 93–415, Title II, § 225, Sept. 7, 1974, 88 Stat. 1123; Pub.L. 94–503, Title I, § 130(c), Oct. 15, 1976, 90 Stat. 2425.

1 So in original. Probably should be a semicolon instead of a period.
2 So in original. Probably should read "no".

Historical Note

1976 Amendment. Subsec. (c)(7). Pub. L. 94–503, § 130(c)(1), added subsec. (c) (7).

Subsec. (d) Pub.L. 94–503, § 130(c)(2), added subsec. (d).

Effective Date. Section effective Sept. 7, 1974, see section 263 of Pub.L. 93–415, set out as a note under section 5601 of this title.

Legislative History. For legislative history and purpose of Pub.L. 93–415, see 1974 U.S.Code Cong. and Adm.News, p. 5283. See, also, Pub.L. 94–503, 1976 U.S. Code Cong. and Adm.News, p. 5374.

§ 5636. Noncompliance of program or activity; proceedings by Administrator

Whenever the Administrator, after giving reasonable notice and opportunity for hearing to a recipient of financial assistance under this subchapter, finds—

(1) that the program or activity for which such grant was made has been so changed that it no longer complies with the provisions of this subchapter; or

(2) that in the operation of the program or activity there is failure to comply substantially with any such provision;

the Administrator shall initiate such proceedings as are appropriate.

Pub.L. 93—415, Title II, § 226, Sept. 7, 1974, 88 Stat. 1124.

Historical Note

Effective Date. Section effective Sept. 7, 1974, see section 263 of Pub.L. 93—415, set out as a note under section 5601 of this title.

Legislative History. For legislative history and purpose of Pub.L. 93—415, see 1974 U.S.Code Cong. and Adm.News, p. 5283.

§ 5637. Use of funds; limitations

(a) Funds paid pursuant to this subchapter to any State, public or private agency, institution, or individual (whether directly or through a State or local agency) may be used for—

(1) planning, developing, or operating the program designed to carry out the purposes of this part; and

(2) not more than 50 per centum of the cost of the construction of innovative community-based facilities for less than twenty persons which, in the judgment of the Administrator, are necessary for carrying out the purposes of this part.

(b) Except as provided by subsection (a) of this section, no funds paid to any public or private agency, institution, or individual under this part (whether directly or through a State agency or local agency) may be used for construction.

Pub.L. 93—415, Title II, § 227, Sept. 7, 1974, 88 Stat. 1124.

Historical Note

Effective Date. Section effective Sept. 7, 1974, see section 263 of Pub.L. 93—415, set out as a note under section 5601 of this title.

Legislative History. For legislative history and purpose of Pub.L. 93--415, see 1974 U.S.Code Cong. and Adm.News, p. 5283.

§ 5638. Continuing financial assistance for programs

Congressional statement of policy

(a) In accordance with criteria established by the Administrator, it is the policy of Congress that programs funded under this subchapter shall continue to receive financial assistance providing that the yearly evaluation of such programs is satisfactory.

Utilization of formula grant funds; limitations

(b) At the discretion of the Administrator, when there is no other way to fund an essential juvenile delinquency program not funded under this part, the State may utilize 25 per centum of the formula grant funds available to it under this part to meet the non-Federal matching share requirement for any other Federal juvenile delinquency program grant.

Contributions by recipient

(c) Whenever the Administrator determines that it will contribute to the purposes of this part, he may require the recipient of any grant or contract to contribute money, facilities, or services.

Methods of payment

(d) Payments under this part, pursuant to a grant or contract, may be made (after necessary adjustment, in the case of grants, on account of previously made overpayments or underpayments) in advance or by way of reimbursements, in such installments and on such conditions as the Administrator may determine.

Pub.L. 93—415, Title II, § 228, Sept. 7, 1974, 88 Stat. 1124.

Historical Note

Effective Date. Section effective Sept. 7, 1974, see section 263 of Pub.L. 93—415, set out as a note under section 5601 of this title.

Legislative History. For legislative history and purpose of Pub.L. 93—415, see 1974 U.S.Code Cong. and Adm. News, p. 5283.

Part C—National Institute for Juvenile Justice and Delinquency Prevention

§ 5651. Institute structure and operation

Establishment

(a) There is hereby established within the Juvenile Justice and Delinquency Prevention Office a National Institute for Juvenile Justice and Delinquency Prevention.

Deputy Assistant Administrator as head; supervision and direction by Assistant Administrator

(b) The National Institute for Juvenile Justice and Delinquency

Prevention shall be under the supervision and direction of the Assistant Administrator, and shall be headed by a Deputy Assistant Administrator of the Office appointed under section 5611(f) of this title.

Coordination of activities with National Institute of Law Enforcement and Criminal Justice

(c) The activities of the National Institute for Juvenile Justice and Delinquency Prevention shall be coordinated with the activities of the National Institute of Law Enforcement and Criminal Justice in accordance with the requirements of section 5611(b) of this title.

Responsibilities of Administrator

(d) The Administrator shall have responsibility for the administration of the organization, employees, enrollees, financial affairs, and other operations of the Institute.

Delegation of power by Administrator

(e) The Administrator may delegate his power under this chapter to such employees of the Institute as he deems appropriate.

Purpose of Institute

(f) It shall be the purpose of the Institute to provide a coordinating center for the collection, preparation, and dissemination of useful data regarding the treatment and control of juvenile offenders, and it shall also be the purpose of the Institute to provide training for representatives of Federal, State, and local law enforcement officers, teachers, and other educational personnel, juvenile welfare workers, juvenile judges and judicial personnel, probation personnel, correctional personnel and other persons, including lay personnel, connected with the treatment and control of juvenile offenders.

Additional powers

(g) In addition to the other powers, express and implied, the Institute may —

(1) request any Federal agency to supply such statistics, data, program reports, and other material as the Institute deems necessary to carry out its functions;

(2) arrange with and reimburse the heads of Federal agencies for the use of personnel or facilities or equipment of such agencies;

(3) confer with and avail itself of the cooperation, services, records, and facilities of State, municipal, or other public or

local agencies;

(4) enter into contracts with public or private agencies, organizations, or individuals, for the partial performance of any functions of the Institute; and

(5) compensate consultants and members of technical advisory councils who are not in the regular full-time employ of the United States, at a rate now or hereafter prescribed for GS-18 of the General Schedule by section 5332 of Title 5 and while away from home, or regular place of business, they may be allowed travel expenses, including per diem in lieu of subsistence, as authorized by section 5703 of Title 5 for persons in the Government service employed intermittently.

Cooperation of other federal agencies

(h) Any Federal agency which receives a request from the Institute under subsection (g)(1) of this section may cooperate with the Institute and shall, to the maximum extent practicable, consult with and furnish information and advice to the Institute.

Pub.L. 93–415, Title II, § 241, Sept. 7, 1974, 88 Stat. 1125.

Historical Note

References in Text. "This chapter", referred to in subsec. (e), was in the original "this Act", meaning Pub.L. 93–415, Sept. 7, 1974, 88 Stat. 1109. For complete classification of Pub.L. 93–415, see Short Title note under section 5601 of this title.

Codification. Subsec. (h) of this section was, in the original, designated as "(b)" and has been editorially changed to conform to the apparent intent of Congress.

Effective Date. Section effective Sept. 7, 1974, see section 263 of Pub.L. 93–415, set out as a note under section 5601 of this title.

Legislative History. For legislative history and purpose of Pub.L. 93–415, se 1974 U.S.Code Cong. and Adm.News, p. 5283.

Library References

Infants (West) 13, 16, 17.

C.J.S. Infants §§ 11 et seq., 17, 18, 93 et seq.

§ 5652. Information function of Institute

The National Institute for Juvenile Justice and Delinquency Prevention is authorized to—

(1) serve as an information bank by collecting systematically and synthesizing the data and knowledge obtained from studies and research by public and private agencies, institutions, or individuals concerning all aspects of juvenile delinquency, including the prevention and treatment of juvenile delinquency;

(2) serve as a clearinghouse and information center for the preparation, publication, and dissemination of all information regarding juvenile delinquency, including State and local juvenile delinquency prevention and treatment programs and plans, availability of resources, training and educational programs, statistics, and other pertinent data and information.

Pub.L. 93--415, Title II, § 242, Sept. 7, 1974, 88 Stat. 1126.

Historical Note

Effective Date. Section effective Sept. 7, 1974, see section 263 of Pub.L. 93—415, set out as a note under section 5601 of this title.

Legislative History. For legislative history and purpose of Pub.L. 93—415, see 1974 U.S.Code Cong. and Adm.News, p. 5283.

§ 5653. Research, demonstration, and evaluation functions of Institute

The National Institute for Juvenile Justice and Delinquency Prevention is authorized to—

(1) conduct, encourage, and coordinate research and evaluation into any aspect of juvenile delinquency, particularly with regard to new programs and methods which show promise of making a contribution toward the prevention and treatment of juvenile delinquency;

(2) encourage the development of demonstration projects in new, innovative techniques and methods to prevent and treat juvenile delinquency;

(3) provide for the evaluation of all juvenile delinquency programs assisted under this subchapter in order to determine the results and the effectiveness of such programs;

(4) provide for the evaluation of any other Federal, State, or local juvenile delinquency program, upon the request of the Administrator;

(5) prepare, in cooperation with educational institutions, Federal, State, and local agencies, and appropriate individuals and private agencies, such studies as it considers to be necessary with respect to the prevention and treatment of juvenile delinquency and related matters, including recommendations designed to promote effective prevention and treatment;

(6) disseminate the results of such evaluations and research and demonstration activities particularly to persons actively working in the field of juvenile delinquency; and

(7) disseminate pertinent data and studies (including a periodic journal) to individuals, agencies, and organizations concerned with the prevention and treatment of juvenile delinquency.

Pub.L. 93—415, Title II, § 243, Sept. 7, 1974, 88 Stat. 1126.

Historical Note

Effective Date. Section effective Sept. 7, 1974, see section 263 of Pub.L. 93—415, set out as a note under section 5601 of this title.

Legislative History. For legislative history and purpose of Pub.L. 93—415, see 1974 U.S.Code Cong. and Adm.News, p. 5283.

§ 5654. Training function of Institute

The National Institute for Juvenile Justice and Delinquency Prevention is authorized to—

(1) develop, conduct, and provide for training programs for the training of professional, paraprofessional, and volunteer personnel, and other persons who are or who are preparing to work with juveniles and juvenile offenders;

(2) develop, conduct, and provide for seminars, workshops, and training programs in the latest proven effective techniques and methods of preventing and treating juvenile delinquency for law enforcement officers, juvenile judges, and other court personnel, probation officers, correctional personnel, and other Federal, State, and local government personnel who are engaged in work relating to juvenile delinquency;

(3) devise and conduct a training program, in accordance with the provisions of sections 5659, 5660, and 5661 of this title, of short-term instruction in the latest proven-effective methods of prevention, control, and treatment of juvenile delinquency for correctional and law enforcement personnel, teachers and other educational personnel, juvenile welfare workers, juvenile judges and judicial personnel, probation officers, and other persons (including lay personnel) connected with the prevention and treatment of juvenile delinquency; and

(4) develop technical training teams to aid in the development of training programs in the States and to assist State and local agencies which work directly with juveniles and juvenile offenders.

Pub.L. 93—415, Title II, § 244, Sept. 7, 1974, 88 Stat. 1127.

Historical Note

Effective Date. Section effective Sept. 7, 1974, see section 263 of Pub.L. 93–415, set out as a note under section 5601 of this title.

Legislative History. For legislative history and purpose of Pub.L. 93–415, see 1974 U.S.Code Cong. and Adm.News, p. 5283.

§ 5655. Advisory Committee of Institute; functions

The Advisory Committee for the National Institute for Juvenile Justice and Delinquency Prevention established in section 5618(d) of this title shall advise, consult with, and make recommendations to the Deputy Assistant Administrator for the National Institute for Juvenile Justice and Delinquency Prevention concerning the overall policy and operations of the Institute.

Pub.L. 93–415, Title II, § 245, Sept. 7, 1974, 88 Stat. 1127.

Historical Note

Effective Date. Section effective Sept. 7, 1974, see section 263 of Pub.L. 93–415, set out as a note under section 5601 of this title.

Legislative History. For legislative history and purpose of Pub.L. 93–415, see 1974 U.S.Code Cong. and Adm.News, p. 5283.

§ 5656. Annual report by Deputy Assistant Administrator; time; contents; summary to President and Congress

The Deputy Assistant Administrator for the National Institute for Juvenile Justice and Delinquency Prevention shall develop annually and submit to the Administrator after the first year the legislation is enacted, prior to September 30, a report on research, demonstration, training, and evaluation programs funded under this subchapter, including a review of the results of such programs, an assessment of the application of such results to existing and to new juvenile delinquency programs, and detailed recommendations for future research, demonstration, training, and evaluation programs. The Administrator shall include a summary of these results and recommendations in his report to the president and Congress required by section 5614(b)(5) of this title.

Pub.L. 93–415, Title II, § 246, Sept. 7, 1974, 88 Stat. 1127; Pub.L. 94–273, § 2(27), Apr. 21, 1976, 90 Stat. 376.

Historical Note

1976 Amendment. Pub.L. 94–273 substituted "September" for "June".

Effective Date. Section effective Sept. 7, 1974, see section 263 of Pub.L. 93–415, set out as a note under section 5601 of this title.

Legislative History. For legislative history and purpose of Pub.L. 93–415, see 1974 U.S.Code Cong. and Adm.News, p. 5283. See, also, Pub.L. 94–273, 1976 U.S. Code Cong. and Adm.News, p. 690.

§ 5657.   Standards for juvenile justice system

Functions of Institute

(a) The National Institute for Juvenile Justice and Delinquency Prevention, under the supervision of the Advisory Committee on Standards for Juvenile Justice established in section 5618(e) of this title, shall review existing reports, data, and standards, relating to the juvenile justice system in the United States.

Report by Advisory Committee to President and Congress; contents

(b) Not later than one year after September 7, 1974, the Advisory Committee shall submit to the President and the Congress a report which, based on recommended standards for the administration of juvenile justice at the Federal, State, and local level—

(1) recommends Federal action, including but not limited to administrative and legislative action, required to facilitate the adoption of these standards throughout the United States; and

(2) recommends State and local action to facilitate the adoption of these standards for juvenile justice at the State and local level.

Availability of information of Federal departments, etc.

(c) Each department, agency, and instrumentality of the executive branch of the Government, including independent agencies, is authorized and directed to furnish to the Advisory Committee such information as the Committee deems necessary to carry out its functions under this section.

Pub.L. 93–415, Title II, § 247, Sept. 7, 1974, 88 Stat. 1127.

Historical Note

Effective Date. Section effective Sept. 7, 1974, see section 263 of Pub.L. 93–415, set out as a note under section 5601 of this title.

Legislative History. For legislative history and purpose of Pub.L. 93–415, see 1974 U.S.Code Cong. and Adm.News, p. 5283.

§ 5658.   Records; restrictions on disclosure and transfer

Records containing the identity of individual juveniles gathered for purposes pursuant to this subchapter may under no circumstances be disclosed or transferred to any individual or other agency, public, or private.

Pub.L. 93–415, Title II, § 248, Sept. 7, 1974, 88 Stat. 1128.

Historical Note

Effective Date. Section effective Sept. 7, 1974, see section 263 of Pub.L. 93–415, set out as a note under section 5601 of this title.

Legislative History. For legislative history and purpose of Pub.L. 93–415, see 1974 U.S.Code Cong. and Adm.News, p. 5283.

§ 5659. Training program; establishment, purpose; utilization of state and local facilities, personnel, etc.; enrollees

(a) The Administrator shall establish within the Institute a training program designed to train enrollees with respect to methods and techniques for the prevention and treatment of juvenile delinquency. In carrying out this program the Administrator is authorized to make use of available State and local services, equipment, personnel, facilities, and the like.

(b) Enrollees in the training program established under this section shall be drawn from correctional and law enforcement personnel, teachers and other educational personnel, juvenile welfare workers, juvenile judges and judicial personnel, probation officers, and other persons (including lay personnel) connected with the prevention and treatment of juvenile delinquency.

Pub.L. 93–415, Title II, § 249, Sept. 7, 1974, 88 Stat. 1128.

Historical Note

Effective Date. Section effective Sept. 7, 1974, see section 263 of Pub.L. 93–415, set out as a note under section 5601 of this title.

Legislative History. For legislative history and purpose of Pub.L. 93–415, see 1974 U.S.Code Cong. and Adm.News, p. 5283.

§ 5660. Curriculum for training program

The Administrator shall design and supervise a curriculum for the training program established by section 5659 of this title which shall utilize an interdisciplinary approach with respect to the prevention of juvenile delinquency, the treatment of juvenile delinquents, and the diversion of youths from the juvenile justice system. Such curriculum shall be appropriate to the needs of the enrollees of the training program.

Pub.L. 93–415, Title II, § 250, Sept. 7, 1974, 88 Stat. 1128.

Historical Note

Effective Date. Section effective Sept. 7, 1974, see section 263 of Pub.L. 93–415, set out as a note under section 5601 of this title.

Legislative History. For legislative history and purpose of Pub.L. 93–415, see 1974 U.S.Code Cong. and Adm.News, p. 5283.

§ 5661. Enrollment for training program

Application

(a) Any person seeking to enroll in the training program established under section 5659 of this title shall transmit an application to the Administrator, in such form and according to such procedures as the Administrator may prescribe.

Admittance; determination by Secretary

(b) The Administrator shall make the final determination with respect to the admittance of any person to the training program. The Administrator, in making such determination, shall seek to assure that persons admitted to the training program are broadly representative of the categories described in section 5659(b) of this title.

Travel expenses and per diem allowance

(c) While studying at the Institute and while traveling in connection with his study (including authorized field trips), each person enrolled in the Institute shall be allowed travel expenses and a per diem allowance in the same manner as prescribed for persons employed intermittently in the Government service under section 5703(b) of Title 5.

Pub.L. 93–415, Title II, § 251, Sept. 7, 1974, 88 Stat. 1128.

Historical Note

Effective Date. Section effective Sept. 7, 1974, see section 263 of Pub.L. 93–415, set out as a note under section 5601 of this title.

Legislative History. For legislative history and purpose of Pub.L. 93–415, see 1974 U.S.Code Cong. and Adm.News, p. 5283.

PART D—AUTHORIZATION OF APPROPRIATIONS

§ 5671. Fiscal years 1975, 1976 and 1977; juvenile delinquency programs

(a) To carry out the purposes of this subchapter there is authorized to be appropriated $75,000,000 for the fiscal year ending June 30, 1975, $125,000,000 for the fiscal year ending June 30, 1976, and $150,000,000 for the fiscal year ending September 30, 1977.

(b) In addition to the funds appropriated under subsection (a) of this section, the Administration shall maintain from the appropriation for the Law Enforcement Assistance Administration, each fiscal year, at least 19.15 percent of the total appropriations for the Administration, for juvenile delinquency programs.

Pub.L. 93–415, Title II, § 261, Sept. 7, 1974, 88 Stat. 1129; Pub.L. 94–273, § 32(b), Apr. 21, 1976, 90 Stat. 380; Pub.L. 94–503, Title I, § 130(a), Oct. 15, 1976, 90 Stat. 2425.

Historical Note

1976 Amendments. Subsec. (a). Pub.L. 94–273 substituted "September 30, 1977" for "June 30, 1977".

Subsec. (b). Pub.L. 94–503 substituted "subsection (a) of this section" for "this section" and "the appropriation for the Law Enforcement Assistance Administration, each fiscal year, at least 19.15 percent of the total appropriations for the Administration, for juvenile delinquency programs" for "other Law Enforcement Assistance Administration appropriations other than the appropriations for administration, at least the same level of financial assistance for juvenile delinquency programs assisted by the Law Enforcement Assistance Administration during fiscal year 1972".

Effective Date. Section effective Sept. 7, 1974, see section 263 of Pub.L. 93–415, set out as a note under section 5601 of this title.

Legislative History. For legislative history and purpose of Pub.L. 93–415, see 1974 U.S.Code Cong. and Adm.News, p. 5283. See, also, Pub.L. 94–273, 1976 U.S. Code Cong. and Adm. News, p. 690; Pub. L. 94–503, 1976 U.S.Code Cong. and Adm.News, p. 5374.

Library References

Infants (West) 13, 16, 17.

C.J.S. Infants §§ 11 et seq., 17, 18, 93 et seq.

§ 5672. Prohibitions against discrimination; required provisions in grants, contracts and agreements; enforcement

(a) No financial assistance for any program under this chapter shall be provided unless the grant, contract, or agreement with respect to such program specifically provides that no recipient of funds will discriminate as provided in subsection (b) of this section with respect to any such program.

(b) No person in the United States shall on the ground of race, creed, color, sex, or national origin be excluded from participation in, be denied the benefits of, be subjected to discrimination under, or be denied employment in connection with any program or activity receiving assistance under this chapter. The provisions of the preceding sentence shall be enforced in accordance with section 2000d–2 of this title. Section 2000d–2 of this title shall apply with respect to any action taken to enforce such sentence. This section shall not be construed as affecting any other legal remedy that a person may have if such person is excluded from participation in, denied the benefits of, subjected to discrimination under, or denied employment in connection with any program or activity receiving assistance under this chapter.

Pub.L. 93–415, Title II, § 262, Sept. 7, 1974, 88 Stat. 1129.

Historical Note

References in Text. "This chapter", referred to in subsecs. (a) and (b), was in the original "this Act", meaning Pub.L. 93–415, Sept. 7, 1974, 88 Stat. 1109. For complete classification of Pub.L. 93–415, see Short Title note under section 5601 of this title.

Effective Date. Section effective Sept. 7, 1974, see section 263 of Pub.L. 93–415, set out as a note under section 5601 of this title.

Legislative History. For legislative history and purpose of Pub.L. 93–415, see 1974 U.S.Code Cong. and Adm.News, p. 5283.

Library References

Civil Rights (West) 3.

C.J.S. Civil Rights §§ 5, 12 to 14, 16, 17.

SUBCHAPTER III—RUNAWAY YOUTH

§ 5701.   Congressional statement of findings

The Congress hereby finds that—

(1) the number of juveniles who leave and remain away from home without parental permission has increased to alarming proportions, creating a substantial law enforcement problem for the communities inundated, and significantly endangering the young people who are without resources and live on the street;

(2) the exact nature of the problem is not well defined because national statistics on the size and profile of the runaway youth population are not tabulated;

(3) many such young people, because of their age and situation, are urgently in need of temporary shelter and counseling services;

(4) the problem of locating, detaining, and returning runaway children should not be the responsibility of already overburdened police departments and juvenile justice authorities; and

(5) in view of the interstate nature of the problem, it is the responsibility of the Federal Government to develop accurate reporting of the problem nationally and to develop an effective system of temporary care outside the law enforcement structure.

Pub.L. 93–415, Title III, § 302, Sept. 7, 1974, 88 Stat. 1129.

Historical Note

Short Title. Section 301 of Pub.L. 93–415 provided that: "This title [enacting this subchapter] may be cited as the 'Runaway Youth Act'."

Legislative History. For legislative history and purpose of Pub.L. 93–415, see 1974 U.S.Code Cong. and Adm.News, p. 5283.

Library References

Infants (West) 13.

C.J.S. Infants § 11 et seq.

Code of Federal Regulations
Grant and contracting procedures, see 45 CFR 1351.1 et seq.

§ 5702. Promulgation of rules

The Secretary of Health, Education, and Welfare (hereinafter referred to as the "Secretary") may prescribe such rules as he considers necessary or appropriate to carry out the purposes of this subchapter.
Pub.L. 93–415, Title III, § 303, Sept. 7, 1974, 88 Stat. 1130.

Historical Note

Legislative History. For legislative history and purpose of Pub.L. 93–415, see   1974 U.S.Code Cong. and Adm.News, p. 5283.

PART A—GRANTS PROGRAM

§ 5711. Authorization for grants and technical assistance; purposes; amount of grant; priority

The Secretary is authorized to make grants and to provide technical assistance to localities and nonprofit private agencies in accordance with the provisions of this part. Grants under this part shall be made for the purpose of developing local facilities to deal primarily with the immediate needs of runaway youth in a manner which is outside the law enforcement structure and juvenile justice system. The size of such grant shall be determined by the number of runaway youth in the community and the existing availability of services. Among applicants priority shall be given to private organizations or institutions which have had past exerience in dealing with runaway youth.
Pub.L. 93–415, Title III, § 311, Sept. 7, 1974, 88 Stat. 1130.

Historical Note

Legislative History. For legislative history and purpose of Pub.L. 93–415, see   1974 U.S.Code Cong. and Adm.News, p. 5283.

Library References

United States (West) 82.   C.J.S. United States § 122.

§ 5712. Eligibility; plan requirements

(a) To be eligible for assistance under this part, an applicant shall propose to establish, strengthen, or fund an existing or proposed runaway house, a locally controlled facility providing temporary shelter, and counseling services to juveniles who have left home without permission of their parents or guardians.

(b) In order to qualify for assistance under this part, an applicant shall submit a plan to the Secretary meeting the following requirements and including the following information. Each house—

(1) shall be located in an area which is demonstrably frequented by or easily reachable by runaway youth;

(2) shall have a maximum capacity of no more than twenty children, with a ratio of staff to children of sufficient portion to assure adequate supervision and treatment;

(3) shall develop adequate plans for contacting the child's parents or relatives (if such action is required by State law) and assuring the safe return of the child according to the best interests of the child, for contacting local government officials pursuant to informal arrangements established with such officials by the runaway house, and for providing for other appropriate alternative living arrangements;

(4) shall develop an adequate plan for assuring proper relations with law enforcement personnel, and the return of runaway youths from correctional institutions;

(5) shall develop an adequate plan for aftercare counseling involving runaway youth and their parents within the State in which the runaway house is located and for assuring, as possible, that aftercase services will be provided to those children who are returned beyond the State in which the runaway house is located;

(6) shall keep adequate statistical records profiling the children and parents which it serves, except that records maintained on individual runaway youths shall not be disclosed without parental consent to anyone other than another agency compiling statistical records or a government agency involved in the disposition of criminal charges against an individual runaway youth, and reports or other documents based on such statistical records shall not disclose the identity of individual runaway youths;

(7) shall submit annual reports to the Secretary detailing how the house has been able to meet the goals of its plans and reporting the statistical summaries required by paragraph (6);

(8) shall demonstrate its ability to operate under accounting procedures and fiscal control devices as required by the Secretary;

(9) shall submit a budget estimate with respect to the plan submitted by such house under this subsection; and

(10) shall supply such other information as the Secretary

reasonably deems necessary.

Pub.L. 93–415, Title III, § 312, Sept. 7, 1974, 88 Stat. 1130.

Historical Note

Legislative History. For legislative history and purpose of Pub.L. 93–415, see

1974 U.S.Code Cong. and Adm.News, p.
5283.

§ 5713. Approval of application by Secretary; priority

An application by a State, locality, or nonprofit private agency for a grant under this part may be approved by the Secretary only if it is consistent with the applicable provisions of this part and meets the requirements set forth in section 5712 of this title. Priority shall be given to grants smaller than $75,000. In considering grant applications under this part, priority shall be given to any applicant whose program budget is smaller than $100,000.

Pub.L. 93–415, Title III, § 313, Sept. 7, 1974, 88 Stat. 1131.

Historical Note

Legislative History. For legislative history and purpose of Pub.L. 93–415, see

1974 U.S.Code Cong. and Adm.News, p.
5283.

§ 5714. Grants to nonprofit private agencies; control over staff and personnel

Nothing in this part shall be construed to deny grants to nonprofit private agencies which are fully controlled by private boards or persons but which in other respects meet the requirements of this part and agree to be legally responsible for the operation of the runaway house. Nothing in this part shall give the Federal Government control over the staffing and personnel decisions of facilities receiving Federal funds.

Pub.L. 93–415, Title III, § 314, Sept. 7, 1974, 88 Stat. 1131.

Historical Note

Legislative History. For legislative history and purpose of Pub.L. 93–415, see

1974 U.S.Code Cong. and Adm.News, p.
5283.

§ 5715. Annual report to Congress

The Secretary shall annually report to the Congress on the status and accomplishments of the runaway houses which are funded under this part, with particular attention to—

(1) their effectiveness in alleviating the problems of runaway youth;

(2) their ability to reunite children with their families and to encourage the resolution of intrafamily problems through counseling and other services;

(3) their effectiveness in strengthening family relationships and encouraging stable living conditions for children; and

(4) their effectiveness in helping youth decide upon a future course of action.

Pub.L. 93—415, Title III, § 315, Sept. 7, 1974, 88 Stat. 1131.

Historical Note

Legislative History. For legislative history and purpose of Pub.L. 93—415, see   1974 U.S.Code Cong. and Adm.News, p. 5283.

§ 5716. Federal and non-Federal share; methods of payment

(a) The Federal share for the acquisition and renovation of existing structures, the provision of counseling services, staff training, and the general costs of operations of such facility's budget for any fiscal year shall be 90 per centum. The non-Federal share may be in cash or in kind, fairly evaluated by the Secretary, including plant, equipment or services.

(b) Payments under this section may be made in installments, in advance, or by way of reimbursement, with necessary adjustments on account of overpayments or underpayments.

Pub.L. 93—415, Title III, § 316, Sept. 7, 1974, 88 Stat. 1132.

Historical Note

Legislative History. For legislative history and purpose of Pub.L. 93—415, see   1974 U.S.Code Cong. and Adm.News, p. 5283.

PART B—STATISTICAL SURVEY

§ 5731. Scope; report to Congress; time for report

The Secretary shall gather information and carry out a comprehensive statistical survey defining the major characteristic of the runaway youth population and determining the areas of the Nation most affected. Such survey shall include the age, sex, and socio-economic background of runaway youth, the places from which and to which children run, and the relationship between running away and other illegal behavior. The Secretary shall report the results of such information gathering and survey to the Congress not later than June 30, 1975.

Pub.L. 93–415, Title III, § 321, Sept. 7, 1974, 88 Stat. 1132.

Historical Note

Legislative History. For legislative history and purpose of Pub.L. 93–415, see 1974 U.S.Code Cong. and Adm.News, p. 5283.

Library References

United States (West) 82.

C.J.S. United States § 122.

§ 5732. Records; restrictions on disclosure and transfer

Records containing the identity of individual runaway youths gathered for statistical purposes pursuant to section 5731 of this title may under no circumstances be disclosed or transferred to any individual or to any public or private agency.

Pub.L. 93–415, Title III, § 322, Sept. 7, 1974, 88 Stat. 1132.

Historical Note

Legislative History. For legislative history and purpose of Pub.L. 93–415, see 1974 U.S.Code Cong. and Adm.News, p. 5283.

PART C—AUTHORIZATION OF APPROPRIATIONS

§ 5751. Amounts for grant program and statistical survey

(a) To carry out the purposes of part A of this subchapter there is authorized to be appropriated for each of the fiscal years ending June 30, 1975, and 1976, and September 30, 1977, the sum of $10,000,000.

(b) To carry out the purposes of part B of this subchapter there is authorized to be appropriated the sum of $500,000.

Pub.L. 93–415, Title III, § 331, Sept. 7, 1974, 88 Stat. 1132; Pub.L. 94–273, § 32(c), Apr. 21, 1976, 90 Stat. 380.

Historical Note

1976 Amendment. Subsec. (a). Pub. L. 94–273 added "and" preceding "1976" and substituted "September 30, 1977" for "1977".

Legislative History. For legislative history and purpose of Pub.L. 93–415, see 1974 U.S.Code Cong. and Adm.News, p. 5283. See, also, Pub.L. 94–273, 1976 U.S. Code Cong. and Adm.News, p. 690.

Library References

United States (West) 82.

C.J.S. United States § 122.

BIBLIOGRAPHY

Abramson, H., *The Use of LSD in Psychotherapy and Alcoholism*, Bobbs-Merrill, N.Y., (1967).

Ackerly, W.C., and C. Gibson, "Lighter Fluid Sniffing," American Journal of Psychiatry, May, 1964.

Adriani, J., *Narcotics and Narcotic Antagonists (Chemistry, Pharmacology and Applications in Anesthesiology and Obstetrics)*, Charles C. Thomas, Springfield, Illinois, (1964).

Agnew, D., *Undercover Agent—Narcotics*, McFadden-Bartell, New York, (1959).

Alexander, M., *The Sexual Paradise of LSD*, Brandon House, North Hollywood, Calif., (1967).

Alpert, R., and Cohen, S., *LSD*, New American Library, N.Y., (1967).

Andrews, G., and Vinkenoog, S., *The Book of Grass—An Anthology of Indian Hemp*, Grove Press, N.Y., (1967).

Anslinger, H.J., *The Protectors*, Farrar, Straus and Giroux, Inc., N.Y., (1961).

Anslinger, H.J., and Oursler, W., *The Murderers, (The Story of the Narcotic Gangs)*, Farrar, Straus and Giroux, Inc., N.Y., (1961).

Anslinger, H.J., and Tompkins, W.F., *The Traffic in Narcotics*, Funk and Wagnalls, N.Y., (1953).

Anslinger, J., and Gregory, J.D., *The Protectors*, Farrar, Straus & Company, New York, (1964).

Aptekar, Herbert H., *The Dynamics of Casework and Counseling*, Houghton-Mifflin, Boston, (1955).

Attardo, N., "Psychodynamic Factors in the Mother-Child Relationship in Adolescent Drug Addiction: A Comparison of Mothers of Normal Adolescent Sons," Psychotherapy and Psychosomatics, XIII, (1965).

Barker, G., and W. Adams, "Glue-Sniffers," Sociology and Social Research, (1963).

Barman, M., and N. Sigel, D. Beedle and R. Larson, "Acute and Chronic Effects of Glue-Sniffing," California Medicine, (1964).

Bartlett, S., and F. Tapia, "Glue and Gasoline 'Sniffing' the Addiction of Youth," Missouri Medicine, (1966).

Becker, Howard Saul, *The Other Side; Perspectives on Deviance*, Free Press of Glencoe, N.Y., (1965).

Becker, Howard Saul, *The Outsiders*, Free Press, Glencoe, Illinois (1963).

Becker, Howard Saul, *The Outsiders*, Free Press of Glencoe, London, (1963).

Beckman, H., *Dilemmas in Drug Therapy*, W. B. Saunders, Philadelphia, (1967).

Berne, E., *Games People Play*, Grove Press, N.Y., (1964).

Bett, W.R., Howells, L.H., and MacDonald, A.D., *Amphetamine in Clinical Medicine, Actions and Uses*, E. & S. Livingstone, Great Britain, (1954).

Birnbach, S.B., *Drug Abuse—A Dead End Street*, A student's guide to narcotics information; H.K. Simon Co., Box 236, Hastings-on-Hudson, N.Y. 10706. An accompanying Teachers Manual is also available.

Blaceslee, Alton, *What You Should Know About Drugs and Narcotics*, The Associated Press, (1969).

Blachly, Paul H., *Seduction,* Charles C. Thomas, Springfield, Illinois, (1970).

Bloomquist, E.R., M.D., *Marijuana,* Glencoe Press, (1968).

Blum, R., et al., *The Utopiates,* Atherton Press, N.Y., (1964).

Brown, T.T., *The Enigma of Drug Addiction,* Charles C. Thomas, Springfield, Illinois, (1961).

Brozovsky, M., and E. Winkler, "Glue-Sniffing in Children and Adolescents," New York State Journal of Medicine, (1965).

Burchinal, Lee G., (Ed.), *Rural Youth in Crisis: Facts, Myths and Social Change,* U.S. Department of H.E.W., Washington, D.C., (1965).

Cameron, Mary O., *The Booster and the Snitch,* Free Press of Glencoe, N.Y., (1964).

Carter, Robt. M., and Wilkins, Leslie (Editors), *Probation and Parole,* Wiley & Sons, N.Y., (1970).

Catanzaro, Ronald J., *Alcoholism: The Total Treatment Approach,* Charles C. Thomas, Springfield, Illinois.

Chambers, Francis T., *The Drinker's Addiction: Its Nature & Practical Treatment,* Charles C. Thomas, Publisher, Springfield, Illinois.

Chein, I., et al., *The Road to H,* Basic Books, Inc., New York, (1964).

Clinard, M.B., *Anomie and Deviant Behavior,* Free Press of Glencoe, N.Y., (1964).

Clinard, M.B., *Sociology of Deviant Behavior,* Rinehart, N.Y., (1957).

Cloward, Richard A., and Oblen, Lloyd E., *Delinquency and Opportunity: A Theory of Delinquent Gangs,* Free Press, Glencoe, Illinois, (1960).

Cohen, Albert, *Delinquent Boys: The Culture of the Gang,* Free Press, Glencoe, Illinois, (1955).

Cohen, Albert K., *Deviance and Control,* Prentice-Hall, Englewood Cliffs, N.J., (1966).

Coleman, James S., *The Adolescent Society,* Free Press of Glencoe, N.Y., (1961).

Connell, P.H., *Amphetamine Psychosis,* Chapman & Hall Ltd., London, (1958).

Conrad, John, *Crime and Its Correction,* University of California, Berkeley, (1965).

Constitution of the United States of America (prepared by Legislative Service, Library of Congress), U.S. Gov't. Printing Office, Wash., D.C., (1964).

Council of Judges, *Model Rules for Juvenile Courts,* N.C.C.D., N.Y., (1969).

Cowen, Emory; Gardner, Elmer; Zax, Melvin, *Emergent Approaches to Mental Health Problems,* Meredith Publishing Company, N.Y., (1967).

Creamer, J. Shane, *The Law of Arrest, Search and Seizure,* S—— & Co., Philadelphia, (1968).

"Crime In The United States (Uniform Crime Reports)," Federal Bureau of Investigation, Dept. of Justice, Washington, D.C., (1965) and (1968).

Cruickshank, Wm. H., and Johnson, G.O., *Education of Exceptional Children and Youth,* Prentice-Hall, Englewood Cliffs, N.J., (1958).

Diagnostic & Statistical Manual of Mental Disorders, American Psychiatric Association (2nd Ed.–DSM II), Washington, D.C., (1968).

Donohue, John K., "My Brother's Boy," Bruce, St. Paul, Minn., (1963).

Dressler, *Practice and Theory of Probation and Parole,* Columbia University Press, N.Y., (1969, 2nd Ed.).

Dressler, David, *Readings in Criminology and Penology*, Columbia University Press, N.Y., (1964).

Drug Abuse—A Call for Action, American Social Health Assn., 1740 Broadway, N.Y., N.Y., 10019.

Drug Abuse—A Primer for Parents, National Education Assn., 1201—16th St., N.W., Washington, D.C., 20036.

Drug Abuse—Escape to Nowhere—A Guide for Educators; Drug Abuse—A Manual for Law Enforcement Officers, both by Smith, Kline and French Laboratories, (1968), SKF Labs, 1500 Spring Garden Street, Philadelphia, Pa., 19101.

Fact Sheet—Drug Abuse Control Amendments of 1965, Public Law 89-74, 89th Congress, U.S. Dept., HEW, FDA, (1965).

Forney, Robert B., and Hughes, Francis W., *Combined Effects of Alcohol and Other Drugs*, Charles C. Thomas, Publisher, Springfield, Illinois.

Frank, Lawrence, and Frank, Mary, *Your Adolescent at Home and In School*, Viking Press, N.Y., (1956).

Friedenberg, Edgar, *The Vanishing Adolescent*, Beacon Press, Boston, (1959).

Fromme, Allan, *The ABC of Child Care*, Pocket Books, N.Y., (1956).

Garber, Sheldon, "Adolescence for Adults," (A report by Blue Cross), Blue Cross Assn., Chicago, Illinois, (1969).

Ginott, Haim, *Between Parent and Child*, MacMillan Co., N.Y., (1965).

Ginott, Haim, *Between Parent and Teenager*, MacMillan Co., N.Y., (1969).

Giordano, H.L., *The Dangers of Marijuana—Facts You Should Know*, Bureau of Narcotics, 633 Indiana Ave., N.W., Washington, D.C., 20226, (1968).

Gitchoff, G. Thomas, *Kids, Cops and Kilos*, Matter-Westerfield Publishing Company, San Diego, California, (1969).

Glasser, William, *Reality Therapy, a New Approach to Psychiatry*, Harper & Row, N.Y., (1965).

Glasser, William, *Schools Without Failure*, Harper & Row, N.Y., (1968).

Gottlieb, D———, and Ramsey, Charles, *The American Adolescent*, Dorsey Press, Homewood, Illinois, (1964).

Hanna, John Paul, *Teenagers and the Law*, Ginn & Company, Boston, Mass., (1967).

Harms, Ernest, and Schreiber, Paul, *Handbook of Counseling Techniques*, Macmillan, N.Y., (1963).

Harris, Thomas A., *I'm OK—You're OK: A Practical Guide to Transactional Analysis*, Harper & Row, N.Y., (1967, 1968 & 1969).

Hayman, Max, *Alcoholism: Mechanism and Management*, Charles C. Thomas, Publisher, Springfield, Illinois.

Hentig, Hans, *Crime, Causes and Conditions*, McGraw Hill, N.Y., (1947).

Hickerson, Nathaniel, *Education for Alienation*, Prentice-Hall, Inc., Englewood Cliffs, N.J., (1966).

Hoffman, L. Wallace, *Children and the Family (Under Ohio Law)*, Juvenile and Domestic Relations Court, Toledo, Ohio, (Revised Edition, 1963).

Holmes, Grace W., *Student Protest and the Law*, (Institute of Continuing Legal Ed.), R.W. Patterson Printing Company, Benton Harbor, Michigan, (1969).

Hush, Joseph, *Opportunities and Limitations in the Treatment of Alcoholics*, Charles C. Thomas, Publisher, Springfield, Illinois.

Ilg, Frances, and Ames, Louise Bates, *Child Behavior,* (The Gesell Institute), Dell Publishing Company, N.Y., (1962, 3rd reprint).

Jeffee, S., *Narcotics, An American Plan,* Paul S. Erickson, Inc., New York, (1967).

Johnston, N., Savitz, L., and Wolfgang, Marvin E., *The Sociology of Crime and Delinquency,* Wiley, N.Y., (1970).

"Juvenile Court Statistics," U.S. Department of Health, Education & Welfare, Childrens Bureau, (1963 and 1967)

Kenney, John P., and Pursuit, Dan G., *Police Work With Juveniles and the Administration of Justice,* Charles C. Thomas, Publishers, Springfield, Illinois, (4th Edition, 1970).

Kessler, Jane W., *Psychopathology of Childhood,* Prentice-Hall Inc., Englewood Cliffs, N.J., (1966).

Kinsey, Barry A., *The Female Alcoholic; A Social Psychological Study.*

Klotter, John C., and Kanovitz, Jacqueline R., *Constitutional Law for Police,* W.H. Anderson Co., Cincinnati, Ohio, (1968).

Knudten, Richard D., (Ed.), *Criminological Controversies,* Appleton-Century-Crofts, N.Y., (1968).

Kolb, L., *Drug Addiction,* Charles C. Thomas, Springfield, Illinois, (1962).

Kron, Y.J., and Brown, E., *Mainline to Nowhere,* A Meridan Book, (1967).

Kvaraceus, Wm. C., and Miller, Walter B., *Delinquent Behavior,* National Education Assoc., Washington, D.C., (1959).

Lander, Bernard, *Toward An Understanding of Juvenile Delinquency,* Columbia University, N.Y., (1954).

Leake, C.D., *The Amphetamines, Their Actions and Uses,* Charles C. Thomas, Springfield, Illinois, (1958).

Lefton, Mark, Skipper, James K., Jr., McCaghy, Charles H., *Approaches to Deviance,* Appleton-Century-Crofts, (Mereelith Corp.), N.Y., (1968).

Lindesmith, Alfred R., *The Addict and the Law,* Indiana Univ. Press, Bloomington, Indiana, (1965).

Louria, D., *Nightmare Drugs,* Pocket Books, Inc., (1966).

Manual on the Law of Search and Seizure, prepared by Legislation and Special Projects Section, Criminal Division, U.S. Dept. of Justice, (1970).

Martin, John M., *Delinquent Behavior: A Redefinition of the Problem,* Random House, N.Y., (1965).

Martin, John M., *Juvenile Vandalism,* Thomas, Springfield, Illinois, (1961).

Maurer, David W., and Vogel, V.H., *Narcotics and Narcotic Addiction,* Thomas, Springfield, Illinois, (2nd Edition, 1962).

Mead, Margaret, *Culture & Commitment,* Doubleday & Company, N.Y., (1970).

Medicinal Narcotics, Pharmaceutical Manufacturers Association, Washington, D.C., (1965).

Mental Health Monograph 2: *Narcotic Drug Addiction,* Public Health Service, Publication No. 1921, (1965).

Mental Health Monograph 3: *Rehabilitation in Drug Addiction. A Report on a Five-Year Community Experiment of the New York Demonstration Center,* Public Health Service Publication No. 1013 (revised 1964).

Merton, R.K., *Social Theory and Social Structure,* Free Press, N.Y., (Revised and enlarged edition, 1949).

Mullan, Hugh, and Sanginliano, Iris, *Alcoholism: Group Psychotherapy & Rehabilitation*, Charles C. Thomas, Publisher, Springfield, Illinois.

Murphy, Gardner, and Bachrach, Arthur J., *An Outline of Abnormal Psychology*, Modern Library, N.Y., (1954).

Mussen, Paul H., *The Psychological Development of the Child*, Prentice-Hall, Inc., Englewood Cliffs, N.J., (1963).

Myren, Richard A., and Swanson, Lynn D., *Police Work With Children*, U.S. Department of Health, Education & Welfare, Childrens Bureau, Washington, D.C., (1962).

Nash, John, *Developmental Psychology*, Prentice-Hall Inc., Englewood Cliffs, N.J., (1970).

Nordin, Virginia D., (Ed.), *Gault: What Now for the Juvenile Court?*, Institute of Continuing Legal Education, Ann Arbor, Michigan, (1968).

Peck, Harris B., and Bellsmith, Virginia, *Treatment of the Delinquent Adolescent*, Family Service Association of America, N.Y., (1954).

Perlman, Harvey S., and Allevyton, Thomas B., (Ed.), *The Tasks of Penology*, University of Nebraska Press, Lincoln, Nebraska, (1969).

Petit, George A., *Prisoners of Culture*, Scribner's, N.Y., (1970).

President's Commission on Law Enforcement and Administration of Justice, *The Challenge of Crime in a Free Society*, U.S. Govt. Printing Office, Wash., D.C., (1967).

Proceedings—White House Conference on Narcotics and Drug Abuse, September 27 and 28, 1962, U.S. Government Printing Office, Washington, D.C.

Rafferty, Max, *Classroom Countdown*, Hawthorn Book Inc., N.Y., (1970).

Rafferty, Max, *Suffer, Little Children*, Devin-Adair, N.Y., (1962).

Ratcliffe, James M., *The Good Samaritan and the Law*, Anchor Books, Garden City, N.Y., (1966).

Reckless, Walter C., *Criminal Behavior*, McGraw Hill, N.Y., (1940).

Reckless, Walter C., *The Crime Problem*, Appleton-Century-Crofts, N.Y., (1950).

Redl and Wineman, *Children Who Hate*, Free Press, N.Y., (1951).

Redl and Wineman, *Controls From Within*, Free Press, Glencoe, Illinois, (1952).

"Report of The National Advisory Commission on Civil Disorders," U.S. Gov't. Printing Office, Washington, D.C., (1968).

Riese, Hertha, *Heal the Hurt Child*, University of Chicago Press, Chicago, Illinois, (1962).

Riessman, Frank, *The Culturally Deprived Child*, Harper & Row, N.Y., (1962).

Rische, Henry, *American Youth in Trouble*, Revell Co., Westwood, N.J., (1956).

Rosenheim, Margaret K., *Justice for the Child*, Free Press, Glencoe, N.Y., (1962).

Rubenfeld, Seymour, *Family of Outcasts*, Free Press, N.Y., (1965).

Rueger, Melvin G., (Ed.), *Schneider's Ohio Criminal Code*, W.H. Anderson Co., Cincinnati, Ohio, (1963, 3rd Edition).

Ruitenbeek, H.M., *Varieties of Personality Theory*, E.P. Datlon & Company, N.Y., (1964).

Saltman, J., *What We Do About Drug Abuse*, Public Affairs Pamphlets, 381 Park Avenue, S., N.Y., N.Y., 10016.

Schmidt, J.E., *Narcotics, Lingo and Lore*, Charles C. Thomas, Springfield, Illinois, (1959).

Schneiders, Alexander, *The Psychology of Adolescence*, Bruce, Mil., Wisc., (1951).

Schur, Edwin M., *Crimes Without Victims*, Prentice-Hall, Englewood Cliffs, N.J., (1965).

Schur, Edwin M., *Law and Society*, Random House, N.Y., (1968).

Schur, Edwin M., *Narcotics Addiction In Britain and America*, Indiana University Press, Bloomington, (1962).

Schwartz, Louis B., and Goldstein, Stephen R., *Police Guidance Manuals*, University of Pennsylvania, Phila., Penn., (1968).

Shaw, Clifford, and McKay, Henry, *Juvenile Delinquency and Urban Areas*, University of Chicago Press, Chicago, Illinois, (1942).

Shaw, Clifford, *The Jack-Roller*, University of Chicago Press, Chicago, Illinois, (1930).

Sheridan, William, *Standards For Juvenile and Family Courts*, U.S. Dept. of HEW, (1966 revised).

Short, James F., *Gang Delinquency and Delinquent Subcultures*, Harper & Row, N.Y., (1968).

Short, James F., and Strodtbeck, Fred L., *Group Process and Gang Delinquency*, University of Chicago, Chicago, Illinois, (1965).

Shulman, Harry M., *Juvenile Delinquency in American Society*, Harper & Row, N.Y., (1961).

Siragusa, C., and Wiedrich, R., *The Trail of the Poppy—Behind the Mask of the Mafia*, Prentice-Hall, Inc., N.Y., (1966).

Social Dynamite, National Committee for Children and Youth, Washington, D.C., (1961).

Sterne, Richard S., *Delinquent Conduct and Broken Homes*, College & University Press, New Haven, (1964).

Sutherland, E.H., and Cressey, D.R., *Criminology*, Lippincott, Phila., Pa., (8th Ed., 1970).

Sutherland, E.H., *The Professional Thief*, University of Chicago Press, (1937).

Sutherland, E.H., *White Collar Crime*, Dryden Press, N.Y., (1949).

Task Force Report: Juvenile Delinquency and Youth Crime, U.S. Government Printing Office, Washington, D.C., (1967).

The President's Advisory Commission on Narcotic and Drug Abuse: Final Report, November, 1963, U.S. Government Printing Office, Washington, D.C.

The President's Commission on Law Enforcement and Administration of Justice: *Task Force Report: Narcotics and Drug Abuse*, 1967, U.S. Government Printing Office, Washington, D.C.

Thrasher, F., *The Gang*, University of Chicago Press, Chicago, Illinois, (1927).

Toffler, Alvin, *Future Shock*, Random House Inc., N.Y., (1970).

Tompkins, Dorothy, *Juvenile Gangs and Street Groups*, University of California, Berkeley, (1966).

Tompkins, Dorothy, *The Offender*, University of California, Berkeley, (1963).

U.S. Treasury Department, Bureau of Narcotics: *Prevention and Control of Narcotic Addiction*, Government Printing Office, (1964).

Vaz, Edmund W., *Middle Class Juvenile Delinquency*, Harper & Row, N.Y., (1967).

Vogel, Dr. and Mrs., *Facts About Narcotics and Other Dangerous Drugs,* Science Research Associates, Inc., 259 E. Erie St., Chicago, Illinois, 60611.

Wertham, Fredric, *The Circle of Guilt,* Rinehart, N.Y., (1956).

West, D.J., *The Young Offender,* Penquin Books, Baltimore, Maryland, (1967).

White, Robert, *The Abnormal Personality,* Ronald Press Co., N.Y., (1964).

WHO Expert Committee on Addiction-Producing Drugs, 13th Report, (1964).

Whyte, W.F., *Street Corner Society,* University of Chicago Press, Chicago, Illinois, (1943).

Wilkins, Leslie T., *Evaluation of Penal Measures,* Random House, N.Y., (1969).

Wilner, D.M., and Kassebaum, G.G., *Narcotics,* McGraw-Hill, Inc., N.Y., (1965).

Winick and Goldstein, *The Glue Sniffing Problem,* American Social Health Assn., 1740 Broadway, N.Y., N.Y., 10019, (1967).

Winick, C., *The Narcotic Addiction Problem,* American Social Health Assn., 1740 Broadway, N.Y., N.Y., 10019, (1966).

Wolfgang, Marvin E., *Crime and Culture,* Wiley, N.Y., (1968).

Wolfgang, Marvin E., *Crime and Race,* Institute of Human Relations Press, N.Y., (1970).

Yablonsky, Lewis, and Haskell, Martin R., *Crime and Delinquency,* Rand-McNally, Chicago, Illinois, (1970).

Yablonsky, L., *The Tunnel Back,* The MacMillan Company, N.Y., (1965).

Yablonsky, Lewis, *The Violent Gang,* MacMillan, N.Y., (1962).

INDEX

(References are to sections)

ABUSED CHILD, 18.2(d)

ADJUDICATORY HEARINGS, 19.10

ADOLESCENT BEHAVIOR PROBLEMS
Conflicts of adolescence, 5.1, 9.1, 9.2, 12.1, 12.2
    Need for independence, 5.1, 5.3
    Need for parental support, 5.1
    Sexual development, effect, 5.1
Identity crisis, 5.3
Independence, need for, 5.1, 5.3
Marriage, necessity of postponement, 5.2
Peer groups, identification, 5.2
Rejection of parents, results, 5.3
    Attachment to outsiders, 5.3
Sex identification, 5.2

AFFLUENT DELINQUENCY
(See Suburban Delinquency)

AGE OF CHILD, JUVENILE, 18.2(b)

ALCOHOL, ROLE IN DELINQUENCY
Alcoholism
    In general, 10.3
    Juveniles, 11.2
        Medical treatment on arrest, 11.4
        Withdrawal symptoms, recognition of, 11.4
Legal control, state laws, 11.1
Prevention, 11.1
Treatment, 11.4
    Medical, on arrest, 11.4
    Psychosocial, 11.4

AMPHETAMINES, 10.3

ARREST, 16.2, 17.2, 19.4, 19.7

BAIL, 19.5, 19.8

BARBITURATES, 10.3

BLACKS, 3.5, 9.1, 9.2

CAMPUS VIOLENCE, 8.1, 8.2

CHILD PSYCHOLOGY
Adolescent behavior problems, 5.1-5.3
Beating by parents, result, 4.3(b)

489